One Day in China

"Picking Leaves," a woodcut by Liqun (pseud.) made for and published in the original *One Day in China* (Shanghai, 1936), opp. p. 11.54.

ONE DAY IN CHINA: MAY 21, 1936

Translated, edited, and introduced by
Sherman Cochran and Andrew C. K. Hsieh with Janis Cochran

YALE UNIVERSITY PRESS
NEW HAVEN AND LONDON

Published with assistance from the foundation
established in memory of Philip Hamilton
McMillan of the Class of 1894, Yale College.

Designed by James J. Johnson
and set in Palatino Roman type.
Printed in the United States of America by
The Alpine Press, Inc., Stoughton, Mass.

Library of Congress Cataloging in Publication Data

Chung-kuo ti i jih. English.
  One day in China, May 21, 1936.

  Translation of: Chung-kuo ti i jih.
  Bibliography: p.
  Includes index.
  1. China—Social life and customs—1912–1949
I. Cochran, Sherman, 1940–   . II. Hsieh, Andrew
C. K., 1941–   . III. Cochran, Janis, 1947–
IV. Title.
DS775.2.04313   1983   951.04'2   82–48901
ISBN 0–300–02834–2
     0–300–03400–8 (pbk.)

10 9 8 7 6 5

Dedicated with love to our mothers,
Alice Cochran, 封佑葵 , and Bertha Fye

April, 1995
To Alison Dray-Novey,
in thanks for a wonderful
Radcliffe Externship—
Jennifer Burns

Contents

Acknowledgments

In preparing this book for publication, we have had the privilege of receiving comments on it from a wide variety of readers. The first to see any part of it were our students at Cornell University and Grinnell College. We distributed our translations in our classes between 1976 and 1982—adding a few each year—and every semester our students imaginatively incorporated material from our translations into their papers for our courses. Their insights and their willingness to work with us on a project before it was in final form served as an inspiration for us.

Once a complete draft of the manuscript for the book was finished, we continued to share it with our students, and we began to show it to our colleagues. In response, several of our colleagues commented on the manuscript, and we found especially useful the suggestions made by Beatrice S. Bartlett, Knight Biggerstaff, Wen-t'ao Cheng, Parks Coble, Lloyd Eastman, Wai-kam Ho, Parker Po-fei Huang, Michael H. Hunt, John Israel, Daniel Kaiser, Carol Kammen, Perry Link, Susan Naquin, Diane Perushek, Harold Shadick, Robert J. Smith, and Jonathan Spence.

In revising and adding to the manuscript, we were aided by James Bollback and Louisa Vinton, who helped with proofreading; Shelly Yogman, who designed and drew the maps; and She Yue-fung, who wrote the handsome Chinese characters that appear on the title page and on the first page of each part of this book.

After submitting our manuscript to Yale University Press, we were fortunate to receive reassuring encouragement from Charles Grench and sensitive and meticulous editing from Sally Serafim.

We wish to thank all of our students, colleagues, and friends for their contributions to this book, but most of all we wish to acknowledge the debt that we owe to the Chinese people who have made the book possible: the members of the editorial board responsible for the original Chinese version of *One Day in China*, especially the editor-in-chief, Mao Dun; the contributors to the original book whose pieces are translated here; and the people whose lives are the subjects of these pieces.

Introduction: Two Versions of
One Day in China

Truly! From the main streets and back alleys of cities, from the tall buildings and thatched huts, from the deserted little marketplaces of small towns, from the broken-down walls and dilapidated houses of farming villages, from the schools, from the sleeping quarters of the unemployed, from the army barracks, from the prisons, from the companies and the government offices, from the factories, from the markets, from the small shops, from the old families governed by strict family rules—from every single corner of China there have arisen anguished and strong calls to arms, grief-stricken utterances, bitter cursing, tearful smiles, restrained but boiling passions, the sleeptalking of those leading lives without a sense of purpose, the charlatanism of religious converts, the sardonic laughter of heartless ones! This is the spectacular orchestra heard on one day in today's China, but it is not confined only to this one day!

> Mao Dun, "On the Editorial Process," *One Day in China* (1936)[1]

In the spring of 1936, newspapers and magazines in all parts of China began to carry advertisements calling for contributions to a record of a single, specific day—Thursday, May 21, 1936.[2] The advertisements were signed by two groups: the Literary Society, known for its distinguished journal, *Literature*;[3] and the editorial board of "One Day in China," whose members included some of the most famous intellectuals of the time, led by the editor-in-chief of the project, Mao Dun (1896–1981), a novelist acclaimed as China's leading writer of realistic fiction and one of

1. For a translation of "On the Editorial Process," which served as the editor's introduction to the original *One Day in China*, see Appendix C below.

2. For a translation of the complete text of this advertisement and a comment on the extent of its distribution, see Appendix A below.

3. The Literary Society (*Wenxue she*) was founded in 1933 as a successor to the Literary Research Association (*Wenxue yanjiu hui*) which had been dissolved in 1931. Its journal, *Literature (Wenxue)*, has been acclaimed by literary critics as one of the most sophisticated, influential, and durable Chinese periodicals of the 1930s. See C. T. Hsia, *A History of Modern Chinese Fiction, 1917–1957*, pp. 125 and 576–77, n. 6; Marián Gálik, *Mao Tun and Modern Chinese Literary Criticism*, pp. 117–18; and Bonnie S. McDougall, "The Impact of Western Literary Trends," pp. 55–58.

the most important writers in modern Chinese literature.[4] Explaining that this record would eventually be published as a book under the title *One Day in China* (*Zhongguo di yi ri*), the advertisements noted that *Literature* had sponsored similar writing projects in the past but that the purposes of "One Day in China" would be somewhat different:

(1) "One Day in China" is intended to reveal the entire face of China during one day. The day that has been selected was chosen at random . . . *May twenty-first*.

(2) Events and phenomena, large or small, which occur within the twenty-four hours of *May twenty-first* within the territory of China, whether at sea, on land, or in the air, all can be used as material for this book. Of this day's astronomy, weather, politics, diplomacy, happenings in society, gossip from back alleys, scheduled entertainment, people's comings and goings, none is to be excluded as material for this book.[5]

To achieve this goal of revealing "the entire face of China," the advertisements appealed for contributions from "people in all vocations" whether or not they had ever published anything before. The contributors were urged to draw upon a wide range of sources: their own personal experiences at work or elsewhere, their private correspondence and reflections, and their first-hand observations of commercial advertising and "supernatural happenings . . . concerning various local customs, practices, and superstitions, etc."[6] Contributions were limited to two

---

4. Like Mao Dun, the other ten members of the editorial board of "One Day in China" were all prominent writers: Wang Tongzhao as an author of short stories and translator of English poetry; Shen Zijiu as an editor and perhaps the most famous female journalist in China; Zou Taofen as an editor, a journalist, and, according to a survey sampling Chinese student opinion in 1937, the third most popular author of nonfiction in the country (behind Hu Shi and Lin Yutang); Fu Donghua as a literary critic; Qian Yishi as a historian; Zhang Naiqi as an economist; Tao Xingzhi as an educational theorist; and Jin Zhonghua, Liu Shi, and Zhang Zhongshi as journalists. For biographical, literary, and bibliographical information about Mao Dun and these other editors and their writings, see C. T. Hsia, *A History of Modern Chinese Fiction*, pp. 140–64 and passim; Gálik, *Mao Tun and Modern Chinese Literary Criticism*; John Berninghausen, "The Central Contradiction in Mao Dun's Early Fiction"; Chen Yu-shih, "Mao Dun and the Use of Political Allegory in Fiction"; Margo Speisman Gewurtz, *Between America and Russia*; Howard L. Boorman and Richard C. Howard, eds., *Biographical Dictionary of Republican China*, vol. 1, pp. 87–90; vol. 3, pp. 110–15, 243–48, and 319–21; and vol. 4, pp. 117, 321–23, 347–48, and 365–66; Donald W. Klein and Anne B. Clark, *Biographic Dictionary of Chinese Communism, 1921–1965*, pp. 191–194, 387, and 759–64; Harold R. Isaacs, ed., *Straw Sandals*, pp. lxiii–lxv and lxviii–lxix; Hsu Kai-yu, ed. and trans., *Twentieth Century Chinese Poetry*, pp. 253–56; Yang Yiming, ed., *Wentan shiliao*, pp. 164–69, 189–90 and 250–51; Liu Bao, ed., *Xiandai Zhongguo renwu zhi*, pp. 322–23 and 335; Union Research Institute, *Who's Who in Communist China*, pp. 38–39, 153–55, 460, and 562–65; and Institute of International Relations, *Chinese Communist Who's Who*, vol. 1, pp. 159–60 and vol. 2, pp. 156–59.

5. See Appendix A below.

6. Ibid.

thousand characters on any topic except the last, "supernatural happenings," for which they were limited to one thousand characters. If the contributions turned out to be as varied as expected, the advertisements predicted that *One Day in China* would

> encompass a cross-section of today's China. In this, we'll see the things that make us happy, the things that make us sad, the things we love, and the things we hate . . . things of every shape and color throughout all of China on one day—a big picture.[7]

These were high goals, but the advertisements produced a surprisingly strong response. More than three thousand people from all strata of urban and rural society and almost every province of the country contributed pieces totaling more than 6 million Chinese characters. Unable to publish so much, the editorial board selected 469 original pieces of writing (800,000 characters) along with sixty-one pages of excerpts from newspapers and seventy illustrations and rushed them into print in a single thick volume entitled *One Day in China*, published by Life Publishing Company (Shenghuo shu dian), and released it in Shanghai in September 1936 at a price of $1.60 in Chinese currency (U.S. $.50). From this book, no portion of which has been translated previously, come the eighty-four written selections presented here.

In selecting, translating, and annotating the pieces, we have tried to bear in mind the goals of the original project—to reveal "the entire face of China," to encompass "a cross-section of today's China," and to present "a big picture." In this introduction, it therefore seems appropriate to consider the differences between how the editors attempted to achieve their goals in the Chinese version of *One Day in China* and how we have attempted to achieve the same goals in this partial translation of it.

The Editorial Approach to the Original Version of One Day in China

In his editor's introduction to *One Day in China*, Mao Dun concluded that it was a product of "a general mobilization of minds."[8] This phrase is especially poignant in light of attempts at two other kinds of mobilization being made by Chinese leaders

7. Ibid.
8. Mao Dun, "On the Editorial Process," in Appendix C below.

during the same period: military mobilization by the Guomindang leader Chiang Kaishek, who sought to mobilize troops in the late 1920s and early 1930s to unify China under his command and wipe out the Chinese Communists in a series of "extermination campaigns"; social mobilization by the Communist leader Mao Zedong, who sought to mobilize peasants to participate in a social revolution, first in Southeast China during the early 1930s and, after evading Chiang's troops on the legendary Long March, again in the Northwest beginning in 1935 and 1936.[9] But Mao Dun and the other editors of the "One Day in China" project had no backing from either the Chiang Kaishek government (which controlled Shanghai, but not the International Settlement within Shanghai where the book was published)[10] or Mao Zedong's Communist base area in Northwest China (from which no pieces were sent to the "One Day in China" project), and they mobilized minds not by activating members of military or political organizations but by appealing to all Chinese to re-cord the history of one day.[11] This process of intellectual mobilization guided the editors in their approach to every phase of the project: their adoption of the idea of "One Day," their solicitation of pieces for it, and their selection of those to be published in the book that grew out of it.

The idea for "One Day in China" came from the idea of "One Day in the World" which was proposed by the Russian writer Maxim Gorky. Gorky introduced his idea in 1934 at the First Congress of Soviet Writers (the same conference in which he coined the term "socialist realism") as a device for stimulating collective writing. For this purpose, he recom-mended choosing a day at random, rather than selecting a day commemorating the founding of a nation, an armistice between nations,

9. On attempts at mobilization by Chiang and other non-Communist Chinese leaders in the early twentieth century, see Lloyd E. Eastman, *The Abortive Revolution*, pp. 272–75 and passim; and Philip A. Kuhn, "Local Self-Government under the Republic," pp. 276–98. On Mao's attempts at mobilization in the 1930s, see Ilpyong J. Kim, *The Politics of Chinese Communism*, chaps. 5 and 6; Mark Selden, *The Yenan Way in Revolutionary China*, chap. 3; Carl E. Dorris, "Peasant Mobilization in North China and the Origins of Yenan Commu-nism"; and the classic account based on interviews conducted at Yanan between June and October 1936 (the very time that *One Day in China* was being prepared for publication) by Edgar Snow, *Red Star over China*.

10. The International Settlement consisted of foreign concessions which were governed under foreign—not Chinese—law. (On foreign concessions, see "Diary of a Middle School Student," n. 5.) The Chinese publishing houses located there, including Life Publishing Company, did not suffer from the Guomindang government's censorship as much as pub-lishers located outside the International Settlement. See Isaacs, ed., *Straw Sandals*, pp. xxxii–xxxiii.

11. The sponsor of the "One Day in China" project, the Literary Society, was politically independent in that it was not affiliated with or backed by the Guomindang government, the Chinese Communist Party, the League of Left-Wing Writers, or any other politically or ideologically committed organization in China. See Yang Yiming, *Wentan shiliao*, pp. 395–96; and Xuanmo, "Wenxue yanjiu hui ji qi zhongyao fenzi," pp. 229–38.

or any other occasion officially or customarily deemed "historic." "Any day will do: September 25, October 7, or December 15, they're all the same," Gorky casually remarked in his proposal, leaving the date of "One Day in the World" unspecified.[12] Subsequently the date of September 27, 1935, was chosen, and in June 1935 in Paris, at the International Congress for the Defense of Culture, which was a meeting of major Western writers including André Gide, André Malraux, E. M. Forster, Bertolt Brecht, and Alexei Tolstoy,[13] Gorky and his fellow Soviet writer Mikhail Kolzov began work. Kolzov's prospectus for "One Day in the World" soon reached Mao Dun, who translated it from Russian into Chinese and published it in the Chinese journal *Translations* on the eve of the "One Day in China" project, in March 1936.[14] Six months later, in August 1936, after the "One Day in China" project had been completed and the manuscript for the book was about to go to press (and a year before the results of the "One Day in the World" project were to be published), Mao Dun acknowledged in his editor's introduction that Gorky's idea had served as his original inspiration.[15]

Although indebted to Gorky for the idea of "One Day," Mao Dun and his fellow editors succeeded in mobilizing far more people to write about "One Day in China" than their Russian counterparts did to write about "One Day in the World." The book that resulted from the Russian project, *One Day in the World* (*Den mira*), had greater geographical scope, incorporating articles from more than fifty countries (one of which was China), but it included few pieces prepared specifically for the publication. Instead, it drew almost all its material from articles that were published in newspapers and magazines on the chosen day, September 27, 1935. The Russian editors edited them, translated them into Russian, and presented them in a geographical format, devoting each chapter of *One Day in the World* to a different country.[16] By contrast, the editors of the

12. Quoted by Mikhail Kolzov, "Den mira" (One Day in the World). We are grateful to Louisa Vinton for translating this passage.

13. Jurgen Rühle, *Literature and Revolution*, pp. 421–23.

14. M. Heercaofu (M. Kolzov), "Shijie di yi ri" (One Day in the World).

15. Mao Dun, "On the Editorial Process," in Appendix C below.

16. All the 595 pages in this book consist of republished articles and illustrations except one 31-page chapter which contains letters and articles by prominent writers. See Gorky and Kolzov, eds., *Den mira*.

In 1960, Russian publicists celebrated the twenty-fifth anniversary of this original "One Day in the World" by publishing another volume in Russian by the same title, *Den mira*, which contained 800 pages of letters, pictures, charts, and other items sent in from around the world about September 27, 1960 (the same day of the year as the original "One Day in the World" but twenty-five years later), plus an interview with the premier of the Soviet Union at the time, Nikita Krushchev, about how he spent that day. See Editorial Board of *Izvestiia*, ed., *Den mira*.

"One Day in China" project, after receiving more than three thousand pieces written specifically for their project, chose to devote their book almost exclusively to a selection of this hitherto unpublished material.[17]

Mao Dun took pride in both the number and the variety of people mobilized to contribute to the Chinese project. In particular, he was struck by the diversity of their vocational and geographical backgrounds. According to his statistical breakdown, of the more than three thousand contributors, 34.9 percent were students, 15.5 percent teachers, 1.7 percent workers, 9 percent merchants, 0.4 percent peasants, and 4.7 percent professional writers. The remainder (33.8 percent) were "free-lance" professionals, soldiers, police, and people of undetermined vocations. The geographical spread was also wide, with pieces arriving from every province or region in China (as Chinese then defined their country's boundaries) except Xinjiang, Qinghai, Xikang, Tibet, and Mongolia. Additional pieces came in from Overseas Chinese in Japan, Hong Kong, the Southeast Asian archipelago, and Thailand.[18]

Pleased to have mobilized such a diverse body of contributors, the editors sought to make the most of this diversity. Their first editorial principle was to give precedence to content over literary style. The second was to include as great a number of subjects as possible, and, insofar as they could, to include more than one perspective on a given subject (for example, accounts of factory life by a worker and a clerk as well as one by an industrialist). Third, contributions had to deal with events occurring on May 21, 1936, and these events "had to have social significance or at least reflect the living conditions of a segment of society." Fourth, contributions from "frontier provinces" such as Yunnan were to be given precedence over those from provinces "with a comparatively high degree of culture" such as Jiangsu and Zhejiang. Fifth, contributions about "the utterly absurd and superstitious" were to be included without exception. In addition, to highlight the pieces' geographical diversity, the editors classified them according to place of origin and organized the book along geographical lines, devoting each chapter to the contributions from one city, province, or region.[19]

Acting on these principles, the editors selected for the most part pieces written by authors who had never before published anything. They generally rejected pieces by previously published writers from Chi-

17. Of the 801 total pages in the original version of *One Day in China*, only 61 pages were devoted to news summaries and excerpts from newspapers, 26 to prefatory material and credits for illustrations, and all the rest (714) to previously unpublished pieces written by contributors.

18. Mao Dun, "On the Editorial Process," in Appendix C below.

19. Ibid.

na's major coastal cities (accepting only sixty-three of the more than six hundred entries from Shanghai, for example) and used a higher percentage of pieces by authors whom Mao Dun characterized as "untried people" living in places distant from Shanghai "who made their debut" in *One Day in China*. According to Mao Dun, the results of the project proved that the Chinese people—amateur writers as well as professionals—had ample creativity and needed only to be mobilized and given the opportunity to express it. "We came to the profound realization," he remarked, choosing the same metaphor that Mao Zedong was later to use in urging all Chinese to speak out and voice complaints during the One Hundred Flowers campaign of 1956, "that our people have latent talent which, if conditions improve, will bloom and produce literary blossoms several times more beautiful than anything we have ever seen before."[20]

Mao Dun clearly was not alone in admiring the success at intellectual mobilization achieved by the project, for it was soon imitated. *One Day in China* was one of the first collections in a genre new to China in the 1930s—reportage (*baogao wenxue*), a style of narrative writing based on direct observation of the lives of common people. In fact, according to an authoritative survey of new genres in Chinese history by the literary historian Wang Yao, it was the very first "collectively written piece of reportage" to be published in China.[21] Once in print, it immediately gave rise to a kind of "One Day" subgenre, including *One Day in Shanghai* (1938), *One Day in Central Hebei* (1940), and *One Day in Anping* (1941).[22]

Now, four decades later, we too are impressed with the success of the original project and pleased to be able to add our version of *One Day China* to this subgenre.

Our Editorial Approach

Our editorial approach resembles that of the original editors in that we have tried to do justice to the original contributors' writing, and, accordingly, we have translated each piece included here *in toto*, resisting the temptation to excerpt

20. Ibid.
21. Wang Yao, *Zhongguo xin wenxue shigao*, vol. 1, p. 294.
22. See Zhu Zuotong et al., eds., *Shanghai yi ri*; and Linda Ann Grove, "Rural Society in Revolution," pp. 127–29.

or abridge. In addition, again like the editors of the original, we have tried as much as possible to include pieces whose authors come from more than one social stratum and more than one region of China; as a result, the percentage of pieces by contributors from any one vocation or region in our version corresponds closely to its counterpart in the original.[23] But the differences between our version and the original need to be explained more fully than the similarities. Besides being smaller—less than one-fifth the size—our version differs from the original in organization, interpretation, and overall structure.

Our organization is topical, not geographical. We have selected and arranged these pieces according to their relevance to four topics: women, local government, popular religion, and perceptions of the enemy. Such a format appeals to us partly because we have been impressed by the number of times these topics have come up in the pieces that we have read (which include only the 469 published pieces, not the more than 2,500 unpublished ones submitted to the project in 1936). But most of all it appeals to us because it calls attention to topics of central importance in the daily lives of ordinary people, especially in rural China where 80 percent of the population has always lived. As Mao Zedong observed in his "Report on the Investigation of the Peasant Movement in Hunan" (1927), three "systems of authority"—which resemble our first three categories—directly affected the lives of peasants:

> A man in China is usually subjected to the domination of three systems of authority: (1) the state system (political authority), ranging from the national, provincial, and county governments down to that of the rural township; (2) the clan system (clan authority), ranging from the central ancestral temple

23. Proportionately fewer of our pieces are by urban workers and more are by rural people and women, but otherwise the percentages of contributors from various vocations in our selection closely parallel the percentages compiled by Mao Dun on the project as a whole (cited earlier). (Incidentally, the percentages are about the same magnitude for the vocations of the contributors published in the original *One Day in China*.) Where possible, we have given the sex and vocation of a contributor at the beginning of each piece. However, we do not note (as every reader should) that the people heard speaking in these pieces are more numerous than the contributors. In some cases contributors have enclosed other people's writings—letters they've received, students' essays they've graded, handbills they've been given, advertisements they've seen—and in other cases contributors have quoted conversations involving other people, including some illiterate or semiliterate people who could not and did not write their own contributions to *One Day in China*.

As an indication of the geographical distribution here, it is worth noting that we have included pieces from every one of China's major regions: the Northeast, North, Northwest (from areas outside the Communist soviet based at Yanan), Upper Yangzi, Middle Yangzi, Lower Yangzi, Southeast Coast, South, and Southwest. For definition and analysis of these regions, see G. William Skinner, "Regional Urbanization in Nineteenth-Century China," pp. 211–49.

and its branch temples down to the family head; and (3) the supernatural system (religious authority), ranging from the King of Hell down to the City Gods and Earth Gods belonging to the other world and from the Emperor of Heaven down to the strange Immortals of the spiritual world. As for women, in addition to being dominated by these three systems of authority, they are also dominated by men (the authority of the husband). These four authorities—political, clan, religious and masculine—are the embodiment of the whole feudal-patriarchal system and ideology, and are the four thick ropes binding the Chinese people, particularly the peasants.[24]

The contributors use different approaches to women and the family, local government, and popular religion than Mao does here—providing concrete descriptions and narratives rather than abstract analysis—but their interpretations, like his, lead to the same conclusion: these three topics, plus perceptions of the enemy, were central concerns in the daily life of ordinary people, especially of peasants.

In addition to organizing the pieces by topics, we have added our own introductions to each of the four parts. These introductions are designed to suggest what the contributors' viewpoints and intentions might have been, by exploring the meanings of a key term that recurs frequently in the pieces in each part: "family" in Part I, "heads" in Part II, "superstitions" in Part III, and "Chinese traitors" in Part IV. As translators, we find this approach appealing because it focuses on the nuances and ambiguities of language and serves as a reminder that the contributors do more than report their observations and express their opinions. They give meaning to their experiences and make subtle appeals to their audience by endowing certain terms with heavy emotional overtones: "family" refers to an oppressive institution, "heads" to abusive local leaders, "superstitions" to wasteful or misguided religious practices, and "Chinese traitors" to treacherous collaborators with the enemy. By analyzing the contributors' use of these terms, we try to show the common thread running through the pieces in each part and the place each part has in the historical context of the time.[25]

With these key terms in mind, it is possible to view the parts of the book in sequence. Each part seems written from a broader perspective than the preceding part because each term is used to characterize problems on an ever-widening scale: problems with "family," confined to the domestic unit, seem closest at hand; problems with "heads" extend be-

---

24. With minor changes, this translation is taken from Mao Zedong, *Selected Works of Mao Tse-tung*, vol. 1, p. 44.

25. Raymond Williams has called attention to the ambiguities and nuances of numerous terms in the English language in his *Keywords*.

yond households at least as far as "ten-household" units and seem slightly more distant; problems with "superstitions" may or may not physically extend farther from households than problems with "heads," but as described here seem spiritually more distant; and problems with "Chinese traitors" involve connections with foreigners (*waiguoren* in Chinese, literally "people from outside the country") and seem most distant of all.

Thus, this book differs from the original *One Day in China* not only in length but in approach. The original editors did not use a topical organization, focus on key terms, or envision a sequence of four parts on an ever-widening scale as we have done here. Accordingly, although they deserve full credit for mobilizing and publishing all pieces translated here, we—not they—bear responsibility for the organization and interpretations in this book.[26]

The Significance of One Day in China

Like the original editors, we have tried to devise an approach to the pieces from the "One Day in China" project that highlights their significance. Every reader will want to evaluate their ultimate significance—and, with this aim in mind, might wish to read and think about the pieces in a different order than the one found here. For this reason, we don't wish to attempt to make a definitive evaluation of their significance, but we would like to suggest a few possibilities.

In retrospect, the significance of *One Day in China* may be assessed from several different perspectives. Writing his editor's introduction on August 20, 1936, Mao Dun eloquently summarized the picture that the contributors show us and concluded that behind their portrayal of "the ugly and the evil, the sacred and the pure, and the light and the darkness . . . we can see in it optimism, hope, and awakening of the masses of people."[27] Adding a foreword to the manuscript of the book two weeks

26. We regret missing the opportunity to consult Mao Dun about this book. We wrote to him and hoped to ask him about the editing of the original *One Day in China*, the authenticity of the pieces published in it, the whereabouts of the more than 2,500 pieces submitted but not published in it, and other questions. Unfortunately, we were not able to meet with him or hear his answers before his death in Beijing on March 27, 1981.

27. Mao Dun, "On the Editorial Process," in Appendix C below.

later, the scholar and educator Cai Yuanpei approached it from a second perspective, viewing it as a kind of super newspaper which came closer than ordinary newspapers to revealing "the totality of one day."[28]

No one else, so far as we know, has pronounced a judgment specifically on *One Day in China*—even though it has recently been republished[29]—but historians and social scientists have used approaches to the Chinese past that are worth bearing in mind while reading this book. In light of recent historical approaches to twentieth-century China, for example, we might consider whether *One Day in China* contains evidence of an interpretive theme developed by historians: wholesale disintegration, a process well underway by 1936 which undercut not only China's administrative system but also its social institutions, political organizations, cultural foundations, and national ideals.[30] In view of recent observations by sociologists and journalists, we might wish to draw comparisons between the world revealed in *One Day in China* and contemporary China—especially with respect to the ability of local people to ignore, resist, or subvert government programs that have to do with the role of women, local government, popular religion, and relations with foreigners.[31] And considering the success of anthropologists at learning about rural China from written as well as oral sources, we would be wise as we read to heed an admonition from the anthropologist Maurice Freedman, who urged everyone interested in China to "interview the dead."[32]

In reading *One Day in China*, we find all of these scholarly interpretations and suggestions helpful, but in our judgment its ultimate significance lies in the perspectives provided not by scholars but by the contributors and their subjects. To be sure, they are uncelebrated people—people for the most part so obscure that we have been able to find little evidence of their identities beyond what they have written within these pieces. But they are insiders who are writing or speaking for themselves, their neighbors, or at most a Chinese audience which, they as-

28. Cai Yuanpei, "Foreword to *One Day in China*." For a full translation of this foreword, see Appendix B below.

29. The republished version is an exact replica of the original, including no additions or revisions whatsoever. According to the cover of the republished version, it has been issued by Sun Chau Book Company (Shenzhou tu shu gongsi) (Hong Kong, n.d.).

30. See Eastman, *The Abortive Revolution*, pp. vii–xiii and passim; Lloyd E. Eastman, "The Disintegration and Integration of Political Systems in Twentieth-Century China"; and James E. Sheridan, *China in Disintegration*, pp. 18–21 and passim.

31. As a beginning point within the large and growing body of literature on women, local government, and popular religion in contemporary China, see William L. Parish and Martin King Whyte, *Village and Family in Contemporary China*. On current Chinese attitudes toward foreigners, see Orville Schell, "*Watch Out for the Foreign Guests!*"

32. Quoted by G. William Skinner, "Introduction," p. xiii.

sume, is familiar with the general conditions of the time. As insiders writing or speaking for insiders they provide views from the inside: not abstract analyses, but personal reactions and intimate insights. They express themselves in a variety of styles—formal and casual, elegant and crude, flowery and straightforward, pretentious and earthy—but almost all seem to base what they say on their own direct observations of daily life in China.

Whether the perspectives of the contributors and their subjects were shared by many of their contemporaries is difficult to say. After all, by its very design this project probably appealed more to the outspoken and disgruntled than to the contented or complacent. Accordingly, the contributors and their subjects provide a largely critical comment on their society. But whether or not their perspectives permit them to make "objective" or "balanced" interpretations, they share among themselves a common mood.[33] It is a somber mood, and their picture of this one day is painted in dark hues. Some of them seem more despondent than others, but almost all are determined to air their grievances.

Yet, for all their frustration, disillusionment, and bitterness, few of them seem broken. Though in their view China's social institutions might be oppressive, its political organizations tyrannical, its cultural life distorted, and its national ideals betrayed, the authors and subjects of these pieces seem to be willing and eager to fight back.

Insofar as the following pieces are part of their fight and express their feelings, perhaps reading what they have to say will permit us to share some of these feelings—the feelings of the kind of people who, as James Agee showed in a very different context, die without self-congratulations.[34] Whatever success *One Day in China* has at conveying these feelings will serve, we believe, as the proper measure of its ultimate significance.

33. This dark mood is pervasive not only in the 84 pieces translated here but throughout the 469 pieces in the original *One Day in China*.

34. Coincidentally, Agee also wrote about people in 1936, but they were tenant farmers in the American South whom he and Walker Evans portrayed in their classic, *Let Us Now Praise Famous Men*.

Notes on the Text

Romanization. Chinese words used in this book have been transliterated according to the Pinyin Romanization, which is becoming the established international system for Romanizing Chinese as pronounced in Mandarin. Exceptions have been made here for the names of Confucius and Mencius, which have long been Latinized, and of Sun Yatsen and Chiang Kaishek, which have long been Romanized according to pronunciation in other dialects of Chinese. Otherwise Pinyin has been used throughout, even in rendering the following names of people, places, and organizations, which may be more familiar to some readers by the spellings given in the right-hand column:

Pinyin	
Beijing	Peking
Beiping (alternate name used in republican China for the above city)	Peiping
Chongqing	Chungking
Dalian	Dairen
Guandong	Kwantung
Guangzhou	Canton
Guanyin	Kuan-yin
Guomindang	Kuomintang
Jinmen	Quemoy
Lu Xun	Lu Hsün
Manzhouguo	Manchukuo
Mao Dun	Mao Tun
Mao Zedong	Mao Tse-tung
Shantou	Swatow
Shenyang	Mukden
Taibei	Taipei
Xi Shi	Hsi Shih
Xiamen	Amoy

Xian   Sian
Yan Xishan   Yen Hsi-shan
Yangzi River   Yangtze River

Abbreviations. In the footnotes, the sources have been cited in abbreviated form. For full citations of all sources, see the Bibliography.

Signs of anonymity. Several pieces translated here (and several others in the original *One Day in China* which are not included here) are signed with pseudonyms and have had all or parts of proper names in them replaced by Roman letters (such as "A," "B," "H," "K," "L," "S. S." or, most commonly, "X"). To indicate that these are signs of anonymity, we have added after each pseudonym the notation "pseud.," and we have kept each Roman letter that appeared in the original in the translated text. Wherever we have been able to infer what the missing words were, we have added them in brackets (inserting, for example, the personal name "Shangjie" in Dr. Song XX [Shangjie], and the place name "Huang" in X[Huang]shishan).

We do not know who was responsible for deleting names and adding Roman letters in the original version of *One Day in China*, but it is worth noting that Chinese authors in this period (like Chinese authors throughout Chinese history) commonly used pseudonyms[1] and that the Guomindang government (like Chinese governments before and since) had a formidable record as a censor.[2]

Terminology. In this book, the following terms have been either translated with qualifications or, in the case of units of measure, left untranslated:

"Years of age." Because a Chinese was considered to be one year (*sui*) old when born, we have subtracted one from the age given in the original.

"Little" and "Old." "Little" (*xiao*) or "Old" (*lao*) is frequently used here preceding the name of a person (for example, Little Lin or Old Wang). In this context, the words are not meant to be taken literally: "Little" implies that a person is young but not necessarily small; "Old" does not necessarily indicate that a person is aged. Both terms are used primarily as expressions of affection (much as Americans might use the term "good ol'" preceding a friend's name).

Local Administrative and Subadministrative Units. Though there

1. See Austin C. W. Shu, *Modern Chinese Authors*, pp. ix–x; and Ting Hsu Lee-hsia, *Government Control of the Press in Modern China, 1900–1949*, pp. 81–82.
2. On censorship under the Guomindang, see Isaacs, ed., *Straw Sandals*, pp. xxxii–xxxiii; Ting, *Government Control of the Press*, chap. 5; and Eastman, *The Abortive Revolution*, pp. 24–30.

were significant variations from one locality to another, the approximate sizes of territorial units at the county level and below in China as designated by the Guomindang government in the 1930s are as follows (listed in ascending order from smallest to largest):[3]

Ten-household unit (*jia*): contained 5 to 10 households[4]

Tax-and-labor unit (*li*): contained about 25 households[5]

Watch-group unit (*bao*): contained 30 to 50 households[6]

Village (*cun*): contained about 300 households[7]

Market town (*zhen*): contained 4 to 10 tax-and-labor units or 100 to 1,000 households at a market crossroads (*jieshi*) but did not encompass villages at market crossroads having less than 100 households (which were instead subsumed under the jurisdiction of rural townships)

Rural township (*xiang*): contained 4 to 10 tax-and-labor units or 100 to 1,000 households from one or more villages

Ward (*qu*): contained 10 to 50 rural townships and market towns

County (*xian*): contained 3 to 12 wards (in 1936, excluding Outer Mongolia and Tibet, China had 1,949 counties, which were subdivisions within its 28 provinces)[8]

Military Units. Military organization was by no means standardized in republican China, but the approximate sizes of military units as designated by the Guomindang government in the 1930s are as follows (listed in ascending order from smallest to largest):[9]

Squad (*ban* or *fen dui*): 12 men

Platoon (*pai* or *xiao dui*): 41 men

Company (*lian* or *zhong dui*): 123 men

Battalion (*ying* or *da dui*): 514 men

Regiment or column (*tuan* or *zong dui*): 1,944 men

Brigade (*lu*): 6,250 men

Division (*shi*): 13,597 men

Units of Currency. Several kinds of paper money and coins were used in China in 1936. Of these, the types of paper money most frequently mentioned here are the "dollar" (*yuan*) and "legal tender"

---

3. Kuhn, "Local Self-Government under the Republic," pp. 284–87; Wen Juntian, *Zhongguo baojia zhidu*, pp. 474–75; Li Wenhui, *Zhongguo difang zizhi zhi shiji yu lilun*, p. 67; *"Shen bao" nianjian*, pp. 243–44.

4. Evidence from Jiangsu province. See Wen, *Zhongguo baojia zhidu*, p. 474.

5. Evidence from Guangdong province. See Li Wenhui, *Zhongguo difang zizhi*, p. 67.

6. Evidence from Jiangsu province. See Wen, *Zhongguo baojia zhidu*, p. 474.

7. Evidence from Shanxi province. Ibid.

8. Chien Tuan-sheng, "Wartime Local Government in China," p. 443.

9. Diyi jituanjun zongsiling bu, ed., *Fagui huibian*, vol. 1, pp. 186ff.; Xunlian zongjian bu, ed., *Junshi jianghua*, p. 40; J. V. Davidson-Houston and R. V. Dewar-Durie, eds., *Chinese and English Modern Military Dictionary*, pt. 2, p. 6.

(*fabi*), the former a general term used to refer to currency in China throughout the early twentieth century and the latter a new unit introduced by the Guomindang government in its monetary reforms of 1935 and 1936.[10] The value of these forms of paper money varied from region to region but each equaled approximately U.S. $.30. Only one type of coin, "big money" (*da yang*), is distinguished by name in *One Day in China*. It was given this name when first issued in 1917 because it was meant to achieve universal acceptance in China. But "big money" turned out to be a misnomer, for coins in this series were struck only in Tianjin and Nanjing and in the mid-1930s represented only one of at least five major issues of silver coins in circulation.[11]

Units of Measure. Units of measure also varied in different parts of China, but these are the approximate Western equivalents:

1 *li*	⅓ of a mile
1 *zhang*	10 feet
1 *fen*	.01647 acre
1 *mu*	.1647 acre (10 *fen*)
1 *qing*	.16.47 acres (100 *mu*)
1 catty (*jin*)	1.1 pounds
1 picul (*dan*)	110 pounds (100 catties)
1 *shi*	100 liters (2.84 bushels or 26.4 gallons)

---

10. On the Guomindang's monetary reforms, see Parks M. Coble, Jr., *The Shanghai Capitalists and the Nationalist Government, 1927–1937*, pp. 192–97.

11. H. G. W. Woodhead, ed., *The China Year Book, 1935*, p. 444.

One Day in China

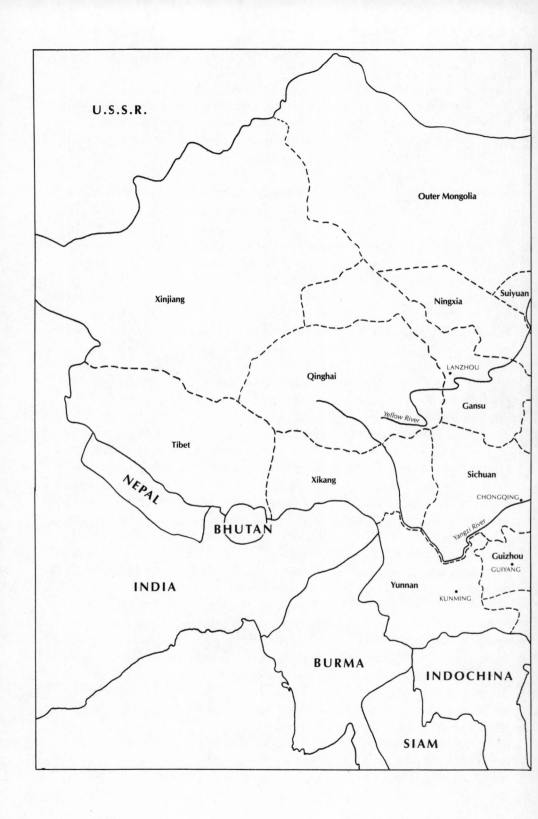

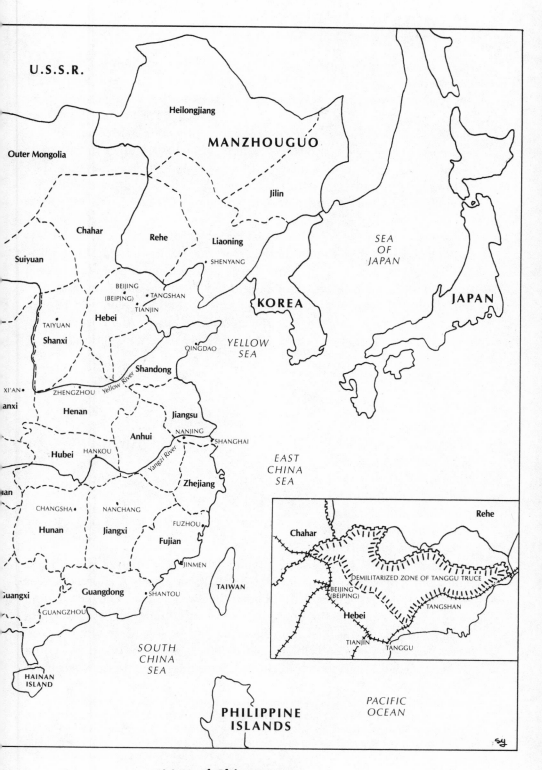

Map of China, 1936

PART I

''Family'' and Women

"Family" and Women

"Family" (*jia*) was used by contributors to *One Day in China* to describe the social institution that dominated women's lives, especially their experience of marriage and work. For several of the women described here marriage had dramatically altered the meaning of "family" because, following traditional custom, they had married "out" of their family of birth and "into" their husbands' families. As a result, according to the authors of the pieces in Section A, a wife was at the mercy of her husband and the members of her husband's family, who sometimes exploited or abused her so badly that she became ill, ran away, sought help from legal authorities, threatened to commit suicide, or, as a last resort, took her own life (nos. 1–8). While there seems to be no escape from the family for the women described in Section A, those dealt with in Sections B and C did hold jobs outside the family, but they did so at their peril. For the uneducated women described in Section B, any employment other than household chores was difficult to find and jobs were confined to a narrow range of tasks that were at best menial and at worst degrading: weeding and planting in the fields, doing piecework in the factories, singing and dancing in the amusement halls, selling their bodies as prostitutes in the streets (nos. 9–15). For the educated girls and women described in Section C, opportunities were considerably greater. Some attended school and others held positions as midwives, teachers, guidance counselors, and journalists (nos. 16–22). And yet, they too were constrained by obligations to the family, for, like the women in Sections A and B, they generally assumed or anticipated assuming the traditional roles of wife and mother. They worked at jobs outside the family in addition to—and without any reduction of—their work within it.

The contributors to Section A identified practices that made a woman subject to the dictates of her husband's family, and they deplored the failure of local government to stop these practices. By such practices as child

3

betrothal, ghost marriages, and arranged marriages, a family—that is, the husband's kinsmen—secured a bride for its own benefit (in the spirit world as well as the physical one) without consideration for the bride's interests. In general, these pieces leave us with the impression that a girl or a woman who was victimized by these practices had no recourse as long as she remained within her husband's family; either she submitted to them or resorted to running away or committing suicide. The two pieces describing suicides (nos. 4–5) show that after a woman's death, her natal family might have had some recourse against her husband's family and that she herself was believed to have the power to return as a ghost seeking revenge. While alive, however, the women pictured in Section A had no effective means of protesting unjust treatment by the family unless they were able to obtain help from governmental authorities.

Some of the contributors described appeals that women made to the authorities. According to laws that were on the books at the time, these women had reason to expect such help, for the Guomindang government's civil code contained reforms promulgated in 1930 and put into effect in 1931 that were specifically designed to eliminate abusive family practices. To end child betrothal, for example, the new laws set the minimum age for betrothal at seventeen for a man and fifteen for a woman and the minimum age for marriage a year higher for each. To prevent arranged marriages, the law stated that man and woman were to make an agreement to marry of their own accord. To make divorce more accessible, the law permitted dissolution of a marriage by mutual consent or on the initiative of either partner. The grounds for divorce included adultery, bigamy, maltreatment, desertion, and other grounds that might have applied to the cases described in these pieces. As scholars have pointed out, the new family law was conservative to the extent that it preserved patriliny, but its provisions gave ample legitimation to the complaints lodged by the women in Section A.[1]

Yet, even though the civil code had been on the books for five years, contributors to *One Day in China* seem skeptical that the women depicted in Section A would benefit from it. They contended that, regardless of what the law said, these women were denied its support because of the

1. The wife's position in divorce law had improved in stages before the 1930s, but she did not have a right to divorce under the law equal that of her husband until 1931. See Tai Yen-hui, "Divorce in Traditional Chinese Law," pp. 79–80. For a full translation of the Guomindang Civil Code of 1931 (promulgated and put into effect between 1929 and 1931), see Hsia Ching-lin et al., trans., *The Civil Code of the Republic of China*. For an interpretation of the provisions in this code pertaining to the family, see M. H. van der Valk, *An Outline of Modern Chinese Family Law*. On the marriage law introduced in 1936 by the Chinese Communists at their base area in Northwest China, see Snow, *Red Star over China*, pp. 225–26.

way it was applied. A woman who had the courage to approach authorities had little hope of receiving a proper hearing because the male authorities at the local level were unsympathetic to women's problems, unhelpful in handling their complaints, or antagonistic toward them for seeking legal solutions to family problems. In the cases of abuse reported to the authorities (nos. 6–8), none of the women seems likely to receive a fair hearing, much less have the case settled in her favor.

In contrast to the uneducated women in Section A, who had no way out of their predicaments in the family, the uneducated women in Section B had options outside the family, but these provided only periodic jobs, not sustained economic independence. Women within the family bore responsibility for paying the bills (no. 9). But in order to work outside the family, rural women had to compete for a limited number of jobs in the fields, fighting for coveted passes that male supervisors issued day by day (no. 10); urban women could be laid off at the factory with no more than a day's notice (no. 11); singing girls and prostitutes were assured of work only so long as they could attract prospective customers (nos. 12–14); and even women owning land—a seemingly secure investment— were not immune to the schemes of men with good connections (no. 15). In sum, for an uneducated woman the prospects of achieving any measure of economic security outside the family were bleak.[2]

Compared to the uneducated women in Section B, the educated women in Section C held jobs outside the family that were more secure, but these women were by no means free of obligations to the family. Instead, they labored under what has been called a "feminine mystique" which defined their roles solely in terms of relations with men—as wives, mothers, and homemakers—and dictated that they carry out undiminished domestic responsibilities within the family whether or not they pursued careers outside the home.[3] Under this double burden, several of the girls and women were drawn back to their family obligations even though they had received an education and were aware of alternatives to their traditional roles. In one piece, for example, family training caused girls in middle school to doubt the value of education for women (no. 16); in another, the family ethic of a submissive wife outweighed an

2. For a rare example of a group of Chinese women who rejected marriage in favor of economic independence in the 1930s (as well as throughout the preceding century), see Marjorie Topley, "Marriage Resistance in Rural Kwangtung."

3. The phrase "feminine mystique," first introduced by Betty Friedan to analyze thinking about women in America after World War II, has been applied to China under the Guomindang by both Norma Diamond in "Women under Kuomintang Rule: Variations on the Feminine Mystique"; and Elisabeth Croll, "'The Feminine Mystique': Guomindang China," chapter 6 in her *Feminism and Socialism in China*.

educated woman's full awareness of the availability of divorce and led her to put up with an unwanted marriage (no. 17); in others, the family ideal of motherhood made women feel guilty about working outside their homes before their children reached maturity (nos. 19–20); and in still another, family chores devoured time needed for professional purposes even for a woman holding a prominent position (no. 22). These concepts of women's family duties were deeply rooted in Chinese history,[4] and we can see here that these ideas were being reinforced in 1936 not only by traditional means but also through the use of modern techniques such as movies and mass political campaigns (nos. 21–22).

Thus, the view of "family" that emerges from these pieces is of an oppressive institution that victimizes women through both its practices and its ideology. Though this gloomy picture of women and the family is painted consistently in the pieces, whether it fairly represents all women and families in China in 1936 is open to question. Section C, for example, is both more and less representative of Chinese women than Sections A and B. On the one hand, it represents women more directly, because almost all of the pieces in it are written by women—unlike Sections A and B, which, like most of the writing about women throughout Chinese history, contain pieces almost exclusively written by men.[5] On the other hand, the women depicted in Section C are, by virtue of their education, less representative of the female population as a whole than are the uneducated women described in Sections A and B. Out of a total female population of approximately 225 million in China in 1936, only 106,075 were enrolled in middle schools, several thousand in normal and vocational schools, and 6,272 in colleges, universities, teachers' colleges, and technical middle schools. Moreover, in rural China at this time only about 2 percent of the female population over age seven had ever attended school and only 1 percent was considered literate.[6] In Section B, the women working in the fields and factories are representative in the sense that during the late 1920s and 1930s women provided about one-quarter of the farm laborers in China and more than half of the factory workers in

4. For a general interpretation of the traditional Chinese family and an up-to-date introduction to more specialized literature on the subject, see Hugh D. R. Baker, *Chinese Family and Kinship*.

5. Our selection includes proportionately more pieces by women than were written for the "One Day in China" project or were published in the original *One Day in China* volume. Women wrote 4 or 5 percent of the pieces submitted to the project (according to Mao Dun's estimate—see Appendix C), and they wrote 8.7 percent of the version published in Chinese (41 pieces) and 14.3 percent of our translated version (12 pieces).

6. Olga Lang, *Chinese Family and Society*, p. 104; and Evelyn Sakakida Rawski, *Education and Popular Literacy in Ch'ing China*, pp. 6–8.

the country's leading industrial center, Shanghai.[7] In all three sections, the women who are married are, by virtue of their marital status, more representative of China's female population than a comparable group of married women in any other large country in the world. In the 1930s, 84.8 percent of the female population of China was married—a higher percentage than in any other large country at the time.[8]

Whether or not the educational levels, vocations, and marital status of these women make them statistically typical, all are characterized here as victims of "family." If, as some scholars have argued, the Chinese family had a brighter side for women—as a source of power, satisfaction, security, or solace—that side is not evident here.[9] Instead, like the other three key terms in this book, "heads," "superstitions," and "Chinese traitors," the term "family" encompasses a set of attitudes and practices of which the contributors disapproved. However, in contrast to the other three parts of the book, the focus in this part is on the most immediate and personal sources and consequences of suffering, for the family was the institution to which the subjects (and the contributors) in *One Day in China* were most intimately bound.

7. See Margery Wolf and Roxane Witke, "Introduction," p. 8; Delia Davin, "Women in the Countryside of China," pp. 246–51; and Lang, *Chinese Family and Society*, p. 103.

8. Lang, *Chinese Family and Society*, p. 128.

9. For an interpretation suggesting that women have not been powerless within traditional Chinese families (because they have been able to gain control over male sources of power by retaining the first loyalty of their sons for themselves), see Margery Wolf, *Women and the Family in Rural Taiwan*, especially chaps. 3 and 10. For additional scholarly analyses of the Chinese family—including discussions of the ambiguity of the term "family"—see the essays in Maurice Freedman, ed., *Family and Kinship in Chinese Society*. For a critique of the Chinese family in the form of a largely autobiographical novel which was published in 1931 (and was popular in China in 1936), see Pa Chin, *Family*.

A. Women Confined within the Family

1. *Betrothal*

by JIXIANG
*(pseud.), a teenage female student
writing from Shanghai*

It was not yet dawn, only about four o'clock.

The children next door were already up, yelling, hollering, and making confused rhythmic beats on the wooden floor with their little leather shoes. Now and then the adults screamed at them once or twice.

Today was the day that Little Tiger from next door would be betrothed.

I groped for the curtain near my bed, pulled it back, and looked outside. The sky was still the color of ink. Several small stars still had open eyes that had been sleepless all night. One corner of the eastern sky showed a bit of white, like the underbelly of a fish, but unfortunately, the roofs of the houses were in the way, so I could see only vague traces of white. Cool morning air penetrated the windowpane, spread on my cheek, and gave me a chill.

I turned on the electric light and saw that Mother was still asleep. All the things in the room seemed to have closed their eyes and nodded off. I couldn't go back to sleep. I thought I might just as well go downstairs and do my shadow boxing exercises[1] for today even though it was a little early.

I tiptoed downstairs, opened the door, and went outside. Lights reflected off the wall opposite No. 20. I would have liked to have gone over and looked in, but I felt that if I as a girl paid a visit so early in the morning people would surely laugh at me. My foot, which had already taken a

1. This type of exercise (*taijiquan*)—a combination of calisthenics and martial arts—has a long history in China and is popular there today.

9

step forward, came back unprompted. At that moment, Little Tiger rushed out of his house wearing a brand-new little Western suit. His hair was well-groomed, he was wearing a bow tie, and on his feet were a pair of shiny black leather shoes, making him the perfect model of current fashion. As soon as he saw me, he rushed up to me, grabbed my hand, bouncing up and down excitedly, and said, "Sister Jixiang, this morning I can watch you do your boxing."

"Today is the twenty-first. Shouldn't you treat me to a drink of the wine of happiness?"

Mother told me to go next door as a guest, saying I must learn some manners and some of the social graces. I changed my clothes and went over to Little Tiger's house. As I was about to go through the gate, Little Tiger led in a band of his little friends, who surrounded me and clamored incessantly for my attention. Eventually Little Tiger's mother shouted out, "Tiger, today you can't run wild! Don't you know that you've now become an adult?" Little Tiger then blushed and led away his band of little friends running down the alley.

I went in and greeted everyone. I began to look around in appreciation at the decorations in the house. In front of me hung a rose-colored silk banner with the two Immortals representing marital harmony[2] embroidered on it and a golden character for Double Happiness pinned in the center. Burning in the incense burner was a piece of incense specially made in the shape of the character for Double Happiness, and on either side a pair of red candles burned brightly. There were two square tables that had been pushed together, and on the one closer to the rear of the house was a pair of transparent, delicate glass boxes. One side of the table was covered with red velvet, on which had been placed six pieces of gold jewelry to be worn on one's hands, and the other side was covered with green velvet, on which had been placed a bankbook and an ivory seal. On the table closer to the front of the house there were four rectangular wooden platters filled with colorful delicacies, the most elaborate being unshelled peanuts, every single one of which was dyed red and had gold paper wrapped around its middle. There were also pyramid-shaped glutinous rice dumplings wrapped in bamboo leaves, each over a foot long, with red and green ribbons tied around them. In short, everything had the aura of happiness.

Four lady matchmakers arrived, instantly giving rise to waves of congratulations. Outside the gate, neighbors from all around crowded to-

2. These two Immortals represented marital harmony in the Daoist popular tradition. On Daoist Immortals, see "A Little Shaman," n. 3.

gether, murmuring among themselves. Some little kids were demanding that their mothers give them goodies off the platters, but their mothers kept them firmly in hand.

After the banquet was over, Little Tiger's mother immediately handed the jewelry and the bankbook over to the matchmakers and repeatedly reminded them to put in a good word over there with the family of the girl betrothed to Little Tiger. Little Tiger's father, constantly stroking the small mustache on his upper lip, was smiling. He was pleased.

Firecrackers went off and green smoke floated off in all directions, leaving behind the smell of gunpowder. The matchmakers, with a person in tow to carry the platters, climbed into two cars, and took off.

At night I chatted with my mother, saying that someone like Little Tiger who is still in his childhood should not be talking about marriage, especially given the depressed state of today's society. Spending more than a thousand dollars in a single day on a son who has not reached adulthood seems extravagant![3]

Mother laughed at my silliness. "Silly child, otherwise what differences would there be in this world between the poor and the rich?" I couldn't help but remember that while we were eating the banquet, two poor children had been begging pitifully at the door. Fortunately Little Tiger had shown compassion and had given them each six copper coins. The two beggar children had stared through dull eyes at Little Tiger and had glanced back once even after they had gone down the alley. Ai! It is a year of childhood for each of the children, but how lucky Little Tiger is and how wretched the beggar children!

The night of May 21, 1936, started and finished in Shanghai.

3. Under the Guomindang government's civil code, which was put into practice in 1931, betrothal was not supposed to take place until a man was seventeen and a woman fifteen, but in this piece Little Tiger is described as not having reached adulthood (*wei chengnian*) and appears to be ten or eleven years old—the age at which betrothal commonly occurred in other parts of China during the 1930s. If he was ten or eleven, then his family was following traditional custom (and thus violating the law) by arranging his betrothal to his mate long before he reached the legal age. See the introduction to Part I, n. 1; and Cornelius Osgood, *Village Life in Old China*, pp. 276–77.

2. *A Comedy in the Midst of Sorrow*

by HUAYING (*pseud.*),
*a woman writing from
Ding County, Hebei*

Great winds blew before noon, loess covered the entire sky, and everything seemed gloomy and dark, quietly waiting for the wild winds to wreak destruction and cause disturbances. A Southerner, I have not been in the North long[1] and I am still not accustomed to this depressing weather, with its blustery winds and drifting yellow sand. In order to keep the dust out, a paper curtain had been rolled down. Inside the house it seemed even darker, and my head felt a bit faint. There was no one to chat with. What to do? Sleep! Yes, that was it.

Ping! Ping! Ping! I felt a wave of pain in my arm. Sitting up and taking a look, I saw Yunwu standing in front of the bed, holding a metric ruler. I felt pain and anger and I sat up, without saying a word. In a low voice, he muttered, "Lazy thing!" He grabbed me and we ran out.

Inside the shabby little courtyard was a crowd of adults and children, all in their best clothes. Boards had been laid out in a corner at the opposite end, and several men were there making the sound *titi tata*, doing I didn't know what. It looked as though they might have been busy eating. From a house to the east, out came a kindly looking old man, his brow tightly knit as though he was deeply worried. When he saw us, the corners of his mouth turned up into a little smile.

"Sixth Honorable Zhang! Congratulations to you!" said Yunwu as he approached with his hands clasped together in a respectful greeting.

"Ai," Sixth Honorable Gentleman's brow knitted even more tightly. "It's nothing to speak of."

"It is very good not only that you are able to achieve something you have always wanted, but that even Muger and his wife can occupy a good piece of land in the ancestral graveyard and in the underworld—and can be of some comfort to you!" In saying these last words, Yunwu was speaking disingenuously.

---

1. Huaying might have been attracted to the North by the project being carried out at this time in Ding County (where this piece was written). This project was designed to improve life in a rural locality and thus resembled experiments in other rural localities during the 1930s, which became known collectively as the rural reconstruction movement. Of all these experiments with rural reconstruction, the one in Ding County—which had American financial backing and was under the "new-style" leadership of Yale-educated James Y. C. Yen—was most deeply committed to transforming traditional Chinese habits and customs.

"Ai. If Muger were still here, then getting a daughter-in-law would certainly make today more festive."

Muger still here—daughter-in-law—festive! These words were very strange! Muger was dead and was still marrying a daughter-in-law? Then the daughter-in-law must be alive? Let's go have a look at the daughter-in-law.

When these strange ideas hit me, they almost made my mouth drop open and made me cry out in surprise. After a moment of exercising control, I calmed down. When I looked around for Yunwu, he was already following Sixth Honorable Gentleman out the main gate. Driven by curiosity, I followed closely behind them.

Reaching a graveyard, they stopped. In the midst of a crowd, two coffins had been put properly in place, and several big men were covering them with dirt. To the left of the crowd were placed people, houses, trunks, and the like, all made of paper.[2]

"Muger's destiny is powerful after all. He is able to marry such a good ghost daughter-in-law. Hasn't she brought along a large dowry?" an old lady in the crowd mumbled, pointing to those things made of paper.

"Isn't that the truth. There are even people from the bride's family to give her a send-off!" came a small voice from the crowd.

"It is said that this young lady has been dead for a year, and because no master could be found at that time and no allowance was made for her to be buried in the ancestral graveyard, all that could be done was to put her body in storage. Now she has been given to Muger through a matchmaker." said a stocky man.

"I must say, Eldest Auntie. It's better to arrange the great affair of a lifetime for sons and daughters. Otherwise, there's no place to bury them when they die." another old lady said, sighing.

Good heavens! When I realized what was happening, the tension that I had felt running throughout my whole body suddenly broke. As it turns out, this is a comedy. The only regrettable part is that it is in the midst of sorrow.[3]

May twenty-first in Ding County, Xiping, Zhugu Village

See Sidney D. Gamble, *Ting Hsien*, which concentrates exclusively on Ding County and is based on data collected between 1926 and 1933; and cf. "A Family Letter," n. 1.

2. Burning these paper objects was believed to transport them to the other world for the use of the deceased. See "The Temple Today," n. 5.

3. This kind of "ghost marriage" in which children are married posthumously is still performed in rural Taiwan. See Arthur P. Wolf, "Gods, Ghosts, and Ancestors," pp. 150–52.

3. A Passage from a Diary

by FEI LEI,
a male teacher writing from Zanhuang, Hebei

Entering my house is like stepping into a sad city devoid of sunlight, where even the slightest bit of fun in life can't be found and disturbing problems are everywhere I look. Two know-nothing children show no consideration for the adults whose hearts have been broken by difficulties and illness, and there are fights at every meal over who gets more and who gets less. My aged father, sitting in a broken-armed chair, was holding his head in his hands. I stood right in front of him, but I didn't dare look straight at him because I was afraid to look into his embittered face with its furrowed brow. I didn't know whether he hadn't seen me or he was thinking about other problems. I was buried under this heavy atmosphere, but the heaviness couldn't suppress my sick wife's moaning which was coming through the window.

Father raised his head, and looking straight at me he asked, "Have you seen Xiujin's sick mother?"

"I've seen her, and her coloring is even worse than it was when I returned home the day before yesterday."

Father once again buried his head in his hands. An invisible fog of sorrow hung all around.

I'm not making a point of cursing my wife. Even though I don't have a deep love for her, I haven't the least bit of bad feelings. What I feel is sympathy that verges on pity. Normally, whenever I see her as she goes about dealing with busy and complicated domestic matters, with a face neither crying nor laughing, this kind of sympathetic pity would naturally rise up from the bottom of my heart. In fact, she has been even more unfortunate than myself. Ever since my beloved mother left this world, all family matters, large and small, have been loaded onto her shoulders. She is young and not as experienced as Mother was, so she hasn't taken care of everything as properly as Mother would have, but she certainly has been unremitting in her devotion to all tasks. She has made the tea, cooked the rice, mended the clothes, spun the yarn, looked after my little brother, raised her own daughter, and been busy with all kinds of work. And on top of everything she has malnutrition, which has damaged her health and made her healthy body gradually become weak and thin. Recently, as a result of childbirth, she has become as sick as this.

When she first got sick, I had already been talking to her about taking care of herself and using medicine as a remedy. She sobbed and sobbed very sorrowfully, and, grief-stricken, she said to me:

"Don't say anything more. Really, how can I take care of myself? In this family both adults and children are short of things to eat and things to wear. If we have some good thing to eat, the two children both act like hungry wolves, and how can I put food into my mouth and let them stare at me?"

I had it in my heart to make a few more dollars for her, but the eight dollars I earn each month from teaching is not enough to support me and cover the family's expenses as well. In addition, the corn that Father said was being saved for seed has all been eaten up. There's no way. All I can give to my wife as repayment is a few drops of hot tears that can't be eaten and can't be drunk.

When I saw her today, she asked me to find some medicine for her to take. She could no longer bear the pain. In the past whenever she even looked at a prescription, her heart would jump. But in her present sickly condition all the dangerous symptoms have appeared, so she wants to take medicine.

After supper, I went to get Fourth Uncle to write her a prescription. He was sitting on a millstone outside the door, chatting with Father and the neighbors. He saw me and asked me first, "Aren't you going to find a cure for your wife's illness?"

"I see that her illness is truly difficult to cure. There's probably not much hope," I said, deeply depressed.

"Is that so! Let her go? Though it's difficult to cure, you can't let her go without trying to find a cure."

I was burying myself in a silent depression when I heard my father let out a long sigh.

Fourth Aunt and Third Sister-in-law, who is from the Wang family next door, were talking. "Death, life, all is fate. If it's not yet time to die, there will be recovery even though the illness is severe," they were saying, expressing the "fatalism" that is commonly invoked by mothers in rural areas. As for me, fatalism no longer is a comfort. I don't need comfort from other people, I know how to comfort myself. What's with this "should die"? What's with this "should not die"? Those who die are those who should die. Those who don't die are those who shouldn't die. But even though I have rejected this kind of "fatalism," which is not even worth bothering to reject, I hope that it will be preserved and will continue to exist because it is certainly a dose of "medicine for calming the heart" for most ignorant and unfortunate people.

I asked Uncle to find a way to cure her. Finally, I went to the Lin Family Drug Store to buy an ounce of large Eastern ginseng and returned home to boil it myself and let her drink it down.

So weak that she didn't look like herself, she was catching her breath, coughing. Her whole body was swollen, especially her legs. She couldn't lie down for long, couldn't easily move around, and, if she lay down for long or moved around, couldn't go from one breath to the next. I could hear short whistling sounds from her lungs, and I couldn't go to sleep with a sense of calm.

At midnight I got up and boiled half a cup of ginseng broth for her to quench her thirst.

A great horned owl in the tree in front of the village hooted from dusk to dawn, and a cuckoo also loudly tootled his flute, shaking the silent night world. These two kinds of birds ought to be shot, frightening and disturbing her, and causing her to sit up and lie down, to lie down and sit up. To comfort her, I cuddled up next to her. Looking up at the window in the ceiling, she whispered to me, "Listen! That's the sound of a noisy friend."[1] I realized that she must feel in her heart an uneasiness about this devil bird, which is considered inauspicious, and so I consoled her, saying, "No, you're wrong, that's the sound of a cannon-firing bug."[2] She cried out despondently, "I'm about to die!" I touched her, silently swallowing the sour tears that were welling up, and, after a moment, soothed her: "Don't talk foolishness, take care of yourself, you'll get well . . ."

4. *A Funeral Procession*

by XIAMIN (*pseud.*),
a male student from Shouyang, Shanxi

From eleven o'clock in the morning on, the usual silence on the motor road outside the school gate was shattered and replaced by a hustling and bustling. Men and women, old and young, drifted off to the west by twos and threes.

On this road, this kind of thing very seldom happens except during the annual West Village drama festival. But the festival won't take place for another half month.

1. [Fei Lei's note:] People in our rural township refer to the "great horned owl," as a "noisy friend," and consider it along with the crow to be an "inauspicious bird."
2. [Fei Lei's note:] The "cuckoo" is commonly known as the "cannon-firing bug" because the sound it makes, *bugu, bugu,* sounds like the words in the local dialect for "cannon-firing, cannon-firing."

My curiosity aroused, I ran up to question passersby and discovered that they were watching a funeral procession. Was there that much to see in a funeral procession? It was just as well for me to go along and have a look, so I joined the crowd passing by.

Weather in the North during early summer is not very hot, and a southwesterly breeze, which was indeed cool and comforting, blew into our faces. On either side of the road, the wind blew the wheat seedlings in turbulent green waves. It was like walking across a narrow bridge over a great river. My heart as well as my body was jostled up and down.

After I had walked one *li* or so and rounded a big bend, there was a village. When I came around the corner of a temple, suddenly the southwestern wind delivered a putrid odor, apparently a greeting for the guests from the dead person. I quickly covered my nose, turned away from the wind, and scurried around to the higher ground behind the spirit tent.

This spirit tent was a twenty-foot square cloth-covered frame. In front of it were several high tables arranged in a straight line. On the tables was sacrificial food. On either side were paper human figures and paper horses strewn about in disarray. It was obvious at a glance that this was not a particularly high-class funeral. But a pious mourner, who was dressed entirely in pure white, knelt in front of the tent and won everyone's respect—under the blazing sun, he unflinchingly maintained an erect posture, kneeling in front of the spirit tent as drips of sweat, or possibly tears, ceaselessly rolled down his cheeks and fell to the ground.

In the area around the spirit tent were patches of grass. To the east, west, and south there was higher ground where spectators had congregated, making it look like a balcony in a theater. I found in this "balcony" some shade under a tree and sat down.

"What's there to see?" I said out loud, at that moment deeply regretting coming for nothing.

What I had muttered drew this unexpected response: "Ai! This is going to throw that guy's family into bankruptcy!"

"Who is the person who died?" I turned and asked the elderly person who had responded.

"A woman in her twenties."

"A woman in her twenties has such a grown-up son?" I pointed to the one kneeling in front of the spirit tent.

"That!" His eyes turned to the place where I was pointing. "That's her husband!"

"Husband!" These two syllables immediately excited me, and unconsciously I rose and peered toward the spirit tent to take a closer look at him. This was the first time in my life that I had ever seen a husband wear such an elaborate mourning gown and kneel in front of his wife's spirit tent.

"You think it's strange for a husband to kneel in front of his wife's spirit tent? In a moment, you'll see that the mother-in-law will have to kneel in front of her daughter-in-law's spirit tent and burn tinfoil—forty dollars worth of tinfoil, to be burned piece by piece. And when the coffin is moved, she has to haul it. These are the conditions that have been laid down by the dead woman's own family!"

The mother-in-law had to kneel and haul for the daughter-in-law. This was even stranger. Upon learning about this peculiar circumstance, I suddenly realized that the hustling and bustling were not for no reason, and I felt that today's trip had a certain value. Just as I was about to try to find out other mysterious and secret things from this old man, sudden-ly—*dong, dong, dong.* The crowd reacted, rising to its feet and looking over toward the sound of the drumming. Several people even walked over there.

Following behind two small drums and two Chinese-style trumpets was a group of people, their black-haired heads undulating along. At the front was a fat man wearing a big straw hat and an outsized long gown, with his arms folded across his chest. He walked in a tiger step and was the leader of the group, as one could tell at a glance. On his left and right were two who looked as though they'd been sent to greet the guests, and both were grinning and making conversation with him.

"That guy walking along over there, isn't he Old Man Sun, who works in the yamen?"[1]

"Right! He is the father of the deceased!"

"Hmm. No wonder! They are well connected."

"Phew! A yamen runner. Nothing more than the leg of a dog.[2] What kind of good connections are those!"

"Huh! What do you youngsters know! Since ancient times it has been said: 'Having a person in a yamen is better than a hundred ounces of silver.' That's really something!"

The youngster seemed not to hear. He was pointing at the guests with his finger, like a shepherd counting sheep: "One pair, two pair,

---

1. A yamen was a large walled establishment within which were the county head's resi-dence, audience hall, court, jail, treasury, and other offices. A retinue of underlings—private secretaries, clerks, personal servants, and runners—served the county head there. Of these, the yamen runner (the position held by Old Man Sun) was lowest on the social scale. See Ch'u T'ung-tsu, *Local Government in China under the Ch'ing,* especially chap. 4.
2. This is a derisive remark. Chinese considered dogs to be lowly beasts.

three pair—ten pair—fifteen pair, sixteen pair. A few days ago during 'Making of the Seven,'[3] this group of hungry devils ate three piculs of the Li family's rice. Today four piculs will probably not be enough. Yi! How come the vegetable seller, Jing Jingwu, is in the group of guests coming for the funeral feast? Oh! Old Wu! Old Wu! How come you—"

From among the guests a pockmarked face suddenly turned and grinned at the youngster. He raised his fist, shook it twice, and then held up two fingers.

"Were you hired for two dimes?"

The pockmarked face nodded, and the two smiled knowingly at each other.

At this moment, the guests all entered the spirit tent, and the crowd immediately closed in around it. The scene became even more exciting than the places where acrobatic troupes and medicine peddlers perform.

Soon another group of people hurried in from the north. They accompanied a woman of about fifty and pushed their way into the spirit tent. The people immediately became excited, and men and women spectators ran forward and formed a ring three or four deep around the tent. Even I let myself become part of the crowd of spectators, and, standing on tiptoes, mouth agape and tongue sticking out, I stared, transfixed, into the tent.

"Kneel down! Kneel down!"

"No! Get up! By order of the head of the militia!" (The head of the militia refers to the leader of the Militia for the Promotion of Public Justice.)[4]

"Kneel down! Kneel down!"

"This is not right, and the Militia for the Promotion of Public Justice will be called in."

"Kneel down! Kneel down!"

"No! Get up!"

"Fight!"

"Fight! Fight!"

Suddenly there was chaos. There were sounds of people screaming and blows being struck. Tables were overturned, chairs smashed, and the whole scene turned into a battlefield.

Everybody became tense, as though a catastrophe were about to strike. By chance, a single-wing Sun-brand [Japanese] airplane flew over,

3. [Xiamin's note:] This is the day for sacrifices on the eve of the funeral during which the members of the family must serve food to anyone who pays a visit to their house.

4. [Xiamin's note:] This is a people's organization that is common in Shanxi. [On this organization, see "My Gramophone's Solo," n. 1.]

but it did not attract people's attention because this was not out of the ordinary. Without thinking, I said out loud to myself, "If a bomb is dropped, I wonder whether this place . . ." Before I finished the sentence, I saw two big eyeballs staring at me, and I realized that this was a warning to me against my uttering such inauspicious words. I quickly averted his gaze and shifted my attention to the spirit tent. Two groups of people made their way out of it and headed northward, breaking through the circle which surrounded the tent.

At this time, except for a group of energetic youngsters who followed them to see what had happened, most of the crowd returned to the original setup and waited to see what would happen next. Meanwhile, in groups of three to five, people began holding discussions:

"When you come right down to it, the Militia for the Promotion of Public Justice has a lot of power!"

"Hey! That was like a dog chasing a rat, butting in on someone else's business!"

"Yuh! That was within their jurisdiction. When a mother-in-law kneels in front of a daughter-in-law, do you call that justice or injustice?"

"Do you mean to say that one who died unjustly must die without getting revenge?"

"Who can say for sure whether or not it was an unjust death. From the dreadful look on the dead person's face, who can guarantee that this is not a case of her going off on her own to look for the ghost Life-Is-Transient?"[5]

"What!" A woman suddenly joined this gabfest. "For a long time, both the mother-in-law and the husband have looked down on her. Now she is dead from poison that was put in the medicine pot."

"Did you see that done yourself?" A youngster reproached her.

"Her ghost has become attached to the body of a servant in her own family who has said it herself. Isn't that truer than what I see with my own eyes?"

"Right! I've heard that the ghost of injustice has haunted her own family for five full days, pleading with them to seek revenge and vent anger on her behalf!"

"Ha, ha! These are really ghostly words.[6] This has all happened because the Li family has nothing going for it. Once you marry, you have a wife. Once you buy, you have a horse. While alive, she was a person in

5. [Xiamin's note:] A colloquial expression meaning to commit suicide. [On this ghost, see "A Procession for the Gods in Cibei," n. 2.]

6. "Ghostly words" is used here as a pun which could be taken to mean words spoken by a ghost or (as the speaker emphasizes) words that are not credible.

the Li family. Once dead, she is a ghost of the Li family. What could any-one named Sun dare do!"

"Hey! This is all because those who have managed matters have done so well. Otherwise they might have ended up with a lawsuit on their hands. Who doesn't know that her father is head runner in the yamen."

"Huh! A lawsuit, X,[7] that would scare anybody!"

"Oh! They're coming out!"

Many eyes once again focused on a large group emerging from the tent. Fat Sun was in front, with two men at his sides. He was leaning back, stomping his feet, pounding his chest, pointing toward the sky and the ground, and screaming as he moved along:

"Heaven above! I, Sun, cannot vent pent-up anger for my daughter. How am I going to face people in this world! . . . Oh daughter! Your worthless dad cannot rid you of your hatred and get revenge for you. If you have a spirit, why don't you reveal your spiritual power now! . . . She, your mother-in-law, pretended to be ill! Even if she were dead she should have had to come out, kneel before the spirit tent, and burn the tinfoil! . . ."

"After recovering from her illness, she will come. After recovering from her illness, she will come. Let her son do it instead." The people on either side of Sun implored him again and again to accept this arrange-ment. Immediately the husband in mourning was dragged over.

"Kneel down! Kneel down! Burn it! Burn it!"

"Burn it piece by piece!"

A haze of blue smoke swirled around, ashes from the paper blew all over, and once again the atmosphere in the sacrificial area grew tense. The spectators closed in as before.

"Bring some clothes to burn!"[8]

A person accompanying Fat Sun broke through the crowd, carrying a large bundle. A crowd immediately formed at another point in front of the tent. Fat Sun bent down, pulled out a woman's cotton jacket, lifted it up, and waved it:

"Look everybody! This is a fine, blue, big, well-padded cotton jacket! Let it burn!"

A person struck a match and set it afire. Then Sun pulled out another piece and waved it in the air:

7. The "X" has apparently been inserted in place of a profane expression.

8. Sun appears to be burning the dowry of the deceased. The act of burning was be-lieved to transport clothes (and spirit money and other objects) to the other world for the use of the dead. See "The Temple Today," n. 6.

"This is a yellow, satin, big skirt!" It was thrown onto the fire. After that, several other pieces were burned, and finally he hauled out a huge red cotton marriage quilt. As before, he waved it in the air and threw it onto the burning pile. Flames immediately shot up, and a puff of black smoke together with the stench of smoldering cloth wafted out onto the spectators, and all rubbed their eyes, held their noses, and retreated. At that moment, a gong sounded three times, *dang, dang, dang,* and the coffin, which had already been removed from the spirit seat, emerged from the tent.

5. *The Ghost of Injustice in a Grand Family*

by YE BUQIAN,
a male elementary school teacher writing from Yi County, Anhui

Dear Sixth Brother:

After reading your letter this time, I feel that lately you seem a bit depressed. I also know that your life is very busy, yet boring, and you are not making ends meet. So, who can blame you? Indeed, our lives have been too difficult, and even coming up with rice—I can't bear to go on! But isn't this what our so-called grand family has bestowed upon us? Ai, I suppose what I just said will surprise you a little! We, the young people who come from this grand family that has fallen, hate to admit that after receiving a bit of education and a smattering of knowledge we lack not only the courage to confront reality but also the willingness to bow down and surrender to old teachings of proper conduct and old customs. As a result, we've ended up at a crossroads and have brought trouble upon ourselves! My dear brother! You think I'm just grumbling again? No. Absolutely not! I'm saying this precisely because this is the common cause of the sickness that people like us have.

On May twenty-first a tragic death occurred in the village. These are the facts: Early last month in our village, Old Xian's family took a wife for his second son. The bride was the granddaughter of Sun Boyuan and came from Guzhu Village. Naturally, this marriage was the kind of union entirely "dictated by the father and mother and arranged by the matchmaker." Predictably, after the bride joined the family, the young couple did not get along. In addition, there was discord between the groom's mother and the daughter-in-law. Someone said it was because she "had a face that was nothing special, couldn't read a word, and brought a dowry that was too meager." Not only did the couple initially lack the courage to resist this kind of unreasonable and disagreeable marriage, but subsequently they were unwilling to surrender to old teachings of proper conduct. As it turned out, the bride's husband's family ruthlessly cut her down and made it seem that everything was her fault. In the end, early on the morning of May twenty-first, she could no longer stand her cruel life. She was so incensed that she hung herself from the lion over the bed.[1] Once the curtain was raised on this tragedy, her clan got the bad news and immediately sent a large group of people to lodge their complaints. There were thirty-five sedan chairs,[2] and each chair was escorted by one person and had a total including occupant and bearers of four people. Another fifty or sixty men came on foot. Including the occupants of the sedan chairs, the bearers, and the escorts, there was a grand total of about two hundred people. Before the group arrived, I was asked by the groom's family to serve as an usher. Because of an old friendship dating from the time we were classmates, I couldn't refuse. The men were received in the Zhushui Garden,[3] and the women were received in the Yizheng Hall.[4] The boisterous and belligerent ones who came from the woman's home were ready to fight. (According to old rural customs, whenever a daughter marries and then unfortunately commits suicide within her husband's family, for whatever reason, the woman's clan sends people to hold an inquest. Upon their arrival in the village, the groom must kneel in front of the sedan chairs and greet the visitors, who use this opportunity to beat him up. Moreover, the tea, snacks, rice, and dishes that the groom's family has prepared are not only left untouched but are smashed to bits by the people accompanying the bride's family. If

---

1. [Ye Buqian's note:] The beds people use in Yi County have the appearance of a niche. There are entrances on both sides of the bed. Atop the canopy on the bed is a small carving of a lion from which a mosquito net hangs.

2. [Ye Buqian's note:] According to the customs of Yi County, whenever a daughter marries and she unfortunately commits suicide within her husband's family—for whatever reason—then the woman's clan always gathers together many clan members and goes to hold an inquest. No matter how far the distance, everyone goes by sedan chair. The cost of hiring a sedan chair varies from two to three dollars to seven to eight dollars, all of which is paid by the husband's side. This is not only to make a show of force but also to increase the expenses for the husband's side. This is a way of venting anger. [For other examples of a woman's natal family seeking revenge after her suicide, see Margery Wolf, "Women and Suicide in China," pp. 112–13.]

3. [Ye Buqian's note:] Zhushui Garden is the security and watch-group office in our village.

4. [Ye Buqian's note:] Yizheng Hall is the name of the ancestral hall.

they go to the dwelling of the deceased, they have to tear down one corner of the roof. As the old saying goes, "May your family have not even three roof tiles left." This act is performed to vent anger and gain revenge.) By negotiating until our tongues were numb and our lips were dry, we mediators managed to avoid a fight. But there was lots of confusion and babbling which can't all be described in detail using brush and ink.

After several hours of negotiations, the bride's side proposed five conditions for settling the affair. These five conditions were:

1. Burn 600 dollars worth of tinfoil;[5]
2. provide a coffin worth more than 150 dollars;
3. provide ten catties of cotton and five bolts of satin;[6]
4. require the husband to be present to hold the head of the deceased at the body-clothing ceremony;[7]
5. perform forty-nine days of sacrifices to release the soul from unjust suffering.

They acquiesced to all of these conditions except numbers 1 and 5, which were too expensive and had to be renegotiated. As for number 4, "requiring the husband to be present to hold the head of the deceased at the body-clothing ceremony," it can't be carried out until we can find the groom, who ran away. When he knelt down at the beginning to receive

5. [Ye Buqian's note:] People in Yi County have always been superstitious. Even if people die of natural causes, about one hundred dollars worth of tinfoil is burned. Death by suicide is believed to give rise to a terrifying ghost. After death by suicide, sacrifices are never made. So, when the members of a woman's clan come to negotiate, they always insist that tinfoil be burned. [This was spirit money. Burning it was believed to transport it to the other world for the use of the deceased. See "The Temple Today," n. 6.]

6. [Ye Buqian's note:] At the body-clothing ceremony, according to the customs of Yi County, the body is wrapped in silk wadding before it is clothed. In general, in the case of death by natural causes, between three and eight catties of wadding are used, depending on one's financial situation. Death by suicide requires something special. The body must always be dressed in traditional clothing. There are three types, cotton, damask, and satin. The upper part of the body is dressed in nine pieces of clothing, and the lower part in seven pieces. Satin is the best. All this is for no other purpose than to cause the husband's side to spend more money. [For details on grave clothes, see J. M. M. de Groot, *The Religious System of China*, vol. 1, chap. 3.]

7. [Ye Buqian's note:] During the body-clothing ceremony, the sons and grandsons of the deceased are required to kneel next to the body and stroke the head. This is called the holding of the head. After the undertaker wraps and clothes the body, it is placed in the coffin. If the deceased has no sons or daughters, a wife "strokes" a deceased husband's head or a husband "strokes" a deceased wife's head. There are cases where a husband doesn't stroke a wife's head, depending on the closeness of the relationship between husband and wife. But in death by suicide, because people fear the evil that the vengeful ghost will do, no one will stroke the head in most cases. [On the popular belief in China at this time that the spirit of a suicide could avenge itself, see Fei Hsiao-t'ung, *Peasant Life in China*, p. 49.]

the sedan chairs and saw the large number of people arriving, he was afraid that he would be humiliated. Ultimately, after much haggling, there was a discount on the price. After 250 dollars worth of tinfoil and seven days of sacrifices, this tragedy was over. According to calculations, the man's side lost over a thousand dollars and was forced to swallow its pride. The woman's side gave up a life and exhausted its lips and tongues.

My dear brother! After reading what I've described, what do you think? Isn't this a kind of perversion? Hasn't the grand family left this as a legacy?

Finally, let me comment on the death of Second Elder Brother this spring. Didn't he lose his life under these same circumstances? Fourth Elder Brother said that he wanted to go to Hankou to negotiate anyway about the death of Second Elder Brother. Oh oh! This is really . . . Please tell him to take a longer and broader view!

My life is extremely mechanical, but the life of a teacher is always like that. A village elementary school teacher's responsibilities are comparatively heavy. The children are extremely mischievous and disciplining them is very tiring. Every day they give me a headache, and I don't even have enough leisure time to read two chapters of a book. But now, all I can do is stick to it. My dear brother! May I persuade you also to stick to it, and together we'll keep on plugging away.

Your Fifth Elder Brother, Buqian

6. *Like Any Other Day—Life on May Twenty-first in the Clearinghouse of the K County Government*

by YUHUO (*pseud.*),
a male clerk writing from Lianshui, Jiangsu

The K County seat is one of China's out-of-the-way cities, and the county head is the highest official in the area. The county head has said: "The clearinghouse is the throat of our county government." It is quite an honor for L and me to be workers in the clearinghouse, in control of this throat. Moreover, the clearinghouse is really interesting, and many of the other workers frequently come by looking for a good time. We are the first to know everything, and we receive and distribute about forty to fifty official documents each day. We read over the contents of the important ones once and commit them to memory. We embellish the interesting ones in telling about them, and, as we work, we talk and joke about them for the fun of it.

All personnel get up at six o'clock, but because part of our work has to be done at night, the county head has given us special permission to get up an hour later. Anyhow, even if we got up earlier, there wouldn't be work to do.

As for today, it was like any other day. Starting at nine o'clock in the morning we began receiving documents. What made us especially happy was the first item, in which the Society of Women's "Lady Xi Shi"—this odd nickname was given to her by L of our clearing-house[1]—led in a young country girl to initiate a lawsuit. The case concerns this young girl (who looks about sixteen years old) who was not willing to follow her parents' orders and marry a thirty-eight-year-old small property owner. We asked this girl her name, age, native place, the ins and outs of her betrothal, and so forth. In fact, these had already been clearly written out in the complaint, and they also had nothing at all to do with our job. But this time, because this young girl had a face like a peach blossom and that "Lady Xi Shi" was also quite a famous "modern woman" in K County, we acted like judges and like two careful military policemen interrogating suspicious-looking characters.

Next came a woman who looked like a beggar. Seeing her ragged clothes and sad face made us shake our heads. Besides, she had come many times before. Because her husband was implicated in a case of banditry, he has been ordered to find a guarantor. She is a person from quite far outside the city who is extremely poor and though she has run around from the countryside into the city and from the city into the countryside, she still can't find a store proprietor to serve as guarantor. For more than ten days she has been constantly at our window—our clearinghouse is like the post office in that no one is allowed inside—crying, sobbing, knocking her head on the ground, and babbling away. If only we could give her a kick and send her to the other side of the sky! To tell the truth,

---

1. This nickname, "Xi Shi," was originally the name of a famous Chinese beauty who was born in the fifth century B.C. in the Lower Yangzi region (the area in which this piece was written) and was familiar to Chinese because of her place in Chinese opera and folklore. Of the many lines celebrating her good looks, perhaps none have been more quoted than the classic couplet by the poet Li Bo:

Her beauty overshadowed the beauties of past and present;
The lotuses were shamed by her color like jade.

Translated by Harold Shadick in Liu T'ieh-yün, *The Travels of Lao Ts'an*, p. 261, n. 4.

too many people have asked us for pity. And so, in order to keep our jobs and rice bowls, we have naturally lost sympathy in our hearts. The most annoying thing to us is the crying and the most pleasing is laughter. So, just as we always do in dealing with annoying people, L shouted at her: "Get out! You mother!" The woman naturally stepped back. L then said in a lower voice, "You have interrupted our discussion of this beautiful woman's divorce case."

Besides beautiful women, what interests us is the most gruesome and bizarre news. An incident of this sort was the next to come up: A twelve-year-old girl had been raped by a man of over thirty. The girl's mother, who came to start a lawsuit, was shaking, shedding tears, and saying that her daughter was about to take her last gasp. This news certainly gave us no small amount of excitement. L immediately rushed out to tell another worker. Soon the clearinghouse was full of people, hustling and bustling, and laughter was rising as high as the heavens. Someone said that the man deserved to be regarded as the number one sex devil under heaven. Someone else said that the girl must have been as beautiful as a piece of jade, and another person imaginatively described and acted out sexual intercourse between them. Finally, on the question of this girl's marriage in the future, everyone agreed unanimously that she ought to marry L as his concubine. Only then did the curtain temporarily close on this comedy, as noise and laughter filled the air.

When it got dark, a ward runner[2] from the tenth ward arrived delivering two official documents. One was a report on a case of robbery and murder which took place last night, describing in great detail the murder of all of a family's members and the theft of all of a family's property. The other one was a balance sheet of the accounts of this ward office for last month. The ward runner had only one eye, his other eyeball bulged out, and his mouth was twisted. The sight was really laughable. After we poked fun at him several times, L said:

"Your salary is not bad, eh—each month eighty dollars divided by ten."

"Reporting to the chairman," he said, standing at attention, "My salary each month is five dollars."

Then I told him that according to the balance sheet his salary should have been eight dollars, and the reason he actually received five dollars was that the ward head was pocketing three. After hearing this, he didn't say anything for a moment. Finally, lips trembling, he said:

2. At the ward level, as at the county level, runners had low status. Cf. "A Funeral Procession," n. 1.

"If, if the chairman had not said this, I would still be in the dark! That mother's fart sucks our blood!" He slowly walked away.

At eleven o'clock at night, a ward runner from the twelfth ward delivered an extremely urgent official document, which said that the workers dredging the river intended to riot tonight and were leaving work together to return home. I hurriedly prepared a summary of it, put a number on it, and recorded the incident in the logbook. Then I handed it to the secretary's runner and asked him to deliver it to the secretary, who was already in bed asleep. Returning to my own bedroom, I said to L, "The workers dredging the river want to riot, which is really no small matter, and among them must be instigators who are Communist bandits." L said, "X hair! You'll see, not a single worker will be absent tomorrow. You think the troops guarding the work don't know how to do anything but eat rice? Let's look at women and go to sleep!"

Just like last night and the night before, L took down from above the head of the bed nude photographs and several movie star pinups which were wrapped in two tickets from the twenty-third airplane lottery. He looked at them one after another as line after line of obscene comments and dirty jokes came rolling out. Finally, as though actually talking to two beautiful girls, he said, "Juanjuan, Qianqian, don't worry about not having money to spend. I've won a prize worth 25,000 dollars and I'm inviting you both to sleep with me tonight—take off your clothes."

Laughing, we slipped under the covers.

7. A Hearing at the Public Bureau[1]

by YE RENHONG,
a male teacher writing from Huizhou, Anhui

After the first class in Chinese literature, as I was passing the side door on my way back to the dormitory, I saw a woman. She had been sitting for I don't know how long on the long wooden bench that had been specifically set

1. [Ye Renhong's note:] In those villages and market towns of the Huizhou area that are comparatively far from the county seat, villagers themselves handle all petty cases, except murder for monetary gain and other serious cases, which have to be reported to and tried at the county or provincial level. Generally the people who handle the cases in the villages are ward heads, who have established some reputation and are respected by the villagers. [It is not clear whether School Head Yang in this piece was a ward head. The designation used in the title of the piece is public bureau (*gong ju*), not ward office.]

up by School Head Yang for people from nearby villages who came to air grievances at the public bureau.

At first she sat facing the school entrance. But when she heard footsteps behind her she suddenly jumped to her feet and whirled around with a painful expression on her face, walked up to me, and said, "Sir, please make it known to Mr. Yang that I am here to see him."

"All right. Have a seat for a moment," I said, heading directly for the dormitory.

School Head Yang had been at school for over an hour. But he has his daily habits—reading from cover to cover a copy of the newspaper *Shen bao,* which is delivered in the morning from the market town, and conducting no business with people before ten o'clock—so whenever I tell him that someone is here to see him, he always says "Fine," pays no attention, and goes on reading the newspaper.

When I returned to the dormitory for the second time, I saw the kitchen servant, Ah Xun, leading the woman in.

Her face was badly scratched. From looking at her you could tell that she'd been in a fight and had been scratched by fingernails. She stared straight ahead, as if her eyes were nailed in place—her every movement suggesting that she was wooden and not at all herself. Anyone would be able to tell that she was under deep emotional stress.

As School Head Yang beckoned her to sit down, she blurted out her grievances: "Sir! I've often heard people say that you, sir, are the one who speaks words of justice on behalf of other people. So I've come —I've come to beg, sir. I am the daughter-in-law of Wang Caixi of the village over there. My husband is called Changfa. He does his business on the road. Three years ago when he came to take me as his bride, he treated me all right—" She stopped abruptly, lowered her head down to her chest, and began to sob out loud. "But now he's had a change of heart and doesn't want me any more. Sir, please, tell me, what kind of a thing is this? He has come home and brought a woman with him."

"Brought a woman home?" School Head Yang interjected. "What is this woman to your husband? Is he taking her as a bride?"

"What else!" The woman nodded in agreement. She reached into her pocket, pulled out a handkerchief, and continuously wiped away the tears that were falling from the corners of her eyes. "He says that people in other places have such a custom. If a man and a woman can't get along, there can be a divorce. From then on, neither one can interfere with the other. So now he has come back, forced me into a divorce, and sent me back to my mother's family. How can I return to my mother's family? What kind of thing is that! In all these years I've been married to him, I've never done a single thing to be ashamed of! Year after year, while he's been out there, haven't I been with my father-in-law, working myself to death and living a thrifty life! Planting fields and leveling hills, is there anything I can't do?"

"So, what do you feel in your heart?" School Head Yang probed.

"Me! I can't leave him like this. My mother has already married me out! How could she permit me to return? I know she'd beat me to death! Ai! Sir, I beg you to think of a way out for me. While I'm alive I'm a person in his family, when I die I'm a ghost in his family. In the meantime, where can I go? People will say ugly things about me."

"What about your man?"

"Him! That black-hearted devil! He'll have it no other way except for me to leave. He beats me to death, scolds me, and causes trouble from dawn to dusk. But—" She swallowed hard. "But, I put up with everything. I'm willing to let him beat me to death! He can swallow me whole! I can't leave him and go away. People would laugh at me for the rest of my life."

"All right! I understand everything. But what you have said just now on your side is not evidence. Tomorrow, you and your husband come to see me together," said School Head Yang authoritatively, and then he began to pace slowly up and down the room.

"Hmm, sir, thank you. Then, I'll come again tomorrow." The woman very gratefully bowed and carefully retreated from the room as though all her most serious problems had been completely solved.

8. *The Pickup*

LÜYI (*pseud.*),
a man writing from Qingdao, Shandong

It rained heavily for two hours on the morning of May twenty-first. The prison was quieter than usual because no one was allowed to go out to "catch some fresh air." Nor was there the sound of roll call or the clanking of chains being dragged by prisoners on the way to the factory where the prisoners glue matchboxes together. Every room of every building was locked in silence. In the prison yard, the guards on duty took cover in the weather shelter, and six or seven warders sat in the office idly chatting.

At about eight o'clock the wind died down and the rain stopped. The sky was still filled with dark clouds. The sun occasionally peeked through cracks in the clouds, but it was immediately covered over by black clouds. Just then a gray sedan sped up the main road south of the prison and parked in front of the prison gates. Out of the car jumped eight tough-looking men. Three of them wore Chinese-style long gowns and had fedoras cocked to one side of their heads, and the others wore shorts and jackets and looked belligerent. After getting out of the car, they lined up along the base of the wall on either side of the gate. The car was parked on the left-hand side of the road as though waiting to pick up somebody. One of the tough guys said, "Hurry up! People are always let out at nine o'clock."

The second floor of the north building in the prison's second compound is the women's jail. Just then more than sixty people were sitting in seven cells there waiting for breakfast. Now and then a few children cried out, breaking the silence. Then a woman impatiently scolded:

"You grown-ups are all dead! You don't look after your own children and you let them wail as if over the dead. You mothers are nothing." This was the women's warder, mincing about on a pair of small squash-like feet, swinging her big ass, wearing a grave expression year in and year out, with her three-cornered eyes and drooping eyelashes. Walking up to the door of cell No. 7, she opened it and pressed her point:

"Watch your kid! Quit screwing around." She slammed the door and, swinging her ass, made her way back to her office to smoke a cigarette.

"You old hag! Is your own child mute? Don't you ever let your children cry?" muttered a woman in her twenties as she wiped away the tears of the child she held in her arms. The child was about two years old.

"Big Sister Zhang, it's all right for you. Today your sentence is up, isn't it? You don't have to put up with her scolding any more. But me, I don't know when I'm going to get out of this hellhole!" sighed a woman serving a seven-year sentence on a murder charge, who also held a child in her arms.

In fact, it was true. Zhang's time was up. Her husband had died five months earlier, and, having no parents of her own since childhood, she had then been secretly sold by her brothers-in-law to a family named Wang, as a pig or cow might be sold. She had no idea of what was happening until she was carried away in a sedan chair and saw for herself. Her second husband was over forty, incredibly ugly, and very bad tempered. Worst of all were the brothers, sisters, and sisters-in-law of her second husband. Because she was no longer a virgin and had "a cooking oil bottle in her," and was "a woman married for the second time," they all humiliated and insulted her in every way and did not treat her as a person. She tolerated the situation for a month, until finally one afternoon she took her child and ran off to a relative's home. But she was immediately found by her second husband, who filed a charge with the court. Convicted of "deserting her husband, running away, and intending to abscond with funds," she received a five-month sentence. Because she had a child, she was put in this detention home rather than in a big penitentiary. Today was her 150th day.

"Big Sister Zhang, after you get out, you must come back here and visit us," six or seven women in the cell all said.

Zhang smiled. She was from a village outside the city. Her figure was slender and graceful, her face was white, her features were properly placed, and her bound feet were like the three-inch golden lotus. After hearing what they said, she replied:

"I'm going, but of course I'll come back to see you. My child and I have been in your care for these many days. Once I get out of here, I'll go to work right away, and I'll never again let anyone sell me. I'll never return to Wang."

"Mealtime!"

A strong voice inside the building interrupted their conversation. All at once doors creaked, lead pots banged, and rice bowls and chopsticks clattered. Each person got the usual: three black-bread buns the size of apricots and a piece of salted vegetable two-tenths of an inch thick and one inch long. If that wasn't enough, then there were rough cornbread and millet gruel. The meal was served under the supervision of the squad head and the woman guard, and each person ate her share. Although the buns had soured and the rough cornbread had sand in it, the women still managed to get them down.

Just as Zhang was swallowing a mouthful of gruel, Warder Wang, who was responsible for roll call, came up the stairs. He walked up to cell No. 7, removed the number-plate marked 501, and said:

"No. 501. Woman Zhang. Pick up your things. Go!"

"Sister, you're on your way!"

"Once you're settled, won't you come back to see us?"

In cell No. 7 all the women put down their rice bowls and gathered around Zhang, creating a commotion. She was handed a blanket and a small bundle of children's clothing. Putting them under her left arm and holding her child in her right, she said to them:

"I'm going, but I'll be back to see you in two days."

Warder Wang looked her up and down and, smiling, said to her:

"You've done your time and your husband's family has come to pick you up!" He turned to the woman guard with the small feet and said, "Women have all the luck. There are people who want to rush over and pick them up! I have never seen anyone rush over and pick up a man."

The woman guard with the small feet, after hearing what he said, immediately broke into a broad grin which exposed her big mouth full of yellow teeth.

This was not what Zhang had expected. It was like being unleashed only to be reined in again. Distracted, she said:

"I'm not going, Warder!"

"Nonsense! This is no hotel! When it's time to leave, you can't stay for another minute."

"Hurry up! Don't cause any trouble," said the guard with the small feet. She then turned toward the cell and yelled:

"Sit down! Eat your food. What are you looking at?"

Zhang's face was ashen. As she followed Warder Wang downstairs, two tears rolled down her face.

In the office, the prison head sat behind his desk with the prisoner's release form in front of him. Warder Wang brought her in, and she stood, dispirited, in front of his desk. The prison head shifted in his seat and said:

"Are you Woman Zhang?"

"Yes."

"How many months were you sentenced to?"

"Five months."

"You've served your time. Put your thumbprint here!"

She extended her right hand and made a thumbprint on the release form.

"That's all. Get out of here!"

Suddenly she fell to her knees, with tears in her eyes.

"Warden, sir! My husband's family has come to pick me up, but I can't go with them. He'll beat me. If things don't work out as he wants, he'll sell me. Please, sir, be merciful. Let me stay here for a few more days."

"What are you saying!" The prison head was displeased. "We're not responsible for your family affairs. You must go!"

"Sir, please be merciful and save my life!"

"Come! Take her away!" the prison head ordered, rising to his feet.

"Get going. You're on your own!" said Warder Wang and Warder Li, as they pushed her out of the office and led her past the two iron gates.

Five or six steps short of the main gate, she stood still, not knowing whether to go forward or backward. The child in her arms began to cry.

On the road outside the main gate, tough guys came from each side, rubbing their hands together and preparing to make the pickup!

A man in his forties, wearing shorts and a jacket, with an ugly face and the coloring of a drug addict, stepped out from amidst the crowd of tough guys, bounded up to her in two steps, and grabbed her hair. The child cried out for its mother, and the blanket and bundle fell to the ground.

"You bitch of a wife, haven't these five months taught you anything? Do you still want to run away? We'll go home and settle accounts."

The woman tried to break loose and cried out in a shrill voice:

"I'm not going with you! I can't bear your beatings and scoldings. I'd rather be in jail! You let me go."

The attempt to break free was useless. Her clothes were torn, but she still remained in the man's grasp. Then the tough guys rushed up, took the child, and picked up the blanket and bundle. Pushing and shoving, they dragged her into the car.

"You rotten woman. You think that I don't want you any longer because I took you to court! That's wishful thinking! See if I don't skin you alive when we get home!"

The door banged shut, the horn honked twice, and the car started up. In the midst of sobbing and tongue-lashing, the car sped off to the south.

The few people who had gathered on the road to watch the action dispersed. Warder Wang, who had stood at the first iron gate to watch this drama, turned around and walked back to his office, remarking to Warder Li:

"Partner, bear in mind that this is the fourth pickup this year."

B. Uneducated Women at Work

9. *Borrowing*

by JIANG ZHEN,
a female elementary school student writing from Hankou, Hubei

After supper, I had just taken out the magazine *New Child* to read when suddenly Mother said to me: "Zhen! There won't be a penny in the house tomorrow, and the money your father is sending still hasn't come today. It's really desperate! Now you hurry over to Auntie Zhang's to borrow a dollar again. Darling child! Hurry there and hurry back!"

"Mother! The money Auntie Zhang loaned us only a few days ago still isn't paid back, and I'm afraid borrowing again won't work! I'm really afraid to see the grumpy looks on their faces," I replied, completely unwilling to go.

"If you don't go, then what will happen tomorrow? Who asked you to be born into a poor family? Not going is out of the question." Mother spoke in this way.

I stood hanging my head, not moving, and not going. Suddenly the sound of a whack scared me. My mother had taken out a ruler. She was slapping it on the desk, and was about to hit me with it. Ai! Now it was impossible not to go, but I begged my mother, saying, "If we get the money, please give me a dime to make a contribution in school. The pressure is really on for us to make contributions for airplanes to celebrate the birthday of Chiang Kaishek!"[1] Mother promised me, and I rushed out.

Arriving at Auntie Zhang's house, I sat for a while and then said to her, "At home things are very difficult. Please lend us another dollar." She said, pretending to be sincere, "It's late in the month now and my

1. This campaign is described in more detail in "An Unscheduled Meeting of the Student Body."

money is gone. Little Sister, my small daughter, is sick, and that costs money. It's very difficult for me these few days too, and it's more than ten days until the first, when the money will come. Between now and then, money will have to be spent." Babbling away, she went on and on, and her face looked troubled and grumpy. I saw she was putting on an act of being poor, and in my heart I really hated her. My elder brother has said that once the war begins all money will belong to the nation. I only hope such a day will come and then the money she hoards away in a box every month will be taken away! I didn't say anything and left, embarrassed. It was dark when I got home, and when Mother saw that I had not borrowed anything, her eyes stared blankly.

I still hadn't read my magazine. Ai! Poor people reading magazines —are we denied even that?

10. *This Day on a Provincial Government Farm*

by GENGSHENG (*pseud.*),
a man writing from Songjiang, Jiangsu

Today was the third day that the farm neighboring ours was sowing seeds. Almost all the women within four or five *li* of here gathered together in groups and hurried to the farm before dawn. Barefooted, with their trousers rolled up high, they have a healthy and vigorous spirit which puts city ladies to shame.

Besides helping their fathers and brothers with daily farm work, the only side-job they have is making Western-style socks. Some go directly to the factory to make them, and some take their work home with them. Usually this pays eighteen cents a dozen, minus the broken needles and other miscellaneous breakage that they must pay for. Those who take their work home with them have to pay a dollar a month to rent the machines. It's said that those who work the fastest, and without stopping, can make at most only two dozen socks a day. So those living near the farm stop making socks and rush barelegged to the farm whenever there is work such as sowing seeds, planting seedlings, pulling and trampling weeds in rice fields. Since the daily wage is forty cents big money, of course it's better than making socks.

The amount of work needed each day on the farm is specified in advance, so naturally not everyone can be hired. The criteria for selection are working speed and familiarity with the work. Each day the people to work the next day are chosen and given "passes to go down to the fields" to show at work in the fields the next day. But some who don't have "passes to go down to the fields" still run over, hoping to be lucky enough to get work. So early in the morning the sounds of people pleading, cursing, and demanding passes all jumble together confusingly, as though something awful were happening.

Nearby lives a farm girl by the name of Ah Mei, who is only twenty or twenty-one and quite attractive. Most of the farm supervisors like to flirt with her, and they have given her such elegant titles as The Flower of A Village, The Village Queen, and the like. Yesterday she didn't show up to sow seeds. Today at ten o'clock she still wasn't there, and everyone felt jumpy without realizing why. They exchanged meaningless small talk among themselves, and wished that someone would go and call her.

"Old Yuan, if you can get her to come, I'll pay the forty cents wages," Old Jin, a horse-faced man, bellowed self-importantly.

"You'll pay forty cents. I'll pay eighty." Old Zheng's face beamed even more happily.

"You'll pay eighty cents. I'll even pay a dollar," screamed Old Niu, a big, fat fellow, jumping up.

"Ha—ha. Two dollars and twenty cents to get a woman to come—that could give us all a lift. It's worth it, it's worth it! Ha—"

"It's a deal! I'll go call her. If I can't get her to come, then I'll pay a fine of a dollar and twenty cents!" said Old Yuan confidently, as he set out to invite the Queen.

An hour later he came running back, grinning. This was a sign of victory. Before he could sit down, Old Niu and others surrounded him and demanded that he report the results.

"I won—she will—this afternoon—come for half—day. The pass to go down to the fields—I have already—given her. You—all see—how? Old Yuan—his—talents—not bad! Ha—" He spoke a line, taking half a day to catch his breath, and sputtered.

"I'll be damned! Is she really coming? That's shameful. If she does that, then for three dollars she'd probably sleep with us. That's a lesson." Fat Niu begrudged paying the dollar that he owed.

"What kind of rubbish is that! Isn't it good that she's coming? It will boost our spirits. Let's hurry up and eat our lunch and get ready to go down to the fields together. Ha—white legs, pretty face," said Old Jin, the most gleeful of all.

"Great! I'll take a photograph of her, and we can each have a copy as a memento. Won't that be good?" piped up Old Zheng, who had been silent for some time.

"Don't be so pleased with yourself. I've heard that Ah Mei has more than a dozen lovers. If those lovers knew you were all going wild, that wouldn't be so funny. If you compete with those dumb villagers, you'll run the risk of getting beaten up! Ha—" warned Old Ni, an old man with a sharp face.

"Bullshit! We don't really want this kind of woman. If we want beautiful women, who knows how many there are in the city! We only want to have a little fun with her!" they protested.

Dang—dang! The gong sounded to start the afternoon's work. Everything was as always. White legs, black mud, and yellow seed, row after row being sown. But in a corner to the east laughter erupted now and then. All the supervisors who oversee work in the fields had gathered in that corner. In the distance row after row was being sown, but in that corner there was no forward movement. A young farm woman with bare white legs stood in the mud joking with the supervisors and holding rice seedlings in her hands.

A camera was set up. It was supposed to be for taking photographs of rice specimens, but, on the pretext of taking specimen photographs, a picture of the Queen alone was taken.

A day of hard work was now over. The women workers came from the fields to get their day's pay—forty cents big money—and hurried home to cook rice and feed the kids. The Village Queen Ah Mei, who worked half a day but received the highest pay, finally left too. The fields again fell silent.

11. *Work Cutbacks in the Datong Textile Factory*

by s. s.,
writing from Chongming, Jiangsu

"Ah Yuan, get up, it's time for the night shift," said her mother, cooking rice, as clouds of steam rose up to a wooden beam and washed the accumulated dust down onto the stove.

Ah Yuan, carrying her lunch box, shuffled out listlessly, her mind occupied with the thought that because she had overslept the day before she had been late for work and had been docked a day's wages. Tonight could it be that she would miss out again? Not a sound was to be heard, and not one of her fellow workers was on the road. Flustered, she rushed to the factory entrance. The factory gate was closed, and the sound of machinery could not be heard. Very surprised, she knocked on the small gate which was used for rice deliveries.

The gatekeeper showed half a face and then, seeing the young Ah Yuan, said, leering, "You have come to work the night shift alone? The night shift is no more. Starting tomorrow there will be a change to a long day shift working five days at a time. Tonight don't go home. You and I will go to the Taian Hotel—"

"Big Uncle, don't talk foolishness. Is it true that there is no more night shift? Yesterday in the machinery area I seem to have heard something about it. Who would have expected it to end so soon?"

The main gate opened suddenly, and Foreman Chen came out. He saw Ah Yuan, and told her that there would be no night shift because cotton was expensive and yarn was cheap, and, on top of that, imported yarn was being sold. So, the factory had no alternative but to keep only the day shift.

Ah Yuan returned home and told her mother, "The night shift has ended. We have to wait five days before there'll be work." Her mother listened, stunned. Last year in late June there were work cutbacks in the factory and there was no recovery until October. By pawning all their clothing and going into debt everywhere possible, they had managed to support themselves for three months of hungry living. This year, it was only May twenty-first and work cutbacks had already begun. The rice money they had promised this morning to repay Chen Shentai now was half gone, and the rice in the storage pot was used up too. How to get by in this life?

12. *A Kind of Business*

by XIONG ZILIANG,
a man writing from Nanchang, Jiangxi

The night of May twenty-first in the twenty-fifth year of the Republic of China [1936].

Since a heavy rain the day before yesterday, the wind has changed direction, so the weather has turned cool and it feels just like early autumn.

My friend Gong, who has come to visit me from Beiping, and I had a snack at Taihe Hall on Zhongzheng Road, and afterward we took a walk around. As we walked we talked and we were happier than I can say. It reminded me of the way we used to take walks on the streets of Beiping three years ago. But then there were two other friends besides Gong, and now there are only the two of us.

When we got to Li Family Alley, we heard the sound of wind and stringed instruments playing the tune, "Three Variations on Plum Blossoms," creating an atmosphere very similar to that at Confucius Temple in the capital [Nanjing].

Driven by curiosity, we entered the alley and discovered the sound was coming from XX Amusement Hall, which had its name on its front gate written out with glass light bulbs. Plastered on the walls were posters showing the names of many singing girls. There was also a black wooden sign with white characters. Large characters gave the price of tea as twenty-four cents per person and described the special features of the place. There were also many small characters: "Comfortable seats, wholesome singing girls, good ventilation, beautiful decor, reasonable prices, well-trained receptionists."

This was a singing girls' hall, just like the ones in the vicinity of Confucius Temple in the capital. Since we had never heard this singing, we were eager to try something new. We entered and found seats, but it was thirty minutes before the waiter served us two cups of tea and gave us hand towels—which had an indescribable smell. Gong took a look at his watch, and it was already nine o'clock, but there were only about ten people in the audience. I realized that it was no longer early, so I asked the waiter when the performance was to begin. He said that there was no set time and that not all the singing girls had arrived because some of them had guests in their homes. But just then came a mixture of girls' laughter, the sounds of high heels *jiji gege*, and the fragrant smells of face powder and rouge.

When the Chinese-style violins began to play, someone on the stage hung up a white iron sign on which was written the name of the singing girl XX and the name of the song "The Wu Family's Hillside," and then a fourteen- or fifteen-year-old girl walked coyly onto the stage and began to sing.

At this time a man in his forties with a notebook and a pencil was walking around in the audience and speaking to people dressed in silk who seemed to be his friends. Some of the friends dressed in silk wrote in his book, some didn't. I found out that this was to put in requests for songs.

After the girl had finished singing, someone hung a larger, copper sign on the stage, on which was written, "Xuedi, please sing two songs."

As soon as Xuedi had finished singing, three or four signs were hung up: "For Yuehong half a dozen," "For Meijin a dozen," and so forth.

At this point, a girl in her twenties came on stage. She had on Western makeup, and her face was passable. She winked at a friend in the silk gown class, and that friend promptly called out "Good!" several times, as though crazed. I thought that he looked a little familiar. Then I recognized him—he was the proprietor of XXX Paper Shop on Zhongshan Road, who had gone bankrupt and run away, it was reported in the newspapers two days ago. And now here he was, talking, laughing, relaxing, and chasing after singing girls, while his precious shop had a sign pasted up, "Inventory check, temporarily closed." After this girl had finished singing, more and more signs were hung up on stage, "one," "two," "three," "five," "six," "eight," "ten"—

Next it was Xiaomei's turn, and she had requests for a dozen. The so-called dozen consisted of no more than a few representative lines from each song. The songs were said to cost a dollar apiece. Tipping was certainly welcomed. By now the house was full, the air was filthy, and we were both sweating. On top of that, the foul odor of the toilet came wafting out and made us feel like throwing up. We noticed the waiter endlessly presenting snow-white hand towels to the friends in the silk gown class, about once every five minutes. But the only time we got them was when we first came in, and then they were not white. While we were hoping for more towels to arrive, the waiter all of a sudden took pity on us and casually tossed us a towel left over from the table next to us. As if obtaining something precious, we each used it to wipe once.

When the time came for them to collect the tea money, we each paid twenty-four cents, the price shown on the gate. But the waiter said it was thirty-four cents. We asked him why, and he said that today was a full-dress performance.

"Then why didn't you write thirty-four cents on the gate?"

"The regulars know. We don't have to bother."

It was already past ten o'clock. Little by little, the audience left. At the same time, there were fewer signs on the stage, and even fewer song requests. That man in his forties had a blank look on his face. He kept looking over at us, perhaps hoping that we would make requests for songs. But it seemed as though he had decided in advance that we would disappoint him because of the well-worn blue cloth jackets we were wearing. By this time, he was sitting at a table in front of us. From his cigarette case he took out a Small Armed Fortress brand cigarette and smoked it. He also took a handful of legal tender out of his pocket and counted it, smiling with satisfaction. I noticed that he counted up to 125 dollars.

At this time, although it was past eleven o'clock, ten more seats had been taken and a few more signs showing requests had been hung up. We wanted to see the so-called full-dress performance, but since we didn't know when it would begin, we decided not to stay for it.

By then, half the shops on the streets had closed their doors, and there were few pedestrians and automobiles. As I walked along, I thought about the situation in the singing hall. Within little more than an hour, more than a hundred dollars was taken in. I understand, I understand. At this time when the economy of farming villages is collapsing everywhere, Nanchang has developed this perverse kind of enterprise, and at a time when the country is in a state of crisis, some of our fellow countrymen are playing this kind of trick.

13. *An Encounter in a Pavilion*

by KONGYAN (*pseud.*),
a man writing from Huizhou, Anhui

In the many years that have passed since I returned to my native village in A County, conditions have changed. Except for the newly built, crisscrossing long-distance telephone wires and the widely scattered lookout towers on the fortifications, which strike the eye and frighten the heart, all else leaves people with the feeling of decay and desolation.

On May twenty-first, although the rain had stopped, it was still very humid. Since it was very uncomfortable to sit at home, I felt it would be better to go out and take a walk. So I decided to visit a friend—a walk of ten *li* or so from my own B Village. Later, returning home, I found the weather unexpectedly becoming even more humid. After walking some distance, I simply couldn't stand it. At the side of the road there was a pavilion, one side of which was unwalled. Although it had had beggars living there and it was dirty and its floor was covered with rotting straw, I had no choice but to go in and rest a while.

The needle-like rice seedlings in the fields were very regular, row after row, and had already grown eight or nine inches above the water line, but they were still a yellowish green color. A soft breeze blew across them, making them all seem to be bowing their heads, deep in thought. There were lonely hills all around, and several black birds rested silently on the telephone wires, motionless against a sky full of white clouds—like a line drawn with ink diagonally across a piece of pure white paper, with several ink drops splashing out. Had they not eventually flown up, spreading their scissor-like tails, no one would have known that they were swallows. With no one passing by, the atmosphere was as lonely as death.

Sitting down on a wooden beam that spanned the supporting pillars in the front part of the pavilion, I gazed out at the hills, the water, the needle-like seedlings in the fields, and the swallows on the wires. After a long while, as I was about to get up and continue walking, a plainly dressed woman suddenly came up.

She was probably less than twenty. Her hair was combed into a bun at the back of her head, very dark but not terribly shiny. She was wearing a gray cloth blouse, neither new nor old, and around her waist was tied a black cloth skirt, neither new nor old. Although it had holes in several places, they had been mended, so it was not very ragged. Her face was not powdered, but both cheeks had rouge on them. Although she was a little sallow and thin, her body was still healthy. At a glance it was apparent that she was a girl from a farm family. She wasn't very beautiful, but neither was she disgusting.

She walked into the pavilion and sat down on another wooden beam that spanned the supporting pillars on the other side. Without making a sound, she trained her eyes on me, looking up and down at my body.

I began to get suspicious. I thought, "My A County has always been a place where proper conduct is valued. I am a male stranger, she is a young woman, and there is no other passerby. So shouldn't she avoid suspicion? Has she also walked to the point where she is too tired to bear it any longer? If so, why is she gazing so steadily at me?" This is a situation that I had never seen before in my A County. Because of the suspicions in my mind, I wanted to find out how it would come out, so I figured I might as well sit for a little longer.

"Ai!" After a moment's silence she began making a long sigh.

"Sir, where are you headed?" she then asked.

"Where is your home? Why are you sighing?" I couldn't hold back my suspicions, and without answering I questioned her.

"Ai!" She sighed again, and her face had a very sad look on it. "Sir, I live in H Township, and this half year I—" She paused for a moment before replying, but again choked up.

"What happened to you this half year?"

She blushed, bowed her head at an angle, and after a moment gave me this answer, "This half year I have not—have not—received—a guest."

I was taken aback and could not utter a word.

"I have a black-hearted one. He abandoned me, he ran away. I can't even find rice to fill my stomach."

"What other people are in your family now?" Since I didn't know what was the right thing to say, I asked this irrelevant question.

"Not many people, only an aged mother blind in both eyes, a father who died last year, that black-hearted one I married, who ran away on his own—I heard that he went to become a soldier, and with Mother completely dependent on me for support, what can I do? Sir, I have a bitter fate! I don't have any kind of great talents, and nobody wants someone to be a helpmate in these times. The wood that I cut, I can't sell for money. Honestly, how can I live?"

After she spoke, she lifted her head a little, with her eyes still fixed on me.

"Where did you come from just now?"

"Sir, this time of year I can pick a few tea leaves for people, but how can that be enough to get by, when I also have to rush home to take care of an aged mother?" She spoke in a very pitiful manner, with tears welling up in her eyes, silently looking at me as though waiting for me to give comfort. But I couldn't find any other good words to say to comfort her. I could only remark, "There is indeed no way out!" This caused me to shudder and almost to shed a tear for her.

For a little while, we both were silent, wordless. Suddenly she spoke again:

"Then if you, sir, don't find it offensive, please, sir—as I've said, there aren't many people in my family."

After saying this, she blushed, but then suddenly on her face appeared a forced smile.

"I have to be on my way. This thing is very distressing!" As I replied, I was thinking to myself, "My rural township is famous as a 'place of propriety and uprightness,' unlike Shanghai. But now how can it be that proper conduct has broken down to the point where her youthfulness is for sale? This is unheard of." But the thing got worse, and she even said:

"Ai! Sir, you are too—you poor thing—then—that doesn't matter—right here—"

After she spoke, she made a motion with her lips, pointing inside, and then bowed her head straight down.

"Sir, do you think I'm very dirty? But I have not—have not—whatever you, sir, wish—"

I didn't know what to say. I gave her a dollar, and we went our separate ways.

14. *Chronicle of a Wild Flower*[1] *with Scarlet Tears*

by ZENG NAIDUN,
a man writing from Fuzhou, Fujian

May twenty-first was an ordinary day on which took place an ordinary event.

At about 9:30 in the morning, two policemen came into the reception room, one officer and one policeman. The policeman had two people in tow: one a man and the other a woman—the man getting on in years and blind, the woman cute, with a sallow face from which the bloom of youth had not quite faded.

At 10:05 a message came from the clearinghouse that the arrested parties should be taken there, so the whole group went. The clearinghouse clerk asked the officer, "What's the charge?" The officer said, "I've caught a private unlicensed prostitute!" He was proud of himself and so was the policeman. But the woman hung her head, and the blind man sighed. After the clearinghouse clerk had inquired about the details of the case and their names, he handed down a slip of paper and said, "Officer, take them to the holding tank for the time being."

At about 11:50, in a dark corner of the holding tank, an old woman, shaking, pulled out ten small dimes and said, "Here's a dollar that Ahua earned last night. Take it and use it! In a yamen[2] you need money." As the man groped for the money, he began to complain. "It's all your fault! You're the one who forced Ahua to stoop to this business. She's been at it for only a few days and already she's been arrested."

"You can't see. As an old woman, what can I do? If we don't push Ahua, where will our rice come from? Who wants to push her own daughter into a fiery hell?"[3]

"If we die of starvation, then we die of starvation! In our family we've had educated people in every generation, and now we've lost face!"

"What's to be done? You can't eat face."

The old lady looked at her daughter, who was weeping in a corner.

At 2:40 several clerks in the office had the following playful discussion.

The first said, "That private prostitute arrested this morning is very pretty!"

The second said, "Let's go to watch the trial at four o'clock."

The third said, "Why bother! Since the banning of prostitution in this

---

1. "Wild flower" was a euphemism for prostitute.
2. A yamen was a complex of government quarters. See "A Funeral Procession," n. 1.
3. "Fiery hell" was a euphemism for brothel.

county, lots of private prostitutes have been picked up. There are so many that you can't see all their trials."

The fourth said, "They say that this prostitute didn't know enough not to talk with the policemen and detective about the money for seeing her body,[4] so she was arrested."

The fifth said, "Naturally! For instance that girl Yuying that we play around with is also a private prostitute. But because she has finesse and backing, even though she has people publicly coming in and going out, the men in uniform wouldn't dare touch a single hair on her!"

"Oh!" sighed the solemn old recordkeeper.

At 4:50 the military tribune took his place on the bench. The first person sent before the judge was the young woman.

The military tribune asked, "Are you Chen Ahua?"

"Yes!"

"Where is your native place?"

"I am a native of this place."

"How old are you?"

"Seventeen."

"As young as you are, isn't there something else for you to do? Why do you have to stoop to this kind of shameful business?"

Tears as big as beans dripped down from her eyelashes. The sound of sobbing was her only reply.

The second person sent in front of the military tribune was the blind man.

"You are a holder of the first-level imperial degree.[5] Why do you want your daughter to stoop to this kind of shameful business?"

"Your honor! I have nothing to say. Ask that stinky old woman of mine! Ai!" (A long sigh.) "I can't sum up everything in one word!"

The third person sent in front of the military tribune was that old woman.

"Why do you want to do harm to your own daughter by asking her to become a prostitute?"

---

4. "Money for seeing her body" was a euphemism for money paid to have sexual intercourse with a prostitute.

5. This man earned a *xiucai* degree (literally "cultivated talent") by passing the civil service examinations which the state administered in imperial China until abolishing the examination system in 1905. Under this system, candidates took examinations to earn official degrees at three levels: the lowest at the prefectural level (which the man in this piece passed); the second at the provincial level; and the third at the metropolitan level in the capital. For interpretations of this examination system and bibliographical guidance to additional literature on the subject, see Johanna M. Menzel, ed., *The Chinese Civil Service*; and Miyazaki Ichisada, *China's Examination Hell*.

"We have to eat rice!"

"Do you realize that being a prostitute is the most despicable thing anyone can do?"

"Sir! I know. But we have to survive, so we can't concern ourselves with all of these matters."

"Do you realize that prostitution is prohibited in this county?"

"I know!"

"If you already know, how dare you break the law?"

"Sir! We have to eat rice!"

"Isn't there another kind of rice for you to eat?"

"Where is there rice for us to eat?"

"Nonsense! There is rice everywhere under heaven!"

"Sir! We can't get that kind of rice!"

"Nonsense!" The military tribune banged his gavel, and the old lady burst into tears.

15. *Records of a Land Survey on One Day*

by LUJUN (*pseud.*),
a man writing from Wujin, Jiangsu

The weather in May is humid and hot, and on the morning of Thursday the twenty-first, on the other side of North Street, a crowd had gathered, looking busy and animated in the midst of the dead silence.

"Auntie! You be patient! And take the long view! If your own son succeeds in the world, it will take no more than a month or so to rake back in[1] these several *fen* of land! In a rural area now one *mu* sells for only thirty dollars or so."

After the land survey in the morning, the land of Second Aunt of the Li family decreased by three or four *fen*. All that was ripped off by Zhang Baigeng, the devil who is a lamp operator![2] That great gentleman[3] didn't say a word or give himself a headache, and Second Aunt of the Li family could only get furious. She didn't cry. She fully understood that personal

1. [Lujun's note:] To rake back in (*pa huilai*): in colloquial usage, to buy back.

2. [Lujun's note:] Lamp operator (*kai denger*): one who operates an opium den.

3. [Lujun's note:] Great gentleman (*da xiansheng*): the common term for a local bully (*tu hao*).

"Woman Spinning Thread," a woodcut by He Baitao, from *Lu Xun shoucang Zhongguo xiandai muke xuanji, 1931–36* [A Selection from Lu Xun's Collection of Modern Chinese Woodcuts, 1931–36] (Beijing, 1963), p. 28.

connections in rural areas are always like this. Zhou Yucai, an old man, holder of the first-level imperial degree,[4] consoled her in these words as if putting the matter to rest and perhaps hoping to get a few more puffs of opium in payment from Zhang Baigeng.

Second Aunt replied, "I know that you pack of dogs only know how to smoke opium. You can't manage anything else, and still you want to mediate! Pack of dogs! What have you given us? Others add three or add four *fen*.[5] We can't even add two or add one. The dispute is not over this land, but in the end you should keep some old face for the next generation to see. That devil will not become rich as a result of this. If I don't sell this piece of my land, then I'll get my revenge on you pack of dogs."

Second Aunt of the Li family was in an uncontrollable rage, and she cursed without restraint. The several great gentlemen felt that they had already successfully completed their task. Her cursing? It meant nothing to them.

In the afternoon, bitter yellow colors emanated from the sun, and the barometric pressure rose. People busy sweating became fuzzy in the head.

In a small, quiet, out-of-the-way alley off East Street, curled up at the foot of a wall inside an old, plain building, several guns[6] were already shooting target practice at this time. This was the great gentlemen's reward for half a day of bitter work.

On the other side of town, in a tiled building at the end of North Street, the sighs of a middle-aged woman could be heard. She was Second Aunt of the Li family, and she could no longer maintain her self-confidence as she recalled the words with which she had boasted to her son:

"You relax. Who will dare take advantage of me! Whoever dares come and struggle over the fields and steal land away from me, I'll fight him to the death with this old life of mine."

Now she was utterly out of control. She felt unable to face her son, unable to face herself, unable to face the situation with her usual courage. If only she could slap that pack of dogs across the face—but she understood everything about rural areas and about personal connections.

The weather slowly darkened. A few stars were caught between soft black clouds which seemed to drip with water. One day was about to

4. This degree had been received under the state examination system which was abolished in 1905. See "Chronicle of a Wild Flower with Scarlet Tears," n. 5.

5. [Lujun's note:] Add three or add four (*jia san jia si*): that is, the practice of expanding the original land by three or four *fen*.

6. [Lujun's note:] Guns (*qiang*): opium pipes.

end! The angry sounds of Second Aunt of the Li family and the laughter of Zhang Baigeng broke the silence on this night. What has the land survey given people? Yes, unanticipated harvests and unanticipated losses.

The marketplace was quiet, and several new wooden stakes had been added in the fields.

C. Educated Women at Work

16. *Diaries of Middle School Girls*

by TANG GONGXIAN,
a male middle school teacher writing from Jinhua, Zhejiang

Nowadays the most troublesome, time-consuming, and onerous task for a middle school class master[1] is reading and writing comments on several scores of diaries every day. Let me make a candid confession. Having read middle school students' diaries for more than three years, though I make no claim to be fast enough to read "ten lines at a glance," I can read at least three or four lines at one glance. I'm afraid that I don't have the energy to read them closely and write comments in detail. So I always feel guilty about it. But if I quit, I would have trouble finding rice to eat!

This day—May twenty-first—presented me with a good opportunity to force myself to read very closely and write comments on several scores of diaries. Within them was much good material. Although they are only brief and casual remarks, these are representative of the girls' general mentality. Now let me copy down some brief excerpts and offer them to "One Day in China." Maybe this will not be totally meaningless.

As we left the school grounds, wearing our scout uniforms,[2] a classmate remarked, "This is embarrassing." But, according to the teacher, it is most glorious to be wearing scout uniforms.

1. The "class master" (*ji zhuren*) was the teacher in an elementary, middle, or high school responsible for assigning grades and meting out discipline to each room of students. Class masters read and wrote comments on the daily diaries or weekly journals that all Chinese students were required to write as part of their schoolwork.
2. Beginning in 1934, all middle school students were required to join the scouts (*tongzi jun*)—girl scouts or boy scouts. As a result, the organization expanded dramatically in the

We go into the streets, and frequently people say about us, "These men who aren't men and women who aren't women, what are they all about?" Ah, I understand that society here still heavily values men and undervalues women!

This semester the school has really been quite rigorous in the training of scouts. My classmates who are not accustomed to this style of life often comment to this effect: "Are they trying to tell us that we women will be going to fight on the battlefield?" I say, "Why can't women fight on the battlefield? Didn't Mulan[3] go into battle on behalf of her daddy?"

Though we were taught only one chapter in algebra, we still did badly on the exam. The instructor teaching us was so angry today that his face turned red and blue. It's difficult to be a teacher!

I most fear arithmetic. What I like is playing games. Aren't women's brains the same as men's?

I don't know what's wrong today. After three chemistry classes in a row, I really feel dizzy! Rather than go to school like this, I'd prefer to cook for somebody else.

People who want to study and know how to study have no chance to. I don't know how to study but am forced to. Heaven only knows why!

Standing behind the art teacher, I watched him sketch very casually, and a beautiful vase of flowers instantly appeared. But when the brush came into my hand, it seemed to weigh several dozen *jin*. I could hardly make it move.

During the first afternoon class, many of my classmates put their heads down on their desks and slept. The teacher, a funny man, then rapped on his lectern and recited a popular poem to the class: "Spring is no time for studying. Summer is hot and good for sleeping. Autumn brings mosquitoes and Winter brings snow. Lock up the book in a trunk and enjoy the New Year." After that none of my classmates dared sleep any more.

1930s. See John Israel, *Student Nationalism in China, 1927–1937*, p. 99; and Eastman, *The Abortive Revolution*, p. 65.

3. Mulan was the semilegendary young woman warrior who disguised herself as a man and went with the army to fight battles in place of her father. On the "Mulan complex," see Roxane Witke, "Transformation of Attitudes toward Women during the May Fourth Era of Modern China," pp. 45–49.

Some of my classmates seem to study merely for "grades." If their grades are a little low in a certain subject, they sob and sob. This morning, outsiders would have thought that there had been a death in the school. Ha ha!

The three days I spent lying sick at home seemed like three years! Since the day I was born, I've never been able to do anything better than other people. But in getting sick, I surpass all others.

The kitchen is really annoying. The dishes are always stinky and the rice is always scorched. This morning's rice gruel was again stinky!

Because this morning's rice gruel was very stinky, we all starved. Women, after all, are the weaker ones!

Mother hasn't written for over a month. I've been having dreams night after night, and haven't been able to sleep!

When I got up this morning, I saw that all my classmates were beaming. It's because we're going to have a party tomorrow.

I went for a walk around the school grounds after dinner with a few classmates. The soft breeze came and went, making people comfortable. Fish in the pond swim to and fro and are truly free.

After supper I played some games in the schoolyard. I saw many of my classmates gathered together in a corner of the schoolyard, and I immediately went to see what was happening. They were watching a crazy old woman on the other side of the wall.

It was past ten o'clock at night and I was reading when the couple next door had another quarrel. I thought to myself, no wonder China is in such bad shape. Even one couple can't get along and always has to fight.

Two weeks ago, because of the death of Mr. Hu Hanmin,[4] during the flag-raising and flag-lowering ceremonies we all had to observe a

---

4. Hu Hanmin, a revolutionary leader and close associate of Sun Yatsen, died on May 12, 1936. The government in Guangdong province gave him a lavish state funeral, and the Guomindang government proclaimed that all Chinese should honor him in a period of national mourning. The elaborate ceremonies seem to have been related to a power struggle at the time between Chiang Kaishek (whose capital was in the Lower Yangzi Valley at Nanjing) and regional leaders in Southwest China, for each side sought to identify Hu with

three-minute silence. This went on for three days. To our surprise, during these past few days we have also been required to observe a three-minute silence. This really had me confused. Then in the afternoon, during the flag-lowering ceremony, I heard my classmates say that this was for the good health of the Leader.[5] Oh, for a moment I thought that yet another great man had died.

Abyssinia has been swallowed up by Italy, but many people praise Mussolini's heroism and bravery.[6] I say he's more vicious than a tiger. I'll never, ever like him.

Younger Brother is only fourteen. He has always said that he is determined to go to war against Japan. Today I received a letter from him saying that he has qualified for entrance into the Central Naval Academy. How wonderful!

This morning during the flag-raising ceremony, the flag reached half-mast and then suddenly fell down. I couldn't help but let out a deep sigh. I'm afraid North China is going to go!

17. *The Woman's Dilemma*

by CHUANHENG *(pseud.),*
a female student writing from
Shanghai

Hunched over piles of books, I slowly raised my head and took a peek at the watch that lay ticking on the corner of the desk. How

---

its cause. In June 1936, immediately after Hu's death, the Southwest revolted against Chiang Kaishek's rule. See Eastman, *The Abortive Revolution*, pp. 251–62.

5. This is apparently a reference to Chiang Kaishek, for the term "Leader" (*lingxiu*) was widely used in China during the 1930s to refer to him. On Chiang's and some of his follower's attitudes toward enshrining one man as the supreme leader at this time, see ibid., pp. 41–44 and 278–82.

6. After Italy invaded Abyssinia (Ethiopia) without a declaration of war in October 1935, Chinese students showed a keen interest in the leaders of both countries. Some preferred Benito Mussolini, the Italian dictator, because he sought for his country the strength it had had under the Roman empire; and others preferred Haile Selassie, the Ethiopian emperor, because he tried to resist the Italian invasion and preserve his country's independence. In different ways each thus appealed to Chinese students as a nationalist hero. See the survey of 1,600 students at twenty-two Chinese universities and eight high schools done by Olga Lang in 1937 in her *Chinese Family and Society*, pp. 278–79.

strange! Today the time on this watch seemed to have stopped. As though to tease me, the long hand and the short hand endlessly pointed to five o'clock!

Five o'clock! The sun cast shadows as it angled to the west. Within half an hour I'd be able to see my elder sister.

But now time seemed like an out-of-breath old cow, ambling along slowly, pausing after each step long enough to have taken three more. Finally, I almost felt that time was running backward.

In her recent letters, Elder Sister had again and again written these lines:

"Children are a most heavy cangue[1] on women. It is locked on me and prevents me from moving.

"The husband-wife relationship, based on emotion, cannot hold up. It's like building a sand castle at the seashore. One day we may both simultaneously feel that life is empty, as empty as a bottomless pit.

"Ten years of a slave's life is enough. I want to fly!

"I want to be a 'real person!' "

I understood Elder Sister's feelings. I also quite understood why Elder Sister wrote what she wrote. So her sudden rush to Shanghai to see me made me especially happy. As it flashed across my mind's eye, I saw a white sea gull extending its wings and freely soaring into the blue sky!

I'd thought up many words of encouragment to say to Elder Sister. In my mind, I'd devised a whole pile of plans for her life after she had left her family. I'd been telling myself that I must use the small amount of strength that I possess to start a fire, to help her, and to allow her to become a "person." I was also thinking how happy I'd be to see her this time. I wanted to hug her tightly while my eyes filled with tears of happiness. Today, for the first time, I tasted joy. It was like watching a person reach the shore after nearly drowning in the ocean.

At 5:30 I hastily gathered up the things on my desk and rushed to the Yangzi Hotel, where Elder Sister was staying.

As the door opened, I was stunned.

Two people were in the room—Elder Sister and Brother-in-law. They stood up together and greeted me with avuncular concern:

"Ah Qian, how are you?"

---

1. The cangue (*jia*) was a rectangular collar made of heavy blocks of wood which encircled the neck, rested on the shoulders, and projected out so as to prevent the wearer's hand from reaching his or her face. The wearing of the cangue, like the wearing of the stocks in the West, was a form of punishment designed not only to discourage wrongdoing but also to humiliate the offender. See Derk Bodde and Clarence Morris, *Law in Imperial China*, pp. 95–96 and 99.

Elder Sister was no different, she hadn't changed. She didn't mention a thing that had been in her previous letters. It was as though nothing at all had happened. She did nothing more than ask me in detail about my health, what I had been eating, and how I had been sleeping, displaying the particular tenderness that only a young wife can show.

I couldn't bear it any longer, and I seized the opportunity to ask her:

"Elder Sister! What's going on?"

Brother-in-law coolly remarked:

"That was a beautiful soap bubble!"

In the evening, the three of us went to see Charlie Chaplin's *Modern Times* at the Rialto Theater. At the end, I was deeply moved by the final scene, which showed the actors walking off on a road of light.[2] I said earnestly to Elder Sister:

"Sis, you see, everyone is walking along the 'road of light,' and only you, after thinking a bit about it, have covered your eyes with your own hands."

Elder Sister closed her eyes, and, after a long pause, she whispered these two words:

"The contradictions!"

Oh! The contradictions! How many people are sinking into this bitter sea and are unable to rise up!

This event occurred on the evening of May 21, 1936.

18. *Diary of a Midwife*

by CHEN HAN,
a female midwife writing from Jiashan, Zhejiang

I am a graduate of a school of midwifery, and last winter I came to serve at West Pond Hospital in Zhejiang Province, Jiashan, West Pond. Needless to say, in my profession I've seen and heard not only about pregnant women but also about patients and medicine. But by

2. *Modern Times*, now regarded as a classic film, was first released in the United States on February 5, 1936. In the scene described here, Charlie Chaplin and his new-found friend, played by Paulette Goddard—"a gamin," as he calls her—walk down a sunlit road toward the horizon as though trusting in the future. For a still photograph of this scene, see Gerald D. McDonald et al., *The Films of Charlie Chaplin*, p. 203.

paying attention to the patients' language and behavior, one can learn a great deal about customs and human relations in a place.

At eight o'clock in the morning the gate for outpatients opened. First came several little kids between one and three years old. Held by their mothers, they were coming to get smallpox shots. As they entered the examination room, I began to prepare to give the shots. I was very amused when the mothers asked me, "Are you giving shots in both hands? Or giving shots in both hands and at the same time in both legs?" To me their questions seemed odd indeed! Then I said to them, "One shot in the arm will be enough, at the most two shots. Why do you want so many?" They said, "The day before yesterday we saw that the several little precious babies next door had a gentleman come to the door especially to give them shots in both hands and both legs, leaving a total of eight flower-shaped marks. At that time, our children had a fever, and some of them were coughing, so they weren't given shots. If they got shots in the hands and the legs, then wouldn't it be unnecessary for them to get shots in the future?" Hearing this, I couldn't help but laugh, but I didn't care what special method had been used to give shots by that Mr. Shot-giver, and I said to them straight away, "One shot will be enough for this year. But in the future one shot will still be needed each year, and that's for the best. Getting many shots all at once right now would be useless."

Oddest of all was that among those who came today for examinations, whether children or adults, several were wearing bright red shirts and trousers or long gowns, which were very eye-catching! Since I had never seen this before, I couldn't help but be driven by curiosity to ask them about it. They told me, "Here in West Pond there is a festival on the third day of the fourth month on the banned calendar.[1] It is for the King of Grain over there in the Temple of the King of Grain. How potent the King of Grain is! When any of us gets sick, although we ask a doctor to look us over and we take medicine, we still must go burn incense, ask for blessings, and make promises before the King of Grain over there. All those people who have made promises to the god must wear red clothes and be the bodhisattva's prisoners during the four-day festival. Today is the first day of the fourth month, and it is the first day for us to be prisoners."

During lunch, my colleagues told me that the festival on the third day of the fourth month here is the most prosperous and happiest day of the year in West Pond. It's more lively than any other festival. Except for the drug stores, all the shops and peddlers seize this opportunity to make

1. The traditional lunar calendar was officially banned by the Chinese government in 1912. See the introduction to Part III.

a lot of money, and the cloth shops in particular sell lots of red cloth before the festival! Today is the first day of the festival, and not many "prisoners" can be seen. When the day after tomorrow comes, if you stand in front of the main gate for a little while, all you'll see will be these red-clad prisoners!

After lunch, I stood at the main gate with two or three of my colleagues, and, sure enough, one-third of the people coming and going had already become red-clad prisoners!

Oddest of all, even women with curled hair and leather shoes who think of themselves as modern also were wearing bright red Chinese-style high-collared dresses with a slit up the side. I don't know whether in the end this is modern—or contradictory![2] Ultimately, it left me perplexed. In addition, there were some youths who looked like members of the educated class and wore red shirts under their long gowns, with the shirts exposed at the "collar" and the "cuffs."[3] I thought to myself: If they were sincere in keeping their promise, why didn't they wear the red shirts over their long gowns?

At about nine o'clock at night, we went across the river to a family named Gu to deliver a baby and found a woman on the verge of childbirth bleeding from placenta previa.[4] When we arrived, the woman was already in extremely critical condition, and the fetus's heartbeat could no longer even be heard. This woman had been injured doing heavy lifting, and she was also giving birth prematurely. Under normal circumstances, we would have been lucky to save the mother, so we said to her husband, "This kind of difficult delivery is very rare. The woman giving birth is now in extremely critical condition. We propose to operate, but her body is too weak. Once the operation is underway, we're afraid she won't hold up. But without an operation, she will certainly die. If we operate, there is still some hope. What do you think?" He was then willing to let us operate and signed a consent form. But still he said to his wife,

2. Here Chen Han is making a pun. The words for modern (*modeng*) and contradiction (*maodun*) sound similar.

3. Here Chen Han is making a play on words. If the word for "collar" (*ling*) and the word for "cuff" (*xiu*) are combined, they form a single expression meaning leader (*lingxiu*) which was an oblique reference to Chiang Kaishek. See "Diaries of Middle School Girls," n. 5.

4. Placenta previa (*qianzhi taipan*) is a condition in which the placenta containing the fetus is attached to the lower uterine segment (rather than high up in the uterus as in a normal pregnancy). It is the most common cause of bleeding during the later months of pregnancy and is regarded as a grave complication which can be fatal to the mother as well as the child.

"Don't you be afraid. We have blessings from the bodhisattva Guanyin."[5]

So we began to sterilize the instruments, and we gave her a shot before operating. In the end the mother was saved. But at this time, needless to say, she was very weak. Later we gave her two shots, a heart stimulant and a blood coagulant, and told her to rest quietly. But small gongs and something we didn't recognize were being vigorously struck downstairs. Were the patient's relatives perhaps giving thanks to the bodhisattva down there in the belief that the woman's salvation had been achieved entirely by the bodhisattva Guanyin?[6]

19. *Changzhen's Birthday*

by LIU HENG,
a female teacher writing from Nanchang, Jiangxi

Today is Changzhen's third birthday.

After more than two months of the rainy season, the grass in the courtyard has turned into a green carpet, but everything both inside and outside the house is so damp that it is covered with mildew. Today was a rare sunny day. The golden rays of morning sunshine were comforting as I took Changzhen onto the balcony for some morning exercise.

"Zhen, today is your birthday. You are another year older."

"Mama, what happens on a birthday?"

"Well, on a birthday, you eat birthday noodles and father sends you new clothes. But you also have to give Mother a most respectful salute."

"O.K., here's a scout salute."

For breakfast, she ate a small bowl of birthday noodles and two eggs. At eight o'clock she rode in a car with me to school. She wore a green

5. Guanyin (known as Avalokitesvara in Sanskrit and often called the Goddess of Mercy in English) is the Buddhist bodhisattva who embodies the principle of compassion and assists Amituofo in the Western Paradise according to the teachings of Pure Land Buddhism. See also "A Record of Digging Up Graves," n. 1; and "May Twenty-first in Taicang," n. 1.

6. For a more detailed description of religious practices surrounding childbirth in China at this time, see an article on the subject originally published in Chinese in 1936 and recently translated by Nancy Gibbs in Patricia Buckley Ebrey, ed., *Chinese Civilization and Society*, pp. 302–03.

spring dress, white socks, black leather shoes, and a red flower-shaped ribbon in her hair. In the schoolyard, I asked my colleague, Mr. Yubin, to take several photographs of her. After that, she ran and skipped her way to class at the kindergarten next door.

In the evening, she said that she wanted to write to her father because she had done a drawing of him and wanted to send it to him! After that, I don't know when Fourth Cousin Maomao said to her, "Today *Tarzan and Jane*[1] is on. Many lions and tigers fight with Tarzan. What fun! Hurry up and ask your mother to take you to see it!"

Yes, this film does have lions, tigers, snakes, elephants, monkeys, rhinoceroses, African blacks, and also that Tarzan who swings through the trees. It's worthwhile for the kids to see. It's a lucky coincidence that it's showing on her birthday, and it will give her pleasant memories.

When she saw Tarzan flying from one tree to another as if on a swing, she was thrilled, and she jumped up and down and clapped her little hands. She said, "That black person is wearing a gold earring even on his mouth." This remark made the elderly woman sitting next to her laugh. The woman patted her on the head, saying, "What an adorable child!"

On the way home, she was so tired that she fell asleep in my arms.

Today she is very satisfied!

Time has indeed passed too quickly. Now Changzhen is already three full years of age.

I still remember ten days before January Twenty-eighth.[2] Qi and I came back to Nanchang to visit the family. I was already five months pregnant. Originally we had planned to return to Shanghai in two weeks. Who would have guessed that the world would change within the space of ten days? The house where we lived in Zhenru was completely destroyed in a battle, so we had to stay temporarily in Nanchang.

It was at ten-thirty on the evening of May twenty-first of that year that Changzhen was born, so we named her to commemorate the place where we had lived after our wedding, the place in Zhenru that was destroyed soon thereafter.

---

1. This is one of several movies that have been made about the adventures of Tarzan, a white man who lived in an African jungle (based on a character originally described in the early twentieth-century novels of Edgar Rice Burroughs). It is probably the movie starring Johnny Weismuller and Maureen O'Sullivan which was released in 1934 and was entitled *Tarzan and His Mate*. *Catalogue of Copyright Entries* (*Cumulative Series*), *Motion Pictures, 1912–1939*, p. 841.

2. In the January Twenty-eighth Incident of 1932, Japanese and Chinese troops clashed in and around Shanghai. See "A Never-to-Be-Forgotten Class," n. 6.

My child, people say that trouble begins at birth, but even before you were born you faced a crisis!

Thank heaven the child is growing up without incident. During the past three years, this is the impression she has given me: submissiveness, gentleness, warmth, liveliness, and intelligence. Day after day she continues to grow, day after day she becomes more mature, like a willow in early autumn on the lakeshore, blown by the spring wind and sprinkled by the spring rain, sending out little branches and putting forth tender, green leaves overnight. Whenever I consider her height, the firmness of her legs, and the darkness of her skin, I realize that physically she is not bad. In evening sessions that I have with her under the lamp these days, she can already recognize about one hundred characters, and she knows stories about pigs, dogs, chickens, and cats. She also has a mind of her own. Since enrolling in kindergarten this spring, she has learned to sing a few songs about flowers and grass, and she has learned to do a few dances in which she imitates birds and butterflies.

But when I think of it, what kind of mother have I been during the past three years? I myself am uncertain and can't say for sure. In order to raise her myself, I should stay with the family and take responsibility for being a mother. But for the sake of my own independence and because of the need to make a living, I can't help but leave the family every day and go to my job.

Ai! My child, I am only sure of one thing—that I have not completely fulfilled the obligations of motherhood!

20. *A Family Letter*

by JINGJUN (*pseud.*),
*a female guidance counselor writing from
Zhouping, Shandong*

My dear son Qi,

Are you well now? Has your mood improved? My dear child, did you really think that I wanted to leave my own child? Absolutely wrong. Although outwardly I appeared decisive as I set foot on the road to come here, by the time the ricksha reached the west compound, tears were gushing uncontrollably from my eyes. I managed to control myself, but after I boarded the train, even before it got underway, I was sobbing.

During the trip everything I looked at made me sad, and my heart and mind were centered on my child. I thought of your loneliness, I hated myself for my cruelty, and I feared that you would become sick. When I reached here, everything I saw disappointed me (because Mr. Liang Shuming[1] hasn't yet returned from Japan, I am acquainted with no one here, and even the Hao brothers aren't here), and once again my tears flowed uncontrollably. It took me a while to regain my composure before I managed to exchange a few words with the others, and I thought to myself, "I can't cry in front of you people. But once I get to my room I'll cry my eyes out." I thought about Little Du (Mme. Chen Hengzhe's child),[2] and I thought about Lili and Daidai (Mme. Liu Qingyang's children).[3] Are they not their mothers' beloved children? How are they doing now? Aren't they growing up all right? Also, aren't your two little sisters living apart from their mother? It's better to part, for how can we live forever within the narrow confines of love between a mother and a son? The great wheel of duty in our times waits for us to push it forward! People awaiting our help cry out in the villages! They scream! I can only give myself over to striving for their sake. I can only take the narrow love that I have for my children and extend it to a great number of people and strive for those who need me to strive on their behalf.

My dear child, be strong! From now on we'll each strive and strive to be a person. You have relinquished the right to enjoy a mother's love. You must become a leader of youth! Study hard! Build up your body, prepare for the work of the future. Haven't you always taken pride in yourself for having this as your goal? A true man, a great man—how can one who thinks of himself as a great man live day after day within his mother's embrace? We're not hedonists! We must sacrifice for the future of the race and the country! Strive! Please awaken your mind! Regain your health! Put away your dependence on narrow mother love! Be a youth of iron! My dear child, depression, sorrow, melancholy are most

1. Liang Shuming was a leader in the rural reconstruction movement in China between 1927 and 1937. His experiment in Zhouping County (where this piece was written) was independent of the Guomindang government and was the leading example of rural reconstruction under "old-style" Chinese leadership in the 1930s. See Lyman P. Van Slyke, "Liang Sou-ming and the Rural Reconstruction Movement"; and Guy S. Alitto, The Last Confucian, chap. 11. Cf. "A Comedy in the Midst of Sorrow," n. 1.

2. Chen Hengzhe (1890–), China's first female professor, taught history at Beijing National University and National Southeastern University; founded the journal Independent Critic; and published many essays, short stories, and poems. See Boorman and Howard, eds., Biographical Dictionary of Republican China, vol. 1, pp. 183–87.

3. Liu Qingyang participated in the student movement in the late 1910s and 1920s. She also helped to lead the campaign for National Salvation in the 1930s. See Union Research Institute, Who's Who in Communist China, vol. 1, pp. 437–38; and Institute of International Relations, Chinese Communist Who's Who, vol. 2, pp. 28–29.

damaging to health! Lift up your spirit! Keep your morale high! You must always be happy! Happiness will fill your body and mind with peace and tranquillity! So then naturally you will be free from all sickness.

Strive, my child! We are all members of society. I am not only your mother and you are not only my dear son. I love life here. I have gotten a real taste of life. I'm afraid I will work forever in the village—as long as people want me to—and I will no longer work in the city. I have decided that when summer comes I'll have your younger sister and eldest brother join me to enjoy the happiness of the village.

My dear child, are you still going back to Beiping? You will have many opportunities to return to Beiping. After you finish this semester in Jinan (five weeks from now), wouldn't it be better for you to come here to spend the vacation with your eldest brother and the others, catch up on your schoolwork, and play around for a while instead of returning to Beiping? I won't return to Beiping in the near future. I must finish what must be done here. I'm afraid I'll have other work to do and will not return within the next two or three years. So you will simply have to come here and live the life of the real people. The countryside is really precious. Living here instantly brings contentment and happiness.

I live in the research institute because the house nearby isn't fixed up yet.

The youngest students training to be teachers are eleven or twelve years old and are all hale and hearty. They are all village kids through and through. Their clothes, made out of blue flower-patterned cloth with blue cloth lining, truly remind me of the society in which I lived as a child.

Since yesterday I've been dispirited because of spending more than half a day in a ricksha and train—no, it was entirely because of your fussing, and today I still haven't recovered. In particular, my head is spinning. I won't write any more. Let me stop here.

With love forever,

Your Mother
The twenty-first

(Enclosure with the author's letter):
Mr. Editor:

I'm more than forty years old. At the invitation of Mr. Liang Shuming (I originally worked for the Shandong provincial government), I have come to the Zhouping Women's Training Center to serve as guidance counselor. When my child and I parted, it was really a matter of life and death—because he didn't want me to come. This is a letter I wrote to him after coming here which I finished writing, by coincidence, on the twenty-first. I'm sending a copy to you. Please publish it so that society may know that not all women lead lives without a sense of purpose.

Every day I work myself to death and I have no time to write more. Please be understanding.

Jingjun

The twenty-ninth

21. *Seeing* New Woman

by HUANG MING,
a man writing from Guiyang, Guizhou

On the day of May twenty-first I was in Guiyang. I even went to see a movie that night. The movie I saw was one that many people have said isn't bad, but I'd been too lazy to go see it—*New Woman*.[1]

"Being too lazy to go see it" doesn't mean I didn't find it appealing. The fact of the matter is that I'm near-sighted. It's not just that I can't make out the subtitles clearly; even the actors on the screen are out of focus. So rather than not get full satisfaction from the movies I see, I have simply given up movies altogether.

All along this has been my general rule about movies. But as soon as a friend with my interests at heart begins to talk me into going, I start to waver.

This time going to see this movie that I'd been "too lazy to go see" was certainly no exception. The friend with my interests at heart was a woman I work with named Chen. In Guiyang, a semicivilized place, I'm not sure whether an unmarried couple going to see a movie together is a topic for gossip. But I know that Chen herself has progressive ideas. By "progressive," I don't mean she has reached the stage where she has romances that create contradictions of the kind that women have in the big

---

1. This was one of the most successful Chinese films of the 1930s. Written by Sun Shiyi and directed by Cai Chusheng, it starred the actress Ruan Lingyu in the role of Wei Ming. The film historian Jay Leyda has remarked that Ruan "was one of the great actresses of film history, as perfectly and peculiarly adapted to the film as we recognize Greta Garbo to be," and that *New Woman*, her last film, "was possibly her best." See his *Dianying*, pp. 87, 95–97, and 371. For the complete script of this movie, see *Xin Nüxing* in Xianggang wenxue yanjiu she, comp., *Zhongguo xin wenxue daxi xubian*, vol. 10, pp. 363–405.

Ruan Lingyu as Wei Ming in the film *New Woman*, from *Asia* 35.10 (October 1935): 614.

city. I mean she has strong willpower, and she is able to use a silence which seems almost like passivity in resisting the old notions of proper conduct. Because of her silence, people who shouldn't be backward but still are do not quite reject her.

I think that I can easily guess the reason she wanted to see this movie. Naturally, she wanted to understand what the "new woman," as presented by the movie company from the big city, was all about.

The movie started at seven o'clock and ended at nine. It seems unnecessary to write down the plot[2] because I imagine that anyone who reads this book will perhaps have seen this film.

2. The plot of *New Woman*, as summarized by Jay Leyda, was as follows: "Wei Ming is an educated wife whose husband has left her with an infant daughter. She gets work as a music teacher in a girls' school and hesitates to marry again, though she is offered pity and

Seeing it was a great pleasure because Chen recited every word in the subtitles to me, which gave me a deeper understanding of the film than I had expected to have.

After seeing the film, she said to me dejectedly:

"How can a person like Wei Ming qualify to be called a new woman? She is simply a weak girl! A new woman would surely never have died except for a cause. Nor would she ever have dealt with an issue by merely saying 'I want to live.'"

"Yes, I very much agree with you," I said, "but you have distorted the central idea of this film. Just because the film is entitled *New Woman*, you can't say that the heroine should be a new woman. The meaning of the film is to use "Song of the New Woman" to encourage Wei Ming to become a new woman, but she fails to. It uses satirical counterpoint to identify the weaknesses of women intellectuals in the big city and to show the general public that you can only live when you have the courage to put up resistance. Otherwise all you can do is die."

A great many people saw the movie that night, especially women. Later on, local newspapers also published many reviews of this film which expressed opinions similar to Chen's. I think that our screenwriters should take note of this.

22. *Two Letters*

by SHEN ZIJIU,[1]
a female journalist and editor writing from Shanghai

Soliciting articles, editing articles, sending articles to press, greeting guests, holding meetings, and answering phones, plus keeping track of indispensable petty everyday family items: fuel, rice, cooking oil, salt, sauces, vinegar,

---

jewels by the school's principal. Burdened with debts and the illness of her six-year-old daughter, she writes a novel, which is accepted by a publishing friend, though no payment is possible then. To get some immediate cash she finds a procuress, but the first customer is the school principal. . . . In despair she takes her own life; as she lies dying in the hospital she hears the shouting newsboys under the window, 'Famous woman writer commits suicide.' The last scene: 'Many women-workers, after reading the news of her, walk together to the morning sun!'" Leyda, *Dianying*, p. 96.

1. Shen Zijiu was a female journalist who served as an editor not only of *Women's Life* (as mentioned in this article), but of other Chinese publications in the 1930s including the

sugar. Every day from the time I open my eyes it's as though I'm on an endless treadmill, which keeps me spinning and makes me dizzy.

As a rule, not until after ten o'clock in the evening do things calm down, and then I am able to write short essays and answer letters. Tonight was as usual with one exception: In tonight's pile of correspondence, I discovered two unusual letters. One was from a friend who was traveling in the Soviet Union reporting what she had seen and heard. One passage in the letter said:

"The appetite for food and sex is human nature.[2] Every woman here has a job (with a few exceptions, of course). Every woman has the freedom to choose her own loving companion. Thus, the most important problems in life are solved. Especially, the most important problem for women, child-rearing, has been solved because daycare centers are everywhere. Everyone has a happy existence diligently striving forward. This new kind of life startles and excites a person like me coming from the old world, even to the point of making me feel half my age. When I see the excitement generated by May Day festivities, I particularly wish that I could live this new kind of life forever. But I am a tourist. Before long I must return to the old world to live the old life of suffering!"

Another letter was sent to me by a reader of *Women's Life*[3] who lives in Gansu province.

Perhaps because the address on the envelope was smeared, the letter, though mailed in mid-March, only reached me today, May twenty-first! By coincidence it's like the other letter in that both talk about "new life." Although the words are the same on the surface, the meanings are entirely different. This unusual letter was written as follows:
"Dear Mme. Editor:

"When you hear that your *Women's Life* has reached remote and barren Gansu, won't you just jump for joy? The March 8 special International Women's Day[4] issue that appeared within the February edition

---

periodical *Guomin zhoukan* (National weekly). She also served—along with Mao Dun and nine others—on the editorial board of *One Day in China*. On her career, see Union Research Institute, *Who's Who in Communist China*, vol. 2, pp. 562–63; Institute of International Relations, *Chinese Communist Who's Who*, vol. 2, pp. 156–57; and Meicun (pseud.), "Shen Zijiu," pp. 250–51.

2. This line is an allusion to a comment by Gao Zi in *Mencius*, book VI, part A, number 4. We have used, with slight modification, the English translation of this line by D. C. Lau in *Mencius*, p. 161. See also the translation of *The Works of Mencius* by James Legge in *The Four Books*, p. 397.

3. *Women's Life* (*Funü shenghuo*) was a Chinese periodical for which Shen Zijiu served as editor. See n. 1.

4. The practice of celebrating International Women's Day was inaugurated in 1910 and introduced in China in 1924. Jonathan D. Spence, *The Gate of Heavenly Peace*, p. 289.

made a particularly big splash in this dead and desolate XX County in Gansu. ([Note inserted by Shen Zijiu:] This deletion has been made because the reader asked me repeatedly to keep the name of the county secret.) On March 8 of this year, there was a small celebration here. In general, the program resembled the ones described in the March 8 special issue, except that there were speeches by representatives of the Party [Guomindang] and government organizations. Who would ever guess that the lyrics from the March 8 festival song, 'Do not listen to the lies of the three states of women's dependence and the four female virtues,[5] do not sacrifice your whole life for the children and in the kitchen,' would be considered rebellious and heretical by the local leaders of the New Life Movement.[6] It is said that headquarters has been asked to ban this song for the following reasons: '(1) The New Life Movement has as a principle the promotion of traditional morality. The three states of women's dependence and the four female virtues are the traditional morality for women. How can you not obey? (2) The New Life Movement has the goal of promoting work and service. Child-rearing and cooking are women's work ordained by heaven. How can you ignore this? . . .' Who wouldn't want to jump out of the old life and into a new life! But ultimately what is 'new,' and what is old? We are really mixed up."

In this routine yet busy life, discovering these two letters that have come by chance and that have both discussed "new life" leaves me not knowing whether to laugh or cry. I've been reeling for a long time!

5. These phrases appeared in ancient texts, the Book of Rites (Li ji) and the Book of Songs (Shi jing). As interpreted in the twentieth century, the three states of a woman's dependence were: dependence on her father before marriage; dependence on her husband after marriage; and dependence on her son after the death of her husband. The four female virtues were: proper female behavior, proper female speech, proper female demeanor, and proper female achievement. See Morohashi Tetsuji, ed., Dai Kan-Wa jiten, vol. 1, p. 150.

6. The New Life Movement was inaugurated by Chiang Kaishek on February 19, 1934, and had the avowed aim of reforming popular attitudes and thus regenerating China. The vocabulary for the movement was drawn from Confucian morality, and was in this case invoked against the March 8 festival song. On the ideological basis for the New Life Movement, see Arif Dirlik, "The Ideological Foundations of the New Life Movement." For an example of other Chinese women having similar reactions against the New Life Movement's Confucian slogans on this same International Women's Day (March 8, 1936), see the account of a meeting in Beijing in Helen F. Snow (pseud. Nym Wales), Notes on the Chinese Student Movement, 1935–6, p. 181.

PART II

"Heads" and Political Authority

"Heads" and Political Authority

"Head" (*zhang*) as the term was used by contributors to *One Day in China* is a title designating a local political or military leader at the county level or below in rural China (where at least 80 percent of the population has always lived), such as county head, militia head, bureau head, ward head, tax-and-labor head, township head, village head, watch-group head, ten-household head, or family head. Though the term had long been used for positions of authority (dating back to the Han dynasty, 206 B.C.–A.D. 221, when the title "county head" was first introduced),[1] these authors gave it negative connotations by presenting consistently unfavorable evaluations of the role that heads played in local government. Heads were depicted as at best ineffectual and at worst destructive in all the governmental functions that they performed at the local level: the propaganda campaigns they carried out through the schools and the armies (nos. 1–6); the public works projects which they supervised, such as the improvement of agriculture, the introduction of schools, the construction of roads, and the building of fortifications (nos. 7–14); and the public security programs in which they recruited and commanded troops and led crusades against Communism (nos. 15–20).

The heads' attempts at propaganda work, as characterized in Section A, were insulting to educated teachers and students and incomprehensible to uneducated peasants. Teachers resented township or village heads for forcing them to present the government's case to local students and peasants and for requiring the teachers to sign loyalty oaths and make anti-Communist pledges in order to retain their jobs. Students and soldiers, while showing a keen interest in political issues, feared that heads in their schools and military units held the wrong positions on these issues, took the subordination of youth for granted, and failed to appreci-

---

1. Morohashi, ed., *Dai Kan-Wa jiten*, vol. 11, p. 664.

ate young people's perspectives on politics, the military, and foreign affairs.

Though we are given no more than glimpses of heads in Section A, the descriptions do not generally inspire respect for holders of positions of authority. In one piece, for instance, a village head was drowned out by peasants who began to chat as soon as they realized who it was that was trying to speak (no. 1). In another piece, heads of military units dodged the pressing issues of war and peace in their addresses to young recruits (no. 6).

The heads appearing in Section B were also described in unflattering terms. Charged with supervising agricultural, educational, and construction projects, they avoided these responsibilities or imposed unrealistic solutions, conscripted peasants to work without pay, and confiscated land without adequately compensating the owners. Moreover, though the heads mouthed clichés about the value of such projects to the public, the peasants described here remained unconvinced and complained that the time required to build roads and fortifications would be better spent at spring planting. In other words, the peasants' view was that the so-called public works projects in actual fact served only the selfish interests of the heads at one level or another rather than the interests of the people whose labor and land were used.

Section B contains portraits of heads that are fuller but not more favorable than the ones in Section A. The most favorable evaluation was by an author who purported to be a tax-and-labor head (no. 12), but even he was ambivalent about the value of the project under his supervision, and the heads portrayed by the other authors in Section B were shown to be incompetent, complacent, threatening, or vicious: the foreign-educated official who was utterly naive about agricultural conditions in the Chinese countryside (no. 7); the illiterate and stubborn ten-household head who blocked efforts to improve rural education (no. 8); the smooth-talking watch-group head who protected his superior, the township head (no. 11); the bureau head who had his men whip an old man for protesting land confiscation (no. 14).

The heads characterized in Section C were still more menacing than those in Sections A and B. Responsible for public security, the heads in Section C performed police functions and had access to weapons; thus, they had not merely the means to threaten people but the power to use armed force. So armed, these heads in charge of public security were, paradoxically, sources of public insecurity, for it was they who drafted young men into the army, fought battles that took the lives of innocent bystanders, and dragged friends or loved ones off to jail. Some of the heads in Section C were given credit for setting local government straight and restoring order—notably in the piece written by a man claiming to be a member (and apparently the head) of a government team carrying out an anti-Communist rural purge (no. 19). But most of the heads in Section C, like the ones in Sections A and B, were presented as unappealing characters: the two smug township heads, each sporting a pistol on his hip, who were suspected of being arbitrary and irregular in conducting military drafts (nos. 15–16); a martinet responsible for training draftees who lost his temper when they came forward with a constructive suggestion (no. 17); the snobbish commanders-in-chief in charge of "exterminating" bandits who would not have deigned to visit a poor mountain village if they had not been assigned there (no. 18); and the military heads of every rank who brutally tortured their victims into confessing that they were Communists (no. 20).

Why heads at subcounty levels performed so badly was explained by the contributors only by implication. Recent historical research on the subject suggests one possible explanation: Chinese political leaders at the provincial and national levels in the 1930s (like earlier leaders in the central government of imperial and republican China during the nineteenth and early twentieth centuries) had tried but failed to discipline local heads.[2] But the authors of the pieces in this part of *One Day in China* did not pronounce judgment on heads at higher administrative levels. They made occasional references to heads of government at the provincial, regional, or national levels who have since come to occupy important places in the historical record: at the provincial level, Yan Xishan (mentioned in no. 1), a warlord whose armies had controlled Shanxi province in Northwest China since 1911;[3] and (nominally) at the national level, Chiang Kaishek (mentioned in no. 3), leader of the Guomindang government which had set up its capital at Nanjing on the lower Yangzi River in 1927 and which claimed to control 25 percent of China's territory and 66 percent of its population by 1936.[4] It is true that by 1936 the governments of Yan Xishan and Chiang Kaishek had tried to penetrate more deeply into

---

2. Historians have evaluated several attempts by leaders in China's central government to reverse the trend toward ever greater power at the local level. On attempts in the nineteenth century, see Philip A. Kuhn, *Rebellion and Its Enemies in Late Imperial China*. On attempts in the first decade of the twentieth century, see Mary Clabaugh Wright, "Introduction"; and Ichiko Chūzō, "The Role of the Gentry." On attempts in the early republican period (1912–16), see Ernest P. Young, *The Presidency of Yuan Shih-k'ai*. On attempts in the republican period under the Guomindang government (1927–37), see Eastman, *The Abortive Revolution*; Tien Hung-mao, *Government and Politics in Kuomintang China, 1927–1937*.

3. For a biography of Yan, see Donald G. Gillin, *Warlord*.

4. See Eastman, *The Abortive Revolution*, p. 272.

Chinese society than any central government had ever done before, for they had appointed officials to serve within the formal administrative structures of their governments not only at the county level (the lowest level at which officials had been formally posted in imperial China) but also at the ward level (with each county subdivided into three to twelve wards).[5] Moreover, every county under Guomindang control in 1936 was supposed to have four bureaus—education, construction, public security, and finance—each with a bureau head operating at the county level.[6] Yet, if the characterizations of the heads given here are any indication, these attempts at bureaucratic penetration into rural China did not succeed in disciplining local heads or inducing talented and effective people to become heads in local government. On the contrary, the contributors showed no respect for the heads holding official appointments (the county heads, ward heads, militia heads, and bureau heads) or for those holding unofficial, subadministrative posts not formally sanctioned by the provincial or central government (the tax-and-labor heads, township heads, village heads, watch-group heads, ten-household heads, and family heads).

In retrospect, the analysis of the interaction between China's central government and local administrative systems (which included 1,949 counties in 1936)[7] has posed fascinating problems for historians,[8] but on May 21, 1936, the contributors to *One Day in China* were concerned less with the reasons behind the low quality of rural leadership than with its effects on local society. Although the Guomindang government had only begun to revive the traditional system of subadministrative control in the early 1930s, these contributors took for granted the existence of a well-established informal structure of authority dating from imperial times and supposedly governing everyone in rural China. It took the form of an ever-ascending pyramid, in which each person belonged to a household, each household belonged to a unit of 10 households, each unit of 10 households belonged to a unit of 100 households, each unit of 100 belonged to a unit of 1,000, and so on; and at every level, heads were responsible for tax collection, labor conscription, population registration,

5. Kuhn, "Local Self-Government under the Republic," pp. 284–86.

6. See "*Shen bao*" nianjian, p. 234.

7. The figure of 1,949 counties excludes those in Outer Mongolia and Tibet and is taken from Chien, "Wartime Local Government in China," p. 443.

8. For a suggestive comment on the interaction between the central government bureaucracy and local administrative systems as a theme in Chinese history from 1800 to the present, see Philip A. Kuhn and Susan Mann Jones, "Introduction."

and mutual surveillance.[9] Implicitly if not explicitly, some of the contributors indicated that they disagreed with policies (such as loyalty oaths) which came down through this authority structure and which had presumably originated with some regional or national leader (such as Yan or Chiang). But in their generally negative characterizations of heads, they emphasized that local government was ineffective not merely because the leadership at the top was misguided or because the orders sent down from above were inappropriate, but because the caliber of heads at the local level was appallingly low.

9. On the Guomindang's revival of the system of mutual surveillance (*baojia*) between 1932 and 1934, see Tien, *Government and Politics*, pp. 94, 101, and 111–13. On the functioning of this system in the nineteenth century, see Hsiao Kung-chuan, *Rural China*, chaps. 2–3 and passim.

A. Reactions toward
Propaganda Campaigns

1. *My Gramophone's Solo*

by LIANG JIMIN,
a male elementary school teacher writing from Xin County, Shanxi

Today, as part of my job, I lectured for fifteen minutes on the cruel schemes of the Communists. The listeners were bored and the speaker had absolutely no interest either. But I had to do it the way I did it. Like a gramophone, once cranked up, I could only go on running and singing.

On the night of the seventeenth, our village chapter of the Militia for the Promotion of Public Justice[1] (of which I, as an elementary school teacher, am the ex-officio secretary) received an order sent jointly by the county chapter of the Militia for the Promotion of Public Justice and the county government. It stated that by order of the headquarters of the Militia for the Promotion of Public Justice, all village heads, village militia heads, and secretaries were to propagandize for the prevention of Communism. Attached to it was a document about propaganda methods, which established five guidelines. Among them, the second guideline was, "The villages and the village militia heads are to act in accordance with *The Work during the Period of Preventing Communism and Outlines of Propaganda, Chairman Yan Xishan's Letter to the People of Shanxi Province Re-*

---

1. The name Militia for the Promotion of Public Justice (*Zhuzhang gongdao tuan*) was given to the militias in Shanxi province in 1935 by the warlord Yan Xishan (mentioned in the introduction to Part II), whose army had dominated that province since 1911. He intended that every village of the province should have such a unit, and by May 1936 the units had recruited members who numbered in the hundreds of thousands. The avowed purpose of these organizations was to compete with the social reforms advocated by the Chinese Communists. See Gillin, *Warlord*, p. 152.

garding the Extermination of the Communists and other documents, and are to join together with school teachers, and these three parties are to take full responsibility for explaining to the people in the village line by line in detail until it is understood." Guideline number three states that "the daily propaganda in each village is to be the responsibility of the village head, who is to take advantage of free time at lunchtime or before bedtime in the evening, and is to summon the people to a public place or to the stage of an outdoor theater to listen to hour-long lectures. In each lecture the village militia head and the teacher one after the other are to take responsibility for giving detailed explanations." Guideline number four states that "during the period of propagandizing, within ten days after the day that the order is received, it is imperative that all listeners be made to understand thoroughly. Qualified males under age thirty-seven also should learn by heart the songs for the prevention of Communism, and when the period of ten days is up, the results should be reported to and checked by the county head and the county militia head."

According to guideline number four of the order, there should have been a meeting of village people on the eighteenth to explain the official methods handed down for the prevention of Communism. But because of long-standing inefficiency in the administration of the rural township, official correspondence and legal instructions of any kind have been regarded as "nothing special," so not until the twenty-first did a portion of the villagers gather and did I start my gramophone singing its solo.

At about seven o'clock on that night, evening colors filled the universe, and the wind roared its usual angry roar. Although it was already early summer, the wind blew right through people, and blasts of air left them in discomfort.

The villagers who came, numbering about thirty, gathered in our only classroom. In every mouth was a long smoking pipe from which hung down a pouch of tobacco. They blew out puff after puff of thick white smoke which spiraled upward and reached the ceiling, came back down, and then spread throughout the entire room. The classroom, less than thirty feet square, was completely filled with the extremely smelly tobacco smoke. It was suffocating.

"Sit down! Everybody sit. We can begin now," came an order suddenly over the din, and for the moment, everyone quieted down. But after realizing the voice was that of the village head, everyone began to chat among themselves, and the situation returned to what it had been before.

Then the village head again said: "Be quiet, everybody! Today Generalissimo Yan Xishan (Shanxi people generally call Chairman Yan "Generalissimo") asked us to gather everyone together for lectures on methods of preventing Communism. Everyone must pay close attention to what Mr. Liang has to say." As he finished, he called me to the platform to speak. I felt that the militia head was a person who ought to speak too, so I asked him to speak first, but he repeatedly declined. With no alternative, I could only mount the platform and bow to the audience. At this point, everyone fell silent as though they were expecting something.

Composing myself, I said: "Now that the Communist bandits have all been cleared out,[2] Chairman Yan has ordered that each village gather everyone together to hear lectures for the purpose of making everyone understand the Communist bandits' maliciousness and cruelty and the importance of avoiding their trap. Although our Xin County has never been trampled by the bandits, mere mention of their cruelty and maliciousness is enough to make everyone turn pale. Concerning the Communist bandits' maliciousness and cruelty, we have the Chairman's *Letter to the People*, which can be explained to everybody. Now I'll begin to talk about what is in it, so that everyone will see clearly the real face of the Communist bandits."

After this preface, I explained line by line Chairman Yan's *Letter to the People of Shanxi Province Regarding the Extermination of the Communists*.

"The Communist bandits deceive people by first giving them a taste of honey and then spices." Thus did the gramophone start, and, line by line, the loud voice took the place of the noise heard earlier.

After a while only a very few people were listening attentively and changing the expressions on their faces. There were people whispering among themselves, but whether they were discussing Communist bandits or swapping family secrets I couldn't tell because I was busy making my gramophone sing.

There were also some people who were clearly dissatisfied with what I was saying, and they stealthily sneaked out. By then, the gramophone I was playing was gradually drowned out by the noise that everyone was making, to the point where it could no longer be clearly heard. I had not intended to give this talk, and, seeing that everyone was unenthusiastic about it, I then announced that the talk was over and stepped down from the platform.

2. After the Chinese Communists completed their Long March and began setting up a base in Shaanxi province in 1935, they sent an expeditionary force of 34,000 men across the frozen Yellow River in January and February of 1936 to persuade Yan Xishan to fight the Japanese in the Northeast as well as North China. Once in Shanxi, they defeated Yan's troops and occupied eighteen counties. Yan then turned to Chiang Kaishek for help, and Chiang responded by sending his central army into Shanxi. Under attack by the combined forces of Yan and Chiang, the Red Army withdrew from Shanxi and returned to Shaanxi in April of 1936. Ibid., pp. 220–22.

"Listen, everyone," the village head again spoke up. "We'll be lecturing for ten days. Today is the first day, and you are not quite concentrating. You are talking among yourselves. I hope that you will not act like this in the future." The village head paused and went on to say, "Furthermore, today we only talked a little about the *Letter to the People Regarding the Extermination of the Communists*. After we finish this, there are two more books, *A Letter to the People after the Extermination of the Communist Bandits* and *The Work during the Period of Preventing Communism and Outlines of Propaganda*. I urge all of you to come every day until you achieve a thorough understanding. Otherwise, since I have orders from higher-ups, I won't be easy on you!"

Before the village head seemed to have finished, twenty or thirty people's heads began to look this way and that. The noise they made was even louder than before. Meanwhile, some people began to move toward the door and leave.

Then we also walked out of the classroom, and I heard village people whispering among themselves. Amidst the whispering, I thought I heard: "What was said today? Wasn't it about the Communist Party coming again and some sort of tax being levied?"

2. *Depressing Weather*

by XIAOAN (pseud.),
a male elementary school teacher writing from Ding
County, Hebei

When I woke up from my afternoon nap, it was already about three o'clock.

The wind had not stopped blowing since it started just before 11:00 A.M. The desk top, which had been dusted before naptime, was once again covered with a layer of yellow dust.

There was no other sound outside except the wind roaring through the air *hu—hu*, and I could see through the glass window that the sky had turned yellow. Depressing weather!

Sitting down in a chair at the desk, I intended to continue to edit *Teaching Methods for a Short Course in the Chinese Language in Elementary Schools*, which we were eager to finish. But no matter how hard I tried, it was impossible to concentrate.

I put on my hat, braved the wind, and went looking for Teacher Li at the elementary school, intending to borrow some novel or another from him.

"Hey, you're working so hard! Didn't you even take a nap?" Teacher Li was hunched over his desk carefully writing something. But he immediately put down the writing brush, stood up smiling, and said very courteously:

"Oh, cousin![1] Please have a seat!"

"Don't be polite, don't be polite. I've interrupted you," I said, and, walking over to his desk, I pointed at his unfinished work. "What is this?"

"This thing?" he said, as he made his way over to pour some water for me. "It is *The Pledges with Regard to the Problem of Communism*. What an awkward title." A humorous expression appeared on his face. Then he handed me a Baby[2] brand cigarette. I immediately stood up to thank him.

I sat down, and he did too. We both lit our cigarettes and had a smoke.

I couldn't get out of my mind the awkward title that he had just mentioned. I asked:

"What regard to what, Comm-what party, pledges for what?"

"Cousin, you take a look!" He unfurled on his desk a roll of coarse paper on which was mimeographed: "Hebei Province, Ding County Government Order!"[3]

I sensed that he intended to hand it to me, and I quickly said to him with a smile:

"I don't want to see that thing."

"Cousin, really! This is something that we have to know about. Come, I'll read it to you."

Before I could let him know whether or not I was willing to listen, the old gentleman cleared his throat twice and then intoned in a loud voice:

"Hebei Province, Ding County County Government, *Re* Education No. 713. Order to Xiping, Zhugu Village Elementary School.

"According to the Hebei Provincial Ministry of Education, Order No. 624 issued on April 10 of this year, which states that according to Hebei Provincial Government No. 2087 issued on March 27 of the twenty-fifth

1. [Xiaoan's note:] Those of the same surname address each other as "cousin" (*dangjia*) [literally "the one in charge of the family"]. "*Dang*" is pronounced with the third tone.

2. In the original text, Xiaoan included the name of this brand in Chinese followed by the words "The Baby" in English.

3. Ding County was the site of an experiment with rural reconstruction and had American financial backing, but as this piece shows, it was not invulnerable to Guomindang political control. On rural reconstruction in Ding County, see "A Comedy in the Midst of Sorrow," n. 1. On Guomindang repression of other experiments with rural reconstruction in the 1930s, see Alitto, *The Last Confucian*, chap. 10.

year of the Republic of China [1936], which states that according to Jicha Council for Political Affairs Order *Re* Politics No. 873 issued on March 16 of this year the Communists have recently brought about chaos by periodically fomenting violence and spreading heterodoxy. Intellectuals often are swayed and end up taking the wrong path. In order to stop this process, it is necessary for intellectuals to distinguish between right and wrong and to reaffirm their convictions. Faculty and staff of schools in each locality have the responsibility to give direction to the thinking of others, and they are public servants obligated to obey their higher officials."

"I suppose this means an official here, an official there, officials everywhere." Teacher Li laughed, and I did too. He again cleared his throat twice and continued to read:

"During this extraordinary time, they should make an example of themselves in order to provide leadership for the students. Those whose convictions are shaky should be removed immediately and unequivocally, and measures should be taken to put their houses in order so that teaching will be done on the basis of correct principles and the behavior of the learned will be upright. Herewith are three kinds of pledges devised by this council with regard to the problem of Communism. The first kind is intended for the use of those who are anti-Communist. The second kind is intended for the use of those who have joined the Communist Party and have already turned themselves in or are considering turning themselves in. The third kind is intended for the use of those who are in the Communist Party—" When he reached this point in his reading, I broke in, laughing, "But don't have their hearts in the Communist Party."

"No interruptions." He also laughed. But he went on:

"—for the use of those who are in the Communist Party or those who are not in the Party but agree with Communist principles—"

"This kind of thing really—"

"Don't interrupt, listen carefully!" He tossed his cigarette butt into the spittoon and continued to read:

"Each of these pledges will be handed by the government to the Ministry of Education for duplication, and all teaching and administrative staff members of each school are ordered to fill in these forms voluntarily according to the procedures before a set deadline, so as to show their orientations—"

"All right, cousin, wouldn't you like to take a break?" I was getting a little impatient.

"What? You don't like listening?"

"From the beginning I wasn't the least bit interested in listening."

But Teacher Li seemed greatly interested in this matter. He picked up a small piece of paper off the desk and also something that was mimeographed:

"You take a look at this one."

To be polite, I took it. On it was printed:

"Voluntary Pledge of Intention to Be Anti-Communist (when duplicated, space should be left after each of the six following items)

—Down with the Communist Party which has brought catastrophes to our country and harm to our People

—Down with the Communist Party which has sold out the Chinese race

—All Communists are the maggots of the human race

—Communists are the ruination of society

—I pledge not to join the Communist Party, not to collaborate with the Communist Party, and not to join any organization that has not been sanctioned

—If violating any of the above, I agree to receive the most severe punishment."

I read it over once and handed it back to Teacher Li without saying anything. Teacher Li took it, read it over once, and slowly put it down on the desk without saying anything either.

The wind outside seemed to be blowing harder and harder. Paper in the window set a certain rhythm, making *ta ta* sounds that were sometimes fast, sometimes slow.

1936, May twenty-first, nighttime in Ding County, Xiping, Zhugu Village

3. *An Unscheduled Meeting of the Student Body*

by BAISHUI (*pseud.*),
a male elementary school teacher writing from Wuxi, Jiangsu

This incident took place in a village elementary school which was in a so-called model county.[1]

Several times orders came down from

---

1. Experiments were conducted in this county as part of the rural reconstruction movement. On this movement, see "A Comedy in the Midst of Sorrow," n. 1.

higher-ups—from the bureau of education[2]—asking elementary school students to make contributions for airplanes. But such utterly destitute village children didn't have half a copper of candy money to save and would not have been able to come up with so little as a dime or two even if they spent nothing on food for as long as two or three days.

Who would have expected these things to come faster and faster, to the point where yesterday urgent orders arrived from the bureau of education! "Every elementary school student must contribute at least fifteen cents, and every teacher must contribute at least one dollar" for the purpose of buying airplanes to celebrate the fiftieth birthday of Council Head Chiang Kaishek. The deadline for collecting the money is the twenty-fifth, and it will all be sent to the bureau of education.

Since we received this official correspondence, we have been utterly frantic. The fact is that we cannot stall or make excuses. But those of us who have worked hard in the elementary school of this village know that there is no way to collect tuition for the school. Some of our kids even owe money for books bought at the beginning of the semester and still haven't been able to pay for them. Now there is absolutely no way to extract additional funds from them to make the contributions. Altogether we have over 180 kids and six adults. If everyone contributes according to the regulations, there should be a minimum of thirty-some dollars in legal tender. But no matter what, we have no means to raise this amount of money.

Deng! Deng! Deng! The meeting bell sounded, and immediately all of our kids rushed into the hall to participate in the student body meeting. The meeting began at 8:20 on the morning of the twenty-first. Ordinarily each class is holding its morning session at this time.

At student body meetings, the responsibility for serving as chairman, recording secretary, master of ceremonies, or whatever, rotates among our kids. But this time the meeting of the student body had not been scheduled, and a rather detailed explanation was in order. Therefore, after the chairman made some simple remarks, the school head took the platform and presented in detail the facts about making donations for buying airplanes in celebration of the birthday.

Then all our kids understood the purpose of calling this unscheduled meeting. After the school head stepped down from the platform, the atmosphere in the hall was heavy with silence.

"We have no power to change the rule about making contributions.

2. Under Guomindang rule, bureaus were organs of government at the county level. See the introduction to Part II.

What we must discuss now is how we can carry out this order," the chairman said.

"Let me say this in all seriousness." One of our kids, who was wearing worn-out canvas sandals with no socks and a torn green jacket with some buttons missing, spoke up: "It's impossible to come up with fifteen cents. As the saying goes, how can you squeeze oil out of a rock?"

"That's true. I think we can only manage one-tenth. Perhaps it's possible for each one of us to give one and a half cents." Another of our kids spoke in a seemingly playful tone, but in fact he was addressing himself to painful realities.

"We can't come up with even a single copper. If the government really wants contributions of fifteen cents, then we'll all take off our clothes, go to town, and put them in hock to get the money. If we can't get fifteen cents, then we'll sell our bodies to the pawnshop." The class head of the fifth grade was red in the face and grumbling.

After that, more than ten of our kids expressed their opinions.

"Quit making comments that are beside the point. Let's come up with something." The chairman was reminding everyone of the problem at hand.

Eventually, after much contention, it was decided that each of our kids would try to come up with six coppers before the twenty-fourth. Three individuals were put in charge of collecting. At the same time, fearful that the higher-ups would say something, it was decided that when the money is submitted to the bureau of education, the school head will write an official letter reporting our true situation.

Has the problem been solved? This will depend on whether or not our kids hand over the money in the amount specified. Will the higher-ups agree to change our quota to the amount specified by the students?

As for the one dollar expected from the teachers, no one can fall short by even half a penny. Weren't the contributions for famine and flood relief and the contributions for prison construction deducted from our monthly salaries last year? This month our regular budget will surely be six dollars short.

Oh! In giving a birthday present to Council Head Chiang Kaishek, we shouldn't be so stingy, but realities have forced us to act contrary to our desires.

4. *Stirring and Disturbing News*

by WEN WANLAN,
a male student writing from Guiqi, Jiangxi

After lunch, everyone lay down to rest as usual. Naturally, the cranked-up gramophone might as well be turned on at this time.

After all, Lei Kexia is a talker, no, actually a propagandist, and speeches came rolling out once again on subjects such as the Japanese soldiers' occupation of North China, the inevitability of war between Japan and Russia, this kind of ism, that kind of ism. We were all tired of listening and only occasionally made an effort to respond, "Hmm—yes," but he kept rambling on and on. As he was getting worked up, suddenly the sound of footsteps could be heard in the room, and no one knew who was coming. When we recognized the special feature on his face, we immediately greeted him:

"Pockmark Zeng, please sit down, please sit down."

"Those with matches bring them over." Pockmark Zeng spoke in his usual carefree way.

"Have you brought along any Golden Dragon brand cigarettes?"

Lei Kexia, who doesn't like to smoke, showed no particular interest in his arrival and continued to expound theories interminably.

"Stop blabbing. I have heard that two hundred men will be immediately inducted into the air force, and there will be a two-million-student army! Huh, we'll all have to go." Pockmark Zeng, looking for a match, reported his news the moment he heard classmate Lei's grand theories. This was certainly fresh news, and Lei Kexia immediately asked:

"How do you know?"

"Of course I do."

"Listen, how did you find out?"

Pockmark Zeng couldn't find a match and he left, perhaps because he was dying for a cigarette.

"We are wanted as soldiers?"

"Once we become soldiers, we'll fight the *wo*X [Japanese dwarf pirates]!"[1]

"Hmm, fight the *wo*X—but what about my lover?"

We all agreed that this news was only a bubble, so we didn't pay much attention. Lei Kexia, having no rival, also quieted down.

---

1. On the term for Japanese dwarf pirate (*wokou*), see "The 'Roar' of the Little Imps," n. 4.

Scarcely five minutes had passed since the bell rang for our study hall. We were just fanning ourselves to cool off, talking loudly and laughing loudly. Suddenly a face with glasses and Western-style hair appeared at the classroom door, and at a glance anyone would know that Teacher Zhang, our dean of studies, had arrived. The classroom became solemn and silent, and our eyes were all nailed dead on our books, as we prepared for roll call and getting the business over with. But no, Teacher Zhang walked to the platform and, with a somber look on his face, said:

"Attention, all of you: I have just received a piece of important news." As soon as we heard the speech begin like that, our eyes shifted from the books and became nailed dead on Teacher Zhang's mouth —what kind of news might it be? The classmates who had been in our room probably were thinking back to the news that classmate Zeng had reported, and exchanged glances.

"Mr. Liu, the training officer, sent a letter from XX, stating that the central government now wants to recruit a two-million-student army and wants all those who have received military training to join. Those joining up should sign up immediately, and the deadline is the twenty-fifth. I believe that each of you wholeheartedly loves our country and that you will certainly be willing to go." Pockmark Zeng's news was confirmed after all.

"What are we going to be trained for?" asked one of my classmates.

"You'll be making preparation to oppose outsiders. After you are trained, you will train the people. When you go to fight in the war, you'll be at least company heads or platoon heads."

"Let's go, let's all go!"

"We want to go kill the enemy!" Everybody was aroused, but one classmate stood up and said:

"Teacher Zhang, about joining up, I'm certainly willing to join up, but is it to oppose outsiders or not.[2] If—"

"Of course it is to oppose outsiders. No, at any rate, if you love the country and want to save it, this is a kind of obligation. Isn't it?" Teacher Zhang replied in this way.

"Yes, we all want to join up!"

"If we go, then down with XX [Japanese] imperialism!"

"Anybody who won't go has no guts."

"Yes, I know that each of you loves the country and doesn't want to

2. This student seems to be expressing a preference for fighting the Japanese rather than the Chinese Communists and other Chinese rivals of the Guomindang government. On the controversy at the time over the Guomindang's policy toward the Japanese, see the introduction to Part IV.

be left behind by the others. Now that we have all agreed, I will immediately submit your names to the higher-ups," said Teacher Zhang. He was about to leave when Lei Kexia stood up and asked:

"I'm near-sighted, so I probably can't go?"

"It may be possible. That will be determined," he said and left.

"Hey hey! The blind man is such a sweet fellow."[3]

"Useless, no guts."

"Only knows how to sing at a high pitch!"

We all badgered Lei Kexia until finally he had to stand up and defend himself:

"I was just asking whether my near-sightedness would make me ineligible."

"Don't say another word."

"Don't say another word. That's that!"

Then there was another round of laughter and angry shouts, and, for a while, the whole classroom turned into our battlefield, and our voices almost raised the roof off the building.

"We must go to fight XX [Japanese] imperialism!"

"Let's get on with this life-or-death battle."

Then someone voiced a different opinion. "I'm not going. What's the use of going anyway? We'll just be fighting against our own people!"

"I'm not going either."

"I'm definitely not going."

"You are all cowards." Those who had agreed to go opened their mouths, cursing.

"I'd rather be a coward." The quarrel quickly spread, and no conclusion was reached by the time study period ended.

I was a little troubled. Should I go or not? If I go—what about my tuberculosis, which is in its first stage? If I don't go, I can't quite become reconciled in my heart. These two conflicting ideas clashed in my mind momentarily. In the end, I decided not to go, to avoid ending up dying in vain. So, preparing a draft in my mind, I went with fear and trembling to the dean of studies' office to request a leave of absence, with the result that verbal permission was granted. But my heart was still unsettled—in the end, to go or not to go? All the way to bedtime, I was still troubled by this. My classmates were still hollering, laughing, and fooling around endlessly. At the window, stars were already blinking their eyes, and across the edge of my pillow, I heard a train chugging along.

3. Lei Kexia literally means "Lei the blind."

5. *An Ordinary Day*

by LONG GANG,
a male soldier writing from Changsha, Hunan

"1936"—people say—"is an extraordinary time." And so we all feel somewhat "extraordinary."

To be sure, leaving school and living on my own was extraordinary, but as time has passed it's become ordinary.

Today as the blazing sun rose, we also rose. In this way, ordinary life began once again.

Following instructions, my fellow trainees and I, wearing recently issued shirts, left troop headquarters and went to the parade grounds. First we ran one lap on the public playing field, and then we did morning exercises—Chinese martial arts. After one signal from the bugler, morning exercises ended, and, after another signal from the bugler, we all formed up and conducted the flag-raising ceremony.

Then the deputy column head gave us a lecture. Yesterday a medical officer from the medical corps had a fight with some trainees for some reason. The medical officer was injured and his glasses were smashed. "What have you all turned into? After only three months of training, you have beaten up a medical officer. Upon graduation, do you intend to beat up your company and column heads? Rebellion, isn't this a rebellion!" The deputy column head's face was long and red. The upshot was that one student, Jiang Jinggui, was expelled. The charges were humiliating an officer and breaking discipline. His platoon head was also given a demerit. But the opinion of his fellow trainees was that the medical officer deserved to get punched. Some of the trainees gave the medical officer the nickname "Emperor of Medicine" because only by striking the emperor does one become a "rebel."

After the lecture, we had breakfast.

Before noon, physical training, study, and military techniques—hand grenade throwing.

After noon, bivouac. Subject: intersquad war games, on the offensive.

We then regrouped and conducted the flag-lowering ceremony.

The officer of the day reported that supper was to be earlier than usual. At 5:40, every column was to fall in and participate in a speech contest.

The contest began. Eleven trainees who had survived earlier rounds of elimination participated in it. I thought to myself, perhaps these eleven individuals represent all the types of people among the more than two thousand of us. Among them, there is a little of everything. They spoke on all kinds of topics: "This Place (where we are being trained) and the Northeast," "The Restoration of the Nation and Education for Farming Villages," "How to Make Sacrifices," "The Coming Sino-Japanese War," "Why China Will Emerge Victorious," "A Pressing Problem among Youth in Modern Times: The Quest for Education," "What Young People Should Do for National Salvation," "Ally with Japan? Be Neutral? Ally with Russia?," and "The Restoration of the Nation and the Future of Youth." One of them spoke as follows: "The 'December Ninth Incident,' which resulted from the conflict between Japan's oligarchs' clique and the junior officers' clique, is one reason why we shall ultimately be victorious." This is a serious mistake. Internal conflicts within the ranks of the enemy will only determine how soon the invasion will come. These will definitely be of no benefit to us. Besides, he was so careless that he mistakenly cited the December Ninth Incident when he meant the February Twenty-sixth Incident.[1] While I was pretending to be deaf and dumb, however, someone won my respect. One of "our little buddies" (the youngest trainee in the entire ourfit) delivered a speech entitled "Ally with Japan? Be Neutral? Ally with Russia?" and said: "We dare say that allying with Japan and attacking Russia is a Chinese traitor's approach. Neutrality is without a doubt impossible."

By the time the contest was over, darkness had descended upon us, but we weren't aware of it.

We returned to the barracks, washed up, held roll call, and went to sleep.

An ordinary day had passed in an ordinary way.

1. The author is correct in pointing out that the speaker confused the two events. The December Ninth Incident of 1935 occurred in China (not Japan) when about two thousand college and high school students in Beijing demonstrated against Chiang Kaishek's appeasement of Japanese aggression and in favor of the Guomindang's forming a united front with the Chinese Communists against Japan. The February Twenty-sixth Incident of 1936 (which the speaker meant to cite) started when young Japanese army officers rebelled against the government in Japan, led 1,400 troops into the streets of Tokyo, killed several cabinet members, occupied several official buildings, and kept the city under siege for three days. For details on the December Ninth Incident, see John Israel and Donald W. Klein, *Rebels and Bureaucrats*, pp. 1–2, 87–95, and passim. For details on the February Twenty-sixth Incident, see Ben-Ami Shillony, *Revolt in Japan*.

6. *One Day in a Training Camp*

by QIAN LUOHUA,
a male soldier and college student writing from
Suzhou, Jiangsu

In the wake of the talk about pacts for the prevention of Communism in North China, we were sent to a concentration camp. Up to today, ten full days have passed. During these ten days, we have led the life of soldiers. Because we were leading the life of soldiers, it wasn't easy for us to get permission to step outside the barracks. We weren't allowed to read any magazines and only a few daily newspapers. Even the newspaper *Li bao*[1] was on the black list. We were abruptly cut off from social reality!

It is said that under this kind of training one "sacrifices one's own small self" for the purpose of "obeying and following the leader" in order to "restore the nation." In listening to speech after speech by the company head, the battalion head, and the regiment head, however, one did not even hear the phrase XX [Japanese] imperialism stated in its entirety. It was as though their omitting it would make us forget about it. But I still haven't forgotten that on the day we entered the camp, newspaper headlines reported on the second step toward the implementation of Hirota's three principles,[2] as though these were meant to be "advice given with good intentions."

On this, the eleventh day, we again followed orders, packed up our gear, and prepared to carry out a troop movement from Suzhou to Nanjing to "receive instruction."[3] Everyone busied himself because this order was not to be disobeyed. But the looks on several hundred faces showed what was in several hundred different hearts.

From dawn to dusk it was busy, leaving not a single moment for rest. New orders frequently canceled previous orders issued only an hour earlier. As a result, the sleeping quarters were swept as clean as possible.

---

1. *Li bao* was a newspaper started in 1935 which was characterized in 1936 by Lin Yutang as "small and a tabloid in format, . . . but [it] makes an attempt to give the most important political and social news of the day at a price low enough to suit the purse of the common man." See his *A History of the Press and Public Opinion in China*, p. 141.

2. Hirota Kōki was Japan's foreign minister between 1933 and 1936 and became its prime minister in February 1936. On October 4, 1933, he drafted three principles as the basis for Sino-Japanese peace negotiations. Widely discussed at the time, the principles called for: (1) China's cessation of anti-Japanese activities; (2) China's de facto recognition of Manzhouguo; (3) Sino-Japanese cooperation in suppressing Communist activities. See B. Winston Kahn, "Doihara Kenji and the North China Autonomy Movement, 1935–1936," p. 180.

3. This phrase, as used in Guomindang official pronouncements, had strong moral overtones.

"Personal items"[4] were arranged as neatly as they could be. We changed into new uniforms—we were wearing the old uniforms only an hour ago—so new insignia and other things had to be put on. The white insignia had to be replaced by the red, for reasons which I still don't understand. Slung over the shoulder was a mess kit, a canteen, and an army blanket, with a cup and towel hanging down. Around the waist was a leather belt which had to be placed between the last and next to last buttons on the army shirt. Beneath the shorts was exposed skin which was suntanned and beneath that were puttees wound three times around the calves. Feet were covered with a pair of cotton socks and straw sandals. Hands were covered with snow-white gloves.

In the midst of the evening's abyss, we marched to Suzhou Railroad Station, sporting a military appearance of the kind that I have described. Along the way we sang songs that did not clearly distinguish between "Enemy or Friend."[5]

By the time we reached the station, it was almost nine o'clock. In the midst of farewells, a unit of middle school students that was leaving first was given its send-off. They were traveling by truck. We are fortunate to

---

4. [Qian Luohua's note:] "Personal items" (*neiwu*) refers to the act of putting one's personal items in order in the barracks. Failing to follow the specific order in which items are to be arranged is a violation of orders and discipline. Arranging these things is extremely bothersome, and often takes half an hour. But it is said that this is at the heart of self-cultivation. Accordingly, this marks the first stage in the process that includes "regulating the family, governing well the states, and bringing about peace and tranquillity under heaven." But some of my fellow students who do not possess "self-respect" deliberately screwed up their personal items because training had been so exhausting that they wanted to be "locked up in isolation" for a few days to get a rest. Being "locked up in isolation" means sitting in a dark room and is the most severe punishment in the camp. [The quotation within this note concerning the family, the states, and heaven is an allusion to one of the Confucian classics, *The Great Learning*. Our translation of this quotation is based upon that of James Legge, *The Four Books*, pp. 357–59.]

5. Here Qian Luohua is implicitly criticizing the Chinese leadership's approach to Sino-Japanese relations as it was expressed in an article entitled "Enemy or Friend" (*Di hu, you hu*). This article was circulated and published (in the supplement to *Waijiao pinglun* [Foreign Affairs Review]) at the end of 1935 under the authorship of Chiang Kaishek's personal secretary, Xu Daolin, and it was representative of Chiang Kaishek's views at the time (according to his close associates as well as his critics). Throughout 1935 and early 1936 Chinese intellectuals and students attacked the article for doubting that Japan was anything but China's enemy, and by May 1936 these critics used the article's title, "Enemy or Friend," as a sardonic code phrase to express their contempt for Chiang Kaishek's policy of nonresistance against Japanese aggression in China. See Chen Bulei, *Chen Bulei huiyilu*, pt. 2, p. 41; and Parks M. Coble, Jr., "Suppression of the Anti-Japanese Movement in Nationalist China, 1931–1937," pp. 9–10. On Chiang's foreign policy and Sino-Japanese relations in the 1930s, see the introduction to Part IV below.

be college students, so the government has been especially kind, inviting us to ride in the third- or fourth-class passengers' car.

While resting in the station, with songs being sung all around, I hurriedly dashed off a letter. At the end of this letter, I wrote the following words: "One hundred fourteen days ago we also had many students riding in a 'special car.' Our 'National Salvation Propaganda Corps from the Universities and Middle Schools of Shanghai' walked in a week from Shanghai to Suzhou in the midst of a snowstorm. We slept for one night in Suzhou and then were taken to the train station by the military police, who had been especially dispatched to pick us up. After being 'legally' beaten up, each student was picked up by two military policemen and was hauled into a 'special car,' which went directly to Jiangwan."[6]

Soon after I finished the letter, the "special car for those receiving instruction" was ready. The order was given and we climbed on board.

We all are sleeping safely and soundly. We can sleep safely and soundly because we don't have to worry about the tracks being ripped up or water from the steam engine being drained out. Also the train is traveling very fast, unlike the train chartered from Shanghai to Wuxi for Fudan University petitioners, which took four days and four nights.[7] Along the way they had to do "illegal" repairs on the tracks.

I will sleep safely and soundly through the twenty-fourth hour of this day.

6. Judging from his description of this episode, Qian Luohua apparently participated in the patriotic demonstrations against Chiang Kaishek's policy of appeasing Japan which were started by students in Beijing on December 9, 1935 (and therefore, are often referred to as "the December Ninth Movement"—see "An Ordinary Day," n. 1). Students from Shanghai (apparently including Qian Luohua) and from other Chinese cities responded to the events in Beijing by demonstrating for the same cause in December 1935 and January 1936 and by joining the students from Beijing in a march across the snow to present their demands at the Guomindang's capital in Nanjing. For details, see Israel, *Student Nationalism in China*, chap. 5.

7. Wuxi is only about seventy-five miles from Shanghai. Here Qian Luohua is apparently referring to an episode during the student demonstrations of December 1935. In that instance, the mayor of Shanghai (Wu Tiecheng) complied with a request from 200 Fudan University petitioners that he ask officials in Beijing to release imprisoned demonstrators, and he ended the students' occupation of Shanghai's North Station by granting them transportation to Nanjing on a train—the train that is described here. It never reached Nanjing, for it was turned back by officials at Wuxi. See ibid., p. 130.

B. Resentment toward Public Works Projects

7. *"Pest Extermination"*

by LU HEFENG,
a male peasant writing from Chongming, Jiangsu

Today a "fake foreign devil"[1] who was said to be an "official" in the county government came to our village in order to "exterminate pests" in our village. He told us villagers that when planting rice we should leave a four-foot-wide space between the rice plants and told us to catch pests in the fields. He also told us to place in the fields a "three-legged stand" with a lamp lit in it, put under the lamp a wooden bucket filled with water, and pour in the water a little kerosene. This was to "trap" the pests and kill them. We villagers have had plenty of trouble with pests, but we are really not happy about being asked to use this method of extermination. We villagers at the moment don't even have money to light lamps at home, so what money is there for lighting lamps out in the fields? We asked this "fake foreign devil," "Don't you have some kind of liquid medicine to spray on and kill the pests altogether?" The "fake foreign devil" shrugged his shoulders and smiled, and we all smiled.

1. This was a common smear term used by Chinese to refer to those Chinese who wore foreign clothes and affected foreign mannerisms in China. For a memorable fictional characterization of a "fake foreign devil," see Lu Xun, "The True Story of Ah Q," p. 77 and passim.

8. A Page from the Life of a Rural Elementary School Teacher

by DONG CHENGYU,
a male elementary school teacher writing from Feng County, Jiangsu

I got out of bed at five o'clock today.

The report on the second inspection has to be completed soon and sent to the bureau of education,[1] and on the twenty-fourth, the second meeting of the Society for the Promotion of Education has to be convened at which there will be a competition testing general knowledge and seminars focused on a problem: "The Abolition of Corporal Punishment for Children and the Methods of Breaking Out of Bondage of All Kinds." My research findings have to be organized to be presented for discussion at that time, and I have been given the responsibility for drafting questions testing general knowledge. In addition, I have to go to Fan Village this afternoon to participate in a talk for the watch-group heads and the ten-household heads in which plans will be made to establish a tuition-free school.[2] Ai! These things cannot be postponed and are also very complicated. How can they be done with good results?

Thinking about setting my daily schedule, I made this decision: this morning, work on the report on the inspection; tomorrow, organize the research problems; and the day after tomorrow, draft the questions for testing general knowledge.

While I was concentrating on drafting the report, a rough voice called out, pounding into my ears: "You're up so early, School Head!"

I looked up and saw that it was a group of eight country bumpkins, each one full of fear and consternation. After asking about their reasons for coming, I learned that all were ten-household heads in the eighth watch-group, and because thieves had stolen desks and stools from the People's Reading Class last night, they were coming specifically to see me and find a way to deal with the theft. Ai! The more one becomes afraid of having things to do, the more things there are to do. If I refuse to get involved, that would run contrary to the principles of administering rural education. Moreover, I have the responsibility of supervising the People's Reading Class and cannot get out of helping solve this crime concerning it. But if I agree to get involved, I won't have enough energy for it! What

---

1. The bureau of education was one of the four organs of government at the county level. See the introduction to Part II.

2. These heads were in charge of units that were responsible for mutual surveillance and security. See the introduction to Part II, especially n. 9.

to do? After giving it a moment's consideration, I finally agreed to help and they were then willing to go home.

This thing cannot be put off! The earlier it is started, the easier it will be to crack the case. All right, let's go! Putting away the draft of the report, I rode my bicycle to the place where the things had been lost and took a look around. The total losses consisted of a pair of elm doors, four ash boards (used as desks), and six benches. The approximate value was twenty dollars. The thieves made off with them though the gate had been locked. The boards were very heavy, and one person would not have been strong enough to move them. I suspect that the number of thieves must not have been small. The dog didn't bark in the night, and I suspect that those who did the stealing must not have been strangers. Then who? A house-to-house search? That would be a waste of energy. If you think about it, would they dare store stolen goods at home! Must be in a place far away! But how to crack the case? Thinking it over and over, I had no good solution except first to bring the two ten-household heads of that village back to the school together with a nearby neighbor named Jiqun. I am not a local administrative official, nor am I a judge, so I have no authority to hold trials and hand down sentences. How to deal with this? Hey! Temporarily lock them up in the library and question them later, after hearing what goes on out there!

At about eight o'clock, three elderly, bearded peasants arrived. They were willing to complete all arrangements and procedures concerning bail for the release of the two ten-household heads who will take responsibility for conducting investigations and searches. I couldn't help but grant bail. So far no one has asked about the one named Jiqun, probably because he is subject to a lot of suspicion. I'll wait until tomorrow to see what people in local society have to say about this thing before I do anything with him.

During lunchtime, a small shop on South Main Street caught fire as a result of carelessness. Most of the townspeople were just standing by, looking on, and watching the excitement. Even the few people fighting the fire either had close relationships with the person whose place had caught fire or were afraid it would spread to their own houses. Fortunately, there was no wind today, so only two houses were burned down, and no one was hurt.

These people are so devoid of the spirit of cooperation and so lacking in sympathy. How to reform them, train them, and bring them along is indeed the mission of those administering rural education and the problem urgently in need of solution.

But this fire worried me to death, and my voice became hoarse from shouting directions to the fire fighters. I decided to organize a fire-fighting team next month in order to make the locality safe and secure. One popular lecture will be given each week in order to develop the people's consciousness.

In the afternoon, I went to Fan Village to participate in the talk session for the watch-group and ten-household heads. Those attending included three watch-group heads and seventeen ten-household heads. Six of them could read. At the outset, I reported on the importance of education for children and the parents' responsibility for the education of their sons and daughters. A report by Watch-group Head Zhu Benli followed, on the purpose of the talk session being held. Finally, there was a discussion of the question of plans for establishing an elementary school. But although I expended the energy of nine oxen and two tigers and spoke many persuasive and encouraging words, in the end they were still stubborn and unwilling to take the initial responsibility. All I could do was to go back to school to think up some other good strategy. I had always hoped that the school would be established as expected so that children would have a place to study and education would flourish.

By the time I got to school from Fan Village, it was already past six o'clock. My energy was entirely exhausted, and I was about to go into the bedroom to take a rest when Watch-group Head Sun from Sun Walled Village arrived at school to discuss with me his assigned duty which was to confiscate the Temple of the Fire God and make it public property. Although I had very little energy at this time, I still had to receive him. What the shrewd Sun said included these lines: "School Head, I really can't get involved in this affair. Now all the plowmen's households are cursing me, saying that I have taken payoffs from officials who want the land confiscated and that I have forgotten the welfare of my beloved neighbors. Everyone is furious, uttering harsh words and giving stern looks, and also saying that no matter who comes to confiscate our land, we'll fight to the death. School Head, do you see what I should do about this matter?" At the moment, I could give no satisfactory solution in reply and could only equivocate, muttering a few lines, saying some comforting and encouraging words, and agreeing to help out.

Ordinary people in local society all say that Watch-group Head Sun is very crafty and also that he cultivates two *mu* of the temple land. Whether what he told me was fabricated by him or was really uttered in the plowmen's households is certainly open to question. Maybe he has deliberately found an excuse to avoid the task and is threatening me because he wants to protect his own two *mu* of temple land, but there is also the possibility that people who are generally ignorant, stubborn, and stupid said these words. Now that the problem has arisen, I should be thinking about ways to solve it. How to persuade them and make them obey is, however, a difficult problem.

After giving it some thought, I decided to bring the members of the plowmen's households together, have a talk on the afternoon of the twenty-third to find out their attitudes, and then decide how to handle it. So I ordered the watch-group heads to go back and notify each plowman's household to be in attendance at that time.

Today's three incidents are too complicated, so although a lot of energy has been wasted, no solutions have been reached. I have really learned many lessons which have made me more aware of affairs in the world and human relations in society, and I can comfort myself on this point.

The rural elementary school is the center of rural culture, and it has the mission to reform rural culture. It should have the educational scope to include all the people in rural areas, and should bring the power of education fully to bear upon all the people themselves in rural areas.

This school district is located in the southern part of Feng County, and the former courses of the Big Sand River and the Yellow River cut across the district, causing the livelihood of the people to be impoverished, their culture to be backward, their customs to be ingrown, and their language and behavior to be vulgar and barbaric. In such a farming village, of all kinds of education—concerning village administration, welfare, language, and health—which one does not need to be provided, which one does not need to be promoted!

Practical problems all come out in practical living, and many of them are in need of our solutions. The spirit of the administrator of rural education is "clearly recognize the problem, solve the problem, and research the problem." I deeply believe that "rural teachers should use difficulties to develop thought and the spirit of struggle." Therefore hardships and problems can only give us courage to strive for improvement and deepen our commitment to experimentation.

Friends, look, the reactionary current is at floodtide everywhere, the lingering influence of feudalism is everywhere, and in this society, which is filled with the black smoke and pestilential vapors of confusion and corruption, our diligence is needed everywhere! We must adopt the attitude of striving for improvement while groping down the dark road, going through difficult passes one after another, and rebuilding the old farming villages in accordance with the ideal of reason!

9. *The Fourth Day of Drafting Workers for Road Construction*[1]

by SHEN TIANYU,
a man writing from Wuxi, Jiangsu

Early in the morning, the powerful sound of brass gongs clanged madly in certain farming villages around Wuxi. A few minutes later over thirty thousand peasants with iron hoes over their shoulders reached the fields. There were waves of wheat but no ripe kernels to kiss the peasants' stocky legs. They swung their iron hoes and slowly transformed their wheat fields into a big road. They seemed to be very experienced at this kind of work. In fact, they have built public roads, ward roads, and rural township roads, all with their own hands.

The ground was covered with green wheat kernels and bean pods. On the side of the road in disorderly piles were pitiful green corpses —trees that had been cut down from the graveyard and mulberry bushes.

Last night the township head attended a meeting at the army's company headquarters and did not return until eleven o'clock. It was announced that on either side of the road a water ditch two feet five inches deep has to be dug. The surface of the road has to be covered with cinders, which the common people have to transport from the city. The work has to be completed before June 10. The company head said that this is construction for "national defense," in preparation for fighting the XX [Japanese] people. Therefore, who could say anything about it?

At noon more than thirty township heads, foreign-style black umbrellas in hand, inspected the entire road up and down and called the roll—one person from the roster on the doorplate of each household.[2] Twelve soldiers who sat in the shade of the trees supervised the construction work and asked girls passing by for tea and water to quench their thirst. Under the sun, the peasants worked themselves to death, digging up, removing, and piling up their own land. The sweat, the curses, and the anger of thousands upon thousands of people mixed together with thousands upon thousands of baskets of dirt. This was the foundation for six big roads for "national defense."

Yesterday Ah X from X Family Village was beaten almost to death by

1. Both Chinese and foreign observers in China during the 1930s commented on the Guomindang government's zealous promotion of road construction and its conscription of labor and confiscation of land for this purpose. See Eastman, *The Abortive Revolution*, pp. 209–12.

2. In the 1930s, as in earlier Chinese history, doorplates were used to register the rural population; see Wen, *Zhongguo baojia zhidu*, p. 475. On the origins of this system in imperial China, see Hsiao, *Rural China*, pp. 50–61 and passim.

"Road Construction," a woodcut by Wang Shikuo, from Zhongguo quanguo muke xiehui [Chinese Woodcutters' Association], comp., *Kang Ri ba nian muke xuanji* [Woodcuts of War-time China, 1937–1945] (Shanghai, 1946), p. 46.

the construction supervisor for disobeying orders. If it had not been for everybody begging on their knees, he would be dead as a dog! This bizarre piece of news happening in this world of great peace immediately spread up and down the entire road.

"Those mothers! When the XX [Japanese] come, it will be no worse than this!" someone swore under his breath.

In the afternoon students from the XX Elementary School were doing problems in arithmetic:

1. 124.933 *li* [length of the road] × 180 × 3.125 *zhang* [width of the road] ÷ 60 = 1,169.56 *mu*
2. 1,169.56 *mu* × 100 dollars [price of land] = 116,956 dollars
3. 1,169.56 *mu* × 0.8 *shi* [weight of small wheat produced] × 8.4 dollars [today's market price] = 935.648 *shi* × 8.4 dollars = 7,859.443 dollars
4. 360,000 man-days of labor [the lowest estimate for the man-days

of labor needed for the entire road] × ⅓ dollar [wages per day] = 120,000 dollars

5. 1,169.56 *mu* × 0.8 dollar [average land tax per *mu*] × ? years = ???

Early in the evening, the setting sun was as red as the fresh blood on Ah X's head. A brown cavalry horse carrying a "national hero" galloped down the newly constructed big road for "national defense." In the distance, the gong marking quitting time made a feeble sound, and exhausted peasants, dragging their iron hoes, baskets, and carrying poles, returned to their homes to await the sound of tomorrow's gong.

A white-haired old lady wept as she touched her only property, several mulberry bushes lying along the roadside.

The fourth day of drafting workers for road construction was over.

May twenty-first, nighttime

10. *A Sketch of Road Construction*

by KANG YIMIN,
a man writing from Wuxi, Jiangsu

The soft breeze of early summer blew against small, weak wheat plants, and slave-driver birds[1] flew up and down through the air chirping incessantly *kuai kuai bogu* (hurry, hurry, plant the seeds). Village men and women, with carrying poles made of mulberry branches on their shoulders or with baskets made of mulberry branches in their hands, trotted along the footpaths separating the fields. Occasionally I could see groups of white-haired old ladies wearing long gowns and carrying incense candles, on their way to the East Buddhist Nunnery to burn incense—all these things are reminders that today is the first day of the fourth month on the lunar calendar.

Suddenly the sound of a gong floated up and down the streets and alleys, abruptly breaking the early morning silence, as though to indicate that some extraordinary event was about to occur.

Shouts erupted from the village, "Go build the road! Go build the

1. Slave-driver birds (*cui mang niao*) are known in English as goatsuckers.

road!" After that, a group of peasants carrying hoes and rakes went to the wheat field, through which a line had been drawn with gray powder.

A peasant who had arrived late spoke to the person who sounded the gong: "Qian Erguan, all you watch-group heads and ten-household heads[2] must be really pleased. You only have to use your mouth to make assignment after assignment, and the real work gets done without your touching a thing. Think about it. Now is the time when the spring silkworms are having their big sleep, the leaves are opening, and families are worried about being short of hands to help with this and to help with that. Who would expect a big thunderbolt to come out of the blue, requiring household after household to send people to build that mother of a road!"

"Old He," the person who sounded the gong said as he walked along, "Don't talk like that! These days it isn't easy to manage public works projects in this remote and poor village. The poorer the common people, the more the tricks by higher-ups. Once this road is constructed, how many fields will again be wasted? We cultivators' lives depend on the fields, and whoever's field is taken away might as well be losing his life. Among those who have had one *mu* or half a *mu* of their fields taken away this time, who hasn't gone to the township head to speak bitterness and shout out complaints? In actual fact, the township head is only carrying out public affairs with a public spirit. If he himself had been the one to initiate this kind of project, he would have been beaten to death and no lives would have been asked in return."

"In the end it is we common people who suffer a bitter fate. We conscientiously, diligently planted a crop of wheat and eagerly waited for it to ripen so it could be taken to market and converted into cash for household expenditures. Who would have expected that just as the green plants were about to form wheat kernels, it was as though they were suddenly struck by a disease that transformed them from green wheat plants into weeds and required that they be pulled up out of the ground by the roots! Wouldn't you say that this is evil-doing? Those whose fields are in the western part of the village are lucky because their fields are far away from the pond and the river, so they haven't been affected in the least. Now spring silkworms are about to be put on the racks where they spin the silk, and in this especially busy season if I don't come out to work on the road, where will I be able to hire a person to do road construction in my place!"

2. Ordinarily watch-group heads and ten-household heads were responsible for mutual surveillance and security. Apparently in this case they also supervised road construction. See the introduction to Part II, especially n. 9.

"Right, those whose land has been affected are the unlucky ones. Have those who merely provided workers lost much? Isn't this true—it's an old story. In the spring of the twentieth year of the Republic [1931], I spent 143 dollars to buy 2.135 *mu* of land from Wang Xiangji, and less than two months later construction began on the Wuxi-Shanghai Road. It took more than 1.8 *mu* of my land and made me so mad that I almost passed out. Later, even though I copied down the number on my land deed and sent it up through official channels, I still haven't got the faintest idea what has happened to it. Now the field can't be cultivated and yields no income, but I still have to pay the land tax the same as before, year after year—you think about that. How is this account going to be settled?"

"In the road construction being done this time, someone has said that the township head is being unfair. Because he himself has fields in the eastern part of the village, he drew a line for a road that circles around the western part of the village. No wonder people owning fields in the western part of the village have been cursing him day after day and are prepared to fight to the death against him!"

"This charge is unjust! In reality, what power does the township head have over this decision? Wasn't it those several gentlemen who surveyed the land, came to the village, and did an inspection three days ago who changed the gray powder line? Naturally they followed their own thinking. Going to the eastern part of the village requires crossing the pond and the river, and now they can build one less bridge and save some public funds. But they have caused suffering for those of us common people who till land in the western part of the village. However, in good conscience, I'll say that going toward the eastern part of the village will damage the Zhang family's fields and going toward the western part of the village will damage the Li family's fields. Lamb's wool comes off the lamb's body, and in the end we common people who get our rice from tilling the land bite the dust."

"Look, a group of people are gathering together over there. What kind of problem are they causing this time?" Old He quickened his pace and ran toward the crowd in the wheat field.

"Isn't that Zhou's Old Wife? She is making a big ruckus again, whining away. Wang Xiangji is also there making a scene. What's the use of their quarreling with the township head!" Qian Erguan threw up his arms, hung his brass gong on the branch of a tree along the river, and made his way into the crowd. Several small barefoot children who had rushed over to see the commotion picked up the drumstick to the brass gong and played with it, striking the gong.

The number of people in the wheat field continued to grow, and they formed a big circle along the river bank as though watching a magic show. The major actors in this drama were Wang Xiangji, who was standing in the middle, gesturing wildly, Zhou's Old Wife, who was screaming to the high heavens, and the township head, who was shaking his head in frustration.

"Township Head, go ahead and do your own thing," said Wang Xiangji, with sweat pouring from his forehead, as he tightened his fists and rolled up his sleeves. "I haven't broken any law. Whoever wants to take my ancestors' graves and build a road through them, I'll fight that person to the death!"

"I've told you before." The township head seemed impatient. "You are using your mouth and tongue for nothing. These are public affairs being done in the public spirit, and not only graves but even houses where people live are being torn down. What's the use of your fighting to the death against me!"

"I'm not afraid of my house being torn down, but it won't be so easy to touch my ancestors' graves!" Wang Xiangji saw that having argued half a day with the township head hadn't scored him half a point, and then he turned to the people to plead his case: "Every one of you here think about it. Who doesn't have ancestors? Who doesn't want sons and grandsons? How are my sons and grandsons to show their faces if I'm forced to dig up my ancestors' graves? If coffins and corpses are turned over like this, will the younger generations live out their days?"

"Xiangji." Qian Erguan, seeing no end to this scene, made his way out of the circle of people and sought to become the mediator. "If I may put in a few impartial words, the road construction must definitely go on. Even the township head doesn't have the power to change the line of the road. I wonder whether we can ask the township head to go to the higher-ups, clear matters up a bit, and get a few more days so that Xiangji can choose a good, auspicious day to dig up the coffins. Otherwise, violating the earth and making members of a family suffer some kind of disaster isn't fair either."

"That can't be done," the township head said sternly. "The higher-ups have allowed three days for laying the foundation for this section of the road. If he is allowed to choose a day, nobody will know what day is auspicious. If the deadline isn't met, won't it be the township head who once again bites the dust!"

"Township Head, what's to be said about my affairs?" Zhou's Old Wife had been weeping to one side, forgotten by everyone. "I don't want ancestors, I don't want sons and grandsons, I only want to have rice to eat. Although I have only this .725 *mu* of rice fields, which even in a good year only produces enough to feed a mother and a son for half a year. Now that it will all be taken up by the road construction, what are we going to live on?"

"What can be done? Your family is not the only one whose fields are being affected. It's not the township head who is doing you harm."

"I don't care about anything else. I only know I want to find rice to eat. If you really want to touch this .725 *mu* field of mine, I'll smash myself to death against this big tree!" Zhou's Old Wife grasped her head tightly, let out a scream, and thrust her head forward, really intending to smash it against the big tree along the river.

"Oh-ah, Zhou's Old Wife, it isn't worth this! Hurry up and call her son over here." Qian Erguan and a group of people quickly grabbed Zhou's Old Wife, and the entire circle of people fell into confusion.

"Township Head, Township Head." Suddenly a person dressed like an underling made it to the inside of the circle and said, "The gentlemen who have come from the city to supervise road construction are waiting for you in the township office."

"Everyone hurry up and go build the road! How will this crowding together seem when people see it!" The township head shouted out loudly, turning his face to fix his gaze on Wang Xiangji and Zhou's Old Wife. "You two must bear in mind that continuing to make scenes like this which result in complaints against you for halting construction work and resisting orders is no laughing matter!"

In the wheat fields, the noise of hoes and rakes, *tie ta*, once again resounded, and the atmosphere that gradually spread through the entire area was like the silence following a big rainstorm.

11. *A Small Episode in a Certain Village*

by MINSHENG (*pseud.*),
a man writing from Yishui, Shandong

Ba, the village head, was over fifty years old. His beard and hair had both turned gray, his back was hunched, and his face was full of wrinkles. He had worked his heart out finding provisions, recruiting and assigning men, and handing out and packing around tools for road construction. Now, as he went into the crowd, he immediately noticed a change in the expressions on people's faces.

"Village Head, we're not going. We've found a way out," Li Xiu was the first to blurt out.

"Why aren't you going? Will the township head stand for it if you don't go?" Village Head Ba, having been a village head for more than ten years, knew that orders from higher-ups could not be defied, but if he always behaved like a yes-man, he would antagonize his neighbors, and his conscience would not allow him to do this. If he resigned, the higher-ups would refuse to accept his resignation, but if he didn't carry out his official responsibilities, he would be punished. It was troubling him to death.

"So you're not going. Why? How are you going to get out of it?" He looked into people's faces, sighed, and said, "Ai, I've had enough trouble these past few days. Just as I was beginning to round up provisions, I broke my leg. You tell me what to do. Our village, though small, has over eighty households and thirteen *qing* of land. The big households, I don't worry about. The Liu, Yuan, and Chen families have all handed over their shares. The Liu family has handed over three hundred catties. The Yuan family has handed over five hundred catties. And the Chen family has handed over one hundred catties. These families don't owe another cent." He deliberately raised his voice in the last sentence hoping that everyone would get the point. "But the small households are difficult to deal with! Although as little as one catty of rice is expected for each *mu* of land, all the small households have almost reached the point where they have nothing left in storage. Food won't fall from the heavens, and if I want to borrow, I have no place to borrow from. I understand the bad spot everyone is in, but there's nothing that can be done. Now there's the job of building XX Road for automobiles. Ai, you tell me, recruiting men and handing out tools, are these easy jobs? Am I happy doing all this? Today you say you're not going, but how am I to report what you say to the higher-ups?"

Once the village head had aired his grievances, the crowd seemed moved by what he'd said, and there was a moment of silence.

"We're not going. If we're punished, we'll take the punishment. If we're put in jail, we'll all go," an aroused Hugui insisted.

"I'm afraid that this might not work," Village Head Ba replied, swallowing hard and measuring his words. "In that case, they will say that we're rioting. Isn't that what happened in X[Huang]shishan,[1] right out in

1. The "X" must have been substituted for the character "Huang" judging from the map of Yishui county in *Shandong tongzhi*, pp. 476–77.

the open for us to see!" He looked downcast as he spoke these words. Once again people saw in their minds' eyes the Black Flag Society[2] causing trouble, and the army using big cannons to break it up. Their faces all turned pale.

"Each of you hurry up and pack up your bags so we can hit the road!" The village head spoke again after a moment of silence.

"Ai, if we all go, we won't be able to tend all those nice little rice seedlings. When autumn comes, what will we eat!" said Yue An, groaning. In fact, right now he had nothing to eat and accepted it, but having nothing to eat in the future was something that he could not accept because he felt that it would be imposed on him by other people.

"I've heard that the road bed is supposed to be five feet deep and twenty feet wide. How many days is that going to take!"

"Ai, not only does the road have to be that deep and that wide but it also has to be so compact that even if water is poured on top, none will soak in!"

"This is the busy season in the fields, and they want us to be busy for them! They don't allow us to tend the little rice seedlings, and they force us to build that mother of a road for automobiles!"

Anger welled up and filled everyone's hearts. The village head tried to calm everyone down, speaking in what appeared to be a most judicious manner. "We have to be content. We only have to do the labor. Just think of the fields along this big road. They'll suffer horribly! The road bed is over twenty feet wide plus the shoulders on either side and the big ditches that have to be dug, amounting to a total of nearly forty feet. Imagine how much land that will take up!"

After the village head made these remarks, people seemed to relax a little, but a moment later the plump rice seedlings in the fields reappeared before people's eyes and, as before, anxiety filled people's hearts.

---

2. Japanese observers identified the Black Flag Society as an organization active at this time in southern Shandong. See Elizabeth J. Perry, *Rebels and Revolutionaries in North China, 1845–1945*, p. 269.

12. *A Sketch of Repairs on a Fortress*

by KANG CHENGXUN,
a male civil bureaucrat writing from
Zhengding, Hebei

"Hey! Tax-and-labor Head,[1] get up and take your group to repair the fortress!" There followed the sound of a knock on the door. Startled, I woke up out of a dream and realized that it was the township head's underling coming to rouse me to go supervise the work. But it was still early and the crows hadn't even let out a caw yet. However, I was afraid I wouldn't be able to fall asleep again if I tried, so it was just as well for me to get up.

There's been a severe drought this spring, and raindrops small as cow's hair have fallen only twice, really confirming the ancients' saying, "Spring rain is as precious as cooking oil." In the fields, waterwheels have been going day and night. When the animals are being fed, people are used to do the pumping. Not only are men working in the fields but women and children are also helping with the work. But even so they feel they can't catch up. Who would have expected an official order to come from the county dictating that roads be repaired and a fortress be built? It certainly seems that the busier it is the more there is to do!

Due to the short notice, work is being assigned this time household by household, and even those widows' families that have no men must hire workers to carry out the order.

Even before the sun rose, we moved out. Fifty members of the Iron Hook Unit chatted and laughed as they marched toward XX Village. At a glance, this scene was quite similar to the Feng-Jin Battle of eight years ago,[2] when able-bodied men were drafted to dig military trenches, only then, because soldiers were supervising, no one dared crack a joke. Now, though they are in "extraordinary times" and inhabit a "special zone," people seem to be living not in dreaded wartime but in an atmosphere of peace and tranquillity. It is like "living between the tiger's jaws but being as invulnerable as Mount Tai!"

The glossy green wheat fields swayed back and forth in the soft breeze. It looked as though this year's wheat crop wouldn't be bad. But

---

1. Tax-and-labor head (*li zhang*) was a subadministrative post. See "Notes on the Text" preceding Part I; and the introduction to Part II. On the origins of the post in imperial China, see Hsiao, *Rural China*, pp. 31–34 and passim.

2. The name of this battle includes characters for Fengtian and Shanxi provinces and apparently refers to fighting over Beijing in 1928 when the warlord who had been holding the city, Zhang Zuolin, retreated from it to his base in Fengtian (Liaoning), and other warlords—including one from Shanxi province, Yan Xishan—converged upon it. See Gillin, *Warlord*, pp. 108–09.

while the road was under repair, the foundation would have to be widened to allow for the addition of a parallel road, built specially for large vehicles carrying heavy loads, so a lot of private land was taken up and wheat plants about a foot tall were yanked out and fed to the animals. Although landowners shed tears when they saw the green plants destroyed, and some even fell to the ground, sobbing and refusing to get up, in the end they couldn't resist the force of officialdom and had to yield under the leather whips of the police who supervised the work.

After walking more than ten *li*, we reached our destination. By this time only a few rays of sunlight had appeared, but the workers repairing the fortress had all arrived. Wooden stakes had already been driven in, and work had already been allocated by sections, so as soon as we arrived we began working immediately, without any time for rest.

The area within this fortress was about three square *li*. The wall of the fortress was about eight feet high and five feet wide with a five-foot-wide ditch outside the wall. Because the fortress had been built recently, it was all on land that had belonged to people. Wheat plants, on which kernels were forming, and cotton plants, which were breaking through the surface of the ground, were all dug up. The land was even gouged out so it will not be able to be cultivated.

In fact all those doing this work were peasants who had no desire to destroy the green plants and do harm to the land. Under the circumstances, however, they had no alternative but to harden their hearts and do it.

It is said that when the government takes people's land, it will give compensation for the losses incurred. But the common people, in view of what has happened in the past, naturally disbelieve a hundred and twenty percent of this. They consider it to have been determined by fate.

What great value a "fortress" has for military purposes we don't know. In normal times when small bands of local bandits would hear that villages and rural townships had taken security precautions, they would naturally not dare "pull the tiger's whiskers," but when real war breaks out, this fortress will not withstand a hit from a single cannon shell.

The order to repair the fortress says it is "for the purpose of protecting the area and safeguarding the people." Whether the "area" can be protected is not yet known, but the "people" certainly have not been safeguarded!

After the sun, that Golden Crow, swooped to the west, we quit working. This day's time had really not been wasted, for in the end we did something to "protect the area and safeguard the people."

13. *The Usefulness of a Fortress*

by XINGZI *(pseud.),*
a woman writing from Kunming, Yunnan

At six o'clock in the afternoon, with the sun still above the mountains to the west, white waves shone in the midst of a sea of grass.

Qi and I were going for a walk along the road that encircles the city. The foreign fruit trees growing around Kunming produced a fragrance that was hard to take, polluting the soft breeze blowing in from the south. We stopped at the pier in Da Guan Lou Park. The white wooden boats in Yuan Pond were crowded together like a flock of geese in a pond. Families of boatpeople were building fires, and white smoke curled up along the masts and slowly drifted away.

A long-distance vehicle kicked up clouds of dust on the gravel road, and we quickly stepped over onto the bank to get away from it. On the bank were many chicken coop-like shacks, with families of boatpeople and poor people living in them. Qi, seeing women crowded inside the shacks and dirty-faced children crawling on the ground, said with feeling:

"You see, over there are grand Western-style buildings, but over here are only mud walls and thatched roofs. The tall are too tall, the small are too small, the useless are too many, the useful are too few!"

Words to this effect I'd heard many times from him, so I wasn't moved. Things in this society are all like this, so there was nothing odd about it.

I pointed to the fortress which had been built for military purposes at the side of the road and said, "Let's talk about this thing. What's the use of it?"

"What use it has," said Qi, "is at least to guard against Communist bandits."

"But take a close look. A single cannon shell can blow it up. Can it guard against anything? Have you forgotten the lesson we learned two months ago? If others had mounted a real attack, would our classmates in the fortress have survived? I say that thing is absolutely useless."

"Then it's still good for guarding against local bandits."

"But would local bandits dare come here?"

"Then it's absolutely useless?"

"Yes, I say it's absolutely useless. If anyone insists it has usefulness, then maybe occupying a lot of useful land and wasting a lot of money would have to be regarded as useful."

We walked along the road for a while in silence.

"You say it's useless. But now I see its practical usefulness." Qi pointed to two beggars about to go into the fortress as though he had made a big discovery, and he said in all seriousness, "It had no use before, but now I have made a discovery: It's a beggars' hotel—a free hotel, much better and much bigger than the chicken coops that we just saw. Can you still say now that it's useless?"

"I agree!" I seconded him. "It really is useful."

14. *The Last Day*

by YEHONG (*pseud.*),
a male elementary school teacher writing from Zanhuang, Hebei

Waves of noise came in from outside the school. I went out and found that a whole flock of crows was all over the place. This certainly was an unlucky day. These troops in black shirts had never before come to cause trouble in the school, but today they were filling all the branches and bending down the luxuriant trees abloom with red blossoms. Though I was standing in the courtyard, they were not afraid and still cawed loudly.

"Sir, my mother—requests that you come to see my father—" called an elementary school student, Tian Fa, as he ran up to me in haste. He was wearing no socks and his feet were covered with sweat and dust. On his forehead were beads of perspiration. In his deep and dark eyes he had a look of confusion. His little shoulders trembled inside his torn sleeves.

I knew what was going on. Old Man Jingan must have gone crazy again because the fortress construction was encroaching upon his wheat fields. I nodded to Tian Fa and immediately followed him out. The beautiful May colors, evident in the paths between the fields, were marred by the rough, tough workers who were constructing the fortress. Black-haired heads crowded tightly around the village like an iron chain binding the village together. Cries of "Shovel that dirt" and "Pour that water" reverberated all around and filled the sky. Anger welled up within my heart.

The old lady was already waiting outside the fence. She covered her red, puffed-up eyes with her hand.

"Sir, you—come quickly. Save us—"

Apparently the sobbing caught the words in her throat, and I could

"An Ordinary Tale" (one in a series), a woodcut by Xinbo (pseud.), from *Lu Xun shoucang Zhongguo xiandai muke xuanji, 1931–36* [A Selection from Lu Xun's Collection of Modern Chinese Woodcuts, 1931–36] (Beijing, 1963), p. 33.

see the muscles in her tanned face twitching. She exercised great patience in her struggle with the pain inside herself. She led us through a gate in the fence.

"Aren't you going to invite the gentleman in for me? You mother!" A rude, coarse voice crashed upon my ears like a big wave. I was very familiar with this voice. It was that of Old Man Jingan. It was the same sound I heard in the wheat fields yesterday, only the tone was a little shriller. "Hurry up and ask him to come over here. I want to ask him what day it is today. You mother, Blind Zhang told me it is an inauspicious day. He was even laughing! When he heard that the workers were building the fortress on my wheat field, he laughed again!"

Entering the house, I said, "Today is the first day of the month. It's a lucky day. I'm here. Can you hear me, Uncle Jingan?" The man had not gotten up from his raised-earth bed,[1] and he was lying in a dark corner that the beautiful sunshine could not reach. The face of this sturdy old peasant was covered with bloody scratches. His eyebrows were raised. His brownish hair, difficult to manage ordinarily, was even more messy today.

"It's a good thing you're here!" he said, peering at me through his deep gray eyes. I could almost see his heart pounding. I sensed that a hand was reaching out to grab me, so I quickly took a step back. "Aren't you the one who just said that today is an auspicious day?"

"Yes—" Before I could finish my answer, the old lady tugged at my sleeve. So I pretended to cough and left the house to spit. She followed after me and whispered, "Don't tell him that today is an auspicious day. He's been waiting for an auspicious day to go to the bureau[2] to fight for his life. That's why Blind Zhang said that today is a black day."

I was taken aback and didn't know how to respond. The old man yelled out through the window:

"Sir, don't leave. Today—is an auspicious day."

When I went back into the house, he was already up sitting on the edge of the raised-earth bed, breathing so deeply that his chest heaved up and down. His big, strong hands, caked with dirt, were pressed heavily upon his thighs. His chest was thrown forward, striking a righteous and heroic pose.

This was the same heroic pose that he had struck yesterday sitting in the wheat fields. When the workers sent by the bureau to build the fortress had reached his field and were about to start work, he had said to them:

"These three *mu* of wheat fields have been handed down to me by my ancestors. In a good year, I harvest 2.2 *shi* and in a bad year 1.3 *shi*. All the lives in my family hinge on this piece of land. If you're going to build the wall of a fortress on this piece of land, then you'll be cutting the heart out of me, Jingan, and eating it. You mothers, I won't be able to live any longer. None of us will be able to live any more!"

The construction workers had made bemused faces at each other, and they had immediately begun to dig, using picks and shovels. That

1. The functions of the raised-earth bed (*kang*), which was common in the houses of North China, are aptly summarized by Chen Yuan-tsung: "At night when you spread your bedding on it, it is your bed. During the daytime when you have rolled up your bedding and stacked it on one side, the kang can be used as a place to work, eat, and receive visitors on. A large kang can take up half the space in a room. It is actually a raised room within a room, a split-level room, the inner raised one with a flue beneath it where a fire can be lit for warmth." Chen, *The Dragon's Village*, p. 66.

2. Bureaus were organs of government at the county level. See the introduction to Part II.

poor piece of green-colored wheat field had been instantly transformed into spaded soil. The kernels of wheat, almost ripe and almost bursting, had been left strewn all over the ground. He had picked up a fistful of sand and pebbles and thrown it at the work gang.

"You're cutting down my wheat! You're cutting down my wheat!"

The bureau head supervising the job had come over and ordered the police to lash him in the face with a leather whip. Then the wheat field, its plants already ruined, had become dyed with drops of blood shed by the owner of the land. Several villagers had come over and dragged him away, and they had apologized to the bureau head. The bureau head had then spoken words that had been spoken a thousand times before: "Aren't the repair and the construction of fortresses all done for you common people! The Communist bandits are going to come at any moment, and you are still in a dream world! Aren't you afraid that the Communists will rape your wives and daughters, kill all of you people, and leave things in flames? Look at Shanxi!—"[3] The construction workers had resumed work energetically. Their iron shovels had flown, and soon they had dug a ditch in the wheat field and had used dirt from the ditch to build a solid wall which extended the wall they had previously built, completing a wall in the shape of a circle around the village as strong as iron. Heaven above! Like someone knifed in the belly, the nearly ripe wheat field had pumped out fresh red blood. This blood had blotted out the green wheat plants and had exposed their guts, which had already been slashed.

"Is this an auspicious day?" he screamed, grabbing my hand. Before I could answer him, he let go of my hand and ran out the door. "Digging up the dirt in our own fields and burying us alive. What has it got to do with preventing banditry? It's got us by the neck and is strangling us!"

By the time I'd hurried over and reached him, he had already slugged two policemen, and had already been tied up and turned in at the bureau office by the village head, who wanted no trouble. On the way there, I heard him screaming:

"This is the last day. I've lived to be forty-four. I've never seen force used to seize the common people's wheat fields for construction of fortresses! I've lived enough, lived enough. This is my last day! Last—"

The poor old woman cried and then fainted and fell to the ground. The son, Tian Fa, knelt next to her, wailing with all his might. The leather whip lashed against Uncle Jingan's face and back, and drops of blood dripped down, reddening the sun-baked empty road—

---

3. This was a reference to the Red Army's occupation of eighteen counties in Shanxi province between February and April 1936. See "My Gramophone's Solo," n. 2.

C. Fear of Public Security Programs

15. *A Certain Township Head*

by JIN BO,
a male elementary school teacher and civil bureaucrat writing from Shantou, Guangdong

As a result of losing out in a struggle with my stomach, I came to this rural area and accepted a low-paying job in this isolated place. Here the population is not large, about seven or eight hundred, and almost all the villagers, except those doing business in the market town or staying overseas on the Southeast Asian archipelago, are farmers.

This place is exactly like other places in that it has a rural township office and a township head. However, the township head here is always elected through an electoral procedure that is like a fist fight.

The current township head was elected in this way.

He is a person who has been abroad, and he was once a "third cousin" (Malayan for riffraff) in Singapore. Now he is also a member of the county government's team of detectives. So, he always has a gun on his hip, which makes the rural people's hearts jump.

It is said he once used this gun on Mount Cow Horn to finish off a young college-educated Communist bandit head for whom there was a reward of 2,000 dollars.

"These brothers-in-law[1] are really difficult for people to understand! Why not study books instead of going looking for death?" he said of the

---

1. Brother-in-law is used here as a smear term. The township head meant by this expression to belittle the Communist, suggesting that the Communist was from a family where the women were unvirtuous so that the Communist's sister would be willing to sleep with the township head even though she was not actually married to him (thus making her in a manner of speaking, his common-law wife and making her brother his common-law brother-in-law).

victim, apparently speaking with thirty percent regret and seventy percent self-satisfaction.

The rural township office was originally in the Temple of the "King of Three Mountains," which is in the eastern part of the village. When this township head took the position, the office was moved to this elementary school of mine, where the action is. It was said that the original location was "vulnerable" but lacked "strategic points." Moving to the school, which is in the heart of this village, has made it comparatively secure.

At that time, I was indeed very displeased, but it had the school head's support.

So, at the school entrance there is a sign, "XX County, No. 3 Ward, XX Township Office," which competes with our sign, "XX Private Elementary School." At the same time, there in front of the "protective wall," on a pole that comes to a point, stands a flag with red fringe, a blue background, and yellow stripes. This is the insignia of the Police Reserve Force.

You shouldn't think that he, the township head, is just an old boor, for he, the old boor, holds me in high regard. He talked with me, talked and talked, and then I became the copyist of the township office. It was specifically determined that the salary would be six dollars a month.

But in his own accounts it is clearly written twelve dollars. Only heaven, I, and Old Boor know the secret!

"Mother X! Falsely reporting the salary!" At first, I grumbled within my belly. Then I thought it over: "It is, after all, extra income!" Then I calmed down.

Now I am a teacher and a copyist in the township office.

Several days ago the ward office sent an official document, saying that the County Government Department of Organization and Training ordered that for the third period the able-bodied forces in each rural township "should immediately be recruited and organized, and held in waiting for training."

As a result, Old Boor began to busy himself writing an official document. "For these reasons, the following will be so." He pulled out a stack of household registration forms,[2] scratched his head, blinked his eyes, shuffled around, shuffled around some more, and came up with twelve names. Huh! What is this? On the official document isn't it clearly written

2. Household registration (*hukou biao*, literally "household and mouth registration") had been required of the rural population since late imperial times. See Hsiao, *Rural China*, chaps. 2–3.

that "during this period the rural township in question should recruit *ten* of the able-bodied"?

But Old Boor had his "strategy."

He ordered me to make out "letters of notification" to notify those who had been recruited, "the individuals in question."

"This is a notification: The able-bodied forces for the second period have finished training, and the review has been completed.

"Now

"XX County Department of Organization and Training orders that new recruits be organized and that training be resumed. . . . The person named herein is of suitable age and should be included on the recruitment list. The able-bodied forces for the third period having been accordingly formed, it is appropriate to send notification with the expectation that it will be immediately heeded. Wait for the summons from the government for training, and do not find excuses for avoiding it, otherwise it will lead to prosecution. This is most important! Heed this notice."

So, today quite a number of people came looking for Old Boor. Among the ones I knew were Second Uncle Yixing, who is the proprietor of a shop selling miscellaneous grains in the market town, and Third Brother Cailong, who is the manager of a money-changer's shop.

I sensed why these people came to the office today. Of yesterday's letters of notification, didn't some go to the son of Second Uncle Yixing and the younger brother of Third Brother Cailong?

Second Uncle Yixing said that yesterday after his family received the letter of notification, it was as though someone had died. His wife knocked her head against the stone door frame, knocking and knocking until a big pool of blood poured out. Later she fainted and was out for more than ten minutes. Second Uncle's daughter-in-law threatened to jump into the well. She said that since her husband was "going into the army," she could no longer be a person. And—

"Ai! Township Head! What is to be done? On top of that, the shop is in need of help right now!" added Second Uncle Yixing.

Third Brother Cailong said that his younger brother had recently started coughing and every day had been unable to get rice down. In his words, "He looks like a perfectly healthy person, but he has this latent illness!"

Afterward they went into the township head's office and talked in low voices, talked and talked and talked for more than two hours, and then those two guests left. I don't know what the result was. But from what I have gleaned from my past experience, I know that nothing on this day was dissatisfactory for Old Boor.

The water carrier Ah Niu and the carpenter Nine-fingered Number Four Son came in the afternoon. By chance, Old Boor wasn't there. In accordance with the line from *The Regulations for Self-Government*[3] "always receive the people," I went to receive these two people.

They were also among the able-bodied for the third period who "should be included on the recruitment list."

"Mr. Jin, do a good thing! If we have to drill every day, how are we to make a living? Ai! It's not for one or two days, it's for three whole months!"

"This order is from the higher-ups. Everybody has the duty to receive training, and it's only a matter of when. Also, in the future when you complete your training, you villagers will shoulder the responsibility for security, and the police will be abolished. Then your assigned payment will be lessened," I explained to them.

"But sir, every day I rely only on water-carrying to support my ma and pa!"

"All the mouths in the whole family depend on my wage of fifty cents a day to keep alive!"

"This is—hmm—there is no other way—and—and the township head is not here just now. You go beg him to his face." I really didn't know what to say, and in my mind appeared an image from several years ago of a person in my hometown who was suspected of being a XX [Communist] and was arrested by the army, causing the entire family to go hungry.

Just then the township head arrived. He looked at these two "boors," stuck up his nose, and said:

"What's the matter?"

"Township Head! Do a good thing! We are—are." It looked as though an olive of sorts was caught in his throat.

But the township head, understanding why they had come, did not wait for him to go on. Looking formidable, he said sternly:

"You people don't quite have a 'global' understanding! You are always thinking about 'the means of avoidance.' This 'maneuver' is predict-

3. This was apparently a manual for use in local government. The concept of "self-government" mentioned in its title was introduced in China during the 1890s and became popular with leaders on virtually all points of the political spectrum by the 1930s. See Kuhn, "Local Self-Government under the Republic," pp. 270–98.

able. Huh! Ask you for a few dollars' worth of monthly surtaxes,[4] and you 'fulminate and fulminate in querulous language'! All right! In the future when you yourselves complete your training, the police will be abolished, and I the little township head will ask you for a little less in the way of 'economics'!" The township head used this "cosmopolitan language" to exhort and harangue them.

These two who had "thought of 'the means of avoidance'" could no longer "think of 'the means of avoidance.'"

At night Old Boor asked me to make two copies of a list of names —one for the ward, one for the County Government Department of Organization and Training.

The list did not have on it Second Uncle Yixing's son or Third Brother Cailong's brother with the "latent illness." It had on it exactly ten names —"in accordance with the order."

Not long ago he, Old Boor, rather unexpectedly asked me whether I needed spending money. Then, using the nimble-fingered technique of the shopkeeper who works as a money-changer, he counted out for me six blue dollars showing "posthumous portraits of the Director"[5] from a bulging wad of legal tender.

Tomorrow he will make an entry in his accounts: "the copyist's salary, paid, twelve dollars."

16. *The Draft*

by BUGAN (*pseud.*),
*a male shopkeeper and civil bureaucrat
writing from Xinning, Hunan*

At last it has stopped raining. In the farming villages, rice seedlings are being hurriedly planted. At this time you can hear men and women on every foot-

---

4. These kinds of miscellaneous "surtaxes" (*juan*) constituted the main form of income that rural heads derived from holding posts in local government. Township heads like this one and all other heads below the ward level received no salary from higher levels of government. They, in turn, prevented heads at higher levels of government from gaining control over the revenue that was collected through these surtaxes. Ibid., pp. 290–92.

5. Each of these one-dollar bills in Guomindang currency had on it a likeness of Sun Yatsen, who had been known by the title "Director" (*zongli*) since 1905. On the awarding of this title, which has been reserved for Sun Yatsen alone among Guomindang leaders, see Harold Z. Schiffrin, *Sun Yat-sen and the Origins of the Chinese Revolution*, p. 362.

path singing the spring planting song. But under current circumstances, is it really possible for them to be happy? A new kind of fear has gripped the hearts of all able-bodied young men and their parents, wives, and children—a fear that is electric in its intensity.

After four o'clock in the afternoon, I left my job and returned to XX Street, nearly five *li* away.

The street was uncommonly noisy.

I heard Wang Chunsheng, a convicted criminal recently released from prison, haranguing a crowd, "How many of those in their thirties[1] are left in the streets!" I wanted to ignore him. But the question that came to mind was inescapable, "Could it be that men are being drafted into the army?"[2]

I returned to my shop as usual, and, exhausted, I plopped down in my rattan chair and took off my trousers.

In fact, I had guessed right. Before I had a chance to catch my breath, the woman from across the street came to question me.

"Are the higher-ups drafting soldiers?"

"Maybe not. But I don't know. What's happening in the streets?"

"Every man in his twenties and thirties has been weighed and has been measured with a rope."

Oh, this must be the so-called physical examination. But they had absolutely no idea what a physical examination was. That's why she put it in such a funny way. She went on to say:

"They want the weight to be 82 *jin* and the height to be 4 feet 8 inches."

No wonder Wang Chunsheng was in the streets screaming at the top of his lungs. Maybe they've already been drafted in the lottery? Where are they? Maybe Wang was one of them?

Later I learned that the lottery hadn't yet been held. After Township Head A weighed each man, he pointed to three in the group: Wang Chunsheng, a weaver, and a fellow named Luo, who had just come to town to work in a shop on the lower street.

"Oh, that must be Songming. Really bad luck! Didn't he close his shop and hide out for a whole year in order to avoid conscription last year? Just back, and he runs into this."

1. "Able-bodied men" (*zhuangding*), as defined by the Guomindang government for purposes of its military draft in the 1930s, included all males between the ages of seventeen and forty-four. See Kong Chong, *Xian zheng jianshe*, p. 92.

2. The higher authorities are not identified in this piece, but being from Hunan province, the men drafted probably entered the army of either a local warlord or Chiang Kai-shek's Guomindang government which promulgated a conscription law in 1933 and began enforcing it in March 1936. See Chien, "Wartime Government in China," p. 454.

"Of the three of them, Wang Chunsheng does not have a wife so only one person will suffer, and the weaver is in the same situation. Both of them can go, only—"

"Oh yes! Only Songming is married. On top of that, he's the only person who can run his shop."

"After Songming had been weighed, his head was bowed, his spirit seemed broken, and his face was dark, making him unrecognizable. He's so gentle. How can he possibly be a soldier! For it to be that way is really pitiful. Heavens! Besides, substitution is not allowed."

"In fact, Wang Chunsheng is even more unlucky."

"Oh yes, isn't he the one who was in the streets screaming at the top of his lungs? 'Everyone else who's released from prison eats chicken, pigs' feet, tripe. They eat big meals and small meals to recuperate from prison life. I can't even get enough rice. On top of it all, I have such bad luck. Now conscription has rolled around to me. At home I've got a crippled mother who's sixty-some, and a teenaged sister. What are they going to do? How many people in their twenties are left in the streets!' He certainly is a pitiful fellow. He's been in prison for such a long time, and still his unlucky star continues to haunt him! Those heads higher up are weird, wanting people to go but not caring about their family situations."

"You think that's bad? You haven't seen what it's like in the countryside. In some households out there only one person supports a family, and he may even be reduced to being a porter with a carrying pole on his shoulder. When it comes to conscription, does he have to go? Yesterday didn't Township Head A go to Village X and stir things up, making the chickens fly and the geese quack?"

The longer we continued our conversation the more painful it became. My next-door neighbor, Old Man Bing, heard me come home and rushed over to pose questions. "I ask you, what's the use of having so many soldiers?" he first asked.

I tossed off the reply, "How do I know?"

"Ha! You work for the county office. How can you not know?"

He thought that I was trying to evade his question. In actuality, we who work as copyists mechanically performing tasks have absolutely no time to get involved with any other matters. So there are many things I have no way of knowing about.

Township Head A came again. Accompanied by the township police, he proudly marched in, carrying a pistol.

He came to assemble the reserve forces and conduct a draft lottery. Perhaps there were irregularities in the selection of the three men this morning.

Very soon the able-bodied men in the street were prowling around like disbanded troops. One or two faces were full of fear and sadness. Their fearful hearts, one after another, jumped up and down in their chests.

Wang Chunsheng, the weaver, and Songming were full of great hope as when praying devoutly to gods. Now it was possible to say that luck might be coming their way. They imagined seeing a person on the other side of the group of potential draftees drawing the character *bing* out of a bamboo pipe in front of them which would make him rather than any one of them the draftee. So they were fully relaxed.[3]

Many people were milling around the block headquarters.[4]

The sky was now getting dark, and Township Head A and his pistol had left. The able-bodied men who had participated in the lottery all came out together. At this time their faces all looked as though a curfew had been lifted and a thousand-*jin* burden had been eased. I peered into Songming's face and found a look of serenity. The fear had finally passed.

However, Wang Chunsheng had again drawn the character *bing*, and said, "I was a prisoner and now I'm a soldier."

The sky was already dark.

Listen to this: Tomorrow Township Head A will be going to XX Village to conduct the draft.

17. *The First Day of Training for Able-bodied Men*[1] *in a City Ward*

by WANG WUCHAO,
a man writing from Wuxi, Jiangsu

The big parade grounds were steamed and smoked by cross-currents combining the smells of engine oil from the nearby railroad, coal from the coal storage shed, and gasoline from the auto garage. In the midst of this stench, about three hundred able-bodied men were scattered around.

3. One method of conducting the draft lottery was to fill a wide bamboo pipe (similar to the tally containers in temples) with paper slips. On some were written the character *bing* (soldier); the remainder were blank. If a young man drew a *bing*, he was drafted.

4. A block headquarters (*jie gongsuo*) was responsible for security within one block of a neighborhood.

1. "Able-bodied men" included those between the ages of seventeen and forty-four. See "The Draft," n. 1.

Swirling morning winds pulled down the coal smoke which had been hanging not very high in the gray air, and sent it up each person's nostrils.

Within this diverse group of the able-bodied were people from different occupations: workers, peasants, coolies, ricksha men, barbers, shopkeepers, owners of small shops, students. At first, everybody looked around for acquaintances or those with similar clothes, and they divided themselves up into four or five small groups, talking in low voices with faces downcast. Gradually, the thoughts hidden in each person's heart merged together into one, and the three hundred people, squatting down or standing up, formed one large group.

"People were sleeping soundly but have to come here to smell foul odors—training, training, training, my balls! Soldiers who've been well fed aren't even ordered to the battlefront to risk their lives. What's the use of training good old me. Want good old me to go to the battlefront instead?" Ah Xing, squatting down and pulling out small blades of grass, suddenly became frustrated.

"Isn't that so? Because of this training, we who rely on the strength of our bodies to get rice to eat can't even get five hours' sleep a night and can't be sure our shoulders will be strong enough to lift heavy things during the day. These mothers!" The coolie Little Earth, tugging once at the green sash around his waist and pulling it tight, echoed Ah Xing.

"The boss wants me out of the business. He asked me to buy my own rice to eat while coming to drills." Brother Little Lin, an apprentice in a machine shop, used his fingers to rub eyes that had gone sleepless from working the night shift. Tears rolled out, mixing with dust that had fallen from his eyebrows and forming, as they trickled down, dark circles around his eye sockets. Sticking out his thick lips, he thought of the bitter hunger that would result from being fired from his job.

"Did your boss say the same thing?"

Chunsheng stretched out his long neck, which had been dyed a shiny black by black grit, and fixed his yellow eyes on Brother Little Lin's face.

"Don't all the bosses have black hearts? Do they care whether other people live or die?"

Little Lin yanked up a blade of grass by the roots.

"Don't we have bad luck too? We have to leave our rickshas empty and give up doing business for two or three hours. But the rent we pay on the rickshas can't be one penny short. What's more, our bodies are tired to death. Ai! These days it's really hard to get by!"

Little Number Five Son of Xu, bare feet covered with scabs, squatted down. His old cotton jacket with old cotton wadding sticking out every which way looked like a rotting dog floating down the river.

"Day after day I can't go home until it's too dark to see my way. Lying in bed with aches and pains throughout my whole body, I'm reaching the breaking point. The killer watch-group head comes to knock on the door before there's light in the sky. He doesn't even let me go take a look at the seedlings in the fields and is always in a hurry for me to come, as though I owe a debt to the emperor. He's easy on those who are friendly with him and lets them off. I could get along without connections, if only my wallet were thick and full and I was willing to take out the things he wanted. Once good old me is trained with a gun, this kind of jerk will be sent to death along with the XX [Communist] Reds!" Big Number Three gritted his teeth, formed his rough, strong fingers into a big fist, exclaimed "Hah," and pounded the ground.

"Big Number Three, be quiet—the robber watch-group head just passed by." The white eyebrowed Ah Ding tugged at the corner of Big Number Three's shirt.

"What's to be afraid of? Sooner or later—"

"Hey! How come Brother Xiangsheng is here?"

Three or four people noticed a person coming from the west, wearing a gray cloth uniform and a thick purple wool army cap.

"Brother Xiangsheng, you've come to drill too? Isn't there some silly kind of training at your school?" Big Number Three broke into the kindly smile of a peasant and went up to greet him.

"I don't understand even now!"

"This is good. Once we learn to fire guns well and go to kill the enemy with you as the military adviser, we'll no sooner raise the flag standard than we'll win a victory, and we'll no sooner take the horses there than we'll have success.[2] Ha ha ha!" He seemed to have forgotten the watch-group head over whom he had just been gritting his teeth and to have forgotten the seedlings in the fields. He just closed his eyes and drooled.

"Of course, in order to go kill the enemy for the country, we should come and learn to drill. But I think that this training for able-bodied men is the same as the military training at our school, which is nothing more than a show put on to fool people. Altogether it's only four weeks long, but it has to begin with such useless movements as 'attention' and 'at ease,' and people become tired to death and in the end don't even learn how to shoot a gun. All those in our Volunteer Army in the three prov-

2. This was a popular saying and does not indicate whether or not these recruits expected to use horses in the military.

inces of the Northeast[3] are workers and peasants who have never learned 'attention' and 'at ease,' but they kill the enemy as if the gods were with them. Why is this so? They've learned guerrilla warfare well. Hiding in the mountains and woods, one person shoots down ten XX [Japanese] people."

"Right! We must learn the Volunteer Army's tactics so our sweat won't go to waste!"

"When the old army officer from Hunan comes, let's go beg him and ask him to each guer—whatchamacallit military tactics. We don't have to learn 'attention' and 'at ease.' If he turns us down, we'll all leave together—not a single one of us will stick around!"

"Good, good! Agreed, agreed! Let's have Brother Xiang go and speak up, and Big Number Three and Little Lin go too. If he turns us down, we won't stick around."

A large group of people all were facing east. Brother Xiangsheng was arguing with a monkey-faced army officer. In the end, the army officer waved his white gloves in the air every chance he got, and the morning breeze intermittently carried the sound of his Hunan accent: "It's no good. How can it be done? Those who don't stick around will be rounded up and locked up at the county government."

"That mother. What's no good? Wants to lock us up. Let him lock all of us up. Everybody stick together."

In the crowd, Ah Xing jumped up, rolled his sleeves up past the elbow, and spit a big mouthful on the ground.

"Good! Everybody stick together. Make them teach about the real work of killing the enemy!"

Several hundred people's faces were animated and excited.

"Brother Xiang, what was that old devil talking about? What did he mean by 'It's no good, it's no good.'"

"He said it's necessary to learn 'attention' and 'at ease,' and these are called the motionless positions and are the most, most important subject. In the future, when the county head comes to conduct the inspection, the difference between good and bad depends on this one point, and whether the army is good or bad also depends on this point. Once an 'attention' is called out, even if the mountain collapses, no one can move. How could any of you not learn it well!"

3. The Volunteer Army was participating in the Chinese resistance against the Japanese in the Northeast at this time. See "A Letter from the Northeast," n. 8.

"No wonder—no wonder, no wonder. Our country's army is forever motionless. It is probably concentrating on learning 'attention' and 'at ease'!"

18. *A Night When Troops Arrived*

by GELI (*pseud.*),
a male teacher writing from Qianshan, Anhui

The sun had already hidden behind Mount Wan, and the city was draped in a crimson silk veil. The evening breeze danced elegantly, teasing the green branches.

The noisy sound of rumbling on slabs of stone covering the streets, the bright lights, and the moving shadows portrayed the busyness of this small town's night market.

In the middle of the street, children shouted and jumped around. They were all in formation, imitating the movements of an army. The one at the head shouted, "One, two, three—four!" There followed a loud roar, "One, two, three—four!"

There were no street lights, but occasionally an intense light from a gas lantern streamed out from a family gate and shone onto the wall opposite it, making visible on the wall some posters recently pasted up made of red and green colorful paper, some long and some short, at odd angles:

"Welcome to the 83rd Division, which will exterminate the bandits and save the people!"

"Welcome to Regiment Head X, who will supervise the extermination affairs!"

"The 83rd Division is the savior of the people of Qianshan!"

Now and then four or five newly arrived, tired-looking soldiers in dirty uniforms passed by, and, one after another, sad black shadows were cast across the posters only to vanish immediately without a trace.

Village Detective Fang Haiyan was running up and down the street. Servants in groups of three or four were moving beds, desks, chairs, and similar furniture. A regiment from the 83rd Division was to get into town tonight!

Three people were standing in front of the gate of the Mass Education Hall: Zhijian, Hanyun, and I. The three were of similar age, all about twenty years old, and all had the same yellow thin faces and unkempt hair. Cigarettes hung from their lips and flickered on and off.

Suddenly Hanyun broke the silence and said sarcastically, "Tonight the town will be able to sleep soundly without a care in the world!"

Zhijian and I responded together, "Even if you are afraid, won't it be the same anyway?" I alone went on to say, "In fact, even if we're afraid, so what? If the bandits really come, we might as well stick out our necks and let them kill us. In this world, 'death' is in the order of things, and 'living' is something we have no part in!"

"I'm resigned to this too, but I always have fear in my heart. I really can't help it. But I believe I'm not the only person like this!" said Hanyun, tossing a cigarette butt into the middle of the street and setting off a few dim sparks on the stone slabs in the darkness.

"That's also true," Zhijian said in a very deep voice. We've had trouble in ordinary times. But hasn't it become impossible to overcome now because it's all tangled up with related things? People like us will ultimately end up fading away like shadows. Ai!"

For a moment the three of us sank into silence.

Hanyun, a person who gets impatient if he goes for a minute without speaking, surveyed the sad scene in front of us and spoke again: "I don't know what kind of discipline the 83rd Division has. I've heard they're X XX's troops and very capable of fighting."

"Who cares about this nonsense? By now people in this small county have become used to it. Since last year, the XXX Route Army and the XX Army have taken turns chasing and exterminating. One time a press-gang of eighty soldiers carried arms into the mountains and only forty or fifty returned. As for the bandits, the more they are exterminated, the more there are. Only the 10th Division that came here last time was an exception. It had discipline. At any rate, in recent years people here have become totally numb!" As I reached this point, Hanyun broke in, saying jokingly, "People here, after all, have seen a little bit of the world! For example, last winter there were even two commanders-in-chief stationed in this place to supervise the extermination. If it were not the case that there were bandits here, even if they were given an invitation to this small county in the mountainous wilderness, they would not come!"

"Isn't that so?" I said. "If it were last year, the situation would be different. The coming of a regiment would have created confusion in the streets—especially by the time the bandits had gotten to the Wang Family Arch. If these were ordinary days, all the people in town would have run away long ago. In the beginning when there were bandits in Yaqian (about 100 li from the county), people in the county seat ran away. Later, when the bandits got within 30 or 40 *li*, the people then ran away. And these days there was a time when the bandits got to the edge of town and people were still sleeping and dreaming away. Nowadays people here are completely numb!"

"In fact, there is no alternative. I think that sooner or later Qianshan is in for an extremely bloody drama. We'd better not live in town—" Hanyun was worrying about the future again.

Zhijian suddenly said, "I heard about a strange thing. People in the streets are spreading the rumor that this year there is not one swallow in the town."

I was very surprised. "Not one swallow!"

For a long while there was not a sound, and then the clock inside the gate of the Mass Education Hall struck ten.

Suddenly the sounds of out-of-step footsteps and canteens banging against bayonets resounded on the street across the way. We all shifted our gaze to the front and said in unison:

"The troops have arrived!"

19. "A Rural Purge"[1]

by DENG YAN,
a male soldier writing from Qiongdong, Guangdong (on Hainan Island)

Qiongdong County in Qiong Prefecture is a place that has many Communist bandits. Around the sixteenth and seventeenth year of the Republic [1927–28], the whole place was almost completely reddened, and later, despite several serious [Guomindang] Army extermination campaigns, the Communists haven't been completely wiped out. Even today, bands of three to five men still commit crimes of murder and arson.

As early as March of this year, my unit had already begun a rural purge, and during the past couple months of the rural purge, we have caught several dozen Communist bandits and shot them. But there have

1. The title of this piece (*Qingxiang*) was the name given to the standard procedure used by the Guomindang in its effort at this time to exterminate Chinese Communists in rural China—a procedure which, in the words of Philip Kuhn, "colored the Kuomintang's [Guomindang's] whole approach toward rural administration during the early 1930s." See Kuhn, "Local Self-Government under the Republic," pp. 286–87.

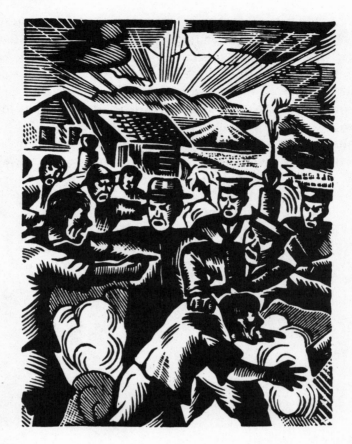

"An Ordinary Tale" (one in a series), a woodcut by Xinbo (pseud.), from *Lu Xun shoucang Zhongguo xiandai muke xuanji, 1931–36* [A Selection from Lu Xun's Collection of Modern Chinese Woodcuts, 1931–36] (Beijing, 1963), p. 34.

been no gold nuggets worth sifting out and recording since the rural purges began. The most eventful, the happiest, and the most exciting day of all is none other than today—May twenty-first.

Yesterday we arrested a township head, a man as hypocritical as a shopkeeper who mounts a lamb's head on his shop but actually sells dog meat. This township head was in fact an important Communist bandit, but he had been very secretive about his activities, so no one had yet found him out. Not only did the people elect him as township head, but until two months ago he concurrently served as platoon head of the reserve forces. A few months ago a certain family in his rural township received two blackmail threats signed by the Executive Committee of the Qiongdong County Branch of the Chinese Communist Party. Meanwhile, someone realized that the handwriting in the threats was his. In addition, another villager found a Communist work report book, and the handwriting in it was recognized as his. So someone secretly came forward and reported him, and he was arrested.

By the end of two sessions of the trial, he had refused from beginning to end to admit that he had participated in the work of the Communist bandits or that he had written the blackmail letters. But when he was asked to write down several dozen characters at random, they were in the same handwriting as the blackmail threats and the report books.

At dawn this morning, he told the soldiers guarding him that he wanted to take a crap. As soon as he returned, he said that he had to go again. This went on for five visits, and the guards thought he must have diarrhea, so they didn't suspect him. But on his last visit he untied himself while he was in the latrine and began to run away. Fortunately, the guards were alert, and they opened fire and gave chase. As soon as the officers and soldiers in the battalion headquarters heard shots being fired in the vicinity of the latrine, they knew that the prisoner had escaped, and they rushed out to join the search. After chasing him for more than a *li*, they captured him and beat him until blood streamed out of open wounds all over his body. At that time, it happened to be a "market period," a really bustling time.[2] When people in the market heard the shots, they thought something had happened, and some took off and some went running, misled by this false alarm.

After he was caught and brought back, the soldier who was the guard said, "He took so many craps that very early on I became suspicious. But when I listened at the latrine door, I heard many poop-poops that certainly sounded like diarrhea. So I didn't think that he intended to escape." Another soldier off to the side said, "You made a mistake with the poop-poops. I, too, can pretend that I've got diarrhea." Then the soldier put his hands to his lips and made a few poop-poop noises that sounded like a diarrhea attack. All the soldiers laughed at that.

At noon the battalion head brought back four Communist bandits guilty of murder and arson. The soldier who was the guard, having learned a lesson in the morning, asked his platoon head for several pair of leg-irons with which to lock them up one by one. A little later on, many villagers came, including the township head, the tax-and-labor head,[3] and also the common people. They came to give testimony or to

---

2. As in many traditional agrarian societies, markets in rural China were periodic rather than continuous. In China, rural markets normally convened every few days but a wide variety of short-term schedules were followed. See G. William Skinner, "Marketing and Social Structure in Rural China," pp. 10–31.

3. Tax-and-labor head was a subadministrative post. See "A Sketch of Repairs on a Fortress," n. 1.

press charges against the four Communist bandits who had been brought back by the battalion head.

The purge of the first ward in Qiongdong came to an end today. At four o'clock in the afternoon, the ward head held a banquet honoring the battalion head's success at the rural purge. At that time, I accompanied him and was seated with him. After we reached the point where the wine was sweet and our ears were hot, I realized that there wasn't any entertainment, so I asked five or six soldiers who knew music to sing Cantonese opera. The ward head himself sang several songs from local Qiong Prefecture opera. Partying it up, what fun we had. We went all the way to ten o'clock, and then the banquet broke up.

20. *One Page of a Diary*

by HEITIAN (*pseud.*),
a man writing from Chongqing, Sichuan

The weather had suddenly become hot and made me feel a bit uncomfortable. Paging through a book, I couldn't read at any length. After looking at my correspondence, I felt even more restless. Inside the house I paced around twice in a circle. Looking at the fierce sunshine, I began to shake, so I lay back down in bed and continued my daydreaming.

"Open the door—" Someone was at the door. I began to wake up. Still feeling groggy, I didn't respond, even though I knew someone was at the door. Then the mailman shouted again loudly from outside, "A letter has come. Open the door!" I heard "A letter has come," and that woke me up. I went out to get the letter.

Yi! I was very surprised. The letter was from my good friend Xi. My friend Xi was arrested last year as a suspected Communist, and seven full months have passed since then. He got out of prison yesterday and is going to the countryside right away to rest, so he can't come visit me and instead has written me this letter. The letter is as follows—

Dear Tian:

This letter I am writing to you will without a doubt surprise you. My friend, let me tell you that yesterday at seven o'clock in the morning I was released from prison, without any explanation. I went into prison

"Prisoners," a woodcut by Xu Tiankai, from *Lu Xun shoucang Zhongguo xiandai muke xuanji, 1931–36* [A Selection from Lu Xun's Collection of Modern Chinese Woodcuts, 1931–36] (Beijing, 1963), p. 39.

without knowing what was happening and I came out of prison without knowing what was happening. I don't know whether I should feel sad or happy! After receiving this news, how would you feel?

As I was about to get out of prison, the military tribune, who was strutting around noisily in his leather shoes with an inflated sense of self-importance, told me, "You are all right now. On the outside, you should use your strength for the sake of the country!" I nodded slightly and was about to respond candidly in these words, "I used to be deeply deferential and looked for nothing more than a bowl of rice to eat and still I almost lost my life. How would I dare use whatever strength I have for the sake of the country!" But the jailer conspicuously pounded his rifle butt on the stone floor, which caused my guts to shrink up. It was all I could do to keep hold of my belongings, keep my head bowed, and make it out the door.

My friend, you must realize that if I don't hurry to the countryside for a rest, before long I'll certainly die. My plan is to leave Chongqing tomorrow, and because of various problems I can't come visit you, my old friend, in person. I am devoting tonight to giving you a general report on what happened between the time I went in and the time I came out so that you will become more knowledgeable and see what has become of one corner of the "new Sichuan"! But, my friend, this is not the new Sichuan that appears in the newspapers. It's also not the new Sichuan that people elsewhere have been talking about. If you pay a little attention and penetrate beneath the surface of society, you will realize that what I am telling about is the true face of the 100 percent real "new Sichuan." My friend, consider this:

Last year on the X day of the X month, while I was working in my office, someone outside the door suddenly called out "Mr. X." The attendant came in to say that a Mr. Xie wanted to see me. As I stood up, two men in short jackets (not in military uniforms) came in, speaking with Hubei accents. At that time I sensed that something was wrong, but my conscience was perfectly clear. I kept my poise and was not afraid. So I simply walked up to them, pointed my finger at my nose, and made it clear that I was X XX. Who would have expected that as soon as the words were out of my mouth, they would draw their pistols and pull out a printed form. I said, "I haven't seen clearly what's written on the form." Speaking with Hubei accents, they said, "Let's go!—" Hey! Wasn't that strange! One pointed a pistol at me while the other used rope to tie my hands, crossed like a pair of scissors, behind my back. Without allowing me to utter a word, they gave me a shove and took me away!

My suspicions were confirmed! Three other men, dressed in the same way, were waiting outside the door. Each held a pistol, and as soon as we came out, they followed behind, making the sound *dide dide*. At that time I still felt unapprehensive, assuming that the present government was enlightened, unlike that under the former Sichuan "local armies." Even if I were implicated in some way, the worst that could happen would be that I would have to explain myself and let them investigate me, and then that would be the end of it. Who would have anticipated the tragedy that followed? My friend, only a stupid fool like me would remain unconcerned even as a big calamity was about to descend upon me. Going on the assumption that only the Sichuan of the past was in the dark ages, I was completely at ease.

After arriving there, I was standing in the middle of a room. Soon a middle-aged man in a yellow uniform came in, sat down at a long desk, and began questioning me about my name, address, and background. Then he asked me what work I did and how many fellow party members there were in this locality. Oh, then I caught on. They had put a red hat on me! But I kept myself under control and in my heart I was still not concerned. I even came back at him, asking why he was taking up this line of questioning. He said that Xie XX had confessed and that I had better speak up. Good heavens! What could I say! If I were a thief, I would have to pick the lock on a door before I would know whether the house was square or round. Before I could explain myself, a fist suddenly came flying at me and landed squarely on the left side of my jaw, sending pain running all the way from my teeth to my toes. After that, a leather boot kicked me in the butt, making it so numb that I couldn't tell whether it itched or hurt! By then, my heart was trembling, and I knew that this was not a good thing.

The fact of the matter was that I had absolutely nothing to say, but he was not the least bit willing to listen to any explanation. Several men lifted me up into the air and left me hanging there, in order to force me to admit that I was a Communist and to make me reveal the names of other party members. My friend, imagine becoming so tired that you thought you were going to die swinging on a swing, but instead I was swinging in the air held by a rope which was hanging from the rafters and was tied to my thumb. This was no fun! While hanging in the air, I sobbed to the point where no more tears would flow. Crying out and screaming were of no avail. I thought I was dead and lost consciousness. That kind of unbearable suffering was indescribable. My friend, I was in no position to be tough! I would rather die than have my whole body hang by one thumb! There was no way out. All I could do was sell myself. I blurted out, "Yes—yes—yes yes—" again and again, hoping that the suffering would stop at least temporarily. Huh! That string of yes's was quite effective. The rope went slack, and I dropped to the ground.

But after gaining an inch, he wanted a foot. Seeing that I had said "yes," he thought that I was giving a true confession. Immediately he ordered Xie XX to be brought out for a confrontation between us. At first, there was fire in my heart, and I was so angry that I wanted to devour Xie XX in one gulp. But then I saw how he looked—his shoulder blades had large and small holes burned in them and both his thumbs were sticking out and were covered with blood—and, in fact, I took some pity on him! When the man in the yellow military uniform questioned him, I could no longer restrain myself and yelled out, "Xie XX! Speak from your conscience." But he still insisted that I was a Communist and that he and I had gone drinking and had had discussions together, clinging to his story as tightly as a man clenches his teeth when he dies. I realized that he really did not want to sell out his conscience and that he acted as he did only because he couldn't stand to be tortured so severely any more. I thought to myself: This is a confrontation. If I again admit to being a Communist, what will happen then? While I was considering what to do, I noticed that a bunch of joss sticks were burning with a red glow and several soldiers were stripping my clothes off. My back was in danger of being treated in the same way that Xie XX's had been. I sensed that the situation was not good. Capital punishment on the basis of unjust accusations was preferable to experiencing this pain that went beyond human endurance! So I quickly said, "I am a Communist. I did go drinking with Xie XX. It's all true!" He was then satisfied and called in a copyist to make an entry in the confession book.

By then I had made it through the first difficult passage.

From then on, we were locked up in Local Court Prison No. 2. During these few months, I led an inhuman life and endured unimaginable suffering. If I wrote everything about this down, not only would my tears soak the stationery but, my friend, it would cause any man to cry out even if his heart were made of iron and stone! All right, these tragic events which are not so important to the facts of the story I will not tell you now.

I don't remember what day we were sent to go on trial at the headquarters of a company attached to X Regiment of the central military police. When we first arrived, we were very happy because this was the central government's military police. This is an organization which imposes order on undisciplined troops. It would certainly exonerate me from the unjust accusations made against me. I had no idea that it would turn out to do the exact opposite! Every squad head, every sergeant, and every common soldier in the military police was qualified to conduct interrogations. They liked to take you out to interrogate you every day, and when they felt like it, they interrogated in the morning and again in the afternoon. The forms of torture that they used were different from the ones at the other place. If you said only, "I'm not a Communist" or you hesitated, then they forced you to sit on a soft stool,[1] carry a flaming caldron on your back, be branded with eight-flower patterns,[2] have your stomach filled with water,[3] and hang in the air, all at the same time.

---

1. In this form of torture, the victim is left hanging from his hands and feet with his buttocks unsupported.

2. In this form of torture, the victim's body is burned in eight different places, branding the victim with eight marks each in the shape of a flower.

3. In this form of torture, the victim's stomach is pumped full of water.

Sometimes, if they were afraid you would cry out, they stuffed a gag of white cloth in your mouth. They didn't care whether you could stand it or not as long as it gave them satisfaction.

My friend, after being interrogated twice over there, I grasped the principle—each time I was interrogated, whether by a company head, a squad head, or a common soldier, from beginning to end I never told the truth, and since they thought I was confessing, I was not subjected to severe punishment even once. This was very fortunate! But I asked my conscience whether I was deceiving others or deceiving myself. I didn't care which because I wanted to die. Three friends there involved in the same case wanted to be vindicated from the unjust accusations against them. Every time they were interrogated, either their thumbs were both pointed upward and covered with blood, or their noses were clogged with clots of blood, or their backs were cracked and crumbling like a clay pot. When I saw these tragic scenes, I almost broke into tears. It was especially bad for Xie XX, who twice had to be carried out to be interrogated, for he could not move on his own. But we were not in the same cell, and there was no way for me to teach them my secret trick, so all I could do was sit by myself and sob.

The inhuman life in Prison No. 2 had already been so bad that I had not been able to bear to think about it. Who would expect that upon reaching this X Regiment of the military police I would enter a truly hellish house, overflowing with people? Eating, sleeping, and shitting were all done in that small room. It was really worse than being a cow or a horse. It was far worse than Prison No. 2. And sometimes I even held in my mind memories of Prison No. 2. My friend, since I admitted to everything, I did not suffer all the cruel forms of physical punishment, but I certainly had my full share of mental anguish, which kills without using a knife. There was no alternative. I had cried until tears would come no more. All I could do was pray for death.

When the military police took a case, it was really "handled with dispatch." If you didn't confess, they might say a lot of things on your behalf and then at the end they simply asked you, "It's true, isn't it?" If you said "yes," then all that he said was recorded by a copyist and that was your confession. My friend, this is a fast method, don't you think? But I believe that if you examined the confession book you would see that not a single confession was consistent.

Whatever he sought, he never obtained proper evidence and a proper confession, so the case was not brought to a conclusion. Something like a month ago we were taken to the military tribunal for a trial. Ah ha! This was the way it should be! After all, this was the military tribunal, and the judge seemed like a human being. When he questioned us, not only did he use no unusual punishment or bogus confessions but he even let us speak our consciences. When he saw the confession book and the serious injuries that had resulted from the torture, he became very angry. He immediately got on the telephone and called Qi XX, and it seemed to me that he wanted to take issue with him. But Qi XX was afraid of being found out, and he avoided him. Time after time, he was always out. Maybe it was our unhappy fate. Once again our case was still not closed.

My friend, do you know of Qi XX? He is the number one criminal and blackheart who persecuted us. He is the scoundrel who started arresting innocent and good people and inflicting cruel punishment on them. But I don't hold any grudge against him now because he has the responsibility to arrest Communists, and if he can't arrest the real Communists, then all he can do is arrest the false Communists. Otherwise, he would not be able to report that he had done his job.

Now I'm out of prison. But I still don't understand why I went to prison and why I'm out of prison! I heard that it's because of the military tribunal, but I'm not sure. My friend, my friend—I can say nothing more than "my friend" over and over. Now in theory I've regained my freedom, but my health has deteriorated badly, and I don't know where my job has gone. What's the use of having regained a hundred freedoms? Reflecting upon the pain and suffering that I endured (which, fortunately, was not as bad as that of the others), the tears that I shed, and the hellish life that I led, I have to cry, whether I want to or not. Oh-oh-oh—

Now I have returned to this world to live as a human being again. If anyone gets me angry again, I will say nothing except to ask him to take this oath: "If I am acting contrary to my conscience, I will put myself at the mercy of the XX [central government's] military police," because the fates that people fear most such as "falling down and cracking your skull" or "being killed by a stray bullet" are not as horrible as that.

My friend! What I have reported to you is really only one ten-thousandth of the story because some parts I can't bear to write, some I don't dare write, some I won't write for fear of depressing you, and some you wouldn't believe. In a word, although I am using my pen at this moment to write my old friend, I still can't be sure that I am the person that I was—I've already lived at least one lifetime.

For this one case, seventy or eighty people were unjustly arrested. I heard that all of them will be eventually released. This is really—

It's almost dawn, and this morning I'll be going on my journey to the countryside, so I must get a little rest. Later, when old friends meet again, all the things I haven't told you which you might be curious about

I'll tell you as stories, so as to avoid the sadness that we would feel now. Won't this be better? I'm putting down my pen and let's shake hands. My friend!

Xi

The night of May twentieth

PART III

"Superstitions" and Popular Religion

"Superstitions" and Popular Religion

"Superstitions" (*mixin*) was used by contributors to characterize Chinese religious beliefs and practices. This choice of words is not surprising, for the term had been used in the advertisement soliciting pieces for *One Day in China*; possible topics, the editors had suggested, might include "absurd happenings on *May twenty-first* concerning various local customs, practices, and superstitions, etc."[1] But whether or not the contributors were echoing the editors in their adoption of the term, not all of them used it in the same sense. Some applied it broadly to condemn not only the beliefs of Chinese popular religion but also the wastefulness of its rituals (nos. 1–8); others applied it more narrowly to condemn popular religious beliefs but were less critical of popular rituals (nos. 9–17); and those who were concerned with Christianity rather than traditional Chinese religion used it to criticize Christian beliefs, which they found disturbing though perhaps not so threatening as the establishment of Christian institutions in China (nos. 18–23).

The contributors whose writings appear in Section A attacked the rituals along with the beliefs of popular religion as superstitions, and characterized these rituals as corrupt and detrimental to the people's welfare. Though as much as 90 percent of the Chinese population resorted to popular religious rites as "occasional practitioners" (if not serious devotees),[2] the pieces in Section A leave the impression that they all were

---

1. *Shen bao* (May 18, 1936). For a translation of this advertisement, see Appendix A below.

2. It is difficult to estimate the number of practitioners of Chinese popular religion. In his study of Buddhism in twentieth-century China, Holmes Welch has noted that serious Buddhist devotees numbered 3,890,000 (less than 1 percent of the population) in the 1930s, but "probably 90 percent of the population occasionally resorted to Buddhist rites and 99 percent were affected by Buddhist contributions to Chinese thought and behavior." If 90 percent were (in Welch's words) "occasional Buddhists," then it seems likely that considerably more than 90 percent of the Chinese population were "occasional" practitioners of

wrong to do so. The chicanery of the priests, the ignorance and foolishness of the devotees, and the commercial exploitation of religious gatherings by peddlers, gamblers, prostitutes, and others were all regarded as symptomatic of superstitions, and were all condemned for draining the people's energy, impairing their health, and separating them from their money. Extravagant feasts, frivolous festivals, costly ceremonies, and gambling binges might have lined the pockets of charlatans and thieves, but from these contributors' perspectives such unproductive activities—inspired by superstitions—were economically wasteful.

Some of the contributors, like advocates of moral reform as early as two thousand years ago in imperial China and even now in contemporary Taiwan,[3] hoped that the government would intervene, abolish the superstitions, and end the waste. But for the state to carry out this kind of reform in rural China was no easy matter, because the hierarchy of popular religion was represented by temples in every rural township and market town. Moreover, in the eyes of the practitioners of popular religion the gods in these temples were the supernatural officials of an otherworldly bureaucracy, which ran parallel to the formal state bureaucracy but reached even farther down, having representatives in smaller territorial units.[4] So, for example, the City God in the City Temple (mentioned in nos. 1, 9, and 12) was popularly viewed as analogous to the county head in the county seat. But at still lower levels, various local deities, including the Earth God (a designation which also may be translated "Locality God") (which is mentioned in number five) were viewed as supernatural officials as well, even though they presided over territorial units smaller than those of the lowest-level officials holding governmental appointments (the county heads or ward heads). Thus, the jurisdiction of these local deities was more comparable to the units presided over by subadministrative heads who did not hold governmental appointments (the township heads and village heads). This highly structured otherworldly bureaucracy and its territorial jurisdictions were purely ritualistic (with no central organization or institutional coordination in China comparable to that, for example, of the Catholic church in the West), but the temples, shrines, and

popular religion (which, as the pieces in this part show, involved deities and rituals associated with not only Buddhism but Daoism and various popular cults as well). See Welch, *The Practice of Chinese Buddhism, 1900–1950*, pp. 357–58, 387–88, and especially p. 393.

3. On early popular religion and its critics, see William Theodore de Bary et al., *Sources of Chinese Tradition*, pp. 113 and 630–59. On anti-superstition reforms in Taiwan, see Stephan Feuchtwang, "City Temples in Taipei under Three Regimes," pp. 287–89.

4. Ibid., pp. 280–81; and Arthur P. Wolf, "Introduction," pp. 6–9.

other popular religious institutions described here nonetheless attracted a loyal following that seems resistant or even impervious to reform.

In light of these differences between the urban-based government and the rural-based religious hierarchy, it is not surprising that the critics of superstitions expressed little hope for lasting reforms. They might have looked to the Guomindang government to lead campaigns against superstitions in years gone by, for its supporters had taken up the cry "Down with Superstitions!" as early as the 1920s, and its leaders had issued decrees against all such practices between 1928 and 1930. One decree, for example, had called for the suppression of unofficial popular cults and temples, another had laid down the "Procedure for the Abolition of the Occupations of Divination, Astrology, Physiognomy and Palmistry, Magic and Geomancy," and a third had required all "vendors of superstition" to stop selling "superstitious merchandise" such as incense and candles. But the contributors to *One Day in China*, like other observers in China during the 1930s, were well aware that these decrees had never been enforced and that unofficial popular temples, "vendors of superstition," and other participants in rituals and related activities all continued to flourish.[5]

Religious practitioners showed their indifference toward or ignorance of the law not only by celebrating particular days but by following an entirely different calendar from that prescribed by the government. Officially, the Chinese government had banned the lunar calendar and replaced it with the Gregorian calendar in 1912, immediately after a revolution toppled the last imperial dynasty and placed a new republican government in power. The change in the calendar had been made, according to Chinese reformers at the time, because it was expected to pave the way for increased national efficiency as it had in Meiji Japan. But whereas the Japanese government, which had adopted the Gregorian calendar in 1873, had largely succeeded in shifting the old festivals to the new Western chronology, the Chinese government had still not achieved this goal by 1936. Even though the Guomindang government regarded Thursday, May 21, 1936, as a working day, on which its offices were open, schools were in session, and all other business was conducted as usual, this official policy did not prevent the Chinese religious practitioners described in several of these pieces from regarding it as the first day of the fourth month of the lunar calendar, nor did it stop them from celebrating it as a festival day. For them it was the beginning of "small fullness," the fifteen-day period in the agricultural growth cycle during

5. C. K. Yang, *Religion in Chinese Society*, pp. 366–67 and 395; and Wolfram Eberhard, *Chinese Festivals*, p. 4.

which kernels of grain form (nos. 1–5, 11, 13, and 15–16). Despite twenty-four years of official policy to the contrary, the lunar calendar still set the rhythm for festivals and thus determined that the day of *One Day in China* was to be a popular religious occasion.[6]

Finding popular religion offensive, the contributors in Section A denounced it, but lacking strong government support they made little headway against it. However much they tried in their roles as teachers and soldiers to inveigh against superstitions, they were no match for the people believing in superstitions. However vehement their criticisms, they acknowledged that superstitions pervaded all levels of rural politics and society and shaped the thoughts and actions of people ranging from county heads and other government officials (nos. 5–6) down to peasants in small villages (nos. 7–8)—including one group of villagers who had once accepted reform-minded leadership and built a new school, but had abandoned all reforms and reverted to superstitious practices as soon as the reformers had died or moved away (no. 8). Such accounts reflect both the contributors' determination to eradicate popular religion and their frustration at being unable to do so.

Unlike these frustrated reformers, the contributors in Section B used the term "superstitions" more narrowly. They applied it not to all popular religious beliefs and rituals but only to what they felt to be false doctrines and dubious beliefs that ignorant and gullible religious devotees accepted uncritically or even blindly. Rather than labeling all popular rituals as superstitions, they described festivals, processions, pilgrimages, and other religious practices sympathetically. They found these rituals at the very least amusing (to the practitioners as well as to themselves), and in some instances they regarded the rituals as expressions of popular attitudes and deep concerns. For example, the practice of bribing a god with opium was taken as a reflection of popular attitudes toward both officials and opium (no. 9); the ritual of putting the God of Epidemics on parade was interpreted as a reflection of popular concern for good health (no. 11); and the ritual of "Burning Busy Incense" was viewed as a reflection of the hopes and fears with which peasants anticipated the next harvest (no. 12).

And yet, though these contributors were sympathetic to—or at least interested in—popular religious rituals, they (with the possible exception of the contributor of no. 14) used superstition as a pejorative term too. Like the contributors in Section A, those in Section B generally identified

6. On the adoption of the Gregorian calendar in China, see Joseph R. Levenson, *Liang Ch'i-ch'ao and the Mind of Modern China*, pp. 113–14; and Derk Bodde, *Festivals in Classical China*, p. 220.

themselves as critics—albeit more sympathetic ones—of the popular religions that they described. This contrast between the opposition to superstitions among the literate contributors on the one hand and the commitment to popular religious beliefs and rituals especially among peasants on the other hand reveals a cultural gap that separates the contributors from the subjects of their pieces and brings to mind a remark made more than two thousand years earlier by Confucius. When ritual is lost among the literate ruling class, Confucius observed, then it may turn up in the countryside.[7]

As opponents of popular religion, the contributors had available to them the option of embracing an alternate foreign religious faith, Christianity. After all, earlier Chinese leaders of movements advocating reform and revolution had often invoked the concepts and symbols of foreign faiths, and during the massive Taiping movement of the mid-nineteenth century and in other instances since then some Chinese reformers and revolutionaries had borrowed symbols and concepts specifically from Christianity.[8] But even though the contributors writing in Section C devoted their pieces to the subject of Christianity, they were unreceptive to it.

In expressing their objections to Christianity, they used the term superstitions (*mixin*) or other, related terms having the same root, "fanatical" (*mi*) and "gone astray" (*mitu*) (in nos. 19 and 21), but otherwise they did not comment on Christian superstitions. In contrast to the pieces on Chinese popular religion, which are primarily concerned with beliefs or rituals, those on Christianity are primarily concerned with organizations and institutions—especially ones designed to penetrate Chinese society and win converts.

The record of the Christian church in China suggests that these contributors had little cause for alarm. It is true that by 1936 the Christian gospel had been preached in all but about 100 of China's 1,949 counties and that several Christian educational institutions had been founded—13 Protestant colleges with an enrollment of 5,800 students, 255 Protestant middle schools with another 44,000 students, and 16,213 Catholic schools (including "prayer schools") with 435,522 students. Moreover, by 1936 the foreign missionaries (6,059 Protestants and 5,411 Catholics) had delegated much of the responsibility for proselytizing to their Chinese counterparts (2,135 ordained Protestant ministers and 6,050 Catholic priests, brothers, and nuns)—a trend illustrated by almost all of the pieces in Section C. But it is also true that in 1936 a mere 536,089 Chinese had con-

7. Confucius's remark is cited by C. K. Yang, *Religion in Chinese Society*, p. 375.
8. On the Taipings' Christianity, see Vincent Y. C. Shih, *The Taiping Ideology*.

verted to Protestant Christianity and 2,934,175 to Catholicism—higher numbers than at any earlier point in Chinese history but still a combined total of less than one percent of China's total population at the time.[9]

Despite the low rate of conversion to Christianity, in almost all of the pieces in Section C, the contributors emphasized the potency of the Christian appeal—the aggressiveness of the church's preachers (nos. 18–20, 23) and school teachers (nos. 21–22), and the strength of its organization (no. 23). Though Chinese Christians were far outnumbered by practitioners of popular religion, the contributors writing about Christianity were disturbed by its capacity both to spread superstitions (as the popular religion had done) and to perpetuate these superstitions through Western-backed institutions.[10]

9. John K. Fairbank, "Introduction," pp. 13 and 18; M. Searle Bates, *Missions in Far Eastern Cultural Relations*, p. 10; F. C. Dietz, "The Roman Catholic Church, 1936."

10. Chinese Christian writers, who are not represented here, felt differently about the role of Christianity in early twentieth-century China. Like several contributors in Sections A and B, they criticized Chinese popular religion and characterized it as superstitious; but unlike some of the contributors in Section C, they did not regard Christian beliefs as superstitious. On Chinese Christians' responses to foreign missionaries and formulations of their own approaches to Christianity in the early twentieth century, see Chan Wing-tsit, *Religious Trends in Modern China*, pp. 183–84; and Philip West, *Yenching University in Sino-Western Relations, 1916–1952*.

A. The Wastefulness of Popular Religion

1. *The Temple Today*

by CHEN JI,
a man writing from Zhenjiang, Jiangsu

It was a gloomy day.

After eating breakfast, I walked northward along South Main Street. Vegetables being borne on carrying poles made the narrow street seem even narrower, and the crowds of pedestrians seemed even greater than yesterday. Within the crowd, people hauled on their backs yellow cloth sacks, one after another, with "Going to the Mountain to Offer Incense" written on them in eye-catching black characters.

They were the reason for the greater numbers: old people hauling sacks or carrying incense, candles, and paper spirit money; young people; small children; men; women—

Yes, today was the first day of the fourth month according to the banned calendar.[1] Oh, it was a day for burning "Incense for the Great Peace."

Some of the people burning incense were praying for blessings. Others, who had appealed to the bodhisattva during serious illnesses and had promised to burn incense once they were well, were carrying out their promises today.

There is no particular place where incense is burned. All local temples are qualified to receive people who burn incense and worship. So, making offerings of incense at one temple is certainly not regarded as "fulfilling all responsibilities." "Incense for the Great Peace" is therefore also called "Incense for Ten Temples," the "Ten" in Ten Temples meaning numerous.

1. The traditional lunar calendar was officially banned by the Chinese government in 1912. See the introduction to Part III.

I finished walking down that long and crowded street, and as I stepped onto broad Zhongshan Road, the sky seemed to become considerably larger.

On the road, many "incense guests" were also passing up and down, some walking and some in rickshas.

I thought to myself:

"I'll go to the Temple of the City God[2] and take a look around."

Turning east and walking, I arrived before long.

In front of the temple: Under the stone bridge, both banks were filled with beggars. Face after face was pale and buried under long hair. Like a swarm of frightened flies around a latrine, they went buzzing off the moment the "incense guests" arrived. There were so many of them, and they were such a nuisance!

When I entered the temple gates, the strong, heavy odor of incense rushed up my nostrils. On either side, standing erectly, were the massive, towering, unreachable bodhisattvas of the South Pole and the North Pole.[3] The few people prostrating themselves at the feet of the bodhisattvas seemed even smaller than they would otherwise.

Walking farther inside and climbing up some stone steps, I reached the main hall of the City God.

Puffs of green smoke came out of a three-legged black vessel and swirled around it; and from time to time a few flames shot up.

Kneeling reverently and huddling together in front of the idol were numerous people wanting to pray for "the end to calamities and the coming of blessings."

They knelt down, knocked their heads on the ground, bowed, and stood up. Then they knelt down again, knocked their heads on the ground—once, twice, patiently worshiping every bodhisattva, large and small, one after another, in the building.

In front of the buddha's niche, red candles burned brightly and incense smoke curled up to fill the room. The faces of both bodhisattvas and people seemed to be obscured in a layer of clouds.

The incense in the burner was not burned up before newly arriving

2. The City God was the most important of the local gods in China's towns and cities, occupying a position in the supernatural hierarchy analogous to that of the county head in the bureaucratic hierarchy. For discussions of his role as protector of the people in the 1930s, see John Shryock, *The Temples of Anking and Their Cults*, pp. 98–115; and Henri Maspero, "The Mythology of Modern China," pp. 282–83. On the City God's place in the supernatural hierarchy, see Arthur P. Wolf, "Gods, Ghosts, and Ancestors," pp. 139–40.

3. These were two of the five lords of heaven, each of whom was a master of one sector of the sky (the other three sectors being east, west, and center). In the hierarchy of popular gods, only the Jade Emperor ranked higher. Maspero, "The Mythology of Modern China," p. 339.

people put another bundle in it. The candles in the candle holders burned only half way down before someone replaced them. Inside the building, the smell of people and the smell of incense became heavier and stronger.

Some old people came dressed specially in brand-new funeral clothes.[4] It is said that if you appear before the god once, then after death when your soul returns to the old place, the bodhisattva will recognize you as a "good person" who has offered incense before and will treat your soul with courtesy.[5]

Some people, after worshiping the god, also burned paper boxes and paper tinsel, saying it was like "making a deposit" and considering it to be money they were depositing in the other world.[6]

Many children in colorful clothes and long skirts had on black cloth headbands, each with a paper flower sticking up from the forehead. One pair of little hands was put in a set of handcuffs made of wood and locked together with an iron chain, giving the appearance of a criminal. Earlier I told about those making promises to the god during an illness. When they came to burn incense and beg forgiveness from the bodhisattva, they acted as though they themselves were the guilty parties. The children, not understanding any of this, were merely live puppets.

I watched these people scurrying around, group after group leaving and group after group coming in.

Feeling that the air was stifling, I became upset and walked out through the temple gate. I realized that countless gray-colored living beings must also have been wriggling around in other temples at this same moment.

On the way home, I encountered still more "incense guests." One of them, carrying a small stool, was huffing and puffing. After each step he took, he sat down on the stool and bowed his head to the heavens.[7]

---

4. [Chen Ji's note:] Clothes made ready for wearing at the time of death.

5. This is a reference to the moment following death when each person's conduct was reviewed by the City God. According to popular religious beliefs in China at the time, whenever anyone died, the City God had that person's soul arrested and brought before him. If the City God treated the soul "with courtesy," that meant he would leave it free; if not he would punish it either lightly (having it beaten with sticks) or severely (condemning it to wear the cangue). See Maspero, "The Mythology of Modern China," p. 372. (On the cangue, see "The Woman's Dilemma," n. 1.)

6. Not only imitation or token paper money but also paper houses, miniature furniture, and other items were sent to the other world for the benefit of gods, ghosts, and ancestors. The practice of depositing spirit money in the Bank of Hell and making other "financial" transactions with those in the other world has a long history in China and is still common in contemporary Taiwan. See Hou Ching-Lang, *Monnaies d'offrande*; and Arthur P. Wolf, "Gods, Ghosts, and Ancestors," pp. 175–76 and 179–82.

7. [Chen Ji's note:] This is called burning-bowing-incense and is done to fulfill a promise made to the god during a serious illness.

After walking some distance, I turned my head by chance and saw that the person who was still burning-bowing-incense[8] and kneeling had not made much headway. I felt a little lost!

2. *Possessed by the Bodhisattva*

by SHILANG (*pseud.*),
a male writing from Suzhou, Jiangsu

In many localities Chinese people still continue the practice of making use of waste materials. For example, today is May twenty-first, but here we still continue to make use of the already banned lunar calendar.[1] In people's minds, the third month on the lunar calendar, which was an intercalary month,[2] has just flown by, and today is the first day of the fourth lunar month. The first day and the mid-month day are certainly special days according to superstitions.

We have a market town here with an auspicious and elegant name, Sweet Dew. Chinese rural townships and market towns always have one or two temples, but our temple here is bigger and more famous than those elsewhere. This is the Temple for the Lie Emperor,[3] which is architecturally grand and has within its jurisdiction people burning incense smoke in eighteen territorial tax assessment units.[4]

Normally on the first day of the month, there is a spectacular Bud-

8. See n. 7 above.

1. The traditional lunar calendar was officially banned by the Chinese government in 1912. See the introduction to Part III.

2. The intercalary month was the solution in the Chinese lunar calendar to the problem that has faced all calendar makers: how to reconcile as much as possible the irreconcilable movements of the sun and the moon. The intercalary month was inserted in the Chinese lunar calendar usually at three-year intervals but sometimes at two-year intervals so that there were a total of seven intercalary months within every nineteen years. See Joseph Needham et al., *Science and Civilisation in China*, vol. 3, pp. 390–408.

3. The Lie Emperor (Liu Bei) assumed the imperial title in A.D. 221 during the Three Kingdoms period. He and others from this period (which Chinese have regarded as an exciting and romantic one in their history) have figured prominently as deities in popular religious cults. See C. K. Yang, *Religion in Chinese Society*, p. 59.

4. This territorial unit (*tu*) originated as early as the Song (960–1279) and Yuan (1271–1368) dynasties, and, though officially abolished during the Qing dynasty (1644–1912), it survived down to the twentieth century in parts of South China (where this piece was written) as a designation for a bounded area of taxable land. This unit varied in size, but in imperial China it generally covered about five hundred acres (three thousand *mu*). See Hsiao, *Rural China*, Appendix I; and Philip A. Kuhn, "Local Taxation and Finance in Republican China," p. 106.

dhist temple fair.[5] Old ladies and other women from every family throughout the entire market town and old farm women from rural areas open their tight fists and spend some hundreds of coins praying for blessings for themselves. At the Buddhist temple fair, every seat sells for fourteen copper coins, and several hundred devout women come. No wonder the temple curate's son sauntering out through the temple gates is as free-spending as a young master from a wealthy household.

Today's Buddhist temple fair made each devout woman feel uneasy because, as at the Buddhist temple fairs on the first day of both the third lunar month and the intercalary month,[6] the body of a young village woman was possessed by the bodhisattva. In each of the past two Buddhist temple fairs, when her body was possessed by the bodhisattva, she spoke on behalf of the bodhisattva, talking like a crazed woman. In response to what she said, the entire temple is now being renovated and will be like new. To be sure, the temple has temple property, but the people managing it feel certain that it is not enough, so several dozen yellow books for entering pledges to the temple have been sent out. Hearing that the bodhisattva has potency, believers have grown in number, and many have written their names in the books. Today the temple's renovations are almost complete. In the near future, the temple will hold an even grander Buddhist temple fair for the purpose of opening the eyes[7] of the new bodhisattva. And shortly after the grand ceremony for opening the eyes, there will be a two-day grand temple fair. The bodhisattva let the coming of these two major events be known through the mouth of the village woman. These events will occur because of chaos in the other world. To restore order, the number of people participating in the Buddhist temple fairs must be greater, and the fairs must be grander. The heart of every devout woman has been frightened into reverence, and it has never occurred to anyone to wonder about the purpose behind the village woman's craziness.[8]

5. "Temple fairs" (*hui* or *miao hui*) were scheduled according to long-term cycles (in this case a monthly cycle), and, as G. William Skinner has pointed out, these were distinct from periodic markets (*shi, ji, xu,* or *chang*), which were scheduled according to short-term cycles. See Skinner, "Marketing and Social Structure in Rural China," pp. 11–12, n. 24; and "A Rural Purge," n. 2.

6. See n. 2 above.

7. "Opening the eyes" (*kai guang*) is a ceremony which invests a new statue of a bodhisattva with potency. In this ceremony, pupils are painted on the image's eyes. See Morohashi, ed., *Dai Kan-Wa jiten,* vol. 11, p. 714.

8. This case was not unique. Writing in the early 1930s, Henri Maspero noted that in Chinese temples processions were often ordered by spirit mediums speaking for the gods. See his "The Mythology of Modern China," pp. 282–289. On Chinese female spirit mediums in contemporary Hong Kong, see Jack M. Potter, "Cantonese Shamanism."

The Chinese people gripe about being poor, but they always are generous when it comes to superstition. Originally the bodhisattva of this temple was a great and loyal official of the Sui dynasty [A.D. 581–618] who died at the hands of a powerful and evil official, and the people's establishment of the temple in his memory is not without meaning.[9] But people have ignorantly worshiped idols, and they have increased the evil power of superstition. So there are people who feed themselves off the bodhisattva, clothe themselves off the bodhisattva, and live their lives entirely dependent on the bodhisattva. For example, many village women who were once visited by the bodhisattva have now become shamans.

3. *The Temple Fair for the God of Good Sight in Zhengzhou*

by SHI PO,
a man writing from Zhengzhou, Henan

On the day of May twenty-first (the first day of the fourth month on the banned calendar),[1] the annual[2] "Temple Fair for the God of Good Sight" held at Orphan's Bridge by the South Gate in Zhengzhou was very lively, despite the news of the emergency in North China.[3]

South of Orphan's Bridge, on both sides of the street, were straw mats one after another, end on end, displaying farm tools, bolts of cloth, jewelry, food, lumber, leather, incense paper, medicines, and books that were falling apart.

This fair was attended mainly by people from farming villages, especially women. The women came for the purpose of burning incense to the Venerable God of Good Sight.

The Temple of the God of Good Sight disappeared long ago. The site of the original temple is now occupied by a women's vocational school. Each year on the day of the fair, all that can be done is to put up a temporary shelter made of straw mats to provide a place of honor for the Vener-

9. Deceased notables were commonly assigned the status of deities in Chinese temples. For other examples, see Arthur P. Wolf, "Gods, Ghosts, and Ancestors," p. 140.

1. The traditional lunar calendar was officially banned by the Chinese government in 1912. See the introduction to Part III.

2. Temple fairs were scheduled according to long-term cycles. See "Possessed by the Bodhisattva," n. 5.

3. The emergency mentioned here is a reference to the movement of Japanese troops, tanks, and other equipment into North China during the last two weeks of May. See Eastman, *The Abortive Revolution*, pp. 250–51.

able God of Good Sight. Several Daoist priests tapped broken ritual instruments. The sounds of the ritual instruments and the old women's chants mingled together.

The women threw into the incense burner[4] incense paper which they had brought with them from the village. The incense burner, made of brick, swallowed up lots of incense paper, incessantly shot out its red tongue, and puffed out blue smoke. The women knelt in the dust and knocked their heads on the ground (many banging their heads so hard that it could be heard). When they stood up and dusted themselves off, the Daoist priest spoke to them with a beguiling smile:

"Venerable devotees! Won't you give a little money? Provide some lamp oil money for the Venerable God of Good Sight!"

These old ladies are generally exceedingly frugal, but once "god" was mentioned they ceased to be tight-fisted. Many of them gave money, and the Daoist priests rolled their eyes and stared coldly at those who did not.

At the entrance to the straw-mat shelter was a large earthenware basin filled with sacred water. All the women rushed over and dipped out water to wash their eyes. The water in the basin had some kind of drug in it which had been added by the Daoist priests. Washing with this water did in fact give a feeling of coolness. Ignorant men and women were fooled by the Daoist priests into believing that the water had been provided by the Venerable God of Good Sight and that all those with eye diseases who washed in this water would find their severe disorders becoming small disorders and their small disorders disappearing altogether.

With water in this basin being used from morning to night, who can say how many people's eyes were washed in it? The water turned from white to black, but people still crowded around to wash their eyes. Those who didn't have a chance to wash felt as frustrated as if each had a bellyful of stifled air, and they said with firm resolve, "That was really bad luck! I'll be sure to come early to next year's fair."

As the sun set, women dragged their tired bodies down the road home, and Daoist priests pocketed their copper coins and went into the city smiling to themselves.

Those who didn't get a chance to wash in the sacred water of the Venerable God of Good Sight might be better off in the end; those who did wash might find after they reach home that they have caught an eye disease! Just think, it went from white to black and countless people washed in it. How unhygienic!

4. The incense burner has commonly served as a ritual object for religious organizations and other communal associations in traditional Chinese society. See Feuchtwang, "City Temples in Taipei," pp. 277–78.

4. *Scenes beyond the Border*

by REN XI,
a male teacher writing from Xuanhua, Chahar

The weather was overcast, and a strong north wind was blowing. I walked into the courtyard and felt unbearably cold, so I immediately went back into the house, put on a cotton jacket, and then felt a bit warmer. This was a summer morning beyond the border.

How strange! On the slopes over on the mountain,[1] groups of people one after another were going up toward the temple on top of the mountain. Now and then I could hear cocks crowing and goats bleating. Which school has come on a trip here?[2] They have arrived early and in such good spirits—I thought to myself. When I ran over to ask what was going on, I learned it was not a trip. It was the day of the Temple-Cleaning Festival,[3] at which time Auntie Buddha bestows mercy, and people from every surrounding village all come, particularly young women. Also each person has to offer a cock or goat or dog or something of that kind.

After lunch, with the school's permission, I went to the mountaintop to take a closer look. As soon as I went through the second door, I heard shouts flying out, "Skip No. 1, let go of No. 2, take No. 3."

"Why are these kinds of sounds coming from a temple?" I asked myself, feeling it was odd.

I then went in. There were really a lot of people inside, like a mountain of people, who had formed a perfectly round circle playing "Press Bets on the Precious Number."[4]

In the other half of the room, to the left of the circle of people, there were offering tables on which were placed various kinds of snacks offered up to a big earthen figure, the so-called "Holy Mother of Sons and Grandsons." Several young women dressed in colorful clothes, with three-inch bound golden lotuses [bound feet], powdered faces, and heads covered

1. [Ren Xi's note:] Outside the north gate of Xuanhua is a mountain called Mount Heng on which there is a temple called Mount Heng Temple, commonly known as North Mountain Temple. It is a scenic part of Xuanhua.

2. [Ren Xi's note:] The schools in Xuanhua always take trips to North Mountain in the spring and in the autumn.

3. [Ren Xi's note:] The Temple-Cleaning Festival is on the first day of the fourth month of the lunar calendar. On this day, all those women who have not given birth to children go to the temple and before the Holy Mother of Sons and Grandsons (Auntie) make vows and offer cocks or other things to the monks of the temple. Later, marks are made on the little earthen person in the temple to complete the taking of vows.

4. "Press Bets on the Precious Number" (*ya bao*) was a Chinese gambling game in which the players placed their bets on a number between one and four to indicate their guess as to how many of a certain number of items (such as beans) would be left over after a large pile of the items was divided into fours.

with flowers, were kneeling down prostrating themselves there, and saying prayers. In the middle, an old monk was standing still, like a wooden chicken, staring at them. "Skip No. 1, let go of No. 2, take No. 3—" Again another wave of shouts came over. Ha, ha! I laughed as I walked down.

At midnight I still can't sleep, and what I'm still thinking is this: In the twentieth century, there are still scenes beyond the border like this!

5. *One Day in Dazhu*

by YINGSAN (*pseud.*),
a male elementary school teacher writing from Dazhu, Sichuan

Last night in the teahouse I argued against several neighborhood friends who advocated the ridiculous idea that "weaponism" and "fatalism" would lead to the loss of our country, until they finally accepted my opinions. We talked on in high spirits until very late. Today when I got up, it was already no longer early. I hastily ate breakfast, grabbed two copies of *Teaching Methods*, and ran to school.

At the school gate, the little Earth God shrine,[1] which I had never noticed before, suddenly caught my eye. The insides of the incense burner and the dirt in front of the shrine were filled with incense and candles. People were still adding new incense and candles and devoutly worshiping there. This made me realize—today is the first day of the fourth month on the old calendar. At the same time, without thinking, I remembered two lines of an old saying used by old Buddhist ladies: "For a bundle of incense on the first day and the fifteenth day/Family members great and small will be safe and healthy." These two lines must be more deeply imprinted in the minds of the common laboring masses than in my own. During this depressing year, no one in any vocation has a way out. The life of the masses day by day has not become more "safe," let alone more "healthy." Besides resisting and struggling, what else can they do other than pray to the bodhisattva for this month's safety and health at the be-

1. The Earth God or Locality God (*tudi gong*) has been characterized by Arthur Wolf as the "prototype of the many gods in the Chinese pantheon . . . a tutelary deity, the governor of a place." He points out that Chinese have identified it with a specific locality—a village in the countryside or a neighborhood in a town or city—and have expected it to serve that locality. According to popular beliefs, it holds a place in the supernatural bureaucracy immediately below the City God. See Arthur P. Wolf, "Gods, Ghosts, and Ancestors," pp. 134–39.

ginning and the midpoint of each month? Speaking of this Earth God shrine, I remember that it was originally a tiled building. When I once left my home village four years ago, it had collapsed. Now, although considerably shrunken in size and built of stone, it is still solemn and at least prevents the Earth God from being rained on. This is fortunate for the bodhisattva and shows the sincerity of the masses' support for him.

I went to the classroom to teach a class in science, and because what I had seen and thought were still in my mind, I branched off without thinking into this question of gods. These young girls had more or less inherited from their mothers and their society some belief in gods, so I attacked their beliefs using a logical method. I first asked them, "What are the characteristics of wood, stone, and earth? Do they have senses?" They all gave the correct answer from the *Textbook for Science*. Then I again asked, "What is a bodhisattva made of?"

"The craftsman who makes statues uses wood, stone, and earth and forms it in the image of a person," they again replied in unison.

I then concluded, "If so, why believe in that thing that has no senses?" Most of the children who had always believed in me were accepting.

"But sir! The bodhisattva has incense smoke which gives it spiritual potency," a stubborn child's voice objected.

I therefore lectured her on the principle of how incense smoke could only blacken the wood and stone. Finally everyone ceased to hold any other opinion. I took the opportunity to launch an all-out attack, telling them point by point how gods originated, how they developed, how they have been used by rulers, and how they hinder evolution. Finally, I urged that they must completely wipe gods out of their heads and, raising both hands up to my forehead, I gestured as though tearing the gods out. They all gleefully made the same gesture. The class ended with all arms gyrating.

One class of arithmetic, and this day's work was over.

On the way home, I passed the imposing main gates of the county government office, which the former county head finished renovating only half a month ago, on which wooden scaffolding was being put up and from which things were being removed. Yesterday someone said, "The new county head has a superstitious belief in geomancy,"[2] and it

2. Geomancy is generally defined as the divination of earthly signs. In some cultures the geomancer divines random lines or dots, but Chinese geomancers sought to place man-made structures in harmony with the physical landscape in the belief that such placement would contribute to prosperity, good health, long life, and successful posterity. The term for geomancy in Chinese, *feng shui*, literally means "wind and water"; on its broader meaning, see Maurice Freedman, *Chinese Lineage and Society*, chap. 5.

was being confirmed. I looked with disgust at the new proclamation in vermilion posted on the wall and felt utterly disappointed and angry.

Whenever a new county head assumes the post, I always have some expectations. Naturally, since "you can't get ivory out of a dog's mouth," I don't expect him to relieve our suffering or do anything that will benefit us. I only want to see what kind of new tricks he has.

Since the news that the former county head had been accused before the provincial government of embezzling funds intended for public roads and dismissed, I saw in the newspaper that his successor would be this X County head, who had a reputation as an "uncorrupt official." Ordinary people were all looking forward to his arrival with eager expectation, and my curiosity was also aroused.

After being expected for almost half a month, this worthy county head finally arrived in the county seat two days ago, riding in a "smooth-ride chair" (a kind of simple sedan chair).

As might be expected of "one whose eminence is not falsely reputed," he made an extraordinary impression on people with his simple, and drab clothes—a wrinkled Sun Yatsen jacket made of green cloth, an old yellow straw hat, and a pair of rather scuffed leather shoes. In addition, his straightforward personality was in keeping with the ideals of us young people. Less than thirty minutes after arriving at the county government office, he posted that eye-catching proclamation in vermilion. Within less than an hour, he called a ricksha rather than a more extravagant form of transportation in keeping with his style of dress and went out into the streets greeting guests. After seeing all this, I knew that his tricks were more highly refined and more terrifying than others'. So I have paid more attention to him.

Yesterday a friend told me that this county head has no less enthusiasm for geomancy than for posting a proclamation in vermilion and greeting guests. After greeting guests, he took a compass, looked around the county government office and the tax bureau of which he is the acting head, and also wrote on the walls marks such as "X mountain, X direction." Finally he made the judgment that the front gate of the county government office was too high and the main hall was too low, and that was the reason why all the county heads' official fortunes had not been good—the arrangement was such that "the slave towered over the master"! He also said that if the former county head had not been so lucky, he would have lost his life here. Therefore, his first step after getting out of the sedan chair was to decide on this "new policy"—renovation of the county government office. The height of the main hall was to be raised, and the front gate was to be lowered. It was also said that the second step would be to change the route to North Gate (a city gate).

Although people have said this is all true, I still didn't believe that his tricks would be so clumsy and poor. But today he really was carrying them out, and except for respecting his spirit of "handle with dispatch," I have had only disappointments.

I was cursing in my heart as I walked home.

In the afternoon I saw in the street a mobile advertisement for the only place of entertainment here—the Sichuan-Shaanxi Theater—which was written in gold characters: "Xiao Cuifang, a famous actor who plays female roles, has come by invitation from Shaanxi to be on stage tonight to perform *The Parting of Father and Daughter.*" The actor was new and even the play's title was unfamiliar, leading even me to become curious, and I don't often see plays. I decided to spend a few copper coins and have a look. Soon after the drama began, I realized that the so-called *Parting of Father and Daughter* was the scene in which Wang Baochuan departs from the prime minister's residence and that the so-called "famous actor who plays female roles" was only an actor who customarily plays military figures converted into an actor playing the opposite sex. We could only grumble about being cheated, but the theater had a full house—a phenomenon which had not occurred during the past several days since the "poison needle" incident.

Speaking of the poison needle incident, it has left everyone mystified. I don't know who intentionally or unintentionally created the commotion by telling this tale: A certain country's people have bribed some Chinese traitors into using poison needles to give injections to people without their feeling them, and the poison in the needle is very lethal, "blocking the throat the moment the poison touches the blood." After this commotion mysteriously occurred in southern Sichuan, all the newspapers gave unverified reports about it, leaving everyone mystified. Then each of the county governments arrested some suspects, all of whom were mystified. Then, unable to tolerate being tortured, the suspects gave confessions that left everyone mystified. Spreading day by day, the commotion reached Dazhu, and, a few days ago, several hypersensitive people said that they had been injected. Then the security authorities stationed police in the streets as though something were really happening, to prevent pedestrians from touching each other. Since then, confusion has reigned throughout the whole city, and everyone feels in danger. This is really bad luck for the theater proprietor. Ordinary people regard places where people gather as dangerous, and only the brave ones dare go see a play.

Now, although the commotion has calmed down quite a bit, while watching a play ordinary people still keep a close eye on people around them. While seeing a play they tremble with fear and then silently return home to go to sleep.

6. *A Record of Digging Up Graves*

by ZHIHEN (*pseud.*),
a male soldier writing from Rugao, Jiangsu

The plan to dig up abandoned graves and make a sports field, which has been widely discussed for a long time, finally was carried out today by soldiers from XX Regiment of the XX Corps and civil officials who are in military training.

At the stroke of ten o'clock, the bell tower sent out pounding sounds. Dressed in gray and grass-green, column after column of soldiers with iron shovels over their shoulders sang "The Song of the Big Road" as they marched through the crowd around the city gate and surged forward grandly toward the old abandoned graves.

The road was filled with men and women, old and young, walking along. Pullers of small carts stood on either side of the road holding up fingers and crying out as though selling something: "Hey! Two copper coins a person to go to the old graves—" Some old gentlemen and ladies, unable to walk, piled into the carts together, and the creaking wheels rolled slowly into the crowd. Old ladies who had taken vows held Buddhist rosary beads in their hands, recited "Amituofo" while taking three steps in place for each step forward, made unpleasant-looking faces, and had hopes that all the orphaned souls in the graves for whom no sacrifices had yet been made would ascend to the Western Paradise.[1]

"The bastard—won't have long to live—even bones and necks of the dead have to suffer from his evildoing. In the future there'll be a reckoning—" cursed Little Number Three Liu, a hay carrier, sitting at the counter of the Yongsheng Wine Shop and holding a pot of Baishaoguogongmi Wine.[2]

---

1. The Western Paradise, also called Pure Land, was the Buddha realm presided over by the Buddha of Endless Light, Amituofo (the Amitabha Buddha in Sanskrit). The realm was free of pain or sin and full of beauty and joy, and all who were reborn there would become free of the cycle of birth and death and could stay there indefinitely and attain their nirvana. Chinese Buddhists believed that they would be reborn in the Western Paradise if they repeated the name of Amituofo wholeheartedly. See Welch, *The Practice of Chinese Buddhism*, pp. 89–90.

2. [Zhihen's note:] The name of the wine.

"Ai! The human heart is not like it used to be in ancient times. The principles of the world are deteriorating day by day, and who can say heaven has no conscience. It's only a question of time," said Old Mr. Zhu, who specializes in geomancy[3] and also tutors students in his own private school, as he picked up a peanut with one hand and held his right knee in the other. These were several undigested lines which had come down from his ancestors that he was pedantically spewing out.

I was told that the site of the graves was 936 *mu*—really not small. I couldn't see from one end to the other. The abandoned graves looked like dirt loaves of steamed bread, scattered around like stars or pieces on a chess board, numbering, it was said, between seven and eight thousand.

Arriving in the area where the ghosts reside along the main part of Ghost Street,[4] the troops first formed a long snake-like line and then took a break. Not long after that, the county head, the [Guomindang] Party committee member, and the others rode up in automobiles. On the main road stood two wooden desks, an incense burner, and two candle stands in which red candles were burning. Four spirit foods including a pig, a lamb, vegetables, and meats, had been placed there. Five minutes later the master of ceremonies cried out loudly for the people to be seated. The master of sacrifices and his assistants gathered in front of the altar, carried out the prescribed ritual, burned the sacrificial odes, and fired the ritual cannon to complete the sacrifice to the ghosts. Then several high-ranking officials held an impromptu meeting in which Company Head X, who is known as a grand military lord, divided the work up among the people.

We were a team of two diggers for the five dirt loaves of bread in the southwest corner.

Suddenly a gust of wild wind blew yellow sand up, covering the whole sky. No one could open his eyes. An old Buddhist devotee watching the commotion, who was holding his hands together with fingertips touching, chanted over and over, "Amituofo! Mercy! Mercy!"

The weather was suffocatingly humid and so hot that it was hard to catch a breath, and beads of sweat rolled off our faces into the dirt. Hawkers selling sugarcane rose to the occasion and did a very good business.

---

3. On the type of geomancy practiced in China, see "One Day in Dazhu," n. 2.
4. [Zhihen's note:] That area has always been called Ghost Street.

7. *A Little Shaman*

by SHUXIN (*pseud.*),
a male student writing from Gu Market Town,
Anhui

One evening, Third Aunt of the Xu family and Ah Cheng's Wife sat under an old ash tree chatting in low voices. I saw that they were speaking as though they knew what they were talking about, so I sat down, joined them, and listened. Ah Cheng's Wife glanced at me and didn't say anything. Third Aunt of the Xu family was oblivious and merely devoted herself to saying in a low voice all the words she hadn't finished saying.

"—Incense Master[1] has great potency in healing people, and since Ah Hong has found him, Ah Hong's time to die has not come. Weren't the pus-filled eyes of Third Wife of the Wang family healed by him? He is a virgin man, so seven or eight young ladies[2] all follow him because the family of the Immortals loves chastity."[3]

"Third Aunt of the Xu family! Is that little bogeyman coming again to heal Brother Hong's illness? I'm going to chase him away," I said, about to leave. Ah Cheng's Wife took another glance at me, but still she didn't say anything. Third Aunt of the Xu family did not expect me to say this, and, shocked, she grabbed me and reproached me right away, saying:

"Evil, evil! Amituofo![4] Little kid, you don't know anything. After reading foreign books a few days, you don't believe in this and you don't believe in that. Where does the wind come from? And where does the rain come from? If there were no Immortals anymore, could we still live? From now on, you hurry up and change! If you anger Third Young Lady,[5] that will be no joking matter!"

"It's true, Ah Xin! Last night Third Young Lady descended, and it was something! Saying that Brother Hong's room was too small and that incense fumes were smoking people out, she grabbed the burning, red-hot incense and put it out. She even knew how to sing army songs, and

1. [Shuxin's note:] A shaman (*wupo*) is commonly called an incense master (*xiangtou*).

2. [Shuxin's note:] "Young ladies" (*guniang*) is the name for the Immortals who accompany a shaman during the performance of a healing.

3. Immortals (*xian*) were fairy-like spiritual beings in the pantheon of Daoist deities who had gone through the process of dying only to the extent of discarding their physical bodies. Known in Chinese immortality cults since at least the Han (206 B.C.–A.D. 221), they were believed to live in the supernatural Realm of Great Purity and at the same time to wander freely in the physical world, assuming various shapes, promoting good, and overcoming evil. See Chan Wing-tsit, "Chinese Terminology," p. 151.

4. "Amituofo" was a Buddhist incantation. See "May Twenty-first in Taicang," n. 1.

5. [Shuxin's note:] Third Young Lady (*san guniang*) is the name of an Immortal by whom the little shaman is possessed when he is healing people's illnesses.

something about a national revolution's successes. We didn't understand a thing. She also knew how to sing Soul-tugging opera[6] and sang exactly the same as Da Maozi.[7] Later, after asking for a cup of boiled water and covering the cup with a sheet of yellow paper, she sang songs to get medicine. After the singing was over, we uncovered the cup and took a good look, and hadn't it come to pass! Bubbles from yellow-colored medicine tablets were coming up from the bottom of the whole cup. Since Brother Ah Hong took this medicine of the Immortals, he has gradually become able to move." Ah Cheng's Wife, who had been quiet for a moment and was afraid that I would say something offensive again, was quick to describe Third Young Lady's vitality and potency.

Brother Hong has serious arthritis and has not moved his arms and legs for over two months. I'm afraid it will be difficult for him to recover if he sleeps in a sickbed all day.

"He has completely fooled you all. Whether it's about Third Young Lady or a fourth young lady, it's all simply nonsense. If he has the power to give me a headache, then I'll believe in it," I snapped defiantly.

"Amituofo. Gods and ghosts are scared of aggressive people. You're now young and strong, but when you get sick, Third Young Lady will be able to give you a headache. You listen to me right now and pray, pray to the tablet of Third Young Lady and tell her that you won't offend Third Young Lady again, and I guarantee that you won't be sick for the rest of your life!" Third Aunt of the Xu family coughed twice and went on to say, "After all, I've eaten a lot more years of salt than you, and I've done more things than you've ever seen. What does a little kid know? I didn't think that Ah Hong should've gone to the foreign devil's hospital last time, and you kept saying how good, how good the foreign devil's hospital was. Ah Hong listened to your sweet talk and regretted it by the time he got back. He said the foreign devil didn't even take his pulse and only used a chicken intestine-like thing with one end plugged into the foreign devil's own ears and the other end pressed here and there on his body, and then gave him two pieces of white candy to eat. And he also had a glass tube—which had a pick on the end, looked like the water gun that all of you play with, and was filled with water—jabbed in his butt. Third Young Lady said that there was a ghostly spirit in his body. Even if the foreign devil has more ability, you think about it, can he use the pick to jab the ghostly spirit away? As things have come to pass, since meeting the little incense master, Ah Hong hasn't died. The ghostly spirit is most

6. [Shuxin's note:] Soul-tugging opera (layun qiang) is similar to Beijing opera and is very effective at appealing to the mentality of ignorant rural people in northern Anhui.

7. [Shuxin's note:] Da Maozi is a famous female actress in Soul-tugging opera.

afraid of the spirit of the Immortals. Without the spirit of the Immortals, the ghostly spirit would not have been driven out. Didn't you hear what Ah Cheng's Wife just said? Last night after Ah Hong took the pill of the Immortals, then—"

In a state of confusion, Ah Shi interrupted Third Aunt of the Xu family before she could finish what she was about to say.

"Third Aunt of the Xu family! Ah Cheng's Wife! It's all over! Brother Ah Hong suddenly stopped breathing while taking the medicine of the Immortals!"

There was no reply.

At intervals, waves of wailing came over.

8. *Strange Phenomena in Shubanfo*

by SUN DICHEN,
a man writing from Zhuji, Zhejiang

At the foot of a mountain range with many peaks is a tiny village settlement, and to the rear of the village is Mount Elephant Trunk, which is planted with pear trees. In the third month, its white pear blossoms and green leaves make a beautiful scene. Behind the village there is a big stream, and clear spring water from it irrigates the fields of the whole village. In the village is an elementary school whose school building was once a nunnery and temple. In the twentieth year of the Republic [1931], the school received a prize of first class from the bureau of education.[1] The total population numbered over four hundred, 90 percent working at farming, and the remainder consisting of merchants plus a small number of intellectuals. Four years ago today, whether because of reconstruction[2] or education, they were very diligent and completely ripped out all feudal elements by the roots. The common people, although they had to work hard year round, ultimately became self-sufficient. Their achievement of these satisfactory results was due to the former township head, Yang Keshan, and to Yang Yiqing, Yang Boxin, and a few others with revolutionary ideas.

1. Under Guomindang rule, bureaus were organs of government at the county level. See the introduction to Part II.

2. Rural reconstruction in China during the 1930s consisted of numerous experimental projects to improve life in the countryside. See "A Comedy in the Midst of Sorrow," n. 1.

And now? Yang Keshan, who worked too hard and took ill, has been dead for two years. Boxin and Yiqing have both gone elsewhere. This new village, which had a youthful vigor, has turned into a superstitious world. Before noon on May twenty-first, I boarded a train in Xiaoshan Station to go to Zhuji and Shidu to see friends and passed through this village's Mount Elephant Trunk. I saw men and women, old and young, walking along in the hills and on the plain, some with incense baskets, some with canes, some laughing, some reciting the name of the Buddha. Out of curiosity, I followed them up the mountain. From the foot of the mountain to the temple was about half a *li*, and the steps were all made of stone. The temple, built in November of last year, has a total of seven buildings in three compounds for the worship of three idols. In the middle was Master Guan, to the left was the Patriarch of Bodhisattvas, and to the right was the Deer-horned Great Immortal.[3] In front of Master Guan sat a man with a yellow face and a thin body whom they call the Living Bodhisattva. Before him many people were knocking their heads on the ground as though smashing a clove of garlic to bits. Puff after puff of incense smoke swirled around him. According to the common people, he is a native of Dongyang, his name is Tuquan, and the bodhisattva says that he is wholeheartedly seeking goodness, so the three gods all speak through him.

The sound, "The bodhisattva is coming," almost broke my eardrums. I looked inside the temple and saw that the many people kowtowing to him all were prostrating themselves on the ground without making a sound. At this moment, all the spectators inside and outside the temple were so quiet that you could have heard even the sound of an embroidery needle hitting the ground.

"Many disciples, what have you come to ask me for?" asked Tuquan pretentiously.

Then a few opened their mouths and said, "In our village there is a lottery that we want to hit tomorrow, and we don't know what number to pick. Will the bodhisattva please reveal it to us?"

"Tomorrow the Beckoning-from-Horseback Container holding the lottery tickets will be opened!" replied Tuquan casually.

Next, an old lady in her sixties spoke up: "Master Guan, my son left

3. These gods were from various religions: Master Guan was the hero of the Chinese tale *San guo zhi yan yi*, translated by Moss Roberts under the title *Three Kingdoms: China's Epic Drama*, and was adopted as a deity by both Buddhists and Daoists in China; the Patriarch of Bodhisattvas was from Buddhism; and the Deer-horned Great Immortal was from the Daoist pantheon.

the village in the first month and there has been no news up to now. Is it known where he is?"

"Your son will not return."

When the old lady heard these words, her tears big as soybeans fell to the ground.

Finally a blind person said as he prostrated himself, "Bodhisattva! My eyes have been blind for three years. Please cure me!"

"Here is some sacred water. You take a bowlful, rub it in three times a day, and soon you will be cured."

On the blind person's face appeared a forced smile.

They stood up, and the temple attendant collected money from them. Some gave forty cents and some paid half a dollar, and within less than an hour the desk drawer on Tuquan's left was filled with coins and paper currency. After that, still more people came. I found it hard to take the wave after wave of carbon dioxide, so I listlessly meandered down the mountain. Arriving in the village, all I saw were two or three small children using dirt to make play incense and going through the motions of begging from the gods and praying to the Buddha. The rest were all on Mount Elephant Trunk. Suddenly I saw an elementary school with the characters written on it, "Shubanfo Private Elementary School of Daxi in Zhuji," but both of its doors were shut and not a single child was around. At a glance it was apparent that the upright and selfless Master Guan was revealing his holiness in Shubanfo and was bestowing blessings on the people of Shubanfo, leaving absolutely no need for education. But the fact that Shubanfo, which I have visited twice within a mere four years, had become so retrogressive and backward I certainly did not anticipate.

B. False Doctrines and Vital Rituals

9. *My Day on May Twenty-first*

by YUXIA (*pseud.*),
a male soldier writing from Hua County, Shaanxi

(Hua County was called Xianlin in ancient times and is located in the southeast corner of Shaanxi at the foot of Mount Shaohua. The city is divided into the new and the old. Both were built out of earth and were quite grand but have not been repaired for years, so there are many run-down areas. In order to do the job of defending the city, soldiers have been dispatched to make repairs. Because of the requirements of my own work, I would not be effective without getting close to the people. Therefore, at all kinds of meetings for all the organizations of the people in Hua County, I always participate, take a look, and investigate, which creates opportunities for me to get close to the people. Perhaps this provided the motivation for me to write this essay.)

Today's weather was very good. Perhaps because the weather was good, the heat caused people to be short of breath. Before noon, I was "in the classroom." The so-called classroom was a vacant area where a blackboard hung on a tree at one end, and soldiers sat on the ground. As one can imagine, such a classroom was not cool. After class, I wanted to rest for a while. But when I walked back to the sleeping quarters, a person from my native place was waiting for me there. She wanted me to go have some fun at the temple fair. I was very tired just then and didn't want to go, but I couldn't bear to refuse her, so I said:

"You're really a little kid. What's there to do for fun at a temple fair?"

"No—we have to go," she replied in a childlike way.

"Why do we have to go in this hot weather?"

"Let's go, go right now. Once we're there, you'll realize that it hasn't been a waste of time!"

So we went. When we reached our destination, I couldn't help but be completely disappointed. I really suspected that she was teasing me. The reason was that there was only a temple—the Temple of the City God[1]— with a pair of stone flagpoles over ten feet tall in front of the gate. There were really a lot of people inside, but they all were ordinary incense-burners, devout men and women. Whenever I go into a temple, what I see is people burning incense, worshiping the gods, paying respects to the gods, having their fortunes told, and taking vows. It's the same all over the country, and there was absolutely nothing special about this one.

We made our way through the temple gate to the rear hall. This hall was similar in size to the ones in each county in other provinces. The difference was that here the gods had no niches, and the City God, the King of Hell, the Judge of Hell, the little ghosts, and the others were all placed decorously on the ground inside the temple. On the statues was streak after streak of dark yellow marks. It seemed it was quite pathetic to be a god or a ghost here. But I still didn't feel that there was anything exceptional. I turned to my companion and asked:

"Anything else in back? Today is as disappointing as 'four winning tickets for the air force lottery.'"[2]

Without replying, she nudged me with her elbow and pointed with her finger. I looked where she was pointing. Oh! I got it! I saw a middle-aged man kneeling in front of an earthen idol with an ugly face which represented a ghost or god whose identity I didn't know. The man had a pale face covered with tears, and from his head drops of sweat as big as soybeans fell down one after another. He searched all over himself like someone up to no good, and his veins were swollen up as big as earth-worms. He looked as though he was about to cry. Then, as though crazed, he shook the clothes he was wearing and, *dong*, a small white tin box fell out. After he saw it, he became as happy as a death-row criminal receiving a pardon. He broke into a grin that covered his whole face, and he quickly picked it up. Just then, again looking as though he wanted to do something without letting people know, he furtively glanced about, and, seeing no one was paying any attention to him, he quickly opened the white tin box, dipped his finger inside, scooped out a large fingerful of dark, yellow-colored, thick glue which looked like some kind of paste and dabbed it on the body of the earthen idol. He kowtowed once, stood up, and ran out of the temple without looking back. I also noticed that,

1. On the City God, see "The Temple Today," n. 2.

2. [Yuxia's note:] The first prize in the air force lottery is worth 25,000 dollars, and four of these would be worth *shi wan* (100,000). "*Shi wan*" sounds similar to *shiwang* (disappointing).

except for the two of us, the other men and women all avoided other people and surreptitiously dabbed this kind of paste-like stuff on the idol before taking their leave. I felt it was very odd, so I asked my companion:

"What's going on? Not burning incense, only kowtowing like this! Stranger yet, each of them is putting dabs onto the earthen idol. What are they using?"

She said with a smile:

"Why don't you get closer and take a look?"

Before I got there and before I could see, the odor made a direct attack on my nostrils. Startled, I couldn't help but cry out:

"Oh! Opium paste."

Those devout men and women, feeling that my outcry was insulting to the god, all scowled at me. But seeing that I was wearing a two-and-a-half footer,[3] they couldn't do anything, daring to be angry but not daring to say anything. My companion seemed to know what they were thinking and she dragged me out of the temple.

Once outside the temple, after asking questions in detail, I found out that 70 to 80 percent of the people in this county are addicted to opium. If those who have not become addicted get sick, they go to opium dens to take two mouthfuls of smoke as a cure for the sickness. The opium den is their only hospital, and opium has become the cure-all elixir of immortality, so everybody is addicted. The common people in Hua County use this reasoning: If living people smoke opium, then gods and ghosts must also enjoy smoking, and if ghosts and gods in other places like spirit money,[4] then ghosts and gods in Hua County naturally like opium paste. Dabbing opium paste on the face of the earthen idol is a bribe. Bribery must be done in secret, so when they are dabbing opium paste, they don't let other people see.

From this small episode I know further how great the power of opium is here!

3. [Yuxia's note:] It is called a two-and-a-half footer because the shirt covering the upper body in most military uniforms is two feet five inches long.

4. Chinese practitioners of popular religion burned spirit money in the belief that it would be transmitted to gods and ghosts in the other world. See "The Temple Today," n. 5.

10. *A Procession for the Gods in Cibei*

by CHEN YUGONG,
a man writing from Ciqi, Zhejiang

Spreading out a map of Zhejiang province, one can see in the eastern coastal area a small county called Ciqi running horizontally. In the northern part of Ciqi is a village called Cibei. There stands a green peak, the last in the Siming mountain range which surrounds the clear waters of Lake Du. The lake supplies irrigation and drinking water for the entire village. Many streams extend eastward and westward from it like jade belts, irrigating thousands of acres of land which look like a bright green carpet.

"Life-Is-Transcient" (a ghost commonly found in religious processions who was believed to serve as the messenger of death), a woodcut by Lu Xun, from Lu Xun, "Postscript," *Dawn Blossoms Plucked at Dusk*, translated by Yang Hsien-yi and Gladys Yang (Beijing, 1976), p. 115.

Villagers in this pastoral setting are all able to live in peace and contentment. After working the land, they gather together in a festive mood and
have a procession for the gods. This group activity is lots of fun and yet it
is superstitious. During periods when harvests are abundant, naturally
they go on an annual binge. Even at this moment, when farming villages
all over the country are going bankrupt, this procession for the gods has
not been canceled.

The procession for the gods in this place was on May twenty-first.
There was really a hubbub on this day. All streets and alleys, hillsides
and level ground were crowded with men and women dressed up for the
occasion. Peddlers raised their voices in all kinds of cries to attract customers and hoped to make lots of money. The river was also crowded
with boats, and the old boatmen did well these few days, busily trans-
porting passengers here and there and making at least three or four dollars of hard-earned cash per day.

With several hundred thousand spectators eagerly awaiting it, the
great procession began to move ahead. It was more than ten *li* long, with
tens of thousands of young people in it and countless eyes focused upon
it. At the front of the procession came a young person holding a huge
banner, over twenty feet high, which fluttered in the wind. On either
side many people walked along with him. Second came loads of food carried on men's shoulders, all with flowery decorations and colorful ribbons
tied around. Third came pairs of gongs, making the resounding noise
dong dong. Fourth came several pairs of official insignia. Fifth came more
than ten tall lanterns of the kind carried by standard bearers in combat,
all covered with colorful decorations and strings of beads that dangled
down and tinkled against each other. Sixth came over one hundred flags,
one for the Party [Guomindang], one for the nation, and the rest flags of
various colors which fluttered in the wind, drove through the wind, and
blotted out the sun. Seventh came more than thirty umbrellas of the
masses,[1] one after another. Eighth came several drum boats, each containing more than ten musicians, beating drums, playing Chinese
stringed and wind instruments, singing, and making a racket as they
passed. Ninth came more than ten platforms about ten feet in height, carried on men's shoulders, with lively little children acting out a Beijing opera on each one. Tenth came more than twenty runners dressed in black
clothing and wearing black hats. Two people dressed as Life-Is-

---

1. Umbrellas of the masses (*wan min san*) were presented to officials in honor of merito-
rious service. The tops of these umbrellas were generally made of red silk or satin and inscribed with the names of the donors in gold.

Transient,[2] one in black and one in white, were made up with blood on their faces, and made ghost faces as they went along, frightening cowards among the women and children and causing them to scream. After that came the ghosts of suicides who had hanged themselves. Dressed in red garments with black vests, they wore their long hair down over their shoulders. They stuck out their tongues, which were over a foot long, hunched their shoulders, and had ashen faces. In addition there were ghosts of opium addicts carrying opium pots and opium pipes in their hands; hungry ghosts on whose heads were placed incense, candles, bowls, chopsticks, and bamboo rice sifters; a Judge of Hell; and a group of satellites from hell, including Horse-face and Ox-head.[3] Eleventh came about a hundred men and women dressed like criminals from olden times in chains and red garments. Twelfth came white elephants baring their teeth and green lions taking swipes with their paws, about ten of them. Thirteenth came more than ten colorful dragons whose heads looked very dignified and whose scales were very lifelike. Fourteenth came several big lanterns each made of nine interlocking rings. Fifteenth came more than twenty pieces of paraphernalia used in feudal times—yellow tridents, white battle-axes, golden claws, silver chains. Sixteenth came twenty-four people on stilts, all less than fifteen years old, wearing yellow uniforms, standing on wooden stilts over ten feet tall, and rocking back and forth as they walked. After that, the sound of gunfire shook the sky, and the idol to be welcomed arrived.[4] Among the spectators along both sides of the road, some knelt and prostrated themselves, some held their hands together in worship, and some knocked their heads on the ground as though smashing a clove of garlic to bits. At that moment, suddenly *peng, peng,* firecrackers went off, and the hustle and bustle of the procession came to an end. The spectators rushed home. The peddlers' distinctive cries were once again heard in the midst of the crowds.

2. Life-Is-Transient (*Wuchang*) may be literally translated "inconstant" or "changeable." It is the name of a ghost that was believed to assume variable shapes and to serve as the messenger of death. For Lu Xun's reminiscences about seeing Wuchang in temples, processions, and operas, see his essay, "Wu Chang or Life-Is-Transient."

3. These ghosts were believed to be dangerous because they were forced by circumstances (especially a lack of descendants who would have cared for them by making sacrifices to them) to prey on the living. See Arthur P. Wolf, "Gods, Ghosts, and Ancestors," pp. 169–76.

4. For descriptions by foreign observers of processions in China at this time that resembled this one, see Maspero, "The Mythology of Modern China," pp. 288 and 362; and Shryock, *The Temples of Anking*, pp. 104–05.

11. *The Honorable Guest*

by ZIMO *(pseud.),*
a man writing from Gaoan, Jiangxi

It has been only half a year since I arrived in Gaoan City. I'm still not very familiar with the local situation—the customs and practices. Fortunately, my friend Lie is a local person, so Lie has told me many interesting things.

Early this morning, as soon as I opened the door, Lie said with eager anticipation:

"Good! Today there is another interesting superstitious practice for you to see. Today is the day for 'Opening the Temple Gates.'"

He then explained to me saying that today was the first day of the fourth month according to the banned calendar,[1] and all of the temple gates in Gaoan City had to be opened to receive "the honorable guest." "The honorable guest" rides in a paper boat over ten feet long. He is the local God of Epidemics.

"This superstition has come down through the past three or four hundred years. It is said that once upon a time a merchant came into the city to buy wheat. The money he carried with him was seen by several disciples of Buddha (riffraff),[2] and thus did bad luck befall this wheat merchant. His money was stolen, and he was murdered.

"After his death, strange things happened. Epidemics spread through the city, and not a single family went without illness. Fortunately, the bodhisattva showed compassion saying, 'You all have done wrong and should suffer evil consequences, but there is a way out: Give shelter in the temple to "the honorable guest" (honorable guest being the title of respect for the wheat merchant because he was from another place), and let him have incense burned to him to calm his spirit which has suffered injustices.' Since then, 'the honorable guest' has been received on the first day of the fourth month, and 'the honorable guest' has been given a respectful send-off on the fourth day of the fifth month in the paper boat on the great river and has floated away to the east, carrying epidemics with him."

"Compared with the health campaign of last week, this method is simpler and more effective," I remarked.

---

1. The traditional lunar calendar was officially banned by the Chinese government in 1912. See the introduction to Part III.

2. Zimo used the term "disciples of Buddha" (*luohan*) (which in standard Chinese refers to mythical and ancient followers of Buddha) and put the term "riffraff" (*liumang*) in parentheses after it, indicating that the local euphemism for riffraff was "disciples of Buddha."

Lie smiled but didn't comment.

In the afternoon I went to the main street to pay my respects at the parade for "the honorable guest." According to Lie, once every five days "the honorable guest" must be paraded in the streets.

Two men in short jackets, one in front and one behind, passed by, holding the paper boat of "the honorable guest." As usual, a certain type of Chinese music was being played in front by musicians who themselves didn't seem to know what type it was. A gong was struck, making a loud sound. The paper boat had rectangular and triangular paper flags sticking out all over it and on them were inscribed aphorisms: "The country is prosperous, the people are at peace" and "Good weather, harvests, and prosperity."

Every family set off firecrackers. Amidst the smoke and fog, "the honorable guest" moved forward on parade.

12. *"On Market Day" and "The Burning of Busy Incense"*

by SHANZHU (*pseud.*),
a man writing from Tianchang, Anhui

This happened to be this county's "market day."[1] Streets within the city are ordinarily very quiet, but today was very different. People crowded together, each person's toes touching the next one's heels, shoulders rubbing against shoulders. Some wore coarse blue woolen trousers and carried baskets at waist level. Some had their pants cuffs rolled up showing their mud-splattered legs and carried cooking oil bottles. Some wore straw sandals and no socks. Some wore dark blue headbands, aprons with red sashes, and old-fashioned shoes with tabs sticking up from the heel. In addition, some had trailing behind them the long pigtail of the Manchus from Qing times.[2] In this county, which has experienced crop failures year after year, all the peasants have suffered devastation resulting from natural calamities and exploitation resulting from excessive taxa-

1. Markets in rural China were periodic rather than continuous, normally convening every few days. See "'A Rural Purge,'" n. 2.

2. After conquering China, the Manchus reigned during the Qing dynasty (1644–1912) and required throughout this period that Chinese adopt the Manchu custom of wearing queues down their backs.

tion. Every year every peasant gives untold amounts of blood and sweat and yet cannot gain warmth and a full belly in return. On this day, the lines on the peasants' faces showed their suffering and pain.

This was not an ordinary day. Every year this day is the busiest day for rural men and women from farming villages, as well as for elderly female spirit mediums, middle-aged spirit mediums, riffraff, beggars, shopkeepers, and peddlers in the streets, because this is the day for "The Burning of Busy Incense," an established custom for many years. After burning incense today, peasants will enter their busiest time: raising silkworms, harvesting wheat, planting seedlings, keeping busy with one thing after another, and having very little time to burn incense. Therefore, incense burned on this day is called "busy incense."

This day of "The Burning of Busy Incense" can be called a day of happiness and it can be called a day of apprehension for peasants. On this day they see all their friends and they look forward to a good harvest. But they also will worry from this day onward that what they will get will be a disappointment.

This day of "The Burning of Busy Incense" was eagerly anticipated by beggars and riffraff. Very early in the morning they were already waiting in front of the Temple of the City God,[3] hoping that people burning incense would give them a few copper coins.

This day of "The Burning of Busy Incense" was a day long awaited by shopkeepers and peddlers. They laid out lots of baskets of fruit, displays of incense, and displays of tobacco, and they hoped the fruit would be eaten, the incense bought, and the tobacco smoked. But this year it was not the same as this day four years ago. Except for what they have to spend on buying a few joss sticks, the peasants' money for tobacco and fruit has already been taken away by landlords and officials.

This day of "The Burning of Busy Incense" was a day for nuns and monks in the temples to receive money. They were hoping that people burning incense would toss in a bit more incense money, but today only a very few elderly female spirit mediums tossed in incense money.

This day of "The Burning of Busy Incense" was a day when various kinds of people were happy, sad, sighing, troubled.

3. On the City God, see "The Temple Today," n. 2.

13. *May Twenty-first in Taicang*

by YAN XICHEN,
a male newspaper reporter writing from Taicang, Jiangsu

Being responsible for gathering news every day, I felt especially excited as I got up today (May twenty-first), for I wanted to gather more interesting news. As soon as I got downstairs, I discovered a small item, which was that the candlestand that was placed on the altar in the living room of the house where I am staying had incense and candles burning in it. Suddenly I remembered that today was the first day of the fourth month on the banned calendar.[1] Going out, I saw incense and candles burning inside many shops as well as in residential households. Indeed, burning candles on the first and the fifteenth day of the month is a custom not limited to Taicang.

Hengjing, more than ten kilometers outside Taicang City, will have a fair tomorrow, so lots of people were preparing to go particularly to see tomorrow's festivities, and this reporter was one of them. At one o'clock in the afternoon, I boarded a small motorboat. The boat was small and the people were many. After having difficulty getting a seat, I already felt extremely uncomfortable. On top of that, the oppressively hot sun started everybody complaining about their suffering. On the way, I saw many boats taking people to burn incense. After more than three hours, I reached my destination.

According to custom, on the eve of the fair, old Buddhist ladies must go to the temple and chant sutras all the way until morning. This is called "staying overnight." At about four-thirty in the afternoon on the twenty-first, many tourists, peddlers, and traveling magicians gathered outside the Temple of the Valiant General. A bodhisattva was placed in front of the temple gate. On the altar were four execution flags on which were written the names of criminals who were to be executed. Many old ladies were crowded together inside the temple. Because it could not hold all the people, a round wooden hall had been built, connected to the temple wall at a point where a hole had been made. The old ladies sitting at a little more than thirty tables, with eight persons per table, altogether numbered over three hundred. More than three hundred mouths (not counting those persons standing) recited in unison homage to Amituofo.[2] They

1. The traditional lunar calendar was banned by the Chinese government in 1912. See the introduction to Part III.
2. "Amituofo" is the Chinese name for the Buddha of Endless Light (known as the Amitabha Buddha in Sanskrit). Chinese Buddhists repeated Amituofo (Chinese for "homage to the Amitabha Buddha") in the belief that if holding nothing else in their minds but

had brought their own evening meal to the temple, so at this time some were reciting sutras, some were eating rice. Mixing boiled water with cold rice, they ate the rice with stir-fried fava beans. On the tables were Buddhist sutras, Buddhist rosary beads, fava beans, and rice in water. In the temple, tea was carried around on carrying poles, with each table served one pot. From each old lady two copper coins were collected. The weather was very hot, the people were many, the building was small, and with smoke from incense fumes on top of this, several old ladies entered phase one of fainting. When this reporter wandered around, he encountered an old lady who had been forced to stop the most important work of sutra reciting. Several of her companions were scratching her back and saying that her capillaries were very serious! But the old lady was taking short breaths and insisting she was all right.

Leaving through the temple gate, I went to my relatives' home for a meal and learned that 80 percent of the residences of this place had the task of "taking care of relatives and friends." At about eight o'clock, rain came down out of the sky, causing people to worry that there would be no festivities for them to see. In the rain I once again went to visit the old Buddhist ladies and found they had not given up. They were now reciting sutras more diligently than ever. They remarked, "When the bodhisattva goes out, it is necessary to clean the road. This is street-cleaning rain, and tomorrow it will be fine. Young master, don't worry. Go to see the fair. Don't worry! Amituofo—A—" In the middle of the sound *mituo*, deep in the night, this reporter walked out the temple gate and rushed to the local ward office to use the telephone to get information from each of the other wards. I dare say that throughout the entire county of Taicang within this twenty-four-hour period no special event has occurred!

14. *A Handbill for Peace*

by XIANGRU (*pseud.*),
a man writing from Hangzhou, Zhejiang

It so happened that today I was given a valuable handbill.

"Smash to bits superstitious sayings. Seek and achieve true peace!"

These ten words, in the second largest print used by printers, form a

---

Amituofo, they would be reborn in the Western Paradise. See "A Record of Digging Up Graves," n. 1.

very eye-catching headline. I believe all peace-loving Chinese people will be eager to see what it is about.

At the end of it in one corner, two lines of words were also printed, "Reprinting is welcomed" and "If you reprint this, you will gain unlimited virtue." The obligation of reprinting it has to be met, so I am showing my respect by washing my hands before recording it here—and I am borrowing one small corner of *One Day in China* in which to place it respectfully before my peace-loving fellow countrymen:

SMASH TO BITS SUPERSTITIOUS SAYINGS.
SEEK AND ACHIEVE TRUE PEACE!

Hear ye, everyone! Peace, peace, it is what everyone is now hoping for, and it is urgently needed. However, no single person or small group of people can achieve peace. Nor can there be a turn of the kalpa[1] in a flash. It is necessary for everyone to pray every moment, reciting "I put my trust in the bodhisattva Guanyin" or "I put my trust in the bodhisattva Guanyin who grants salvation from pain and suffering."[2] It is also necessary for every person to repent sincerely the evil deeds of body, word, and thought that one has committed and to vow that hereafter one will never be malevolent and will be benevolent in all things. The selfishness of the heart and the immorality of all past actions must be forcibly eliminated, like cutting down the grass and pulling out its roots, leaving nothing. Once the craftiness, perversity, and violence in one's established character are rooted out, then goodness and kindness will come into being. The beneficial consequences of peace will naturally be obvious. If we acknowledge that time is linear, we must always be frugal, patient, and diligent, and pray and repent not merely for a moment but pray and repent forever. Then true peace will be achieved. Newspapers have frequently reported that "1936 will be the year of the outbreak of the Second World War." (This year is 1936 according to the Western calendar.) We must smash to bits these superstitious sayings and must follow the above-mentioned words. Pray. (Recite the sacred name of the bodhisattva Guanyin. One recitation will earn one merit leading toward peace. One hundred or one thousand recitations will earn one hundred or one thousand merits leading to-

---

1. The traditional meaning of the term kalpa in Indian Buddhism has been summarized by Susan Naquin: "In traditional Buddhist thought, history was divided into great kalpa periods, each lasting hundreds of thousands of years. Each period was marked by a steady degeneration, and toward the end of each kalpa, Buddhist teachings would appear, prevail at first, and then be gradually undermined. At the end of a kalpa a cosmic holocaust would destroy the world and a new period would begin." As Naquin has shown, White Lotus sects in China adopted this interpretation syncretically, specifying and shortening the length of each kalpa, and predicting that each kalpa would end in great disorder caused by human wickedness and natural disasters, followed by the appearance of the Buddha. See her *Millenarian Rebellion in China*, pp. 11–12 and passim.
2. Guanyin was the goddess of mercy. See "Diary of a Midwife," n. 5.

ward peace. In short, the more the better.) Repent. (Repent all the evil deeds of body, word, and thought.) If everyone will pray and repent, then it will surely be possible to transform this foul and evil world into a compassionate, peaceful, and pure world.

NATIONAL SOCIETY FOR PRAYING FOR PEACE

Reprinting is welcomed.

Hangzhou, West Lake, Longxiang Bridge Buddhist Studies Book Store, printers and distributors

If you reprint this, you will gain unlimited virtue.

Addresses for the Society:
In Nanjing, Nanjing East Gate, behind Shiguanyin, Nanjing Buddhist Laity

In Shanghai, Zhabei, Xinmin Road, World Buddhist Laity

15. *Miscellaneous Scenes during a Temple Fair*

by QIAN JULIN,
a man writing from Lanzhou, Gansu

May twenty-first happens to fall on the first day of the fourth month according to the old calendar.[1] I recall that whenever the time came for the Festival of the Bathing of the Buddha in Jingan Temple in Shanghai, peddlers spread out their straw mats on the street, covering dozens of walkways. People from nearby and far away, the old as well as the young, all came to shop for a few daily necessities. It was really hustling and bustling.

I came to Gansu last winter. In lifeless and lonely Lanzhou, only Mount Wuquan can be considered an attraction that draws men and women.

The mountain is located about five *li* south of the city. It's a rather big mountain. Although it has no grass or trees on it, it does have Wuquan Temple, with buildings, observation points, pavilions, and towers, all of which are very grand. Between the first and the eighth day of the fourth month every year there is also a gigantic temple fair worth writing about.

1. Temple fairs were scheduled according to long-term cycles. See "Possessed by the Bodhisattva," n. 5.

Peddlers come from near and far to spread out mats and set up booths inside and around the temple. Restaurants from the city also set up concessions inside the temple. Traveling theatrical troupes which ordinarily perform only at night now also hurry over there, set up a stage, raise a curtain, and give daytime performances.

So people from all around end up "going to Mount Wuquan." I've heard that people from Lanzhou, no matter how poor they are, all have to go on a binge when the time for the temple fair comes. If someone doesn't go, then behind his or her back people will say "this year he or she can't even go to Mount Wuquan!"

So rickshas, donkey carts, big wagons, donkeys, horses, and people on foot wended their way for two or three *li* on the dirt road from the city. The air was filled with dust. Policemen directed one-way traffic.

In front of the houses on both sides of the road sat young girls all wearing make-up and dressed in what they considered to be the most beautiful clothes—which in fact were old and very out of fashion. They gazed at the tourists in the carts and at the same time let the tourists gaze at them so that they could attract an appropriate mate.

Beggars and aborigine women reached out and pleaded for money. But the gentlemen seldom had copper coins in their pockets. Lanzhou people mainly use paper currency, and the smallest denomination is equivalent to ten copper coins. So the gentlemen did not readily hand any over. How pathetic!

On the mountain, peddlers sold nothing but deep-fried flakey cakes, cigarettes, toy spears and swords for children, clay dolls, and masks, all of very low quality. There were lots of Japanese goods, so we can see that Eastern goods have penetrated every nook and cranny!

On the stage inside the main gate a performance of Shaanxi provincial Qin opera was underway. We Southerners find it very difficult to understand. Inside the main hall, lots of joss sticks were lit. I also saw many people sitting on the steps listening to a person who was giving a speech and gesturing wildly. Was he telling a story? No. He was saying "Christ is the Way." Christians are always taking advantage of opportunities to preach their "gospel."

I was walking from the Sutra Library when I saw a sign, one line of which read: "A High Place Is No Better than a Low Place." I say Lanzhou is no better than Shanghai!

Food concessions were filled with customers eating—all families, eating what they considered to be very expensive meals. Some played drinking games and were in high spirits.

The atmosphere in the teahouse was entirely different. The people here were mostly public servants, military officials, students, and quite a few modern young girls from the south. But mingling with them at tableside were more than a few prostitutes from Nanguan showing off and acting sexy, hoping to attract some guests back to their own fragrant nests.

The temple fair at Mount Wuquan has certainly injected excitement into the dreary atmosphere of Lanzhou. Once these few days are over, life will again become cold, dismal, and drab, the same monotonous routine day after day.

16. The "Small Fullness Theater"[1] in Shengze

by YUQIU (pseud.),
a man writing from Wujiang, Jiangsu

Shengze is a market town under the jurisdiction of Wujiang County in Jiangsu. Its famous product, as everyone knows, is Shengze silk.

A custom, descended through time, is that on the day of the Small Fullness Festival several hundred silk shops in the market town all contribute money to have one day of theatrical performances for the gods. As for this year? The day happens to fall on "One Day in China."

It is said that the Silkworm Goddess is one of the forebears of the silk trade. They want to honor this Silkworm Goddess and hope the Silkworm Goddess will protect the silkworms raised by peasants in the surrounding countryside so that they will have a bountiful harvest. Therefore there is this superstition.[2] But they sponsor it half to benefit themselves and half to develop the overall silk market in Shengze, because if the silkworm harvest is good, then the silk business will go more smoothly for the management.

Nowadays, with the collapse of farming villages, a majority of peasants cannot solve the problem of securing clothing and food. So after a

---

1. Small Fullness (*Xiaoman*) is the term on the Chinese lunar calendar for the first fifteen days of the fourth month (approximately May 21–June 4 on the Gregorian calendar). It designates the period in the growth cycle of grain during which the kernels form.
2. On the Silkworm Goddess in early Chinese history see Bodde, *Festivals in Classical China*, pp. 268–71. Other trades and professions in China at this time besides the silk trade also had protecting divinities like the Silkworm Goddess. See Maspero, "The Mythology of Modern China," pp. 310–33; and Feuchtwang, "City Temples in Taipei," pp. 274–76.

full day's work, the only entertainment they have is smoking their tobacco pipes. Those who can afford to sit in little teahouses are exceptions. They would never imagine going to a theater and spending a day
watching theatrical performances. Today since the so-called Small Fullness Theater is performing in the market town, it is the only day in the
year when you can watch an excellent performance of Beijing opera without paying a penny, as long as you aren't afraid of the sun beating down
on you and you have the energy to stand firm in the crowd.

Hutao Street, ordinarily devoid of activity, was today entirely different. At the Silk Trade Lodge Hall (also known as Silkworm Hall, located
on Hutao Street), there was an audience numbering in the tens of
thousands.

Since the first day of summer,[3] the weather has been gray and cold,
but today was completely different. The temperature shot up from 60 degrees to 85 degrees. The blood-red sun seemed especially fierce. It was
beating down upon the masses who watched the theatrical performance
to the point where everyone's sweat was pouring and everyone was complaining about the heat.

Dongdang, dongdang, the sounds of gongs and drums filled the entire
theater. As people in red robes and green robes made their entrances and
exits on the stage, the audience screamed its approval to them time and
again in shrill voices.

The weather was so hot that peddlers selling fruit and fans all did
more than three times their usual business.

Policemen in the midst of the crowd ceased to be effective in main-
taining order. Fights broke out all over. The head of a branch of the public security bureau[4] came and joined in the festivities, and his long gown,
which was made of fine silk, was torn as a result of the pushing and
shoving in the crowd.

3. On the Chinese lunar calendar, the first day of summer (*li xia*) corresponds to May 5
on the Gregorian calendar.

4. Under Guomindang rule, the public security bureau was one of the county-level organs of government. See the introduction to Part II.

17. *Wu Garden and Xuanmiao Daoist Temple*

by QINGYI (*pseud.*),
a man writing from Suzhou, Jiangsu

There are two places in Suzhou where the masses gather: one is teahouses, the other is Xuanmiao Daoist Temple. Of all the teahouses, the largest and the one with the most tea customers is Wu Garden. Xuanmiao Daoist Temple is a gathering place for the middle and lower classes.

Upon entering the back door at Wu Garden, I saw a sign on the wall on which was written: "To reach the main part of Wu Garden, enter here." Inside there were people seated in several large rooms. Most were chatting in groups of two or more. It was quite uncommon to see a person sitting alone. Those sitting alone had nothing to do, so they paid two copper coins to rent newspapers from the newspaper vendor. Generally five out of every ten of these people read the newspaper *Xinwen bao*, two read the newspaper *Shen bao*, and three read various minor newspapers. Businessmen prefer the *Xinwen bao* and educators and the like prefer the *Shen bao* and other major newspapers.[1] Those wearing Western-style clothing who look like students prefer the minor newspapers for their coverage of people's private lives and trivial matters which were well-suited to their taste.

I walked over to the story-telling area. It was even more hustling and bustling. More than a hundred people were seated in the audience, and two people were seated on the stage in high-backed, overstuffed chairs. One was playing a Chinese zither and the other was playing a moon-shaped lute.[2] They played for a while and then sang for a while. A small table with two teapots on it sat in front of them. A red tablecloth hung over the front edge of it, in the middle of which was inscribed a New Life Movement slogan.[3] On each side was written: "When one is alive, one has anxiety and despair; when one is dead, one has peace and happiness. Contentment with peace is poisonous and should never be yearned for." The listeners below the stage included old as well as young, men as well as women. Some lowered their heads, closed their eyes, and listened attentively. Some sipped tea and smoked cigarettes, sometimes lowering their heads, sometimes looking up, devoid of worldly concerns. Some

1. *Xinwen bao* and *Shen bao* were both published in Shanghai, and each had a circulation of 100,000–150,000, the largest of any newspapers in China at this time. See Lin, *A History of the Press*, p. 145.

2. The Chinese zither (*pipa*) and the Chinese lute (*yueqin*) are both traditional musical instruments.

3. The New Life Movement, inaugurated by Chiang Kaishek in 1934, used slogans like this one to try to reform popular attitudes and behavior. See "Two Letters," n. 6.

laughed, some sighed. All kinds of people were there, and it is impossible to describe them all.

I walked over to Xuanmiao Daoist Temple. In a small booth was a sign, "The Brothers Shop, A Branch of a Store in Shanghai." In front of the small booth one person stood on the left and another on the right both wearing blue long gowns with red sashes over their shoulders and looking very much like soldiers on guard duty in the army. On the red sashes were black characters: One read, "You Are Welcome to Browse," and the other read, "The Price Is Cheap and the Goods Are Fine." The two of them chanted back and forth to each other, always repeating that their price was cheap and their goods were fine. There were seven or eight people standing around looking, but no one went in to shop.

A person walked up and down with an air rifle in his hands, sometimes aiming and shooting it at a target. The target had two red circles, and on either side of it was written: "You Are Welcome to Take Shooting Practice for the Sake of Supporting Our Country and Protecting Our Community." Oh what a highfalutin come-on!

"Listen everybody! I'm going to sing about opium junkies." It was a small seven-year-old child with his head shaven except for three tufts of hair, one in front and the other two just above the ears, some of it long and some short. He was blind in both eyes. Only the whites were visible and sticking out. He had a money bag strapped across his body and a bamboo clacker in each hand. He clacked, jumped up and down, and sang. More than ten people formed a circle around him, and some said, "You little devil, you'd better watch out. There might be some old opium addicts around who will invite you to take a slap on the face!" That little kid replied, "Aiyaya, it doesn't matter. I have an order from Chiang Kaishek to come here to campaign against smoking. Ha, ha."

There was another platform on which a man and a woman were standing. Their bones stuck out like sticks of wood. The woman was over thirty, had gold teeth, had a little rouge on her face, and was singing a rhyming narrative.[4] The man was playing the role of an old lady, wearing glasses with lenses two inches across and taking one doddering step after another, which made the dozens of workers and shopkeepers who were standing below the stage laugh uproariously.

Fortunetellers reading ideograms, storytellers, acrobats, stalls selling cups of tea, birdcages—everything was there. It is truly impossible to describe and to write down!

4. This kind of rhyming song (*tanhuang*) tells a story or relates current events. It originated in the 1850s and was still popular in Shanghai and Suzhou in the 1930s. *Hanyu zidian*, p. 215.

C. The Intrusion of Christianity

18. *Around a Corner*

by HE YI,
a man writing from Chunan, Zhejiang

The sky was clear. The noontime sun was blazing, and pedestrians on the road were sweating.

In this hilly city, I entered a small, deserted alley off a narrow street, expecting to reach XX.

There was no one else walking along this alley. Hot golden sunshine blazed down on the quiet road paved with stones shaped like goose eggs. On both sides were uneven rows of tumbledown houses. I walked half asleep along the walls of the houses. Rounding the corner of a house, I came upon the ancestral temple of the X clan. The upswept corners of the roof on either side of the building appeared in their grandeur before my eyes.

There came the sound of a speaking voice, clear, crisp, and warbling. Stopping and suddenly looking up, I saw many people gathered in front of that ancestral temple's wooden gate. Within the crowd stood a tall Western woman,[1] like a whooping crane in the middle of a flock of chickens. She had a small white hat, glasses perched high upon the bridge of her nose, a long light blue dress, white skin, and red shoes. She held her head high, shifted her gaze up and down, and, as she held a picture up high with her left hand, she pointed at it with her right hand. She addressed the group in halting, not very fluent Chinese. I turned to look at the picture, and it was of the man who was nailed to the cross.

I kept walking because I certainly had no time to listen to her great ideas.

About an hour later I returned from XX and once again passed that

1. Two out of every three foreign Protestant missionaries in China at this time were women. See Bates, *Missions in Far Eastern Cultural Relations*, p. 4.

"Early Summer," a woodcut by Zhang Zaimin, from *Lu Xun shoucang Zhongguo xiandai muke xuanji, 1931–36* [A Selection from Lu Xun's Collection of Modern Chinese Woodcuts, 1931–36] (Beijing, 1963), p. 79.

small alley. I noticed that a lot of people were still standing in front of the ancestral temple's gate, but now the foreign woman was sitting down to rest. A young Chinese woman now addressed the crowd, and she was very short, so she stood on the door-base.[2] She was leafing through a stack of pictures held together by a wooden clamp, and pointing at each one. She knitted her brow, strained to make herself heard, imitated the gestures of the Western woman, and painstakingly addressed the group. Her face was flushed and her forehead was perspiring. I stopped at the side of the road, and a few sentences caught my ear:

2. Practitioners of Chinese popular religion believed that a door-base such as this one (which spanned the area below a door) warded off evil spirits, preventing them from entering a building.

"—in one's heart—if various kinds of things—are wrong. If we do not believe in God, then we will eventually be thrown into hell to suffer—I'm not lying to you, this kind of thing really happens. If you believe in God—you'll be forgiven despite your sins—"

Seeing that sort of thing, I couldn't control myself and almost burst out laughing. But everyone standing there was intently listening, as though her words were well worth hearing and taking to heart.

I stood there a while. Eavesdropping on a conversation in the audience, I found out that the Chinese woman was employed by the church and was paid no less than three or four dollars a month.

In the evening when I was at XX, I saw the couple once again pass by. The Western woman was strolling along empty-handed, and the Chinese woman was following behind, holding two pictures in one hand and clutching a bag of assorted stuff in the other. Her face was red, and she was moving at a trot, gasping for breath.

19. *Notes on Dr. Song's Preaching*

by CHEN RONGZHAN,
a man writing from Taishan, Guangdong[1]

At about 10:30 A.M., the "sanctuary" was already so packed that a drop of water couldn't run through.

The people sitting below the dais were mostly women, especially middle-aged village women. They came to listen to the message perhaps in hopes that their hearts would be comforted. Or perhaps might one say that they came to see what the revered Dr. Song was really like and to hear his vigorous delivery? Naturally most of them came from villages outside the city, but quite a few ignorant women also "traveled a thousand miles." In fact, there were several manly looking women who "followed in his tracks" from Canton here to hear him speak.[2] They are indeed religious zealots. Maybe this shows us Dr. Song's enormous drawing power!

1. This piece undoubtedly describes a visit to Taishan by the Chinese Christian evangelist, Dr. Song Shangjie (1901–44), for his biographer has recounted that Dr. Song preached in Guangdong province and specifically in Taishan during the year 1936. See Liu Yiling, *Song Shangjie zhuan*, p. 186.

2. According to Song's biographer, the evangelist visited Taishan at the invitation of several of his female followers and over the protests of leaders in the local church. See ibid., p. 186.

Even after the bell struck twelve, Dr. Song still had not shown up. They felt anxiety in their hearts, just as if they were "anticipating rain clouds during a big drought." Not until 1:30 did they unhappily disperse.

At 7:30 in the evening, the sermon was finally delivered. Since we had long heard of Dr. Song's "big name," we also had gone to the sanctuary to see what his august appearance was like. By then, it was really bustling and there was hardly a seat untaken. At the podium stood a middle-aged man dressed in a Chinese-style long gown of white silk. His face was thin and his hair was tousled. This was Dr. Song XX [Shangjie].[3] On his left stood a young woman in her thirties(?). I couldn't understand the words that he used and could only watch him wave his arms, stamp his foot, and scream like a traveling medicine peddler. The young woman was an interpreter, and she translated quite fluently what he said in another dialect of Chinese into Cantonese. But he did not wait for the interpreter to finish translating one sentence before he launched into a new one. The faster she translated the faster he spoke. Their voices overlapped, so we didn't know which one to listen to. The longer he went on, the more excited he became, stamping his foot and calling out to heaven—Oh God!—which made him foam at the mouth and caused sweat to drip from his body. After reaching inside his long gown and into his pocket for his handkerchief, he even neglected to re-button his gown. The first part of the sermon was followed by a hymn, ". . . Return home you little lambs who have gone astray . . ." Ha ha, how weird! How could the congregation know how to sing in parts with such harmony? Then I noticed that the only ones singing in parts were the women in several pews at the front—they were Dr. Song's followers. The crusade is to last seven days and nights from May twenty-first to twenty-seventh, with three sermons every day. All members of the troupe (the followers) will do their best to put on a good show.

Dr. Song spoke like a traveling medicine peddler, and his style appealed only to the lowbrow taste of ignorant women. He used "the philosophy of withdrawal from this world and a passive approach to this life" as an anesthetic, and the women who listened to him changed their entire outlook. Since they always had been ignorant and were now being exposed to these "fanatical" words, I wonder where they will end up in the future, for they have "gone astray."[4]

"—Return home you little lambs who have gone astray. Smoking,

3. See n. 1.
4. In these two sentences the author has played upon the double meaning of the character *mi* (which also appears in the term for "superstitions," *mixin*), using it the first time in the sense of "fanatical" (*mi*) and the second time in the sense of "going astray" (*mitu*).

dancing, going to teahouses,[5] and seeing plays—are all sins. Return home you little lambs who have gone astray!" After Dr. Song delivered this message, there was another round of hymns. How unjust! Even seeing plays and going to teahouses are regarded as sins. If so, isn't the whole human race committing sins? I wonder what criminal charges should be brought against those who advocate education through movies? If seeing plays is sinning, aren't those who perform in plays piling sins upon sins? After the sermon, someone invited him to a shop that sells flavored ices. Since he regards going to teahouses as a sinful act, he declined the invitation and went back to have some steamed chicken broth by himself.

He has a doctorate in chemistry from the United States.[6]

20. *Western Gold Coins*

by CHENG CHIHONG,
a woman writing from Suzhou, Jiangsu

At just after four o'clock in the afternoon, I took my nine-year-old son, Yuan, for a walk on a broad street. The sun was shining eastward at an angle on the shops. Pedestrians had just taken off their heavy padded jackets and seemed lively and energetic.

On a walkway where the sun had not reached, a crowd had gathered. Inside the human circle a person dressed in an undistinguished Western suit, wearing glasses with tarnished gold rims, and holding a few copies of a small book with a red and green cover was gesturing wildly and delivering a speech. Behind him was not a shop front but a door that looked as if it had never been opened. Thumbtacked on that door was a colorful picture. The picture showed two roads with many people walking forward on them. The destination on one road was a beautiful city with the two characters "Heavenly City" high on the city wall. People walking on this road all wore clothes that gave them face. The destination on the other road was a fire, painted entirely in red and black colors, which made it all the more frightening. Here there were also two characters, "Fiery Hell." People walking on this road all wore tat-

5. This custom (*yam cha* in Cantonese) involves drinking tea, eating pastries, and engaging in conversation, and it is especially popular among Cantonese.

6. Song Shangjie received his doctorate in chemistry from Ohio State University in 1926. He also received a B.A. from Ohio Wesleyan in 1923 and entered Union Theological Seminary in 1926 before returning from the United States to China in 1927. See Liu, *Song Shangjie zhuan*, pp. 35–37 and 46–51.

tered clothes, and "Sin" was written many times along the way. I could imagine what was going on. Next to the picture was a banner on which was written "XX Church, Preaching Team, Section No. X."

The preacher was talking without a moment's interruption, and the audience was listening intently. My son Yuan wanted to make his way in, so I had to stand there for a little while.

The preacher's hands and feet were moving, the blue veins on his face were popping out, and the longer he talked the more animated he became.

"Western gold coins as big as copper dollars. Western gold coins made of gold." The repeated references out of nowhere to Western gold coins lured me into listening well enough to understand—whereas originally I had been prepared to stand by for just a moment and let my son find out that it was not a game of chance or a new food product for sale before moving on.

The preacher was still speaking without stopping while he waved around the book with the red and green cover:

"He (who this "he" was, was not known) makes many Western gold coins, each as big as a copper dollar, each worth several tens of dollars. He gives these Western gold coins to others. He gives them to many poor people, but he has one condition, which is that he gives only to those people who believe in his word. Otherwise he won't give any. But how is he to give them away? He came up with a good method. One day in the morning he went down under a big bridge. Many people there were coming and going, some of them wealthy and some of them poor. He held up a handful of Western gold coins and shouted:

"'Who wants to buy Western gold coins? Two copper coins buys one. Come quick and buy Western gold coins!'

"Everyone listened, but no one believed it, and everyone said he was a swindler. They thought that no one in this world is such a fool as to have a Western gold coin which he doesn't use himself and instead sells to others for two copper coins. Who would have known that these were real Western gold coins! Seeing no one wanted to buy his Western gold coins, he grabbed a poor person and said to him in all sincerity:

"'This is a Western gold coin. Buy it quick for two copper coins!'

"But the poor person still did not believe his words and angrily said to him:

"'Take your hands off me. If it were a Western gold coin, you'd use it yourself! Don't come along and try to cheat me out of my money.'

"For two days he had Western gold coins for sale under the bridge but couldn't sell a single one, and he sighed:

"'Poor people have no luck. . .'"

Then the preacher caught his breath, the people in the audience also caught their breath, and they all laughed at the poor people who were really out of luck and unreasonably refused to spend two copper coins to buy a Western gold coin. The crowd shifted around for a while but immediately calmed down with the sound of the preacher's voice. He continued to speak:

"On the third day he again went under the bridge to sell. This time a little child who heard he was selling Western gold coins believed his words and used two copper coins of his candy money to buy a Western gold coin. The little child's father, who made a living by working for a silversmith, knew at a glance that it was real gold and immediately took it into the streets to cash it in. Getting forty or fifty dollars made the entire family very happy. Later everybody knew that the child had bought a real Western gold coin and wanted to buy several, but the one selling Western gold coins had long disappeared. Everybody regretted not buying earlier!" The story ended at this point, but the preacher's mouth didn't stop and quickly went on: "Everyone! Just think, these poor people had no luck and didn't get any Western gold coins. What a pity! But a Western gold coin worth only forty or fifty dollars is something that can be eaten up and spent, and there is nothing special about it. What is special is this book." Referring unexpectedly to the book, he immediately lifted up the small book with the red and green cover and showed the cover to people in the outer circle. I saw four not overly large characters written in block style: "Gospel According to Matthew."

The preacher went on: "Once this book is thoroughly studied, it really can't be eaten up or spent. I, your brother, have studied this book for the past several decades and have never suffered. This book is really a precious thing, and now it also sells for two copper coins—" The audience was all listening unwaveringly. Because I had heard the whole story, I called my son to leave. My son came out of the crowd but refused to leave. He paused, looking at the copies of the small book, and then asked me very earnestly:

"Should I use these two coppers of mine to buy this book? Or take them to school tomorrow to give them to my teacher as a contribution for airplanes?"[1]

For a moment, I was speechless.

Twenty-fifth year of the Republic of China [1936], May twenty-first, in Suzhou.

1. This donation probably would have been made to the campaign in the schools to raise money to buy airplanes for the Guomindang government's air force. This campaign is described in more detail in the piece "An Unscheduled Meeting of the Student Body."

21. *The Day of Jesus' Ascension to Heaven*

by ZHANG HUAISU,
a female student writing from Shanghai

Today was the day of Jesus' ascension to heaven. Ours is a church school, so we had a holiday. Ascension Day was a day of joy, and even the sun joined in the festivities by showing his full face and reddening the entire sky very early in the morning.

Today there was a grand sermon. When the big bell in the belltower struck, making deep, heavy, solemn sounds one after another, the student body marched two by two into the holy chapel. Upon reaching the chapel gates, you could hear the music from inside. Looking up, you faced a luminous cross, causing your heart to become calm. The cross was in the middle of the holy dais. On either side of it were vases filled with pure white lotuses, and a deep green curtain formed a backdrop, all giving people a feeling of holiness and solemnity. More than three hundred people, and not a sound. Some knelt and prayed, some sat with bowed heads and meditated. The minister wore a billowing white robe with a purple stole hanging over it. The color purple symbolizes joy, and a purple stole should be worn on Ascension Day. At this moment, all the people stood up. No one spoke, no one laughed, and it was indeed solemn.

First, hymns were sung in deep voices and high voices. If it had been heard elsewhere, this would only be regarded as a pretty sound, good to listen to, but here it gave people a feeling of solemnity. Afterward came praying, reciting of the creed, and listening to the minister's sermon. This minister was an American who spoke broken Shanghai dialect, causing people to have no desire to listen and inevitably making their minds wander off to other places. I was thinking. China has always believed in Buddhism and worshiped Buddhist images. Christianity was imported into China only four or five hundred years ago, but it has spread throughout the entire country. The total number of Christians in the world is about one-third of the world's population, making people realize how influential this religion is. I myself am a person without a conception of religion, and while my family believes in the Buddha, I neither oppose nor endorse it. What I hear and see at school is Christianity. But five years of it has still not made me a Christian. Buddhism and Christianity have the same principle, in that they both seek to achieve happiness for humanity and salvation of the poor through self-denial. But motivations in these two religions differ somewhat, for in Buddhism one acts charitably in order to achieve relief from one's own suffering, repentance of one's own sins, and a life to come. The spirit in which Christians help the poor is certainly worthy of respect but their purpose is to enter heaven and to hope to become faithful children of God. In the same way as the Buddhists they also have superstitions, for aren't kneeling to worship idols and kneeling to worship the cross the same? Heaven and hell are absolutely absurd and laughable. As far as I'm concerned, I absolutely don't believe that there is a Buddha, and I don't believe that there is a Jesus. But I admit that any religion benefits humanity. One day a classmate of mine tried to persuade me, saying, "Hurry up and become a believer. Otherwise you won't be able to go to heaven after you die and never will be saved. I really don't understand why you put up opposition like this!"

I said, "I don't oppose any religion. I have always said that the principle of Christianity is far superior to the principles of other religions and is worth acting upon. But I don't have to become a Christian. I won't have to believe in heaven if I can just look back when I die and see that I have not wasted my entire life. Or if I have done something for people and for myself, then I'll have the spiritual comfort that is the same as going to heaven. The 'life to come' in Buddhism is even more intangible, to the point of being laughable. The life to come is something even more intangible than a shadow. Therefore, I will not become a believer in any religion, and my God or bodhisattva is 'conscience'—"

I was awakened out of my reflections when the student body stood up. The minister had finished delivering his sermon and was about to offer the third prayer. After singing the final hymn, people went out of the chapel as before, two by two, to the sound of music.

Written on May twenty-first.

22. *May Twenty-first in Chengtian*

by YU BAOHUAN,
a male high school student writing from Shaoxing, Zhejiang

The croaking of frogs, *guoguo*, had just quieted down, and the chirping of birds, *jijia*, immediately began to take its place, chasing away the long dark night and awakening people who had been deep asleep. The sky was crowded with dark clouds which made people feel unhappy. But when a gust of wind blew, the clouds broke apart a bit and thinned out a bit, and when the sun came out, they had already gone out of sight. The yellow light shone upon the great earth, and the depressed mood of the past few days suddenly was transformed into happiness.

But unfortunately the lecturer at the morning meeting was once again *him*—an Englishman, Bei XX, a teacher who loves to lecture people. He never steps down off the platform without running over by half an hour into the time for regular classes, and what he says is always something that only he himself understands, screaming his lungs out, high-pitched and low-pitched, making references here, making references there, and in the end making nobody knows what point. Almost everybody in the audience was working on today's geometry or spelling English vocabulary in pencil on scrap paper, and others were leaning on their desks and stealing glances at novels on their laps—*The Water Margin* or *The Dream of the Red Chamber*.[1] But his green eyes were exceptionally sharp. Locking together his eyebrows and fiercely glowering at us, he was quick to use his big, rough, hairy fist to pound on the desk and create a racket that rose up to the high heavens. When all eyes had focused their hatred on him, he began to gesture wildly and said to us: "What I'm teaching you is the way to be a human being, and you may not have to read books, but you have no choice but to hear what I say! For you all have to become human beings!" After this scolding, he forgot where he had left off, and the audience burst out laughing, but this didn't cause his face and ears to redden, and he whispered to a teacher seated next to him asking, "Mr. X, where was I a moment ago?"

He told how "the tomb of Jesus is grander than that of your Sun Yatsen and is worth more money than those ancient Chinese objects that were shipped back from England a few days ago because He uses His blood to wash away our sins. . . ."[2] One student needed to relieve himself

---

1. These two classic novels have been among the most popular of all the fiction available to twentieth-century Chinese readers. See Sidney Shapiro's translation of Shi Naian's *The Water Margin* (*Shuihu zhuan*) under the title *Outlaws of the Marsh*; and David Hawkes's translation of Cao Xueqin's *The Dream of the Red Chamber* (*Hong lou meng*) under the title *The Story of the Stone*.

2. The teacher is probably referring to the Chinese archaeological objects that were displayed in an exhibition held at Burlington House in London early in 1936. Western critics at the time regarded this exhibition as spectacular. See John King Fairbank, *Chinabound*, p. 138.

and was not comfortable either sitting down or standing up and didn't know whether to laugh or cry, but the teacher still vigorously roared on. "Foreign blockhead" was muttered in every corner, but he didn't hear. When he felt he had said enough, he asked us to stand and pray: "Our Father Who art in heaven, . . ."

He asked us to go out onto the grass for our Bible class. We were very pleased but also felt it was strange. Even more strange, he did not stop on the grass. Instead, he tucked away his old leather briefcase and strode off toward the front gate. Making fun of him, we followed at a distance, but he unexpectedly went out through the school gate. Then he turned back toward us, and, waving his hand, beckoned us to race him. With his chest and belly thrust out, he ran forward. We couldn't catch him. Climbing up onto the city wall, he sat down on a corner of it, huffing and puffing. Then he ordered us to sit down around him, and said, "You're useless, useless. When you reach my age, I'm afraid that to walk you will have to have people hold you up! You're useless, useless." This silenced us.

The strong sun shone on our shaved heads, and we all found it hard to take. After he finished talking about the last chapter of Matthew, he stood up and said to us, "Jesus uses blood to wash away our sins. Three days after dying, He rose up, preached to His disciples in the mountains outside the city, and urged them to spread the gospel to all people under heaven. All those who believe in the Lord Jesus Christ will get salvation. If Jesus hadn't used His blood to redeem our sins, I'm afraid I would still be a barbaric person, and the world would have no civilization and no church, and you would have no opportunity to study. Jesus preached to His disciples outside the city, and today I am preaching to you on top of the city wall of Shaoxing, touching your hearts, and touching your eyes. Lock it in your memories!" Ah, we understood his intentions. A villager wearing a dark felt hat was standing alongside, listening out of curiosity to this foreigner's spoken Chinese. He saw the villager and asked him to leave. I asked, "Why not let him listen to the gospel?" He said, "Hmm! This is going to the office."[3] We laughed at his mistake in Chinese as we came down and walked back to the gate. Then he got onto his bicycle and peddled home.

---

3. Here the foreigner made the following error. He said *shang ban* ("This is going to the office") when he should have said *shang ke* ("This is a class"), mistakenly assuming that *ban*, which can also mean "a class," could be used in conjunction with *shang* to mean "having a class."

23. *How Churches Are Establishing Power*

by HE XIN,
a man writing from Shantou, Guangdong

Nightfall—all around the area where I live, a deadly silence descended.

The Protestant church across the street from where I live, however, had its door flung wide open, and its light shone upon the dark streets. Inside was a sprinkling of people. Sitting at the center of the dais in four chairs were two ministers in Chinese-style long gowns and two ministers in Western-style suits (one of them a Westerner). High behind them hung a brass cross about two feet long glittering in the reflected light. The building was spacious and deserted, but it had an aura of piety which kept people silent.

A piano began to play, and more than ten young girls wearing high-collared, Chinese-style dresses of white nylon, holding the *Book of Hymns*, began to sing on the dais. The voices were low and soft, and they made people pensive and humble in the presence of God.

After a prayer, the Western minister rose and began to speak. He looked as though he had mixed Chinese and foreign blood, but he spoke fluent Northern dialect, and another minister translated what he said into local dialect. His topic was "How to Recruit Volunteer Workers."

As a foreigner, his language was not free from "Europeanization," so it was not easy to understand. He spoke in a very deep voice and at a slow pace. The frequent smiles that radiated from his wrinkled face showed that he was an old pro, poised and competent. From my standpoint as a non-Christian, this gentleman was capable of being a manipulator.

"Our church is dying and has not adapted to the current national crisis. It has not been guided by the light of the Lord, which redeems the people of the nation from their sins. Affairs of the church have rested too exclusively upon the minister or the intern. Therefore the work of the church has not expanded and it has stagnated, half alive, half dead. Meanwhile, many youths who once received nurturing, training, and assistance from the church cease to serve the church as soon as they enter society. Why is this so? This is undoubtedly because the church has not made them aware of the work that needs to be done and has not given them work to do. In order not to spurn Jesus' will (Jesus asks us to follow Him, not merely to come to church on Sunday and contribute a little money), we must follow the Lord and work together. Only then will we become good, true Christians.

"Therefore, far more people are needed to carry out this task. These people have to be trained, and we must establish a training corps where various kinds of problems that the church needs to confront will be regularly discussed. In this way, we will produce workers who are true volunteers. I personally know of many youths who are willing to serve the church enthusiastically. A certain church in Beiping has already created three committees in charge of establishing a training corps. Members of these three committees include accountants from banks, clerks from the streetcar company, and ministers. They have decided upon the following five kinds of work:

"1. the problems of children,
"2. the problems of youth,
"3. women and the family,
"4. evangelism,
"5. general methods of governing a church under the elders and minister.

"Since in the past the shortcoming of the church was to put the work too exclusively on the few people in charge and ignore the need to work together and share the work, a situation was created in which the preacher preached to himself and the listeners listened without hearing. As a result, even the most enthusiastic members of the fellowship severed their ties and left the church.

"Therefore, this church must immediately address the following four questions:

"1. Is there a need for recruiting volunteer workers?
"2. What kind of work would they do?
"3. How many people should be recruited?
"4. How can this be done?

"But let me ask you this: Besides the children of the members of the fellowship and those in the church school, do you know how many children there are in the vicinity of this church? Aren't there lots of youths all around us? How might we convince them and help them to recognize God? You must realize that a good and vital church is built upon the wholehearted cooperation of all the people. The minister or the intern cannot do it alone.

"The churches in Beiping, Tianjin, Shanghai, Hangzhou, Guangzhou, Fuzhou, and Xiamen are now conducting enthusiastic discussions on these questions. Some of them are already implementing their ideas. I fervently hope that members of this church will very quickly work out a concrete outline of the work to be done. To be more effective, you might unite with all church members throughout the city and together shoulder the responsibility for getting the work started."[1]

In the midst of the wailing of holy hymns, I walked out. Biting my lip, I thought to myself:

"Religion, like opium, is more than ever poisoning both innocent young people like us and children!"

---

1. Between 1925 and 1936 Protestant mission boards accelerated what they called a "devolution" of the duties in China's churches from foreigners to Chinese Christians. In 1925, the number of foreign Protestant missionaries reached a peak of 8,300 (the majority of whom were Americans), and by 1936 the number dropped to 6,020 (with 2,808 from the United States and Canada). See James C. Thomson, Jr., *While China Faced West*, pp. 35–36.

PART IV

"Chinese Traitors" and the Enemy

"Chinese Traitors" and the Enemy

The term "Chinese traitor" (*Han jian*), which could also be translated as "Chinese evildoer," was used by contributors to *One Day in China* to denounce their countrymen who served as cultural intermediaries between the Japanese authorities and the Chinese population or who benefited legally and economically from personal contacts with the Japanese authorities. Significantly, these contributors did not apply the term to everyone who participated in the process of Japanese penetration of Chinese territory. Instead, they reserved it for the literate elite, as distinct from the illiterate common people. In Section A, those writing from Northeast China (which had been occupied by the Japanese since 1931 and was ruled by a Japanese puppet government under the name "Manzhouguo") and from the so-called "autonomous" areas of North China (which had been controlled by Japanese-sponsored governments since late 1935) acknowledged that the common people as well as the elite were forced to yield to the Japanese. However, they accused only members of the elite, not the common people, of being Chinese traitors (nos. 1–6). Similarly, in Section B, those troubled by Japanese penetration of unoccupied China blamed members of the elite who had become Chinese traitors for facilitating this penetration (nos. 7–13). And in Section C, those describing the opposition to Japanese aggression in unoccupied China celebrated the stands taken by people from a cross-section of the population but highlighted the support for the anti-Japanese resistance among the common people rather than the literate elite (nos. 14–19).

Writing from areas under Japanese political domination, the contributors in Section A did not all use the same criteria for determining elite status, but the people whom they accused of being Chinese traitors were all members of an elite broadly defined. Contributors of two pieces (nos. 1 and 2) identified Chinese traitors as members of exploitative social classes—the urban bourgeoisie and rural gentry—and thereby made a direct connection between Chinese traitors and class conflict (as Chinese Communist writers also did at this time).[1] The other contributors in Section A presented no class analysis of Chinese traitors. Those whom they described served in a variety of positions and performed a variety of functions: Some held paid posts under the Japanese-controlled governments in "Manzhouguo" or the "autonomous" areas of North China as officials and police officers (nos. 1–3); others prepared or published school books, propaganda, or other written materials on behalf of the Japanese (nos. 4–5); and still others owned property and exploited their personal contacts with the Japanese for economic gain (no. 6). All of these were activities that could be engaged in only by literate elites possessing some basis for distinguishing themselves from the common people—if not class status, then education, wealth, or shared cultural background and personal connections.

In Section B, contributors writing from unoccupied areas about Chinese traitors also confined their use of the term to members of the literate elite. According to their descriptions, Chinese traitors formed the cultural bridges over which the Japanese extended their influence into parts of the country not yet under Japanese political domination. Specifically, Chinese traitors were accused of opening the way for the Japanese drive by subscribing in the schools to Chinese-language publications from Japanese-controlled areas (no. 7), by teaching the Chinese language to the Japanese (no. 8), and by preparing and endorsing propaganda for them (no. 9)—tasks that could have been performed only by literate members of the population.

The authors of the pieces in Sections A and B by no means denied —and frequently lamented—the fact that illiterate Chinese served Japan's purposes in China. For example, they noted that Chinese smugglers slipped untaxed Japanese goods past customs barriers, and that Chinese merchants distributed and sold such contraband (nos. 9–13). The smuggling had begun as early as 1934 with the resumption of trade between Northeast China and North China—a trade which had ceased during Japan's military invasion of the Northeast in 1931 and had been barred by military authorities until after the signing of the Tanggu Truce by the Japanese Guandong Army and the Chinese Army in 1933. The scale of the

1. For an example of a piece by a Chinese Communist writer identifying Chinese traitors with the rural landlord class, see the one-act play, "Dadao Han jian" (Down with Chinese Traitors) by Zhao Shuli, which was first performed in the same year that *One Day in China* was written, 1936, and has been published in Xianggang wenxue yanjiu she, comp., *Zhongguo xin wenxue daxi xubian*, vol. 9, pp. 907–17. See also Donald G. Gillin, "'Peasant Nationalism' in the History of Chinese Communism," p. 288.

smuggling expanded enormously in 1936, reaching a peak in the middle of the year (just as these pieces were being written) at which time every week an average of 2 million *yuan* (U.S. $700,000) worth of sugar, artificial silk yarn, kerosene, and other products was shipped without payment of duties from Japanese-occupied areas to the city of Tianjin in unoccupied China. During the entire year, according to the Maritime Customs' report for 1936, smugglers avoided paying (and thus prevented the Chinese government from collecting) a total of 50 million *yuan* (U.S. $17 million) worth of goods.[2] This smuggling, in which Chinese non-elites played a role, served as the basis for many of the observations about Japan's effects upon China in Sections B and C. (In these pieces no Chinese admitted to knowing a Japanese, and only a few seemed to have ever seen one. Not until a year after these pieces were written did the Japanese begin the full-scale military invasion that resulted in their occupation of the heavily populated eastern part of China from Beijing all the way to Guangzhou, and only then, during the Sino-Japanese War of 1937–45, were many Chinese to see Japanese for the first time.)

Nonetheless, however much the common people served as smugglers and facilitated Japanese penetration of unoccupied China, they were not called Chinese traitors. Why the collaborators among the common people were not designated Chinese traitors is not explained in *One Day in China*, but the contributors' descriptions of these people as ignorant, passive, weak, unemployed, or desperate imply that non-elite collaborators were not regarded as Chinese traitors because they—unlike elite collaborators—lacked political consciousness, were easily manipulated (especially by Chinese traitors), and, therefore, were considered innocent of the principal charge against Chinese traitors: moral and political capitulation to the Japanese.

This restriction of the term Chinese traitors to the literate elite may be explained partially, but not entirely, by its past usage. When first coined, probably in the seventeenth century, the term was apparently used to criticize collaborators among the literate elite, namely those officials who agreed to serve China's conquerors beginning in 1644 after the fall of a Chinese dynasty, the Ming, and the founding of the Manchus' dynasty, the Qing.[3] Later it was used more broadly. During the Opium War of

2. See the Maritime Customs, *The Trade of China, 1936*, pp. 7–8, quoted at length in T. A. Bisson, *Japan in China*, pp. 130–34. See also Burke Inlow, "Japan's 'Special Trade' in North China, 1935–37," pp. 150–56.

3. Tanaka Masami has advanced the plausible hypothesis (not yet substantiated) that these were the origins of the term Chinese traitor. See his "Ahen sensōzen ni okeru 'kankan' no mondai," p. 4.

1840–42, for example, Chinese in and around Guangzhou used it to criticize anyone—illiterate as well as literate—who was believed to favor appeasement of the British enemy; and during the decade preceding the revolution of 1911, propagandists used it to attack anyone—again, illiterate as well as literate—who was believed to support the Manchu leaders of the Qing dynasty which the revolution ultimately overthrew.[4] After the fall of the Qing, however, Chinese nationalists applied the term more specifically to Chinese leaders and especially to those believed guilty of capitulating to Japan in negotiations over a whole series of Sino-Japanese conflicts: the May Fourth Incident of 1919, the May Thirtieth Incident of 1925, the Nanjing Incident of 1927, the Jinan Tragedy of 1928, the Wanbao Shan Tragedy of 1931, the Mukden (Shenyang) Incident of 1931, the Shanghai Incident of 1932, the Tanggu Truce of 1933, and the December Ninth Incident of 1935 (each of which is cited in one or more of the following pieces and identified either in the text or in footnotes).[5] If the pieces in *One Day in China* are any indication, by 1936 the term Chinese traitor was used to criticize a group larger than the handful of national leaders at the top of the Guomindang government but no larger than the literate elite in Chinese society. None of the contributors, incidentally, branded Chiang Kaishek or any other national leader in unoccupied China a Chinese traitor, but some—for example in no. 14—showed contempt for the policy of nonresistance with which Chiang was identified in May 1936, and almost all were implicitly critical of China's leaders for not taking a stronger stand against the Japanese at this time.[6]

In Section C, contributors writing from unoccupied China described people representing the antithesis of Chinese traitors: Chinese patriots. While some of the common people described in Sections A and B might have been politically passive, permitting Chinese traitors to dupe them into collaborating with the Japanese, those described in Section C were politically assertive and deeply committed to opposing Japanese aggression. The people appearing in these pieces came from various back-

4. On the usage of the term during the Opium War, see Frederic Wakeman, Jr., *Strangers at the Gate*, chap. 4 and passim; Arthur Waley, *The Opium War through Chinese Eyes*, pp. 222–23; and Tanaka Masami, "Ahen sensō jiki ni okeru kankan no ichi kōsatsu." On the usage of the term during the first decade of the twentieth century, see *Min bao*, vol. 2, pp. 42–43 and passim. (Articles in this journal referring to Chinese traitors appeared every year between 1905 and 1910.)

5. On Chinese students' use of the term to denounce officials in the Beijing government between 1918 and 1922, see Chow Tse-tsung, *The May Fourth Movement*, pp. 106–16; and Madeleine Chi, "Ts'ao Ju-lin (1876–1966)."

6. On other protests in China against Chiang's policy regarding the Japanese at this time, See Israel, *Student Nationalism in China*, p. 158; Israel and Klein, *Rebels and Bureaucrats*, pp. 110–11; and Eastman, *The Abortive Revolution*, pp. 249–50.

grounds but spoke as if with one voice. Children as well as adults, women as well as men, uneducated factory workers as well as educated clerks, and peasants in the countryside as well as students in the cities all denounced the Japanese as a despised enemy—racially offensive, culturally barbaric, politically devious, militarily ruthless. As described in Section C, these Chinese neither capitulated to the Japanese (as had Chinese traitors) nor lacked political consciousness (as did common people collaborating with the Japanese). They constituted a third group ardently advocating resistance against Japan.

These three groups—Chinese traitors, Chinese collaborators among the common people, and Chinese patriots—have taken on special significance in the study of Chinese history. Chinese writing about the history of Sino-Japanese relations still use the term Chinese traitor to condemn the Chinese leaders who handled Sino-Japanese negotiations before the Sino-Japanese War of 1937–45; only recently have they begun to consider alternatives to it.[7] And for Western historians, collaborators among the common people and patriots as well as traitors have assumed special significance because of their possible relevance to a major controversy in modern Chinese history: the debate over the origins of mass nationalism. In the course of this long and lively debate, some scholars have asserted that Chinese from all strata of society had a well-developed national consciousness before the full-scale Japanese invasion in 1937.[8] Others have argued that only urban elites had this consciousness before the Japanese invasion and that peasants were converted into nationalists during the Sino-Japanese War of 1937–45.[9] Still others have maintained that the Chinese population as a whole did not become imbued with nationalism even through their experiences during this war.[10]

The pieces in this part of *One Day in China*, written five years after the Japanese invasion of Northeast China and more than a year before the Japanese invasion of North China, supply evidence relevant to this debate (Section C lending support to the first position and Sections A and B to the second or third positions), but they do not settle it, for they do not indicate the relative numerical strengths of the Chinese traitors, non-elite collaborators, and ardent patriots over a long period of time. And yet, though they do not say how many Chinese collaborated or opposed col-

7. Chi, "Ts'ao Ju-lin (1876–1966)," p. 160, n. 65.

8. See Stuart Schram, *Mao Tse-tung*, p. 203n; and Maurice Meisner, "Yenan Communism and the Rise of the Chinese People's Republic," p. 280.

9. Chalmers A. Johnson, *Peasant Nationalism and Communist Power*, pp. 1–6, 23–26, and passim; and Chalmers A. Johnson, "Peasant Nationalism Revisited."

10. Gillin, "'Peasant Nationalism' in the History of Chinese Communism," p. 280; Lloyd E. Eastman, "Facets of an Ambivalent Relationship," pp. 301–03.

laboration with the Japanese, they do reveal what vehement language opponents of collaboration used at this time. As our introductions to Parts I, II, and III have shown, contributors writing on other subjects also used vehement language to denounce people for abusing their positions as privileged members of a "family," as self-seeking "heads," or as promoters of "superstitions." But judging from the contexts in which they were used, none of these epithets was as damning as "Chinese traitor." It was the worst thing said in *One Day in China* about anybody.[11]

11. Not surprisingly, soon after the Japanese invasion and occupation of China's eastern coastal area (including Shanghai) between 1937 and 1938, the government in Japanese-occupied Nanjing banned *One Day in China*. See Xin min hui zhongyang zhidao bu diaocha ke, ed., *Jinzhi tushu mulu*, p. 102.

A. Collaboration with the Japanese in Occupied China

1. *A Letter from the Northeast*

by MENG WEI,
*a male college student writing near Yingkou,
Liaoning*

My dear friend:

Three days after we parted in Tianjin, I finally reached home safely. Along the way, even though I was stopped, questioned, and followed many times, I managed to get out of many, many tight spots. I am still quite worried about whether I will encounter trouble at home. But, my friend, even though I have been here just a few days, I have seen many things since returning to my home village.

In this letter, let me report to you only two events to make the point: One is what I have seen with my own eyes in Yingkou, and the other is the change that has taken place in my home village during the five years under [Japanese] occupation.[1]

At two o'clock on the afternoon of the tenth, I left on the Beiping-Shenyang Express and then changed to the Yingkou-Goubangzi Line and came home via Yingkou. As I took my seat on the train, I discovered I was being followed by a Chinese-traitor plainclothes detective. He sat next to me and, posing as an ordinary passenger, periodically looked over and spoke to me. At first we chatted casually about everyday matters, and then we gradually shifted to the situation in China proper and recent student movements. He blabbed on and on throughout the whole trip. I disliked him very much, but I had to pretend to be interested. When the

1. China's northeastern provinces had been occupied by Japan since 1931. See the introduction to Part IV.

train arrived in Yingkou, I was immediately grabbed by the XX [Japanese] military police, who took me to the Yingkou Shoreline Police Station. At that moment, my friend, I knew immediately what had given rise to my misfortune. The Shoreline Police Station is located in a building which used to be a school of commerce before the September Eighteenth Incident.[2] Besides myself, a young, husky ricksha puller was there, having been brought in before I was. He was on his knees crouching like a mouse listening to a Chinese traitor tongue-lash him. At first I thought that he had committed a major crime as serious as murder. Later I learned that he had delivered a XX [Japanese] woman to the wrong address. Before they let him go, they beat him severely and fined him two dollars. My friend, when I saw him so humiliated and heard his screams, it broke my heart. But when I looked up at the smug Chinese traitor, I became angry, and it took me a long time to regain control of myself.

My interrogator was typical of the [Japanese] "people from the friendly power."[3] He spoke beautiful Chinese, asking questions more or less similar to the ones that the detective had asked on the Yingkou-Goubangzi train. But this time I had to write down in detail my native place, my address, and the names of my ancestors for three generations. In the end his face became more serious and he said to me, "You are a student. We have universities in Manzhouguo[4] and they are free of charge. Why must you go to China to study? Hey, it's all right if you go to China as long as you report monthly on the situation concerning the Chinese student movement. Otherwise, I will consider you a member of the group that opposes Manzhouguo and resists X [Japan]." My friend, I could not swallow all those insults. I would have been glad to die instead. I refused to be intimidated by him, but in the end my life was not taken.

Not until eight o'clock did I get out of the Shoreline Police Station. Darkness covered the whole world and rain began to fall.

I reached home at noon the next day. My father is already recovering from his illness, so please don't worry about him.

2. The events of September 18, 1931, marked the beginning of the Japanese territorial invasion of Northeast China. See "A Never-to-Be-Forgotten Class," n. 4.

3. Meng Wei used the term "friendly power" (*you bang*) sarcastically, implying that Japan was the opposite—an unfriendly power—in China. Japanese leaders used this term at the time as a literal characterization of their country's relations with China; but Meng Wei, like several other contributors in the following pieces, put it in quotation marks and thus conveyed the impression that the Japanese were hypocritical to describe their relations with China in these words. On Japanese conceptions of their role in China during the 1930s, see James B. Crowley, "A New Deal for Japan and Asia;" and James B. Crowley, "Intellectuals as Visionaries of the New Asian Order."

4. "Manzhouguo" was the name that the Japanese gave to the puppet state which they set up in 1932 to rule Northeast China. See "A Never-to-Be-Forgotten Class," n. 5.

I was away from my home village for five years. Before returning this time, I had already anticipated that things would be bad. But I did not expect it to be utterly depressed, demoralized, and bleak. My friend, my home village, renowned for its prosperity five years ago, is now so poor that hardly any smoke can be seen rising from the chimneys of cooking stoves throughout the village. The peasants in my home village live in fear, hunger, cold, and oppression. The walls in my home village are full of advertisements for opium and heroin. In the streets of my home village, incidents regularly occur in which Chinese traitors and XX [Japanese] bullies[5] force the peasants to buy and sell drugs.[6] In the outlying areas around my home village there are many more people sobbing in grief over new grave sites. Oh, my home village! Everything has changed in my home village.

As a result, the "bandit" problem is extremely "serious." In my home village not only has there been an increase in the power of isolated small bands of "local bandits" who resist the X [Japanese], but also there has been a .daily increase in the power of the People's Revolutionary Army,[7] who are scattered all over, deep in the mountains around my home village. Members of the People's Revolutionary Army are aware of mistakes made by the Volunteer Army,[8] and already have a tightly knit organization and iron discipline. It is said that they do not take encounters with the XX [Japanese] army lightly, and that they engage in encounters only if they are sure of victory. Among them there are no classes and no party affiliations. They are of one heart, and that heart is set on resistance against X [Japan] and on national salvation. Their armies have naturally

5. The Japanese term (*rōnin*) here translated as "bullies" referred to wandering masterless samurai earlier in Japanese history. It is used in this context more broadly to describe any Japanese able to take advantage of Japan's military occupation of Northeast China.

6. In 1936 there was a heavy traffic in drugs within the Northeast and from the Northeast into North China. See "May Twenty-first in Tangshan," n. 6.

7. The People's Revolutionary Army (*Renmin geming jun*) was commanded by Zhang Xueliang, a warlord whose army (and whose father's army before it) had dominated Northeast China in the early twentieth century until driven out by the Japanese invasion of 1931. In May 1936 the officers and troops of the People's Revolutionary Army had their headquarters at Xian in Northwest China. See Wu Tien-wei, *The Sian Incident*, chaps. 1–2.

8. The Volunteer Army (*Yiyong jun*) led the Chinese resistance against the Japanese in Northeast China between 1931 and 1936. The leadership of this resistance shifted during this period. Initially, it was a spontaneous movement under the command of former military officers, police chiefs, and members of secret societies. These commanders were encouraged by the Manchurian warlord, Zhang Xueliang, but he, under orders from Chiang Kaishek to follow the Guomindang's policy of nonresistance, did not have the Volunteer Army under his direct command. Before 1932, the Chinese Communists also played no role in the anti-Japanese resistance in Northeast China, but by 1935 and 1936, they were the predominant element in it. See Lee Chong-Sik, "The Chinese Communist Party and the Anti-Japanese Movement in Manchuria."

won the support of the laboring masses who serve as their base. All the well-to-do long ago became Chinese traitors, and the small merchants are still fantasizing that they will be able to "eat their regular bowl of rice and remain submissive subjects." Therefore, only the peasants are throwing themselves into the revolution more and more every day. The most shameless here are "officials who have forsaken their country." Most pitiful and yet annoying are the petty bourgeoisie, and most admirable are the peasants! This is because the peasants have suffered most.

Yesterday police from the XX Police Station again came to my home and searched it. Even my neighbors became involved. I am not at all certain that I can continue to live here. I hope that my father's condition will improve soon, and then I will immediately get out of this set of tiger's jaws.

I am taking a risk in sending this letter. Although the signature is false, you can undoubtedly tell that it's me. I am not at all sure that you will receive this letter. In any case, we will soon see each other again. My friend, be diligent!

Wei   Sent on May twenty-first

2. *A Letter to Me*

by YIMIN *(pseud.),*
a man enclosing a letter by BAICHUAN *(pseud.) from*
Yutian, Hebei

The following letter was sent by a friend from Yutian County in East Hebei. In this letter, he has given a clear and general description of the situation in East Hebei and also has pointed out the road that we should take. After reading it, I was so moved that tears were almost trickling down. Since by coincidence he wrote this letter on May Twenty-first, I am offering it to "One Day in China" before I have gotten him to agree to it. I imagine that he will forgive me for doing so.

I, Yimin, have written the above and attached it as a note,
May twenty-seventh

Brother Yimin:

At a time when our military and political authorities are walking away from North China, especially East Hebei, as though these were hu-

"China Is in Danger of Being Sliced up like a Melon," a political cartoon from *La Satire chinoise: Politique et sociale* (Beijing, 1933), p. 7.

man excrement, you have paid attention to this area where mountains and rivers have changed color, you have offered comfort, and you have taken pity on those of us who have been abandoned, even though you are not a Northerner, are not from East Hebei, and have no military or political responsibility. How grateful we should be!

Your letter asks about the current situation in East Hebei. Because what I have seen and heard is limited, I'm afraid that it is difficult to give you a satisfactory answer. All I can do is give you a general report on this county and maybe you can infer what the general situation in East Hebei is like.

Our county of Yutian, located to the east of the Beiping-Tianjin Railroad, is on a vast plain that extends as far as the eye can see. Its products are plentiful, its cultural level is rather high, and in the past it could have been called a land of happiness. Despite being looted and pillaged by soldiers and bandits several times since the founding of the Republic [in 1911], it has managed to survive. Unfortunately, in the twenty-second year of the Republic [1933] our government signed the Tanggu Truce with the "friendly power [Japan]."[1] Our county was said to be in the so-called

1. Baichuan used the term "friendly power" sarcastically, implying that Japan was the opposite—an unfriendly power—in China. See "A Letter from the Northeast," n. 3.

"military zone" and was thus heartlessly discarded.[2] During the past two or three years, the fate of the people throughout the entire county has tragically declined! The trouble created by the [Japanese] bullies,[3] the spread of drugs,[4] and the armed robberies by local bandits and by members of the Peace Preservation Forces[5] in the military zone are all death blows to the common people.

Last year the Chinese traitor, Yin Rugeng, and other clowns who have sold out their country and allowed the "friendly power" to lead them by the nose proclaimed the "autonomy of East Hebei."[6] Since then, people throughout the entire county have had a full dose of being slaves in a forsaken country.

In the so-called East Hebei Autonomous Government,[7] as in the illegitimate Manzhouguo,[8] though in principle Chinese traitors take charge and have political power, in reality they only beg for a bowl of rice to eat while watching the expressions on the imperialists' faces. All executive

2. This "military zone" was a demilitarized zone south of the Great Wall which included virtually all of Hebei province north of the Beijing-Tianjin area. It had been established under the provisions of the Tanggu Truce, which was signed by the Japanese Guandong Army and the Chinese Army on May 31, 1933, to end the fighting between Japanese and Chinese troops in the area. By creating this demilitarized zone, the Tanggu Truce brought to a halt the Japanese military advance into China (which had begun with the Japanese invasion of Northeast China in 1931) but only temporarily. Subquently, during the Sino-Japanese War of 1937–45, the Japanese invaded and occupied first North China and then all of eastern China—the richest and most populous parts of the country. See Bisson, *Japan in China*, pp. 43–47.

3. The term translated here as "[Japanese] bullies" (*rōnin*) is from Japanese. See "A Letter from the Northeast," n. 5.

4. In 1936 there was a heavy traffic in drugs within the Northeast and from the Northeast into North China. See "May Twenty-first in Tangshan," n. 6.

5. Some units that were called Peace Preservation Forces were pro-Japanese and some were anti-Japanese. The ones mentioned here seem to have been pro-Japanese. Cf. "A Sketch of May Twenty-first in Beitong County," n. 1.

6. On November 25, 1935, Yin Rugeng, a Japanese-educated Chinese, declared "autonomy" for the demilitarized zone plus the four nearby counties. He thus detached this area from the jurisdiction of the Guomindang government. Though Yin was nominally in charge of this area, the Japanese Army held actual control. See Kahn, "Doihara Kenji and the North China Autonomy Movement," pp. 192–93; and n. 7 below.

7. Yin Rugeng announced the founding of the "East Hebei Autonomous Council for the Prevention of Communism" on November 25, 1935, with himself as chairman. Its name was changed to the "East Hebei Autonomous Government for the Prevention of Communism" on December 25, 1935. This government administered a total of twenty-two counties in Hebei province covering more than 10,000 square miles with a population of about five million. Yutian County, whose local government is described here, was one of these twenty-two counties. See ibid., pp. 192–93; and Inlow, "Japan's 'Special Trade' in North China," pp. 141 and 149.

8. "Manzhouguo" was the name that the Japanese gave to the puppet state which they set up in 1932 to rule Northeast China. See "A Never-to-Be-Forgotten Class," n. 5.

power is in the hands of people from the "friendly power," and Chinese traitors only serve as the tiger's claws! Take our Yutian for example. The county government engages a XX [Japanese] adviser, and he is the real county head. He has absolute power regarding all executive and legislative decision making. All official documents are read and approved by him. Sometimes he even tries cases in person. He is truly a person who has "the power to give life and take it away as he pleases." The county head merely follows orders. Below the county government are various departments and bureaus, and most of these have engaged advisers from the "friendly power." These so-called advisers are in fact the department heads' and bureau heads' daddies. What else? The village normal school and the county middle school have been forced to hire people from the "friendly power" as Japanese language teachers and school physicians. Besides carrying out the policy of cultural invasion and paralyzing the population, their most important responsibility is the surveillance of anti-Japanese and anti-Manzhouguo dangerous elements. The cruel punishment of "execution for gathering to talk"[9] is in force once again today. The army of occupation includes not only the Japanese Regular Army, which is stationed in the county seat, but also several dozen Japanese military police and some members of the East Hebei Peace Preservation Forces. These troops have as their mission to exterminate the "dangerous elements."

Elementary school textbooks have been completely changed since the semester started this spring. The new replacements for the textbooks are a revised version of elementary school textbooks used in "Manzhouguo." The contents promote a spirit of coexistence and coprosperity among China, Japan, and "Manzhouguo," with the ultimate aim of obliterating the Chinese people's national consciousness. The historical materials concerning past national humiliations either twist the facts or ignore them completely. Although middle schools are using the old textbooks at the moment, the books' heads and legs have been chopped off, mutilating them beyond recognition. This is the kind of education that is given to people in a forsaken country.

Activities of Japanese and Korean bullies are everywhere, reaching into every nook and cranny. They openly set up gambling rings, organize numbers games, sell drugs, blackmail law-abiding citizens, and make connections with local bandits—all shameless rackets that they are fully

9. This ancient expression seems to have originated with Qin Shi Huangdi (reigned 221–206 B.C.), a historical figure who was notorious for his Draconian laws. Our translation of the phrase is taken from Ssu-ma Ch'ien, *Records of the Grand Historian of China*, vol. 1, p. 90.

capable of operating. People fear them as though they were tigers, and officials in the government revere them as though they were gods. Here the sun is blotted out, darkness has descended, and we truly do not know what kind of world there will be for this human society!

The economic situation in this county has reached the point of total collapse. This county was famous for producing cloth, and no less than several tens of thousands of people have made their living in the cloth business. Since the dumping of untaxed Japanese goods in large volume, this county's textile industry has gone completely bankrupt. The life of the peasants is even more indescribably painful. Flood and drought have caused famines, and crops have failed year after year. Foodstuffs cannot be imported from outside the Great Wall because that area is controlled by Japan. As a result, the price of food has skyrocketed, and people are in a panic over food shortages. On top of this are oppressive taxes and sur-taxes on every last item, trouble made by bullies, and local bandits as thick as the hair on your head. Peasants have reached the stage where they have no way out. In summer and autumn last year, there were already violent waves of millet and rice riots. This year it goes without saying that the same will be true. Ai, the taste of living in a forsaken country is hard to take!

Finally, let me comment on the reactions of the people in this county to the present situation. In general, the people can be divided into three groups. The first group is the big gentry and landlord class and some intellectuals affiliated with this class. In order to protect their own property and status, they have willingly become the filial sons and submissive grandsons of imperialism. They were the first to welcome Japan. They are also the ones who invoke the enemy's power and oppress people in their own country. Now is a happy time for them. Sometimes their schemes are even more terrifying than those of their masters!

The second group lives without a sense of purpose, numbly, having lost all feeling. Included in this group are intellectuals, workers, and peasants. They are people who are utterly submissive. They are not Chinese traitors, but they don't dare resist. They are barely holding on and keeping up day by day. If someone will encourage these pitiful and weak people, they are not unsalvageable.

The third group consists of the dangerous elements whom the "friendly power" most fears. Included in this group are progressive intellectuals and awakened workers and peasants. They know that they have suffered the tragedy of losing their country because imperialists have invaded and Chinese traitors and thieves willing to sell the country have shamelessly sold out. The Chinese nation has absolutely no way out, and the individual has no way out unless these people are eliminated. With this awareness, the dangerous elements are brave even under extraordinarily hazardous circumstances. Right now they are using various methods and opportunities and are bravely and decisively marching down the road toward national liberation. They will deliver the deathblow to the imperialists. They are the saviors of the Chinese nation. For them, the future is unlimited. Come, let us give them our blessings and pray for their ultimate victory! That's all there is to it. I salute you!

Your brother, Baichuan, May Twenty-first

3. *A Sketch of May Twenty-first in Beitong County*

by HUANA *(pseud.)*,
a man writing from Beitong, Hebei

In front of Guanshu Gate (the south gate of the Tong county seat): Soldiers stood dressed in two different colors. On the left, dressed in gray military uniforms, were members of the Big Sword Forces who had participated in the resistance at the Great Wall. On the right, dressed in olive drab uniforms, were members of the Peace Preservation Forces (that is, the Peace Preservation Forces for the military zone which was formed after the signing of the Tanggu Truce)—sometimes also known as the Public Security Police Force of the East Hebei Government.[1]

The West Granary was a place to store grain during the Qing dynasty [1644–1912]. What has become of it now? Originally it was a vacant field where troops drilled; now it is covered with trees. In the northernmost part are cedar trees planted in a circle. The tree in the middle is the big-

---

1. The Big Sword Forces were anti-Japanese and the Peace Preservation Forces were pro-Japanese. Huana probably bothered to give both names for the latter organization because one of its names, the Peace Preservation Forces (*Baoan dui*), was a source of confusion at this time. This name was used by militia units at the county level under the Guomindang government in areas not occupied by Japan, and it was retained by the Japanese in areas that they occupied as the name for their puppet troops. Accordingly, some military units that bore this name were anti-Japanese and others were pro-Japanese not only in 1936 but throughout the Sino-Japanese War of 1937–45. See Johnson, *Peasant Nationalism and Communist Power*, p. 211, n. 77. On recruitment and organization of the anti-Japanese Peace Preservation Forces, see Tien, *Government and Politics*, pp. 101 and 111. On the Tanggu Truce, see "A Letter to Me," n. 2.

gest. Standing next to it is an enamel plaque which is inscribed in large characters, "Planted by Council Head X XX [Yin Rugeng] of the East Hebei Autonomous Government."[2] On all four sides are plaques next to trees planted by staff officers and secretary-general, X XX, X XX, X XX among others. A little to the southwest there is a grove of fruit trees (including peaches and plums). In the middle is a wooden placard on which is written, "Special Senior [Japanese] Adviser XXXX [Minami] Jirō." On all four sides are the names of [Japanese] advisers, XXX [Itagaki Seishi]rō, and XX [Koiso Kunia]ki.[3] Further south is a grove of cedars and a grove of fruit trees.

On West Street: Several Korean laundries have recently opened. Several Koreans were in front of these laundries. The Metro Bar of a certain [Japanese] nationality[4] had windows of colored glass. Inside a gramophone was playing. A drugstore had at its entrance a huge red advertisement featuring a man wearing an Eastern [Japanese] mustache and four Chinese characters: "University Brand Eye Medicine."[5] To the south was a tent with a triangular roof made of bamboo mats. Over the entrance was written "Japan-Hebei Movie Theater." I went in but found it dull, so I left. One other thing: The Bank of China and the post office mailbox remained unchanged.

By the Drum Tower and Main Street: On all shopkeepers' shirts were badges on which was written, "East Hebei Government Temporary License Number XX."

The Za Bridge, the Gu Building, and the Randeng Tower (built during the Zhenguan year period [A.D. 627–50] in the Tang dynasty) remained unchanged.

In a certain small alley: At the entrance to a ramshackle building hung a sign saying, "Ni yao xi ma? Qing jinlai." [This sign was meant to say, "Do you want to have some fun? Please come in." However,] ("Ni yao xi" should be if written in correct Chinese "Ni yao ne?")[6]

---

2. This was a Japanese puppet government nominally under the leadership of Yin Rugeng, a Japanese-educated Chinese. See "A Letter to Me," nn. 6–7.

3. These three Japanese were generals who held high positions in the Japanese Guandong Army which occupied Northeast China (or "Manzhouguo" as the Japanese called their puppet state there). Minami was the commander-in-chief of the Guandong Army between 1934 and 1936; Koiso was its chief of staff between 1934 and 1936; and Itagaki was its chief of staff between 1936 and 1937. See Martin Bagish and Hilary Conroy, "Japanese Aggression against China," p. 326.

4. "Metro" was written in Japanese in the original text.

5. This Japanese brand name (Daigaku yōyaku in Japanese and Daxue yanyao in Chinese) was well known in China, for the product was widely distributed and advertised there in the 1930s.

6. The author is apparently mocking the Japanese who made this sign not only for making a mistake in writing Chinese but also for inadvertently punning on the word xi. In

At the East Granary a platform was being erected. Maybe some kind of a track meet will be taking place.

Atop the red building in Liushi (the women's normal school of Tong County) flew the [Japanese] flag of the rising sun. There were no students, only soldiers.

In XX Middle School (which was founded by a church), a bunch of big kids taunted a little kid saying, "Shame on you for having a dad who is head of East Hebei Normal School. How dare you come over here to study instead of attending your dad's own school. Shame! Are you afraid of not being able to qualify for advanced study? If so, then your dad shouldn't be a Chinese traitor!"

The little kid could only sob and sputter, "You—you—"

The servant of a teacher at the elementary school that is attached to the XX Middle School (which was founded by a church and belongs to Hebei province) caught a ten-year-old child, took him to a station of the bureau of public security[7] and said, "He climbed over our fence." (I know that he is a student at the elementary school that is attached to East Hebei Normal School.) The police only chuckled and didn't do a thing.

There was a rumor: All the wooden clubs in the streets are being put to use by Koreans to beat people up.

"Toot! Toot!" A truck loaded with goods that had been smuggled and had evaded taxation arrived via the Beiping-Tianjin Highway. On top waved the flag of the rising sun.[8]

4. *May Twenty-first in Tangshan*

by YUANQIE *(pseud.),*
a male high school student writing from Tangshan, Hebei

Tangshan, in a desolate part of our motherland, now has been cunningly detached from our country's jurisdiction. This place is brimming over with all that fills us with feelings of humiliation, hatred, and anger. Therefore, every-

this context, the word *xi* that is used is meaningless. But if one substitutes another word that sounds the same for it (as any reader familiar with the Chinese vernacular might do), then the sentence "*Ni yao xi ma?*" could be construed to mean "Do you want to screw?"

7. This bureau was one of the organs of county government under Guomindang rule (see the introduction to Part II) and apparently under Japanese rule as well.

8. On the smuggling of goods from the Northeast into North China to evade Chinese taxation, see the introduction to Part IV.

thing that happens here gives us nothing but pain, which deepens with every passing day.

This morning I was awakened by the *pai pai* sound of machine gun fire. This was the imperialist army's morning drill once again. Then, as a kind of echo, came reveille for the Peace Preservation Forces of the illegitimate East Hebei Government.[1] This wild and violent music, which is played in harmony and in the same rhythm by the enemy and the Chinese traitors, has become the daily morning ritual that arouses our ire—and today, of course, was no exception.

A moment later came an airplane, and "East Hebei No. 1" circled lower and lower. Then it dropped countless leaflets, leaving a trail that gave the airplane what appeared to be a long tail. People everywhere, adults as well as children, all reached up and waited with eager anticipation for the colorful handbills to flutter down into their hands. I thought to myself, this must be more of the same old confidence game—Kingly Way, Land of Happiness, Coexistence and Coprosperity, the Helping Hand, Kindly Benevolence.[2] Eventually I picked up a torn one and discovered that it was about a display of health products to be held in the Japanese concession area[3] in Tianjin on May 25. It said that the price of the well-known Lion Brand Tooth Powder would be slashed.

Originally I was supposed to be preparing for tomorrow's periodic exam, but outside the school the sound of big cannons was especially loud today. Undoubtedly, this was once again the army of the "friendly power"[4] conducting a military exercise in the large tract of land across from the station. This was like dropping a devastating bomb into our hearts, throwing our already troubled minds into greater confusion, and making it impossible for us to concentrate. This might seem to pose a threat to us. But, on the contrary, we are grateful for it because it supplies us with the food to nourish our feelings of hatred, and it permits us to live forever with the conviction that we will not let ourselves be destroyed or demoralized but will "break out of the demoralizing net, and engage in a battle to the death."

1. This was a nominally Chinese government supported by pro-Japanese troops. See "A Letter to Me," nn. 5–7.

2. These were key terms in the propaganda used by the Japanese in China. For a critique by one of Japan's most eminent scholars of the ideology that lay behind this propaganda, see Maruyama Masao, *Thought and Behavior in Modern Japanese Politics*, chap. 3; and for a discussion of Japanese intellectuals' sophisticated perceptions of Japan's role in China during the 1930s, see Crowley, "Intellectuals as Visionaries of the New Asian Order."

3. A "concession" operated under foreign (in this case Japanese) law. See "Diary of a Middle School Student," n. 5.

4. Yuanqie used the term "friendly power" sarcastically, implying that Japan was the opposite—an unfriendly power—in China. See "A Letter from the Northeast," n. 3.

I couldn't go on studying, so I walked out into the streets to look around and to buy some stationery and books. I passed by an office of the illegitimate East Hebei Government. A policeman stood in front of the gate.

The bookstore was empty and had no customers. Some shop clerks leaned against the bookshelves, speaking softly to each other. Others gathered in one corner around the cashier, chatting. They were probably the owners of this bookstore, so they were particularly concerned about business.

A short guy with a round face said, "These days it is impossible to operate a bookstore in Tangshan. Expenses are high, and you can't make any money."

"Chinese traitors in East Hebei are once again following the orders given by the devils to change all textbooks. Textbooks for middle and elementary schools were all sent by the Shenyang East Asian Culture Association. We can't sell even one copy of our books," a thin fellow remarked.

Another man with a very sad face and dull eyes looked around and said dispiritedly, "Right. Every year our bookstore has earned some money by selling textbooks. Now this means of making a living has been taken away. Isn't it true that the World Bookstore in Tianjin has been forced to close because they can no longer sell textbooks in the East Hebei area?"

"Now all businesses are declining, making it impossible to live. We are almost as thin as skeletons, but the devils still suck our blood, and the Korean thugs still rip our veins out. Ai, it's all over," said a guy who looked like a bookkeeper.

As they talked, their words were touching, like the sound of a sad melody. They didn't pay any attention to me. I picked up a copy of *Tangshan Commerce and Industry Daily* and began reading.

The round face spoke again, "Isn't Tangshan a world that belongs to the devils? [Japanese] bullies[5] and Korean thugs operate opium dens, foreign business houses, and hotels. They sell heroin and hard drugs in the form of pills.[6] No one dares interfere in all this illegal traffic. It is as though they are the masters and we are the slaves."

5. *Rōnin*. See "A Letter from the Northeast," n. 5.
6. Between the signing of the Tanggu Truce in 1933 (on which see "A Letter to Me," nn. 3–4) and 1936, drug smuggling spread from the Japanese-occupied Northeast across the demilitarized zone (which had been established by the Tanggu Truce and in which Tangshan was located) and down into North China. By 1936 the Japanese concession in Tianjin, about seventy-five miles southwest of Tangshan and outside the demilitarized zone, had become the largest manufacturing and distributing center for opium in East Asia. See Inlow, "Japan's 'Special Trade' in North China," p. 143.

This kind of circumstance is too common in Tangshan. Foreign business houses and hotels are sources of crime.

The thin guy craned his neck forward and delivered a speech: "Last winter didn't seven or eight heroin addicts lose their lives in a foreign business house? Koreans carried them out and threw them down the hill. At the time, they were still breathing. Two days later the corpses had been chewed up by wild dogs and were frozen stiff. Why did these Chinese human wrecks get hooked on heroin?"

Another person jumped in, saying, "Foreign business houses are involved in many things. No matter what kind of illegal things you do, once you are in a foreign business house, you're safe. Foreign business houses also are involved in tax collection, and the like. Paying them is the same as paying the public security bureau[7] but cheaper."

"The other day several people in the post office were counting money that they were either about to send or had received in the mail, when a man came up to them and snatched it away and ran around the corner where he ducked into a foreign business house."

"When Old Zhang who works as our cashier went to the post office to mail money, wasn't he robbed of thirty dollars?" The thin man confirmed this unequivocally.

Just then the elementary school let out, and several students in black uniforms came into the bookstore to buy things.

The round-faced guy became excited, his face turned pale, and he finally added, "If we don't drive out the XX*zi* [Japanese devils], there's no way we can live." The whole group nodded.

The children made a lot of noise for a while, and one of them bought a Japanese-made plastic triangle before they left. I followed them out of the bookstore. The streets were filled with advertisements for foreign business houses, opium dens, Benevolent Elixir,[8] University Brand Eye Medicine.[9] Remnants of posters plastered on the wall five months ago supporting autonomy for the five provinces were still visible.[10] All

7. The bureau was an organ of the county government in the parts of China under Guomindang rule and apparently in the demilitarized zone as well. See the introduction to Part II.

8. A brand of Japanese-made pills. See "Benevolent Elixir."

9. A Japanese-made product. See "A Sketch of May Twenty-first in Beitong County," n. 5.

10. In late 1935, the Japanese Army began promoting the "North China Autonomy Movement" to detach the five North China provinces of Hebei, Chahar, Suiyuan, Shandong, and Shanxi from the jurisdiction of the Guomindang government at Nanjing and place them instead under an "autonomous government" with Chinese leaders nominally in charge but the Japanese holding actual control. The "East Hebei Autonomous Government

around, Korean bullies were busy talking and appeared to be plotting some devilish conspiracy. These shameless things, they serve as the claws and the teeth of the tiger and the wolf!

On my way back, I passed the Illegitimate office of the East Hebei Autonomous Government for the Prevention of Communism, and at the front gate there was a new policeman.

5. *A Never-to-Be-Forgotten Class*

by LIU SHIYIN,
a male high school student writing somewhere in the Northeast

When I got up this morning, I was a little dizzy in the head. Staggering out, I hadn't noticed that last night's rain had made the ground muddy, and the moment I got outside the dormitory, I fell, getting mud all over me. What a disaster! Such a bad sign so early in the morning.

I washed my face, and then ate breakfast. I threw rice gruel, steamed buns, and salted vegetables haphazardly into my mouth. Who cares whether these have vitamins or are nutritious?

Before time to go to class, I heard that a certain important person was coming to conduct an inspection. The school janitor was madly trying to clean the entire school in a single breath and make it shine to the school head's satisfaction!

In "History of Our Nation" this morning, my classmates all wore frightened expressions, and the teacher had a pale face as he mounted the lecture platform.

The first sentence in the opening remarks was: "Take out the ink brushes!"

We gave him a strange look—his lips were trembling slightly, a book in his hands was also shaking, and his two weary eyes shot a glance at us. Then he went on to say:

"Open the books—from—"as his voice choked up, he quickly let out a deep breath and went on to say:

"—Chapter Three of this book, 'Diplomacy in the Early Years of the Republic,' Chapter Five, 'Diplomacy Following the European War,'—plus

---

for the Prevention of Communism" was meant to be part of the "North China Autonomy Movement." See Kahn, "Doihara Kenji and the North China Autonomy Movement."

'The Nanjing Incident,'[1] 'Negotiations over the Jinan Tragedy,'[2] 'The Wanbao Shan Tragedy,'[3] 'The Outbreak of the September Eighteenth Incident,'[4] 'Japan's Occupation of the Three Eastern Provinces and the Attitude of the League of Nations,'[5]—plus . . . Ai!"

At the beginning his voice had been too high-pitched. Gradually it became lower and lower, and in the end it was as if something were lodged in his throat, for he barely had the strength to go on!

Our hearts fluttered continuously, but we still didn't quite understand what was to come.

1. The Nanjing Incident occurred on March 24, 1927. When Chinese troops who were participating in the Guomindang's Northern Expedition reached the city, they set off shells that killed a Japanese naval officer and an American academic, and, in response, American and British gunboats laid down a barrage. The incident created tension over the next few months between Chiang Kaishek's government on the one hand and Western and Japanese governments on the other. See Iriye Akira, *After Imperialism*, pp. 125–33.

2. The Jinan Tragedy, also known as the Jinan Incident, occurred during the first week of May, 1928. Just prior to that time the Japanese government had urged Chiang Kaishek not to allow his troops to enter Jinan in Shandong province for fear their presence would threaten the safety of the two thousand Japanese living there, and Chiang had replied that the Japanese residents would be protected, making it unnecessary for Japan to send troops to Jinan. Both governments sent armies anyway and fighting broke out between Chinese and Japanese troops there on May 3 and May 8, 1928. See ibid., pp. 193–205.

3. The Wanbao Shan Tragedy occurred in the summer of 1931. It started in Wanbao Shan, located a few miles west of the city of Changchun in the Northeast. Local Chinese peasants, resentful toward about four hundred Koreans who had recently leased land and dug rice paddies in this area, tried to oust the Koreans on July 1, 1931. As a result, there were fights between the Chinese on one side and the Koreans and the Japanese police on the other side, but no casualties. Subsequently, when Japanese propagandists spread news of the incident within Korea, several hundred Chinese residents there were attacked and killed or injured. These events led to anti-Japanese boycotts in Shanghai but no direct action against Japan by the Guomindang government. See ibid., pp. 290–92.

4. The September Eighteenth Incident, also known as the Mukden Incident or Manchurian Incident, occurred in 1931. On September 18, 1931, a Japanese officer set off explosives along the South Manchurian Railway a few miles north of Shenyang (Mukden). Attributing the incident to Chinese soldiers, the Japanese Guandong Army occupied the city of Shenyang within the next few hours. See ibid., pp. 293–99. For more details, see Richard Storry, "The Mukden Incident of September 18–19, 1931."

5. Following the Manchurian Incident (see n. 4), Japan occupied the three provinces in Northeast China (Manchuria), prompting Chiang Kaishek's government to appeal to the League of Nations for support. After pleading unsuccessfully with Japan to withdraw, the League of Nations sent an International Commission of Enquiry, which conducted an investigation in Northeast China between April 21 and June 4, 1932. By then, the Japanese had created a supposedly Manchu state there, calling it Manzhouguo (as pronounced in Chinese) and making the last emperor of the Qing dynasty, Puyi, its titular chief executive. But the commission nonetheless condemned Japan as an aggressor and declared that Manzhouguo was nothing more than a puppet state under Japanese domination. See James B. Crowley, *Japan's Quest for Autonomy*, pp. 180–86.

"—plus 'The January Twenty-eighth Incident'[6] and 'Japan's Recent Aggression,'—write the two words 'Cut out' beneath these lessons!"

He managed to finish and then on the blackboard he vigorously wrote the two words, "Cut out!" As he turned around, the expression on his face was even harder to look at.

We flipped through our books, found these lessons, and calculated that they made up approximately half the entire book!

We didn't think to ourselves, "Take some more out! Save us the reading!"

Cut these out—it's like cutting flesh out of our bodies. At the moment that we had to write "Cut out," it was as though the ink brush in our hands was a sharp knife being stabbed into our hearts!

"Don't you be upset! I don't want it to be like this! Ai! China? Soon we'll no longer be able to be—" At this point in his remarks, the teacher suddenly lowered his head, and two or three teardrops fell to the lecture platform.

Before long the teacher calmed down and said to us, "Higher-ups have said that a few days from now people from a certain country [Japan] will come to conduct an inspection. I also have discussed this matter again and again with the school head and the dean of studies. However —the final solution has to be like this! Otherwise—I'm afraid we—" And then he went on to say in a deeply serious manner:

"I'm afraid all our lives will be in danger!"

The atmosphere throughout the classroom rose to a fever pitch. Some of my classmates were already silently weeping. Little birds on branches outside the window were also wailing.

When my sorrow and indignation reached the boiling point, I wrote these roughly worded sentences down on a piece of paper: "The country is in grave danger, and in fact can be kept waiting no longer! Anyone who is a part of the country must do everything in his power to save the country!" My tears trickled down the brush, dissolved in the ink, and caused my characters to run.

---

6. The January Twenty-eighth Incident, also known as the Shanghai Incident, started in Shanghai in 1932 when a Japanese naval commander called in the marines to suppress anti-Japanese boycotts and other demonstrations that Chinese had held in Shanghai as protests against the Manchurian Incident (see n. 4). Chinese forces put up strong resistance for about a month before collapsing and allowing the Japanese to occupy Shanghai and Wusong. A little over two months later, on May 5, 1932, a truce was signed by Chiang Kaishek's government and Japan in which the Japanese agreed to withdraw from these occupied areas. See ibid., pp. 159–60 and 167–68. For more details, see "Shanghai: January 28, 1932."

The teacher suddenly raised his voice and told us, solemnly, "Ai! All of you are China's future leaders! Since you have all expressed yourselves in this way—your country will be saved because of your red hearts and hot blood!" Among my classmates, some were still crying, some were staring at the teacher in silence.

The teacher immediately comforted us. "Ai! It is fortunate that for the moment we can still read closely these lessons that will be cut out. All things considered, won't this be the final class for you? Ha!" At the end, as though something in his heart had made him happy, he suddenly broke into a smile.

Some of my classmates also let out a breath.

The teacher then spoke gently to us. "Oh, you have to be careful! Your diaries, compositions, and books that are suspect all have to be well hidden! Or burned! You should all know. These may cost you your lives!"

By this point, most of my classmates had ceased to be sad. The teacher paced back and forth on the lecture platform, and we didn't know what he was thinking in his heart. Sometimes his face was smiling, sometimes it looked upset.

Thus ended this tragic scene.

6. *The Township Head's Misfortune*

by Hu Di,
a man writing somewhere in a Japanese-occupied area

"How can it be like that!" the township head, red in the face, blurted out. He paced up and down inside the house, with his hands held together behind him and his head bowed.

"That little punk! That mother!" echoed the squad head of the Militia Guard,[1] a deadpan expression on his face. He was wearing a yellow uniform, sitting in a chair, and fingering the pistol in his holster.

---

1. The name Militia Guard (*Baowei tuan*) was given to units organized by militarists who controlled territorial bases ranging in size from an entire province to a small locality. See Roy Hofheinz, Jr., *The Broken Wave*, p. 117; and Kong Chong, *Xian zheng jianshe*, p. 90.

There was a loud noise and a group of people rushed into the room. Seven or eight animated faces all were single-minded in their hatred. The house heated up like a pot of boiling water.

"How come he got away?"

"That mother X! That little punk was not raised by human beings."

"He'll have his legs broken and his arms ripped off."

"Even a rabbit doesn't eat the grass around his own hole."

"This little punk doesn't know how to do anything."

"What's going on?" yelled the assistant squad head as he came in, brandishing a .38 caliber gun. The township head stopped pacing and, gesturing, bellowed:

"He says that my family dug up sand and disturbed his family's grave. He also says that we've dug from the official road. Where did that mother get that idea? My family dug sand up only in the sand pits south of the village."

"Isn't he trying to conspire against us?"[2]

"Certainly! Clearly this is blackmail!"

"Hasn't that mother lost every bit of his humanity?"

"As a former local bandit isn't he capable of anything?"

"Which piece of land?"

"The piece near the road in the western part of the village."

"I've heard that the little punk has solid support. He often passes in and out of the [Japanese] battalion headquarters!" said the squad head, slapping the end of his black leather belt against his left hand as though he were beating the rhythm for what was happening.

"He has pull? That little punk! Who doesn't know how many bowls of rice he eats a day?[3] He amounts to nothing more than a guy who has started a numbers racket, organized gambling, opened a foreign business house, pushed heroin,[4] and gone over there [to Japanese military headquarters] to make payoffs! With this kind of backing, he thinks that whatever he says goes and that people are as scared of him as they are of tigers!"

"Him? Huh! Just Wan Ying? What pull does he have?" someone said, laying emphasis on the word *pull*.

2. [Hu Di's note:] "To conspire against" (*pianba*) means [in local dialect] to attempt to blackmail.

3. [Hu Di's note:] "Who doesn't know how many bowls of rice he eats a day" means everyone is familiar with his background.

4. In 1936 there was a heavy traffic in drugs within the Northeast and from the Northeast into North China. See "May Twenty-first in Tangshan," n. 6.

"As far as I can tell, that little punk can't shoot his piss more than thirty feet."[5]

The township head spoke, his lips trembling and his facial muscles twitching. "I didn't know he was like that. Last month they blackmailed Liu Yintang of Fu Village by insisting that he had borrowed 2,500 dollars. They gave him ten days in which to pay up, and after that they sent the XX [Japanese] military police and Peace Preservation Forces[6] to bring him in. In Weili [Tianjin] and Yaoshang [Tangshan][7] Liu got the support of yamen attendants[8] and lay in wait for those coming after him. Today it's already the mother of a twenty-first. Has Liu been arrested yet? Hey hey! Now Wan Ying wants to give me trouble."

A young man in his twenties came rushing in, his heavy shoes covered with yellow mud and his body smelling of sweat. He had barely come to a stop when he asked:

"Where is that bastard Wan Ying?"

"Gone! Gone!" The replies were as countless as raindrops falling.

"Look at what he's done!" he said in a deeply serious and accusatory tone of voice. His face immediately showed his disappointment, and he went on screaming:

"How did he get away? I had finished tamping down the land, and before I could drag the stone roller[9] back, I was afraid that you would let him go." There was a pause. "Why didn't you tie him up and show him how dear, how very dear he is to you?"[10]

"We are all from the same rural township and live on the same land. You don't have to be like that. We are going to find ways to take care of him," the squad head said, rising to his feet. He was a head taller than anyone else in this group.

---

5. [Hu Di's note:] Not being able to shoot piss more than thirty feet means not being very capable.

6. The name Peace Preservation Forces was used by some Chinese military units that were pro-Japanese and others that were not. (See "A Sketch of May Twenty-first in Beitong County," n. 1.) Judging from the context, this unit of the Peace Preservation Forces was pro-Japanese.

7. [Hu Di's note:] Weili is another name for Tianjin and Yaoshang is another name for Tangshan.

8. [Hu Di's note:] Yamen attendants (menzi) means people who have money and power. [The yamen was an official residence and administrative center. See "A Funeral Procession," n. 1.]

9. [Hu Di's note:] A "stone roller" (hunzi) is a farm tool made of stone in an elliptical shape.

10. [Hu Di's note:] "Dear to" (xihan) is a folk term used east of Tianjin as a synonym for "loving." In this context, however, it means beating in order to extract a confession.

"What?" The young man was really put off. Wide-eyed and dumb-founded, he looked deeply hurt.

"Let him think up anything he wants to. There's no way I'll ever be afraid of him!" the township head said, shaking his fist in the air. The young man shook his head, rolled his eyes, and, scarcely before the township head had finished, seized the chance to speak:

"He has pulled tricks that eat the villagers alive and damage the households. We don't have to deal with him in the usual manner. First we beat him up. Then we take him to court. We don't care how many tea guards[11] he has."

"Hey! You're still young. You're still far from understanding how things are. There is no way to avoid dealing with official matters. We can find a proper setting in which to deal with him on the basis of princi-ples!" the squad head said, interrupting. The young man's face looked distraught. He rolled up his sleeves and took a step forward.

"Principles? That mother X. These days who talks about principles any more? They call upon the battalion headquarters and the XX [Japa-nese] military police who come and blackmail us. Is that a matter of prin-ciple? Power is the principle!"

"You can't say that!" said the squad head, as though he'd been slapped in the face. He had a chance to interject these words and was then immediately shouted down by the young fellow's shrill voice:

"That mother! Can't you see how they [the Japanese and Chinese traitors] have ruined the villages on our left and on our right? Numbers rackets, gambling rings, and heroin pushing have not quenched their thirst.[12] And now they've pulled this trick. These days there is really no way for good people to live!"

"If the western army comes over, then it will be all right.[13] I'm sure that they would chop the heads off all these faggots!"[14] the deputy squad head said as he fingered a bullet on his cartridge belt and rose to leave.

"Hey! Placing your hopes on someone else is pointless. I've seen it all! These days, it will only work out if you dare to do it yourself. Don't you see? In one fell swoop at Huo Village they killed three or four [Japa-

11. [Hu Di's note:] "Tea guards" (*chahan*) means people who patronize and support prostitutes. Here it refers to wealthy and powerful people who protect their own running dogs regardless of the circumstances.

12. [Hu Di's note:] "Has not quenched their thirst" (*jiebuliao he*) means has not satisfied them.

13. "Western army" probably refers to the Communists' Red Army, which was based to the west of the region where this piece was written. See "My Gramophone's Solo," n. 2.

14. "Faggots" (*tuzaizi*) was an abusive slang expression which literally referred to a man who played the female role in a homosexual relationship.

nese] devils. They really acted with one heart, and they did their business so secretly that even the gods didn't know what was happening! Wan Ying relies on [Japanese] small devils! These devils don't have three heads and six arms! Aren't they afraid of dying?" The township head had hit upon all the points in question and formed his lips into a smug smile.

"Huh! If we Chinese are of one heart, it won't be difficult to wipe out the devils' dens!" the young man remarked, also grinning.

The squad head sighed, put on his hat, and tried to look sincere. He glanced furtively at the township head and then hung his head. After a moment's hesitation he said to the township head:

"What are you going to do?"

"Whatever Wan Ying does, I'll act accordingly!" the township head again blurted out, his jowls bulging. He looked as though he would not be satisfied until he had crushed his enemy.

"You can't say that. It's better to solve problems than to create problems! Come over here," the squad head said, gesturing to the township head, and they left together.

What remained in the room was confusion and raucous voices.

"Hey! What kind of a principle is that?"

"Wouldn't it be nice to be rid of all those bastards!"

"The day will come!" said the young man with fierce determination.

"It won't be easy."

"What? It can be done as long as we're united!" the young man insisted as before.

"That mother! There's never a time when things are good! We waited such a long time for the heavens to give us a needed rainfall, and now this awful thing has happened and has made everybody jumpy. Ai! Is it really true that peasants aren't worth a copper?" the old man standing at the door said, expressing his gut feeling as he glanced at the placard inscribed in faded gold characters, "On the Barge of Compassion, All May Cross."[15]

Under an old cedar tree, the squad head was making gestures as he talked, but the sound of his voice was so low that it was difficult to hear. Suddenly the township head began to scream:

"You tell Wan Ying that he can do whatever he wants, that mother X! He has power, and I'm putting my life on the line!"

The pure wind that followed the rain carried a wave of fragrance from the locust tree blossoms.

15. This saying, "On the Barge of Compassion, All May Cross," (*Cihang pudu*) refers to the Buddhist belief that Guanyin, the goddess of mercy, ferries all souls that are saved to the Western Paradise. See "Diary of a Midwife," n. 5; and "A Record of Digging Up Graves," n. 1.

B. Subversion in Unoccupied China

7. *Diary of a Middle School Student*

by DAGE *(pseud.),*
a male middle school student writing from Tianjin

Yesterday was too shocking. At night, no matter what, it was impossible to sleep. It was as though I had in my head a great stormy sea in which high waves were breaking and rolling in and out. I was thinking about the two roads, survival and destruction. I don't know what time it was when I got into the dream. Mr. Li seemed to be lecturing on the history of the Southern Song dynasty [A.D. 1127–1279] and on the Chinese traitor Qin Gui who was obsessed with slandering and destroying Yue Fei.[1] All my classmates sitting and listening were angry. For unknown reasons I suddenly became a refugee. A powerful X [Japanese] soldier holding a gun chased me from behind. I was really running fast in flight, with him in pursuit, and we seemed to cross from North China through Central China and South China, all the way over the Sichuan. Finally, at the sound of an explosion, my vision was blurred. It also seemed as though many people were speaking in loud voices, bickering endlessly. At this moment, my half-closed eyes gradually opened up and looked around inside the dimly lit room. Old Li had already gotten up and left. The sparrows boasted of their industriousness, *zizi zhazha*. Outside the glass window, the sky was filled with sorrowful clouds, pale and dispirited. Suddenly it occurred to me that the

---

1. Qin Gui (1090–1144) and Yue Fei (1103–41) are two of the most celebrated figures in Chinese military history, Yue as a patriotic hero who sought to regain the North from foreign invaders and Qin as the arch-traitor blamed for preventing Yue from achieving his goal. They have been prominently featured in Chinese plays and stories as well as historical writing. See Robert Ruhlmann, "Traditional Heroes in Chinese Popular Fiction," p. 154.

sound of Old Li's closing the door and the noise of the birds provided the setting for my last dream.

The first and second hours were for civics, and when Mr. Wu entered the classroom, the first thing he saw was two lines of white characters on the blackboard, "Please, sir, talk about the current situation in North China!" and "Why does this school subscribe to the *Shengjing Daily*?"[2] He was silent for a moment, shuffling around with his lecture notes and his roll book. My classmates were all worked up. They sat up erectly, waiting attentively for a response. In fact my classmates all knew about the subscription to the *Shengjing Daily* and were merely putting the teacher on the spot on purpose. Yesterday at four o'clock in the afternoon a shorty [Japanese] accompanied by a Chinese traitor came to force the school to subscribe to the *Shengjing Daily*, causing an argument. The school administration, afraid of getting into trouble, followed orders and did what it was told. After my classmates learned about this incident, they all pounded their fists and stamped their feet, for they felt that the taste of being half-slaves without a country was already too spiced with poison and was unbearable. Depressed throughout the night, they all wanted to take it out on Mr. Wu. After a moment of silence, Mr. Wu, forcing a smile, said, "He who holds no rank in a State does not discuss its policies.[3] It's better to study our own law, and if only all of us show respect for the law, there will be a day when China is strong." My guts were about to explode. "Chinese traitor! Are you a Chinese or not?" I muttered, unable to restrain myself, but not, regrettably, in a loud voice that he could hear. My classmates ridiculed and taunted the teacher, one dropping a line here, another dropping a phrase there. The teacher himself felt embarrassed, and said, smiling and blushing, "The school's subscription to the paper cannot be helped. Take the case of the municipal government. It was directed to take out one subscription, it resisted subscribing, and in the end it had to take out sixty subscriptions in order not to get into trouble! Who asked that our country be weak? All that can be done is to swallow our anger! In North China there are now forty or fifty thousand X [Japanese] soldiers on the communications network which is being formed by hastily constructing railroads and highways in each of the major cities and along the railroads. It's all over for North China!

2. This newspaper was published in Shenyang, a city in Northeast China that was under the Japanese puppet government of "Manzhouguo." See "A Never-to-Be-Forgotten Class," nn. 4–5.

3. This sentence is a quotation from one of the Chinese classics, *Lunyu*, bk. 8, chap. 14. See the Arthur Waley translation, Confucius, *The Analects of Confucius*, p. 135; cf. the Legge translation in *Chinese Classics*, vol. 1, p. 213.

There is no way! Do you have a way? We'll do it together!" These words were spoken by a high school teacher responsible for providing education during a national crisis! Just then the school head came around to look in on the class, and Mr. Wu blissfully lectured on the law. My classmates held back their anger, with their eyes bulging out and looking straight at the floor.

During the drill period between classes, there came the sound of two red-eyed [Japanese] airplanes in the sky, flying from the east to the northwest, leaving two black shadows in my mind. *Duduhong*—the sound of the [Japanese] soldiers' target practice came at intervals across Beining Road, shattering every deadened heart that has gone into hiding, cowering in weakness!

On the bulletin board in front of the dining hall were posted mimeographed proclamations and handbills, and people crowded around, reading. These were the Student Union's emergency proclamations and policies for national salvation work. The enemy is using "Kindly Benevolence" and "The Helping Hand" as slogans, is using "Self-Government" and "Prevent Communism" as smokescreens,[4] and is using "The Increase of Soldiers in North China" as a scheme. Thus is North China being destroyed without a sound and without a smell. Student who have served as the vanguard to save the lost country should stand up and expose the conspiracy between X [Japanese] imperialism and Chinese traitors. Therefore, the Student Union has now decided to make this propaganda week, in order to call upon the people and communicate with the people and bring them together to save the lost country. The propaganda methods include local propaganda disseminated intensively in the vicinity of the school and flying and leaping propaganda disseminated extensively throughout the city. Prepare to wage a great independent war for national liberation to save our North China! Save our China!

In the afternoon, after classes, I taught third- and fourth-grade mathematics at the People's Elementary School. I made up five questions on the increase of X [Japanese] soldiers stationed in North China, the murder of Chinese workers during the secret construction in the X [Japanese] concession area,[5] the size of the four provinces in the Northeast and the size

4. These and other slogans were used in Japanese propaganda at this time and throughout the Sino-Japanese War of 1937–45. See "May Twenty-first in Tangshan," n. 2.

5. A "concession" was an area for foreign residences that had been expropriated or purchased by the Chinese government and leased in perpetuity to a foreign power. It was administered by foreigners under foreign law and was financed by local taxes levied by foreign authorities. At this time, Tianjin's concession area was under the administration of not only Japan but also six Western European nations. See Albert Feuerwerker, *The Foreign Establishment in China in the Early Twentieth Century,* pp. 2–3 and 8.

of the five provinces in North China.[6] The kids were all aroused. With angry looks in their eyes, they rubbed their fists and cursed the hated enemy. Ah ha! Will China be lost? Just look at these lively and innocent patriots-to-be. It won't be lost!

8. *One Page of a Diary*

by Li Yun *(pseud.),*
a female college student writing from Taiyuan,
Shanxi

At six o'clock in the morning I opened my eyes. Ah ha, the sky was clear! I smiled from the bottom of my heart.

Recently heaven has deliberately teased us. Heaven's face has invariably shed tears as though something were lodged in its heart. Heavy winds blowing sand have provided the accompaniment. Although it is summertime, cotton jackets and the like still have to be kept at hand. Who knows when one might have to say hello to a needed jacket?

Mother knitted her brow and sighed, "Ai, this is the weather of a forsaken country!"

But today it was clear!

The light in the sky was blue, glistening like satin and darting in and out like a thief. The smiling sun was reminiscent of a fat merchant sitting at the cash box in his shop, squinting through eyes that looked as narrow as seams. The wind could barely move the leaves. The weather was neither cold nor hot. The universe was in harmony.

At a little past ten in the morning, suddenly there was the *longlong* sound of an airplane. Then an airplane appeared. From past experience, I knew that the plane was not one of ours. I ran to the courtyard and looked up into the sky: sure enough, a dark gray single-wing plane with a red sun emblazoned on the underside of the left and right wings—an airplane of the "friendly power [Japan]!"[1] The weather was clear so I could get an especially good look at it.

Recently, this "friendly power" of ours has shown "Kindly Benevo-

6. Dage is making reference here to Chinese provinces that the Japanese had already occupied or seemed on the verge of detaching from China through "autonomy movements." See "May Twenty-first in Tangshan," n. 10.

1. Li Yun used the term "friendly power" sarcastically, implying that Japan was the opposite—an unfriendly power—in China. See "A Letter from the Northeast," n. 3.

lence"[2] by using airplanes to send to Taiyuan "military officers" and "advisers" once every two or three days with all kinds of "secret messages." As all of us looked at the airplane of the "friendly power" going on its mission of "Kindly Benevolence" between the two countries and flying freely through our own air space, our hearts weighed heavy as lead and we felt oppressed.

By 11:30 the "mission" had probably been accomplished. The same airplane was flying back to where it had come from.

Oh, this is the tragedy of our motherland!

In the afternoon I went to school for an hour of class.

Graduation is near so students are allowed to hold discussions in class about their plans for the future. This is indeed a serious problem. But the entire nation and race have no future. How can an individual have a future!

These past two days there have been lectures on the famous "Nineteen Ancient Poems." It is not clear to me what these kinds of works reveal to us.

This "education"! This "Chinese education"!

I've long wanted to look up X, but I've never had the chance. Last night in the YMCA's North Building, in the auditorium where the Northwest Drama Club performs, I bumped into him and he said I could come see him.

I went after dinner.

After he graduated last year from the Economics Department in the Faculty of Law, he couldn't find a job for about a year. Although he majored in economics, he likes art and is well trained in woodblock printing in particular. But these days anyone who studies art has no rice to eat, so he is always out of work. Just recently, after expending the energy of nine oxen and two tigers, he found a job as a petty copyist in the headquarters of the Militia for the Promotion of Public Justice.[3] Working more than eight or ten hours a day, he makes a monthly salary of eighteen dollars!

As we were talking about this, he chuckled nervously and said, "As long as people are willing to give us a mouthful of rice to eat, their generosity seems to us to be as exalted as the heavens and as deep as the earth. How can we complain that this job is no good? Ha ha!"

2. "Kindly Benevolence" was one of the slogans used in Japanese propaganda at this time. See "May Twenty-first in Tangshan," n. 2.

3. This was one of hundreds of thousands of organizations by this name which were created by Yan Xishan, a Chinese warlord whose armies controlled Shanxi province between 1912 and 1949. See "My Gramophone's Solo," n. 1.

I remained silent.

Our conversation moved from woodblock printing and drama to literature and art and then to feeding oneself and unemployment. Finally we talked about the Chinese traitors of Taiyuan in recent times.

Some time ago, someone advertised in the newspaper saying they wished to hire some sort of "Chinese language teacher." There were no requirements, and the pay was good. "Interested persons please come to Zhengda Hotel for further information."

At that time we already sensed that this advertisement was evil and subversive. Later someone looked into it and discovered that it was indeed the X [Japanese] who were using the term "Chinese language teacher" as a pretext for buying off Chinese traitors. The salary was quite high, but the work was very secretive.

A friend of mine from college had no place to go after graduation. I heard recently that he has become this kind of "Chinese language teacher." Living on the third floor of the Zhengda Hotel, he always carries a big leather case under his arm, travels back and forth in an automobile, and appears to be very prosperous.

So, if you want to be a "good person," then you'll have no rice to eat—especially when the likes of Yin Rugeng have already provided a clear alternative by setting "examples" for people![4] Therefore, many people who mouth denunciations of Chinese traitors are tempted in their hearts. As people's stomachs shrivel, it is certain that the number of "Chinese language teachers" produced will rise shockingly!

I feel that this is a major crisis for Shanxi province—and the same could be said for North China and for all of China!

It was getting late so I borrowed from him a copy of *The Downfall of the Republic of Itl*, translated by Xu Maorong,[5] and then returned home.

---

4. Yin Rugeng, a Chinese, had been educated in Japan at Waseda University, was married to a Japanese woman, and was known (among both Chinese and Japanese) in North China for collaborating with the Japanese. See "A Letter to Me," nn. 5–6.

5. This was a Chinese translation of a book by the Soviet novelist and dramatist Boris Andreevich Lavrenev (1891–1959). Originally published in Russian under the title *Krushenie respubliki Itl* (The Downfall of the Republic of Itl), it is a novel about a mythical country's struggle to maintain its independence from a foreign invader. We wish to thank Lo Wai Luen and Marilyn Kann for helping us to identify this elusive title.

9. *On Jinmen*

by GUANQIU *(pseud.),*
a man writing from Jinmen, Fujian

Dear Man:

I recall that at a friend's banquet we talked about the social situation in Jinmen, and everyone seemed to agree that Jinmen was a heavenly place with no suffering, complete stability, and total tranquillity. But the hard facts of the past three years have made our earlier view no longer tenable. The society of Jinmen not only no longer bears any resemblance to a heavenly place but is in a state of upheaval. Declining prices of rubber and pepper from the Southeast Asian archipelago have forced banks to tighten credit. The higher incidence of kidnapping, armed robbery, and suicide, as well as the raising of tax and surtax rates to oppressive levels, have all seriously threatened Jinmen and show that Jinmen is no longer the Jinmen that it used to be!

Jinmen is an island between Xiamen and Taiwan. In the XX [Japanese] imperialists' drive into South China, Jinmen is extremely significant from a geographical and military standpoint. Although the enemy has not yet officially swallowed Jinmen, it seems to be within the grasp of the XX [Japanese].

Everyone knows that whenever the XX [Japanese] imperialists want to swallow any given place, first they make connections and buy off local riffraff and Chinese traitors, who clear the way by anesthetizing the uncultured masses. And then they follow up with a military occupation. Now Chinese traitors in Jinmen are publicly and unabashedly promoting the culture of the "Kingly Way"[1] as in this propaganda: "Under the governance of XX [Japan], the laboring masses are contented and happy, politics are not corrupt, at night no one needs to lock his door or fear the danger of being robbed"; "If XX [Japan] occupies Jinmen, peasants will have a chance to improve agriculture, and there will be an endless supply of seafood to eat"; "If you depend only on your father, you'll live, or if you depend only on your mother, you'll live. Why should we be so picky as to discriminate between China and XX [Japan]?" This kind of talk can be heard on every corner. Today lots of XX [Japanese] bullies[2] have come to Jinmen once again. Haven't they probably come, following their masters' orders, to take up the task of advising and supervising Chinese traitors?

In the wake of actions taken by Chinese traitors, the smuggling prob-

1. On the usage of the term "Kingly Way" in Japanese propaganda, see "May Twenty-first in Tangshan," n. 2.
2. *Rōnin.* See "A Letter from the Northeast," n. 5.

lem no longer can be considered minor. X's [Japan's] sugar, matches, and gasoline have poured into Jinmen in large volume. The truth is that Jinmen is merely a warehouse for X [Japan]. X's [Japan's] goods are transshipped to Xiamen and other places from here. Since Jinmen is an island with ocean on all sides, any village—especially the ones on Lie Island between Jinmen and Xiamen—can be used as a warehouse for X [Japan], and has loyal distributors of evil [Japanese] goods. Although the Maritime Customs has antismuggling boats which are effective, X's [Japan's] goods flow in freely, day and night, without the least bit of interference. The smugglers have made deals in advance with the authorities who could have interfered with goods that are flowing in. Not long ago, because bribes were not equally distributed among the Maritime Customs authorities, there was a falling out between the Maritime Customs authorities and the smugglers, which resulted in the Maritime Customs authorities coming once to Jinmen to crack down. But very soon they again became friendly.

Newspapers have paid attention to smuggling only in North China. They have not reported at all on the Chinese traitors' activities or the rampant smuggling in Jinmen. I think, if the situation continues as it is, we'll soon see Jinmen degenerate into a second North China![3]

10. *A Look around Shamian*

by QIN WEI,
a man writing from Guangzhou, Guangdong

I received from my younger brother, a worker in Taiwan, some money he earned by his sweat and blood, and today at about two o'clock in the afternoon, I took the check to the Bank of Taiwan in Shamian to cash it. So I had a chance to take a look around Shamian.

Shamian is just a small sandbar of a size good only for a public park, but in the hands of the imperialists, it has turned into a formidable headquarters for invaders. On this small sandbar are crowded together Western-style buildings, luxuriant green trees, and quiet scenery. But the grounds are covered with armed fortresses, iron barriers used for defense, and barbed wire barricades. Green-eyed soldiers on patrol, armed

3. On the smuggling of goods from the Northeast into North China, see the introduction to Part IV.

with bayonet rifles, flirt with the boatwomen. To us, these are really intolerable insults. The small sandbar is surrounded by water on all four sides, and the only connections with the mainland are two bridges to the east and to the west. Both bridges have heavy iron gates guarded by armed foreign military police who cast suspicious glances at our fellow countrymen passing in and out.

I entered by way of East Bridge, and saw ahead of me over twenty of my fellow countrymen, dressed like peddlers, talking, joking, and walking toward Japanese smuggling headquarters. This is a sad occurrence. Currently in Guangzhou a National Goods Exhibition is being held. Illustrated propaganda and handbills calling for resistance against economic invasion have been posted in all the streets.[1] But at the same time, among the masses there are a great many unemployed who, in order to find rice to eat, become involved in the illicit business of selling smuggled goods without realizing what they are doing.[2] This shows that it is impossible to speak of resisting the invasion if resistance is started at a secondary level without first achieving total national liberation. Only after we form a people's war front can we eliminate Chinese traitors and proceed to bring down imperialism.

With a painful heart, I walked into the Bank of Taiwan. At this time, it was quiet inside the bank, and I was the only person getting money. Seeing Taiwanese clerks humble themselves to the point of trembling with fear before their Japanese superiors brought these detestable words to my mind: "Slaves without a country!"[3]

Picking up the money and walking out of the bank, I strolled by a basketball court and saw ahead of me two Vietnamese and three Frenchmen playing basketball. It was an odd way of playing basketball. One Vietnamese snatched the ball away from another Vietnamese, carried it over and, using both hands, presented it to a Frenchman. The Frenchman took it and raised his thumb in praise, and the Vietnamese bowed while pointing at his own nose with his own thumb. He was so pleased with himself that it was sickening.

1. The National Goods Exhibition was part of a boycott of Japanese goods being held in Guangzhou in 1936. It displayed Chinese-made products that could be substituted for Japanese-made ones. See Bisson, *Japan in China*, pp. 121–22.

2. The smuggled goods were apparently Japanese-made products which had come from parts of China occupied by Japan and were being boycotted in Guangzhou at this time. See n. 1 above; and the introduction to Part IV.

3. Qin Wei seems to be characterizing the relationship between the Japanese managers and the Taiwanese clerks in the Bank of Taiwan as products of the colonial relationship between Japan and Taiwan. Taiwan had been a Japanese colony since 1895 and continued to be one until 1945.

With an indescribable feeling of indignation and anger, I found my-self uttering the same words: "Slaves without a country!"[4]

As I was leaving on East Bridge, a man and a women, dressed like peddlers and carrying suitcases on their shoulders, were by coincidence also leaving on the bridge. I thought that there must be smuggled Japa-nese goods inside the suitcases. The military police on the bridge ordered them to stop. They opened their suitcases for inspection, and I leaned over to take a look. The suitcases contained ragged clothes and something covered up that could not be seen. The military police who conducted the inspection did not lift it up and simply closed the suitcases and let them pass, even though people like these don't live in Shamian and it's un-usual to have such suitcases come along.

No one has forgotten the June Twenty-third Massacre even yet.[5] But what reminds us and prevents us from forgetting is not the stone tablet erected on the roadside on which the words "Do Not Forget This Day" are inscribed, but rather the imperialists' weapons, which have not been removed even yet—the armed fortresses, the barriers, and the barbed wire barricades. These keep the faces of the imperialists ever before our fellow countrymen and are much deeper and clearer reminders than could be made in one thousand words or ten thousand sentences. With the exception of a Chinese traitor, how can anyone who walks into this place, which has been branded with the mark of humiliation, not feel flames of anger and hatred shooting up inside him and not curse the au-thorities who control this small sandbar?

4. Qin Wei seems to be interpreting the exchange between the Vietnamese and French-men in light of their countries' colonial relationship. Vietnam had been a French colony since the 1880s and continued to be one until 1945.

5. On June 23, 1925, a demonstration on the roadway facing Shamian led to a clash be-tween Anglo-French troops and Chinese cadets from the Whampoa Academy in Guangzhou in which fifty-three Chinese and one foreigner were killed. See David Clive Wilson, "Britain and the Kuo-min-tang, 1924–28," pp. 216–23.

11. *The Smuggled Goods of This One Day*

by SONG WUWEI,
a man writing from Tianjin

Smuggling in North China has gone beyond the stage of being an open secret and has become much- publicized common knowledge.[1] The smugglers' sources are several train stations located at the eastern terminal of the Beiping-Shenyang Railroad near the sea. Tianjin is an important place for selling smuggled goods and a center for redistribution. From Tianjin, goods are further transported on railroads such as the Beiping-Suiyuan, the Beiping-Hankou, the Tianjin-Pukou, the Lanzhou-Lianyun (Long Hai), and the Jiaozhou-Jinan, eventually finding their way into farming villages.[2] They are well organized, systematic, and always have armed guards escorting them along the way. A huge quantity of goods is being smuggled in and out daily, and the value of these goods is impossible to calculate.[3] The effects of the smugglers' tax evasion on national tax revenue and the effects of competition from smuggled goods on domestic industries and commerce have created serious problems nowadays. On May twenty-first, thirty trainloads of goods were smuggled into Tianjin East Station, with a total weight of 93,000 kilograms, and thirty-nine trainloads of goods were smuggled out from Tianjin East Station, with a total weight of 112,000 kilograms. Let me now tabulate their accomplishments of the day:

1. One of the various ways that smuggling was publicized at this time was a one-act play by one of China's leading playwrights, Hong Shen, called "Smuggling" (*Zousi*), written in 1936. See Boorman and Howard, eds., *Biographical Dictionary of Republican China*, vol. 2, p. 214.

2. These railroads went from North China into all regions of the country: Suiyuan in Suiyuan province in the Northwest, Hankou in Hubei province in the Middle Yangzi region; Pukou in Zhejiang province in the Lower Yangzi region; Lianyun in Jiangsu province on the coast north of the Yangzi River; Jiaozhou in Shandong province on the coast of North China. For the names of the railroads, see Morohashi, ed., *Dai Kan-Wa jiten*, vol. 2, p. 460; vol. 4, p. 512; vol. 6, p. 1104; and vol. 11, p. 978.

3. The goods described in this and the following piece were smuggled from Japanese-occupied areas into parts of China not occupied by Japan to avoid paying customs duties. This smuggling expanded enormously in 1936 apparently as the result of two changes in policy: At the insistence of the Japanese military authorities, customs officers within the demilitarized zone ceased to carry arms; and, under the leadership of Yin Rugeng, the East Hebei Autonomous Government began taxing smuggled goods at approximately one-fourth the rates of the Chinese customs, thus giving these goods a claim to legality. See the introduction to Part IV; and Bisson, *Japan in China*, pp. 130–31.

1. IMPORTS

Place of Origin	Type of Goods	Number of Trains Used	Weight of Goods (in kilograms)
Qinhuangdao	white sugar	4	13,000
Qinhuangdao	kerosene	2	7,000
Nandasi	white sugar	9	29,000
Nandasi	artificial silk yarn	1	3,000
Liushouying	white sugar	11	35,000
Changli	white sugar	3	6,000
TOTAL	white sugar	27	83,000
	kerosene	2	7,000
	artificial silk yarn	1	3,000

2. EXPORTS

Railroad Line	Station	Type of Goods	Number of Trains Used	Weight of Goods (in kilograms)
Beiping-Shenyang	Beiping	white sugar	2	6,000
Tianjin-Pukou	Jinan	white sugar	4	13,000
Tianjin-Pukou	Botouzhen	white sugar	5	13,000
Tianjin-Pukou	Bangfo	white sugar	4	11,000
Tianjin-Pukou	Zaozhuang	white sugar	1	4,000
Tianjin-Pukou	Sangyuan	white sugar	1	4,000
Beiping-Suiyuan	Xuyuan	white sugar	1	3,000
Beiping-Suiyuan	Shahe	white sugar	1	2,000
Beiping-Suiyuan	Taiyuan	artificial silk yarn	1	1,500
Beiping-Suiyuan	Datong	artificial silk yarn	1	1,500
Beiping-Suiyuan	Baotou	artificial silk yarn	1	3,000
Beiping-Suiyuan	Baotou	white sugar	4	12,000
Beiping-Hankou	Handan	white sugar	1	4,000
Beiping-Hankou	Yancheng	white sugar	4	10,000
Beiping-Hankou	Shunde	white sugar	2	8,000
Beiping-Hankou	Shijiazhuang	white sugar	1	2,000
Beiping-Hankou	Yuzi	white sugar	1	4,000
Lanzhou-Lianyun (Long Hai)	Xian	white sugar	1	2,000
Lanzhou-Lianyun (Long Hai)	Xuchang	white sugar	2	6,000
Lanzhou-Lianyun (Long Hai)	Qilicun	white sugar	1	3,000
TOTAL		white sugar	36	107,000
		artificial silk yarn	3	6,000

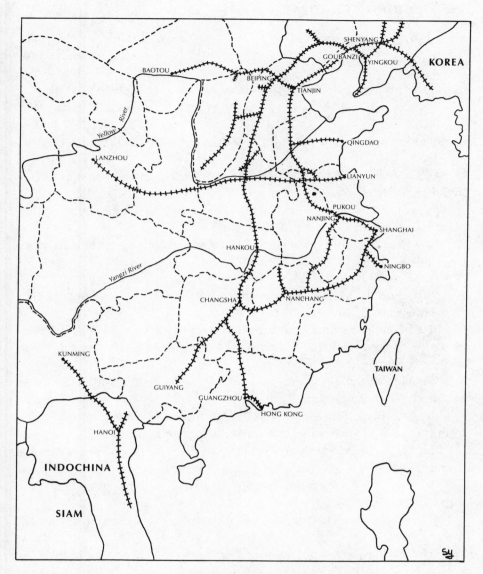

Chinese Railways, 1936

12. *White Sugar*

by ZHANG PAIZHOU,
a male student writing from Xuchang, Henan

One after another, the gray clouds and white clouds slowly broke up. The soft, weak sun showed its red face over the battlements facing west on the city wall. At this moment, a soft breeze blew in my face.

As I arrived at my classmate's, I overheard a conversation between two merchants:

"Manager Hou! I've heard it said that a bag of white sugar in this place has dropped by four or five dollars!"

"It's true, but only one boxcar has come, and it was sold out within two days."

"Sold out? Eh! So fast!"

"Who knows! Maybe every business house managed to get some!"

"How much did you get?"

"Two hundred bags. Aren't they all over there?" said Manager Hou, using his finger to point to a shed on the east side of his courtyard. I saw a lot of bags over there, too.

"Manager Hou, I have come especially to buy sugar. Mine is about sold out. What can be done?"

"If your place has a real shortage of sugar, take forty or fifty bags from me, so that you can stay in business for the moment."

"Shortage, there's no real shortage, but is the imported sugar coming or not?"

"I heard a XX [Japanese] person say it will be coming again within three to five days."

"Three to five days? You don't know whether it will arrive by tomorrow?"

"This is no easy matter! Making it through customs is a lot of trouble. You don't know how insistent the customs people are. If the XX [Japanese] people's soldiers weren't there as escorts, it wouldn't come through at all!"

"How come it wouldn't make it through customs? Didn't it go smoothly before?"

"This is different than before! In days past, each time goods were imported, they had to declare dutiable goods at customs. But now they simply don't declare dutiable goods."[1]

1. This practice was also referred to as smuggling. See the introduction to Part IV; and "The Smuggled Goods of the Day."

"They don't declare dutiable goods? They are allowed to pass?"

"How could they not be allowed to pass? A battalion of soldiers is guarding the train! Each man is armed with a pistol. If the train is not allowed to pass, the guns will open fire.² So who would dare block their way! You think about that. Therefore nowadays wherever imported goods go, they are always priced more cheaply than local goods."

"Oh, I see! That's why the price of each bag of sugar has dropped so much."

13. *Benevolent Elixir*¹

by JIANGFENG *(pseud.),*
a man writing from Nanjing

"I can assure you that nothing will go wrong, boss! Today, the twenty-first, is a good day. In foreign countries, it's the very best number, known as '*chuang da wen*' [a transliteration meant to sound like the English words "twenty-one"].² Anything that has to do with this number is lucky and will give you a chance to make lots of money. For instance, do you know about playing cards? It's a Western game, and if you get '*chuang da wen*' in your hand, you win money. So I say, so I say —don't suppose, boss, that this will be difficult to sell because it is an Eastern [Japanese] product. Don't worry a bit about it. In fact, there's no problem now. C'mon! Today is the twenty-first, a good day! I'm leaving you two boxes, altogether a hundred packs. Each pack sells for a nickel in big money. Hmm, this is a good day so I'll charge you only half price. You can make 100 percent profit! I guarantee that within twenty-one hours you'll sell them all. Mm-hmm. Look, here's a big foreign poster for you to hang up as an advertisement. How gorgeous it is! Ha ha ha ha!"

After washing my face, I sat down by the window and was about to

2. According to the Maritime Customs report for 1936, Japanese and Koreans smuggling sugar and other products were armed with revolvers and other weapons and forced their way past customs officials, who were unarmed at this time. See Bisson, *Japan in China*, p. 133.

1. The title of this essay, "Benevolent Elixir" (pronounced *Rendan* in Mandarin and *Jintan* in Japanese), was the name of a mint-flavored, sugar-coated, all-purpose kind of pill made primarily in Japan and distributed and advertised widely in China.

2. *Chuang da wen* is a transliteration meant to sound like the English words "twenty-one." These three Chinese characters literally mean "to avert disaster."

A cartoon by Taoye (pseud.), drawn to go with "Benevolent Elixir" and published with it in the original *One Day in China* (Shanghai, 1936), p. 2.26.

practice my calligraphy when suddenly I heard this voice coming from the small shop across the street.

My window faces that little shop. The person speaking was a young man from the North. He was holding several boxes of benevolent elixir in his hand and was trying to make a deal with the proprietor. As for the proprietor, he was gaping at the man, his eyes wide open and his old mouth fixed in a half-smile. He was tempted but also afraid, and tentatively, he said:

"I'm only afraid it won't be easy to sell. Haven't Eastern goods been banned? Besides, besides, we have little capital to invest!"

"Don't worry. No problem!" That young fellow loved to say don't worry and no problem. "You can't sell it? No way. This is a well-established Eastern brand of benevolent elixir. It's far better than the various Chinese brands. Look, who buys a benevolent elixir that isn't this brand? As for the banning of Eastern goods, that's no problem. Who'll dare enforce the ban? This benevolent elixir is good medicine which can save lives and raise the dead back to life. Who can ban this? You say you have little capital. Don't let that bother you. I'm leaving you two boxes

—a hundred packs. Just give me a dollar! No, even if you don't pay me, that's all right. I'll be back in two days after you've sold them all. I'm staying at the XX Hotel in Xiaguan—oh, maybe it's better for me to look you up. Come come come, take two boxes!" As he spoke, he put two boxes of benevolent elixir down on the counter, and he took out a note-book. "Your shop is named Mingji, isn't it? What's your name—it's not necessary to write your name down. This is the XX Lake Area, X Zhou Street, Number XXX, the Mingji Shop, two boxes," he said, as he recorded all of this in pencil in his notebook.

"Where is the big foreign poster?" the proprietor asked anxiously, fingering the two boxes of pills.

"Here it is!" The young fellow took an advertising poster out of his canvas bag. "Look at how gorgeous it is. Where do you want it? Let me hang it up for you." He measured the poster against the counter and saw that it didn't fit, so he hung it on the wall outside. "This is a good place to hang it. Look, it's even bigger than your shop sign."

The proprietor smiled and nodded. As the young man threw his canvas bag over his shoulder and took his leave, the proprietor followed him with his eyes and said, "See you later!" He then opened a box of benevolent elixir, picked up one pack, and took a whiff. He arranged all the boxes on a shelf behind him. The air became still.

I opened a drawer, took out a piece of paper, and spread it on the desk. I then heard a Cantonese person over there reading out loud the words in the advertisement and in a couplet posted on that small shop's doors:

"*Yamdan! Dong yeungfo a!*" [In the original advertisement this was "Benevolent Elixir! Eastern Goods!" Pronounced with a Cantonese accent, however, it sounded to the author as though it meant, "Lewd Aphrodisiac! For a Completely Shriveled Thing!"]

"*Mat fa tin bao a! Yen jut dei lang wo!*" [The intended meaning expressed in the written version of this couplet that was hanging on the shop was:

> Everything prospers, Heaven is protective.
> People are heroes, The place is famous.

But pronounced with a Cantonese accent, it sounded to the author like:

> Everything disintegrates, Heaven explodes.
> People are extinct, The place is barren.]

Xuanwu Lake, Twenty-fifth year of the Republic of China [1936]
May Twenty-first, 9:00 A.M.

C. Resistance in Unoccupied China

14. *One Day in the City of Culture*

by Y. CHENG ZE,[1]
a man writing from Beiping

May 21, 1936. Strong wind. In Beiping.

This morning in East Station I once again bumped into that big, tall Sun-brand [Japanese] military policeman.

I've bumped into him more than once. Although previously I had always seen him on the platform of East Station, I had formed only a fleeting impression of him, for I'd never had a close look at his face, his demeanor, or his clothing, nor had I paid any attention to his whereabouts. Moreover, whenever I went to the station, I'd always had things to do, so I'd never had time to examine him.

Yesterday when I went to run an errand at the station, I didn't expect to come across him. As I was walking by the customs loading dock, I looked up and saw him striding along. He was strutting at the base of the ancient city wall, affecting a martial step. His pistol holster rested at an angle on his hip. At his side hung a long sword. He wore a white armband on which two Chinese characters, "Military Police," were written. His big high-topped leather boots stomped on the platform making the sound *kedeng, kedeng*. As long as he is there walking, no one in the station needs anyone else to look at.

Damn it! The less I want to bump into him, the more it so happens that I see him. I saw him not only yesterday but again today. He was on Platform No. 1 probably keeping an eye on the 9:30 A.M. train from Beiping to Shanhaiguan. Before the train got underway, he jumped down

1. The author wrote this pen name not with Chinese characters but with the roman letters "Y. Cheng ze."

off the platform and crossed the railroad tracks, and then jumped up onto Platform No. 2 to wait for the 9:25 A.M. train from Shenyang. He jumped up at the place where I was standing. This head of his was no ordinary head. The average Chinese person is not as tall as he is. Underneath a big red cap was his suntanned yellow face. His skin and flesh were taut and his gaze was fearsome. From the top of his head to the tips of his toes there was not one sign of warmth. My eyes met his once and my heart immediately froze. The wind was strong, and he probably didn't like the chill under the iron shelter over the platform, so he found a place to stand where the sun shone through. I shuffled around, doing my best to calm myself while not letting my angry eyes come close to meeting his.

The train was about to arrive and the platform was bustling. Over the loudspeaker came the loud announcement that the Beiping-Shenyang Express would reach the station at 9:25. Porters, wearing hats with red trim, busily pushed carts on the west side. Hotel representatives also came in. On the west side were employees of the China Hotel. On the east side, the situation was complicated. There were those wearing hats marked "Grand Hotel," and those wearing hats marked "Wagon-Lits."[2] The greatest number were from the Japan Hotel, the Japan-China Hotel, and the Yanjing Hotel.[3] These representatives, needless to say, included Chinese people, as well as women, men, and children wearing [the Japanese costume of] wooden clogs and wide sleeves. The noise contributed to the mass confusion.

At the east entrance, a locomotive blew its whistle and from the tracks came the sound of *zhazha*. Soon the locomotive came raging in, pulling a string of cars, puffing out smoke, baring its teeth, and showing its claws like a poisonous serpent. This was a Nanman[4] [Japanese South Manchurian Railway Company] train. Looking at this kind of train made me think of my home village. It is this kind of train which has drawn more than 3,800,000 square *li* of my homeland into the tiger's mouth! It is this kind of train which has dragged more than 30 million of my elders and brothers into hell! It is this kind of train that has brought in countless [Japanese] products and destroyed China's economic lifeline! It is this kind of train that has brought in thousands and tens of thousands of tigers and wolves! Squatting in Tianjin, Fengtai, Beiping, and other strategically important places, they have made me a slave without a country for the second time! The train growled and shrieked. It wanted to run to

2. The names of these two Western-style hotels appeared in English in the original text.

3. In "Yanjing Hotel," "Hotel" was written in Japanese in the original text.

4. The word "Nanman" appeared in English in the original text.

Changzhou, it wanted to run to Shijiazhuang, it wanted to run to Baotou, it wanted to run to Ningxia. Under its wind of terror, 100 million people in North China all have their necks bound in chains.

Children wearing clogs who had come to solicit business for the hotels were jumping up and down as they greeted customers getting off the train. In the midst of the confusing din, people from the "friendly power" [Japan][5] who had gotten off the train bowed ninety degrees to each other. They were polite to each other, bowing time and time again. Many, many "slaves" busily rushed around, hauling luggage on their shoulders and in their hands. Hotel representatives were busy making arrangements for their various guests. Porters were busy moving the guests' things. People were making their way through the confusion, and by now the tall Sun-brand military policeman was no longer in sight. I took a look inside the train and saw that there were not many passengers. I had heard that many members of the topnotch Sun-brand army who had come enthusiastically to protect us had gotten off earlier at Fengtai.

Again the guests that I had come to meet did not arrive! I wandered aimlessly out the city's Front Gate and into the Legation Quarter.[6] At its entrance were the Golden Fan Dance Hall and the International Transportation Company. Yesterday morning a truck had been parked by the gate. Several shorties [Japanese] wearing yellow wool slacks had been working around the front and rear of a car. But this morning it was deserted and quiet, with no cars and no people.

As I walked down Rue Meiji,[7] the wind became even stronger. There was a barracks on the east side of the road. Affixed atop its gray wall was the [Japanese] flag of the rising sun. The flag was blowing in the wind, and although it fluttered, there were no wrinkles in it. Any passerby could not help but take a look at it. At the gate, besides an armed soldier, there was also an officer of the day who had rank. Mightn't they be welcoming some sort of dignitary?

At 9:50 I left from the north gate of the Legation Quarter, and I wanted to go to Wangfujing Main Street. I suddenly came upon a bunch of yellow things crawling along the side of the street. I was taken aback! I looked more closely to the east and found that outside the walls of the Legation Quarter in the open fields were many, many yellow people in

5. Y. Cheng ze used the term "friendly power" sarcastically, implying that Japan was the opposite—an unfriendly power—in China. See "A Letter from the Northeast," n. 3.

6. The Legation Quarter had foreign concessions within it. On concessions, see "Diary of a Middle School Student," n. 5.

7. The words "Rue Meiji" appeared in English in the original text. Meiji ("Enlightened Rule"), the name of the Japanese emperor who reigned in Japan between 1868 and 1912, is also, by extension, the name given to the period that he reigned.

motion: some running, some standing still. In the distance, blowing in the wind, were targets representing the supposed enemy. The seven or eight soldiers along the side of the road, after crawling for a while, stood up and ran forward. After running for ten steps or so, they again hit the ground. Bracing their rifles with their left hands and holding the triggers with the right, they faced the target and fixed their sights on it. Several other units were carrying out the same exercise. Soldiers with machine guns on the south side also seemed to be shooting, which made the sound *tutu* over there. Some jumped into the trenches along the walls as though carrying out a sneak attack.

One bunch reached the enemy (targets), fixed their bayonets, and charged. They yelled, moving out on the attack. The enemy was very quiet, offered no resistance, and uttered not one word!

Another bunch reached the enemy, fixed their bayonets, and charged. They yelled, moving out on the attack. The enemy was still very quiet, offered no resistance, and uttered not one word!

Still another bunch also reached the enemy. Following the same pattern, they fixed bayonets, charged, and yelled, "Kill!" How appalling that the enemy was still motionless, offered no resistance, and uttered not one word!

After doing this several times, the yellow troops claimed a total victory. Only then did the officers, who were wearing big caps with red trim and epaulets with gold fringe, order these brave warriors to take off their backpacks, prop their guns upright together in groups, and sit down on the grass to rest.

At 10:30 A.M. I stood sadly at the south entrance of Wangfujing Main Street. The streetcars sounded their bells, *dongdong*. People were pushing and shoving as they climbed on and off. Newspaper boys hollered, "Read your copies of Japan's *New Prosperity News*." "Read the *East Hebei Daily*."[8] They stuck the newspapers through the windows of the streetcars, waving them under the noses of the passengers. On Changan Street, cars honked their horns, *wuwu*, as policemen motioned to clear the way. Some big shots had probably been playing around all night, and were only now returning home to sleep. Perhaps they had attended a meeting of the XXXX Association about the XX [Japanese] advisers' plans for building highways and railroads. Perhaps they had been busy negotiating with XX [Japanese]. Perhaps they had been in the park enjoying the camellias and peonies. Perhaps . . . . Horses hitched to rods on large carts moved up and down both sides of the street, groaning, struggling, plod-

8. These newspapers' names suggest that they were published in parts of China under Japanese control. On the "East Hebei Government," see "A Letter to Me," nn. 6–7.

ding ahead, and giving their lives to pull carts full of goods. Rubber tires rapidly whirled around while countless horses became donkey-like, clopping along *didi*, *dada*, giving sweat and shedding blood. The wind was blowing and making a roaring sound. It whistled through the branches of the locust trees, and they, with no place to hide, thrashed at each other, making a *huhu* sound. Blossoms fluttered down from the locust trees, and as soon as they reached the ground, they were picked up and carried off elsewhere by the wind, swirling round and round. The swallows were unafraid of the fierceness of the wind. They flew from the branches of the locust trees up into the sky and glided, glided, glided far into the distance. With one loop-the-loop, once again they soared high, far away, far away, but before long they glided back. Once again they soared high to carry on their struggle with the wind.

Suddenly I thought of December Ninth of last year when the young people of Beiping waged a brave struggle on this street.[9] For whose sake were they cut down by swords and shot down by guns? For whose sake were they punished by being thrown into prison? Are we now willing to serve as slaves without a country? Are we now willing to let people secretly sell us out? Are we now willing to let others secretly make out deeds for the sale of ourselves? It is as though we are in the dark wilderness. All around are many wolves howling at us. If we don't take out the weapons we have with us, what wolf will be willing to back off! Let's take out a match! Let's set the wild grass in the wilderness on fire! Let one spark generate tens of thousands of sparks! Let the fire in the wilderness drive away the packs of wolves, and let the fire in the wilderness burn up this whole filthy world!

On the way home, I passed a house in Neiyi Ward. It had a flag on a pole on its roof. The wind had blown the flag so that it had become wrapped around the pole, leaving half a star barely visible against a red background.[10] I looked up at the sky and was pleased to see that the sky was still there. The sun that shines on China was still high in the sky and shining upon this city of culture.

9. Y. Cheng ze is referring to the December Ninth Incident of 1935. On it, see "An Ordinary Day," n. 1.

10. This flag fits the description of the "five-star flag" used by the Chinese Communist Party throughout its history and as the national flag for the People's Republic of China since 1949.

15. *My Diary for Today*

by Wu Jun,
a policeman writing from Shanghai, Jiangsu

I was in a deep sleep in my iron bed this morning, when suddenly I heard someone screaming in my ear. I was so groggy that I didn't know what was happening, but I was so startled that my heart skipped a beat.

"Get up! Get up! It's nine o'clock!"

After hearing these words, I realized that it was Ah Mao who had come to hurry us down to breakfast—and off to work. As the proverb goes, "Never work for the government if you ever want any comfort." Though sleeping would be preferable, my food and clothes have to come from others. As the saying goes, "When you are given food by other people, your mouth feels too weak to chew it. When you are given things by other people, your hands feel too weak to take them." Everything that we eat and wear is all provided by the nation. Even if we have no concept of nation and society, we still must be devoted to our work because of the need for food and clothing. So I did not hesitate at all and immediately jumped up.

I rubbed my eyes and looked around the sleeping quarters. Oh! How strange! Everyone in the room except myself was already up. They were already busy shining their shoes and putting on their leggings, as though fearful that lagging behind would bring misfortune down on their heads. No wonder! During the past few days the news has certainly not been good. The more the news of the cutbacks is rumored, the more true it seems. Empty words have become fact. All the officers and policemen in this precinct have become filled with apprehension, and each one fears that misfortune will befall him. Indeed, during the past few days everyone is being very careful not to give the impression that he has done a slipshod job, for fear of being let go. Therefore the most important reason that everyone was up early was that they were afraid of being late for work.

After brushing my teeth and washing my face, I looked at my watch and found that it was only 9:20. I felt that it was still early, so I poured myself a glass of boiled water, opened today's newspaper, *Shen bao*, and read as I drank the water. Suddenly I noticed in the classified section an advertisement soliciting essays for your publication. This I found tempting. But as I am a person who never finished school, even if I emptied my stomach and intestines and squeezed all the juice out of my brain, I would not be able to produce an eloquent essay. So I am sending you this entry from my diary.

I arrived at work at ten o'clock. Because several trains scheduled to depart in the morning had already left and it was too early for the afternoon trains to arrive, there were very few passengers in the station. On the long benches set up in the main building for passengers, there were only two or three passengers sitting and dozing. Casually walking around, I kept an eye on the passengers' suitcases to make sure that no bums made off with them.

At 12:30, the express train arrived from Changzhou. It was my responsibility not only to make sure that no bums robbed or cheated the passengers but also to direct traffic. So I stood at the place where the passengers had to pass by and used my hands to motion to passengers to exit along the left-hand side. To be sure, members of the intelligentsia needed no guidance from a little cop, but some of them were still oblivious and others didn't know the meaning of the order as propagated by the New Life Movement.[1] Whenever I tried to stop those who walked on the wrong side, I could hear all kinds of odd comments:

"Ah! I forgot, I forgot."

"Oh, New Life!"

"Why aren't you letting me by?"

"Oh, are you going to frisk me?"

What most attracted my attention were several modern young girls standing on the left, who giggled as they pointed at me, looking me over from top to bottom and criticizing me from head to toe. I suspected that they were making fun of me. They made me blush, and I didn't dare look them straight in the eye.

Later more people came into the station, because two express trains were about to depart.

At this time, two people from the "friendly power" [Japan],[2] a man and a woman who appeared to be a couple, had with them a lively little boy whose clothing was quite extraordinary. Everyone could not help but stare at this little boy. The little boy was certainly very clever and cute! Looking at this darling face alone would make anybody happy. Noticing the way that I walked and acted, he did a very close imitation. People

1. The New Life Movement was inaugurated by Chiang Kaishek in 1934. Its leaders sought to reform popular attitudes by requiring everyone to obey specific rules of personal conduct, including rules for pedestrians. On it, see "Two Letters," n. 6.

2. Wu Jun used the term "friendly power" sarcastically, implying that Japan was the opposite—an unfriendly power—in China. See "A Letter from the Northeast," n. 3.

couldn't help but break into laughter. At the time, I also smiled at him and fell for him.

I never would have expected that his father spoke fluent Beiping dialect.

"If you go on imitating the way he walks, he'll club you!" the father told the child, pointing his finger at me. He then turned to me and said:

"You see how naughty this child is?"

"It's good for a child to be naughty. Being naughty is a sign of intelligence. A stupid child is absolutely incapable of acting like this. He is a clever boy," I said, praising him.

He seemed to want to keep on talking to me. Aware of his friendly attitude toward me, I also felt like talking more to him. I leaned forward and was about to speak to him when I suddenly noticed that he was not very tall, but his stocky build, his hideous face, and his two uncommonly bushy eyebrows were all evidence of the cunning in his heart! He was wearing tapered slacks, which are fashionable for them [the Japanese], and a pair of big leather shoes that were about one-third larger than his feet. Seeing his mannerisms, I couldn't help but think back on many painful events: for example, the extinction of Korea, the Twenty-one Demands, the four northeastern provinces, the January Twenty-eighth Incident, the establishment of the illegitimate state of Manzhouguo, the Tanggu Truce, the problems of North China, and the smuggling that has become commonplace all over our country which is beyond the control of our authorities.[3] Their diplomats' platitude is, "Kindly Benevolence! Kindly Benevolence!"[4] Perhaps what happened here was meant to show the so-called "Kindly Benevolence between China and Japan." I was afraid that he would show me too much kindly benevolence, so I kept my mouth shut.

3. Wu Jun is cataloguing a sequence of events in which Japan penetrated more and more deeply into the mainland during the first third of the twentieth century by annexing Korea in 1910; imposing the Twenty-one Demands on China in 1915; invading China's northeastern provinces in 1931; attacking Shanghai on January 28, 1932; setting up Manzhouguo as a Japanese puppet state to govern China's northeastern provinces on March 9, 1932; and signing the Tanggu Truce with China on May 31, 1933, which left Beijing and Tianjin defenseless. For more on these and related events, see Marius B. Jansen, *Japan and China*, chaps. 4, 6, and 10; the introduction to Part IV; "A Letter to Me," nn. 1 and 4; "A Never-to-Be-Forgotten Class," nn. 1–6; and "May Twenty-first in Tangshan," n. 10.

4. On "Kindly Benevolence," see "May Twenty-first in Tangshan," n. 2.

16. *This One Day*

by YIMING *(pseud.),*
a male worker writing from Taiyuan, Shanxi

In May, dawn always comes shortly after four o'clock.

It was quiet in the courtyard of this typical northern-style "four-quarter house."[1] The streets outside the house were equally quiet.

People were still under their blankets, enjoying the last sweet moments of May twentieth. But God made a slightly startling noise which woke up the wife of an army officer who lived in the east building. Time: a little past five.

This woman held her breath as she moved along on tiptoes.

In the north building, there was a woman waking up, coughing.

"Mrs. Zhang, get up! It's already six!"

She gets up early, and has the habit of setting the clock ahead. Nobody knows why.

"Oh, Mrs. Wang, you're up early!" The voice sounded loud, even though it came from behind a glass window.

Everyone was up, and thus began this fresh but uncelebrated day.

"Mrs. Zhang, the airplanes are coming today. Aren't you scared?"

"Don't you listen to that kind of nonsense! What kind of talk is that! There is no war, no—" she said, comforting herself.

"It's true! They all say that fifty airplanes are coming!" Refusing to accept this fact, she wished to pass the fear on to others.

Yet no one seemed to believe her.

Someone was preparing breakfast in the kitchen. Wives and their husbands all sat around the house chatting, discussing everything from airplanes and bombs to utopia.

"Mr. Wang," someone other than Mr. Wang said, licking tea leaves off his lips, "didn't you also hear that troops have been dispatched north?"

"They were dispatched, and also a brigade of XXX arrived yesterday."

"Then the news about fighting X [Japan] is true! Someone said that X XX [Chiang Kaishek] flew to Shaanxi yesterday to hold talks with [Zhang Xueliang] about dispatching troops."[2]

---

1. A "four-quarter house" (*si he tou*; otherwise known as *si he fang*) was a residential compound built originally for one family (but in this case apparently occupied by members of more than one family) in which there were four separate buildings (the east, west, north, and main buildings) situated around a single, central courtyard. See Morohashi, ed., *Dai Kan-Wa jiten*, vol. 3, p. 8.

2. This rumor apparently was untrue, but it was true that Chiang Kaishek had been flying from one city to another in all parts of China to exhort his troops to "exterminate" the

Yesterday one or two planes did in fact circle around this small city several times. The newspapers also mentioned who were riding up there and where they were going.

"People also say that a big airport large enough for two hundred planes has been hastily built outside West Gate. Is this really true?" asked the army officer's wife, who had spoken to Mrs. Zhang earlier.

"I can't really tell. In any case, Old X [Yan Xishan][3] wants to fight to the death this time."

Mr. Wang set a tone that sounded even more determined than the "Old X" he referred to.

"It's got to be done. There's no alternative but to fight X [Japan]. Otherwise common people will have no way to live!"

"I heard from the wife of Regiment Head Hou that the government has sent 300,000 soldiers to Henan province. As soon as the war breaks out, these troops will immediately be transferred here," said Mrs. Zhang.

"The government has also made an appropriation in the amount of 500,000 to Old X [Yan Xishan] for military supplies. The money will get here within the next two days."

"Old X [Yan Xishan] also knows that no one can live unless we fight the X [Japanese]."

"This is a secret though. Their [Japan's] army officers and teams of spies are all over. Ai!" Then the subject changed. "Chinese people don't have enough backbone. Not all Chinese are of one heart. Some work for the enemy and serve as their spies!"

"The government has asked common people to dig caves—"

"Oh, the pamphlet circulated a few days ago said so," the army officer's wife interjected, but no one seemed to pay any attention to her.

"That's to prepare so that once the war breaks out and the X [Japanese] airplanes come to drop bombs, we won't be afraid—" The conversation took another turn. "When that time comes, we'll go to the villages, and there will be caves more than ten feet deep."

By then, everyone had finished breakfast. (Note, not all at once, so that those still not finished continued talking.) Mr. Wang had gone to his office, but everyone else was still there. Then two guests came in.

Chinese Communists early in 1936 and that he was concentrating his best troops around the Communists' Yanan base in Shaanxi province during May 1936. At this time the warlord Zhang Xueliang and his troops, who were originally from Northeast China and were now based in Shaanxi, preferred to fight the Japanese rather than the Communists and tried to convince Chiang Kaishek to adopt a strategy that would reflect this preference. See Hsu Kaiyu, *Chou En-lai*, p. 114; and Wu, *The Sian Incident*, pp. 41–49.

3. Yan Xishan was the warlord whose armies had dominated Shanxi province since 1911. Although on friendly terms with Japan earlier, Yan had become increasingly antagonistic toward Japan throughout the 1930s. See Gillin, *Warlord*, pp. 208–18.

"Our convoys of trucks will be moving north in the next day or two. The government has really made up its mind this time," said one of the guests. He was apparently a driver in a certain truck convoy.

"Oh?" The host was interested in hearing more.

"The street talk is that the XX [Chinese Communist] Party has sent news saying that they are willing to fight in the front lines [against the Japanese]! Apparently both parties [the Guomindang and the Chinese Communist Party] have settled their disputes."[4]

Two other friends talked in another corner:

"Both sides have come to a tacit understanding and are prepared to end the civil war and join forces up north."

"I'm afraid this is a smoke screen. In fact, the differences between the two—"

"But objectively speaking, this is entirely possible. Because—"

"Under pressure from the people—the smoke screen—is an old trick of the higher-ups."

No one could speak about this with any certainty.

Then the conversation took us to a new place.

"In Tianjin the market for white sugar has no buyers. Chinese sugar sells for eight dollars a bag, but Japanese sugar sells for only five dollars!"

"Smuggling is serious."

"The price of kerosene has come down."[5]

After leaving this elegant house, it was time for us to enter the machine shop with its belts and iron wheels.

Workers don't speak for no reason while they are working because it takes more than ten times the normal effort if they want to be heard. Also, there are all those interruptions.

"Hey, Old Li, the [Japanese] devils are coming. Aren't you scared?"

"I am only scared of rotten pumpkins! Good old me is prepared to carry a gun as soon as the war breaks out. It's much lighter work than what I'm doing here anyway."

"We can't go on living like this any more, let alone waiting for the devils to come. It will be worse once they come. Didn't the newspapers say that the devils force Chinese to work for them, then beat them all to death and throw them into the water as bait for the turtles?"

---

4. On May 5, 1936, the Chinese Communists sent a formal peace proposal to Chiang Kaishek, and, later in the month of May, Communist and Guomindang officials opened negotiations, but they did not settle their disputes at that time. See Hsu, *Chou En-lai*, pp. 114–16; and Wu, *The Sian Incident*, pp. 31–35.

5. On smuggling, see the introduction to Part IV; "The Smuggled Goods of the Day"; and "White Sugar."

"What a rotten thing to do—"

"Just you wait. Not a single foreigner is any good. Sooner or later we've got to throw them out."

"Old Liu, you can't say that. Foreign workers are just like us. Haven't you heard—"

In the afternoon:

A long line of trucks drove from west to east, loaded up with wooden crates, big gunny sacks, and gray clothing. There was a long trail of dust above the dry, gravel road. At this time, this author crossed from north to south heading into this cloud of dust. My nose was plugged, my eyes were shut, and I couldn't see a thing. There was only a strong smell of automobiles and an indescribable smell of sand and dirt.

At night:

This author would like to be able to report to you what opinion some "higher-ups" have of this episode, but I am so sorry, I can't find out a thing.

17. *The "Roar" of the Little Imps*

by Yu Zhijie,
a male elementary school teacher writing from Shanghai, Jiangsu

The fourth-period bell rang in civics class. A group of little imps quickly formed a line like a long, savory cruller which the big mouth of the classroom immediately gobbled up.

"—Smuggling—Little Old Han—Ya Dongyang—Commander Yang Jingyu—"[1]

These cries, clear and sharp, pierced my ears.

1. These were figures popularly identified with the Chinese resistance against the Japanese in Northeast China following the September Eighteenth Incident of 1931. (On the incident, see "A Never-to-Be-Forgotten Class," n. 4.) Little Old Han (Xiao Lao Han) was a Chinese from Liaoning in Northeast China who at 13 joined the Volunteer Army (on which, see "A Letter from the Northeast," n. 8); Ya Dongyang was a nickname which literally meant "Crush the Easterners [Japanese]"; and Yang Jingyu was a military commander who led Chinese guerrillas against the Japanese until his death in 1940 and has been posthumously hailed as a national hero in the People's Republic of China. On Little Old Han, see the play written in 1937 by Wu Zuguang, *Fenghuang cheng*, p. 109; and on Yang Jingyu, see Ling Yongkang and Fu Zhengyu, "Kang Ri yingxiong Yang Jingyu."

Enthusiastic expectations were apparent in every small face, but all were orderly.

We got down to work. The one known to be the most mischievous in the class raised his hand and said, "Sir, tell more news about Little Old Han today."

At this point, one of his old pals stood up and said, "Sir, after you finish talking about Little Old Han, give more news about Ya Dongyang, all right?"

"No, first finish talking about smuggling, and then tell about the other things," said the student who had the title of class head.

I sensed that the majority of the class wanted me to finish talking about smuggling in summary fashion and then continue to report on the actions taken by Little Old Han and Ya Dongyang.

But I decided to tease them.

"You all want me to talk, but I'm afraid you have probably already forgotten what I said last time."

"No, we remember everything in detail. If you don't believe it, just ask us anything."

"How do Little Old Han and Yang Jingyu lead the people in their struggles against the imperialists?" "Why is guerrilla warfare necessary?" "Why do the enemy troops defect?" "Why is it necessary for the Chinese and Korean peoples to unite?" I tested them one by one, and when the little imps saw that I was satisfied, they were proud.

"These are very easy! They are easier to remember than what's in the textbook!"

"If we're tested on these things in the final exam, I'll be very happy!"

It became a bit disorderly. I changed my expression to appear cool:

"What is the use of rote memorization?"

"No, sir, it's not rote memorization at all. I enthusiastically told my dad and mom about what I learned, and they were very happy."

"I told my neighbors. They are workers, and everyone was glad to hear what I said."

"Several of us often use Little Old Han's guerrilla tactics when we play up and down the alleys."

"I—"

"That's very good. Now I'll first give the latest news about Ya Dongyang." As I finished this sentence, several dozen pairs of eyes focused on me.

". . . One night enemy troops sent a telegram to their government, requesting immediate reinforcements. . . Now a division of troops has arrived in Jilin . . . and it has brought with it many weapons of the latest model."

"We're not afraid, even if two divisions come we wouldn't be afraid!"

"Guerrilla warfare scares away weapons of the latest model."

"With his ability, Commander Yang will be able to capture all their weapons again, as he did last time."

I also talked about how Zhao Shangzhi's[2] unit disguised itself as beggars and spied on the enemy and gathered military intelligence. The children got excited.

"I'll disguise myself as a little beggar and find my way in there too!"

"I want to be disguised as a little Japanese and they won't know!"

One or two little imps recollected the story of how Qi Jiguang[3] ordered his soldiers to disguise themselves as peasants and defeated the [Japanese] dwarf pirates,[4] and then interrupted, asking:

"Sir, were Qi Jiguang's military tactics guerrilla warfare?"

"Yes. But today's guerrilla warfare is different from earlier kinds, because the enemy's tactics are different."

Hearing me say that there was no recent news about Little Old Han and the Youth Corps, the little imps were disappointed. I told them the reason was because it is not possible for either major or minor newspapers to carry this kind of news. They yelled out:

"Crooks are hiding something from us, and they are all Chinese traitors!"

"Down with Chinese traitors!"

"Quiet down a bit," I urged. Then I noticed two mischievous ones sitting at a corner table in the back row, not paying full attention and whispering, writing, and making drawings amongst themselves.

I pretended not to notice them, sauntered slowly over there, grabbed that piece of paper, held it up, and took a look at it: there were several encampments and in them hung horizontal and vertical banners which

2. Zhao Shangzhi was commander of the Third Anti-Japanese Allied Army in Northeast China during the mid-1930s. See Boorman and Howard, eds., *Biographical Dictionary of Republican China*, vol. 2, p. 288.

3. Qi Jiguang was a Chinese military official in Ming times who was famed for his success at clearing the coast of Japanese pirates. See n. 4 below; and "Rumors," n. 2.

4. This is a literal translation of the term *wokou* (*wakō* in Japanese). It has commonly been used in China to refer to the freebooters who traded and plundered in Korea and the Chinese coastal provinces of Jiangsu, Zhejiang, and Fujian during the fourteenth, fifteenth, and sixteenth centuries. Although these freebooters have been popularly identified as "Japanese pirates," in actual fact not all of them were Japanese. See So Kwan-wai, *Japanese Piracy in Ming China during the 16th Century*, especially chaps. 1–2.

had "Youth Corps" and "Headquarters of the Commander-in-Chief of the People's Revolutionary Army"[5] written on them. In the left and right corners were sketches of Commander Yang, Little Old Han, and Li Hongguang. These were partially visible behind the big characters which were put on last, "Down with XX [Zhu and Mao][6] and the Reds" and "Down with Chinese Traitors."

I returned the paper to one of them. He shrugged his shoulders, hung his head, and tossed it into his drawer. Everyone couldn't help but look back.

I stood in the middle of this small regiment and gave my orders:

"Jin Genfa and Liang Rujun, report on your private talks. Tell the truth." They seemed embarrassed.

Jin Genfa: "I said I'm always thinking about Little Old Han. If he's nearby, I'll go to see him."

Liang Rujun: "I said if there's a Youth Corps in Shanghai, I want to leave school and join it right away."

This then stirred up the little imps and brought about a decisive response.

"I also want to join!"

"Sir, will you join too?"

Then another one said, "When the war starts, our dads and moms will take us with them to escape and what can we do then?"

"We can hide from them!"

"Talk daddy and mommy into joining!"

"Anybody escaping with his dad and mom is a little Chinese traitor!"

"I won't escape. Anybody who escapes is this." The mischievous one made an obscene hand gesture under the desk.

Just then the bell rang ending the class. "That stupid bell. How come the class goes so fast?" The little imps were disappointed.

"I don't want noon hour. I'm not a bit hungry!"

I couldn't accept their excessive demands. I erased what I had written on the blackboard, said "Goodbye," and left.

> "Arise, . . . Use our blood and flesh . . .
> To build our new Great Wall . . .
> The Chinese people . . ."[7]

5. On the People's Revolutionary Army, see "A Letter from the Northeast," n. 7.

6. Zhu was Zhu De, and Mao was Mao Zedong, the two foremost leaders of the Chinese Communist movement at this time. See Schram, *Mao Tse-tung*, chaps. 6–8.

7. This song, "March of the Volunteers," was originally written in 1934 by Tian Han and Nie Er for the Chinese film, *Children of the Storm*, and it later served as the national anthem of the People's Republic from 1949 until the late 1960s. See Boorman and Howard,

Then the sound of this patriotic song traveled out through the school gate.

18. *Little Sister Is Crying*

by QISHAN *(pseud.),*
a male teacher writing from Lanqi, Zhejiang

At seven o'clock on Thursday evening there was a parents' night at school. Ping's five-year-old little sister, Fen, attended along with her mother.

After supper, the lights in the auditorium were on, and people were chattering noisily. Although it was early summer, one could not smell any sweat in the air because most of those present were women and children.

After the announcements and speeches, the performances on the program began. The audience was quite pleased with the program, and from time to time people murmured to each other about the stories and the personalities of the actors. After doing comedies, they started a tragic drama. Then the atmosphere on the stage became tense and the audience became even more tense.

In the Northeast, the Volunteer Army[1] was gradually retreating as the X [Japanese] Army pressed forward step by step. Before long, the Volunteer Army was surrounded and its members were arrested one after another. The audience held its breath, hoping that there would be a way out. But things never go the way people want. This group of dedicated heroes who fought for the country and the people were tried en masse by a X [Japanese] military tribunal. For refusing to divulge military secrets, they were verbally abused and physically tortured.

The little kids in the audience could not suppress the fire that burned in their hearts, and they all raised their little fists and yelled out "Hate the XX [Japanese]!" and "Down with the XX [Japanese]!"

In this drama, Ping played the role of the head of the XX [Japanese] military tribunal. His face, usually kind and sincere, was now hidden

---

eds., *Biographical Dictionary of Republican China*, vol. 3, pp. 41 and 267. For a full translation of this song, see *Poems from China*, p. 225.

1. The Volunteer Army had led the Chinese resistance against the Japanese in Northeast China since 1931. See "A Letter from the Northeast," n. 8.

behind a mask of craftiness and cruelty. He must have been smiling proudly to himself for giving such a successful dramatic performance. At this time, from Ping's dual perspective, the sadness of the audience was for him a triumph. Therefore, the head of the XX [Japanese] military tribunal on the stage became more cruel and terrifying.

"My big brother is not a XX [Japanese]! My big brother is not a XX [Japanese]!"

From the audience came a pained voice. When Ping looked into the audience and saw that it was his own dear little sister, Fen, who was holding her face in her hands and sobbing, he was stunned. All of a sudden, Ping lost his composure and could not continue to play his role as well as before. Fortunately, the climax of this play had already passed by then, and no one seemed to be aware of the sudden change in his attitude.

Before long, Ping was down with the audience, holding his little sister, smiling in his usual kindly way, and explaining to her what had been happening in the play.

"Big brother! Next time don't play that kind of vicious XX [Japanese]!"

In Ping's arms, Little Sister Fen was smiling contentedly.

19. *Rumors*

by ZHENG YI,
a male elementary school teacher writing from Xianyou, Fujian

Because I got up a little later than usual, it seemed as if something was once again pounding inside my brain. The time for doing my usual reading had come, but I still sat around with the rest of the family, dull-minded and deeply depressed, and participated in their gabfest.

Rumors certainly spread faster than anything else. Originally baseless, once they begin to grow, they become more and more puffed up until people get tired of listening to them. Although newspapers have not reported it, everyone seems to have accepted the following in their hearts:

"The government has decided to resist X [Japan]! Those people [the Japanese] are complete savages. Sooner or later we've got to get tough with them. Relocate, relocate! Before the war breaks out, it is said that both our elderly and our children will have to move to Sichuan—or maybe to Xinjiang."

Along with this rumor that is spreading, an even more absurd rumor is going around. It says that a holy immortal displayed sacred powers in East Village. He first placed against a tree a wooden ladder that he had brought along, and then asked a little girl to climb up on it. When she stepped onto the first rung, she was amazed by the big, tall buildings that appeared before her eyes. Climbing up further, she saw rice and bean fields already golden and ripe. But what a mess—when she climbed onto the third rung, all she could see were corpses with no heads, no hands, and no legs. Oh, the beautiful crops and the grand tall buildings were all washed away in a foul-smelling stream of fresh blood.

Probably because some men with a bit of learning and intelligence were making comments, in less than two days the absurd rumor began to give rise to interpretations.

"Both beans and rice ripened in June, and corpses and fresh blood are the results of war. Huh, terrifying! This clearly means that the war will break out in June! Dead bodies will be strewn all over the countryside, and blood will flow like a river. Oh, houses and crops will all be completely wiped out. The destruction will be even worse than that inflicted by the [Japanese] dwarf pirates[1] in the past. It's going to be unbearable!"

I really don't know why rumors spread so fast, nor what kind of person is responsible for starting them. What might his intentions be? Especially in our small corner, which has been culturally backward and inconvenient to communicate with, most of us neither understood the meaning of such terms as "foreign aggression" and "patriotism" nor did we ever care about them. But recently, even totally illiterate old women and small children all understand what dreadful and despicable things "Chinese traitors" and "XX" [Japanese] are. Ah, isn't it likely that people here feel strongly because this place once suffered from a massacre at the hands of the dwarf pirates? Don't signs of old General Qi Jiguang's warfare still exist?[2] Haven't the stories about suppression of bandits spread from household to household? No wonder old women and little children—as if

1. "Dwarf pirates" (*wokou*) was a term long used to disparage the Japanese. See "The 'Roar' of the Little Imps," n.4.

2. Qi Jiguang (1528–88) was a Chinese military commander who drove the Japanese "dwarf pirates" away from the coast of Fujian and Zhejiang provinces during the late Ming dynasty. In 1567, people in Fuqing County (150 kilometers northeast of the place where "Rumors" was written) showed their gratitude by erecting a shrine in his honor. It was restored in 1733 and again in 1937. See L. Carrington Goodrich and Fang Chaoying, eds., *Dictionary of Ming Biography, 1368–1644*, pp. 220–24.

old women and little children were especially concerned with national affairs—all cry out:

"Hey, this is a good way to do it! The young and able-bodied will go and risk their lives fighting in the war, and we, the old and the little ones, will go far away. It's all right for us to go to Sichuan. Then they won't have to worry about their families, and will be able to concentrate whole-heartedly on what they are doing."

Some with more positive attitudes retort:

"We can work too—cooking, mending, and cleaning, aren't we good at all these things? When the young are fighting the war, we should fol-low behind and help."

Those who want to save China are in the end the people that no one notices in normal times!

After the rumors spread, shocking news comes daily, such as: "A huge army has arrived!" "Trenches have already been dug in such and such a place!"

But the elementary school teachers, who are the models for the peo-ple, are busy with something else: the demand for back pay. However, teachers who in the morning insisted on back pay, in the afternoon se-cretly proposed on their own that classes should resume. The organiza-tion responsible for securing back pay has in effect been dissolved, and what's behind this mystery only heaven knows.

Appendix A:
Appeal for Contributions to
One Day in China

Through newspapers and magazines, the sponsors of "One Day in China" advertized their project widely. Though most publications carrying the advertisement were based in Shanghai, some had nationwide circulation. For example, one publication that carried the advertisement, *Shen bao*, was one of the two most popular daily newspapers in China in 1936, with a circulation of 100,000–150,000 distributed in twenty-four of China's twenty-eight provinces plus Tibet and Mongolia; on the mainland, only the northeastern provinces, which had been occupied by Japan since 1931, were beyond its reach.[1] In addition, some of the periodicals carrying the advertisement—including *Funü shenghuo* (Women's Life), *Yong sheng* (Everlasting Life), and *Shijie zhishi* (World Knowledge)—also passed through extensive distributing networks, for they were published by Life Publishing Company (Shenghuo shu dian) which in the 1930s had fifty-five branches in fourteen provinces.[2]

These publications were accessible to far more Chinese than bare circulation statistics might lead us to suppose. Because of the Chinese practice of renting or reselling newspapers and magazines, observers in the mid-1930s estimated that each copy of a newspaper was read on the average by ten Chinese and each copy of a magazine by a still larger number.[3] Who read newspapers and where will not be known until a systematic analysis is done of the paths that the newspapers followed as they passed from the core cities to the peripheral towns and villages in each of China's regions. However, the available evidence shows that in some towns having less than 10,000 people and in some villages certain units (generally

1. Lin, *A History of the Press*, pp. 145 and 148.
2. Ting, *Government Control of the Press*. p. 155. By 1936, Life Publishing Company had also published books and essays by all of the members of the editorial board of "One Day in China," and in September 1936, it published the book *One Day in China*.
3. See Lin, *A History of the Press*, pp. 148–49. For an example of the rental of newspapers, see "Wu Garden and Xuanmiao Daoist Temple," above.

schools, temples, and government offices rather than individuals) subscribed to newspapers and made them publicly available by posting them outdoors or placing them in reading rooms.[4]

Hoping to reach the broadest possible audience, the sponsors and editors of "One Day in China" published the following appeal for contributions to their project in *Shen bao, Women's Life, Everlasting Life,* and *World Knowledge*[5]:

AN ANNOUNCEMENT CALLING FOR ESSAYS

Fortunate to have had the concern of readers and the support of writers, this magazine [*Literature*][6] is about to embark upon its fourth year. In order to repay our readers for their concern, we previously published *Literature and I* and *One Hundred Issues in Literature* as a token of our appreciation. The authors in this country and abroad who contributed to *Literature and I* and *One Hundred Issues in Literature* made these books successful and beloved among readers. At the beginning of our fourth year, on the one hand, we don't dare do anything but our best to repay our readers as we have in the past. On the other hand, we wish to go a step further and ask for cooperation from authors and readers and support from cultural circles. To this end, we have decided upon the topic "One Day in China" and respectfully request contributions. The editorial purposes and aims of "One Day in China" are as follows:

(1) "One Day in China" is intended to reveal the entire face of China during one day. The day that has been selected was chosen at random. The day we have selected is *May twenty-first.*

(2) Events and phenomena, large or small, which occur within the twenty-four hours of *May twenty-first* within the territory of China, whether at sea, on land, or in the air, all can be used as material for this book. Of this day's astronomy, weather, politics, diplomacy, happenings in society, gossip from back alleys, scheduled entertainment, people's comings and goings, none is to be excluded as material for this book.

(3) In accordance with the purposes stated above, we hope that all writers and unpublished writers who support this project of ours will pay attention to all events big or small on *May twenty-first* that are experienced or observed either on or off the job and will write down their impressions (in a maximum of two thou-

4. On the availability of newspapers in a small Middle Yangzi town during 1920, see Xu Zhucheng, *Jiu wen zha yi*, pp. 25–26; and on their availability in a small North China town, see Lao She, *Huozang*, p. 27. On the availability of newspapers in a South China village during the 1920s, see Daniel H. Kulp, *Country Life in South China*, p. 246. On the unavailability of newspapers in two North China villages in the 1930s, see Ramon H. Myers, *The Chinese Peasant Economy*, pp. 62 and 119. On the circulation of other reading materials, see Rawski, *Education and Popular Literacy in Ch'ing China*, p. 177 (where Kulp and Myers are cited) and passim.

5. See *Shen bao* (May 18, 20, and 21, 1936); *Funü shenghuo* (May 16, 1936); *Yong sheng* (May 16, 1936); and *Shijie zhishi* (May 16, 1936).

6. On *Literature*, see the introduction to this book, n. 3.

sand words). We also hope that artists throughout the entire country will enhance the contents of this book by submitting to us woodblock prints, sketches, cartoons, photographs of landscapes, or photographs of what happens in society which they have made or have taken on this one day.

(4) Materials for writing may be drawn from episodes that take place within personal experiences at work on *May twenty-first*, may be drawn from personal impressions on any aspect of anything in sight on *May twenty-first*, and may also be drawn from private correspondence and personal reflections on *May twenty-first*. Visual materials may be woodblock prints, cartoons, photographs, etc., which are done specially for *May twenty-first* or work completed on this day.

(5) We also wish to include materials about supernatural happenings on *May twenty-first* concerning various local customs, practices, superstitions, etc. (each piece having a maximum of one thousand words). We also wish to obtain interesting commerical advertising (including theater handbills and all kinds of handbills circulated in the streets) found on this one day.

(6) Also to be included in this book are materials on this day's politics, diplomacy, the military, and new books and new magazines, but soliciting such materials would obviously result in redundancies. Therefore, we have decided that the editorial board will make its own selection. But we still welcome reports on new books and new magazines published on this day outside Shanghai in the various provinces.

This is our plan. We hope that this book will encompass a cross-section of today's China. In this, we'll see the things that make us happy, the things that make us sad, the things we love, and the things we hate. We hope during today's so-called "crisis of 1936" that we'll be able to take a look at things of every shape and color throughout all of China on one day—a big picture.

This is no small project, so we sincerely appeal for support from writers, artists, people in all vocations, students, movie actors, theatrical performers throughout the entire country—all those who take an interest in this project.

We hope that all entries will be in the mail by May thirtieth. In return for each of those selected to be used, we shall respectfully send a small gratuity.

Please send entries to the editorial board of "One Day in China," in care of Life Publishing Company, 384 Fuzhou Road, Shanghai.

> Jointly announced by
> The Literary Society
> and
> The Editorial Board of "One Day in China"

Appendix B:
"Foreword to *One Day in China*," by Cai Yuanpei

When we heard of the topic "One Day in China," we thought it was the responsibility of the daily newspapers. After a moment's consideration, we realized that most of what the daily newspapers report are the events of the day before. Occasionally, urgent telegrams or local news received by editors within the first six hours of a working day may be rushed into the newspapers that day, but ordinary news of the day has to wait until the next day to be published. Therefore, what appears in the daily newspapers does not in fact represent the totality of one day. If we take one step back, we'll think of the noontime newspapers and the evening newspapers. I still haven't seen China's noontime newspapers, and therefore cannot comment on them. But since they are published at noon, there would certainly not be time to give reports of news that happened after noon. The evening newspapers that are published in localities where there are no noontime newspapers cover all the news that does not repeat what was in the daily newspapers, so it may appear that the entire day has been covered. But the printing of evening newspapers is always done at four or five o'clock, so the news happening after that must wait until the next day's daily newspapers. Therefore, the entire day is not completely covered. Furthermore, whether daily newspapers or evening newspapers, their space is limited; except for special news, the various aspects of human living can never be reported as fully as one would like. This is very obvious.

Therefore, the editors of "One Day in China" have had to design a special volume and solicit materials for it directly. Since the announcement soliciting essays was made public, over three thousand essays have been received, totaling over 6 million characters. For the convenience of customers, the publisher has made cut after cut, bringing the number down to 490 essays[1] totaling 800,000 characters. This cannot help but be considered a harvest beyond all expectations.

1. The number of essays published in *One Day in China* was 469, not 490. Cai Yuanpei repeated here the (erroneous) figure given by Mao Dun in his introduction to *One Day in China*. See Appendix C below, n. 2.

Also given this harvest and the rapport that has been established between the editorial board and the contributors, from now on, whenever the editorial board needs to conduct a special investigation into a certain locality or a certain matter, it may call upon people who have contributed to "One Day in China" and assign them to do it. Thus, the editorial board's hopes will certainly be fulfilled, and one harvest may develop into countless harvests, something that is unquestionably not beyond the realm of possibility!

Twenty-fifth year of the Republic of China [1936] September 4
Cai Yuanpei

Appendix C:
"On the Editorial Process,"
by Mao Dun

This book has been able to appear before the readers entirely because of enthusiastic suggestions and support from several thousand friends, both known and unknown, throughout the country and abroad.

This project originated from reading about the great Gorky's proposal for "One Day in the World," which is now being carried out, and from the feeling that this is extremely fresh and meaningful, so we will boldly "learn to walk." Yet, because this unprecedented "One Day in the World" has not yet been completed, we, as "the ones learning to walk," still do not have a good model by which to establish concrete editorial principles, and, as a result, we have had to fall back on our poor minds and boldly create. In addition, those of us who are responsible for the work have little talent or wealth compared to others in this country, and this has increased the difficulties. In all honestly, since the announcement soliciting essays for this volume was published, we have been apprehensive, lacking confidence that the project would come to fruition.

Now that this book is finally able to make its appearance before the readers and has also managed not to be a big disappointment, we must reiterate once again in all seriousness that it has depended entirely upon the help and suggestions of thousands of friends who have enthusiastically supported this project.

Between the publication of the announcement soliciting essays and the completion of the editing, a total of no more than three and one-half months has elapsed. The editorial board was established at the outset, and its chief responsibility was to discuss editorial principles and to mobilize contributors from various places to submit essays. Those on the editorial board, however, are nothing but cultural workers who have devoted their lives to writing essays and who have no cultural organization or institution in the country which would have provided clues for how to mobilize essays. Although the members of the editorial board have done their best to draw upon personal contacts and organizational connections to mobilize essays needed to follow the plan, the results were extremely meager. In this respect, even though the editorial board has already exhausted all approaches, it has not done justice to this project, and must apologize to the readers.

By around June tenth, however, the number and range of essays that had poured in from various places throughout the country excited us, gratified us, and made us realize that there were in poor villages and remote areas innumerable nameless heroes working in cultural affairs who responded enthusiastically to our humble call, making us recognize how great our people's latent cultural creativity is!

Of the essays we have received, if we count by the character, the number is no less than 6 million, and, if we count by the piece, the number is over three thousand. With the exceptions of Xinjiang, Qinghai, Xikang, Tibet, and Mongolia, every province and city throughout the entire country has furnished essays. Except those with a special "way of life" such as Buddhists, Daoists, prostitutes, and itinerant peddlers, there is not a single social stratum or vocational way of life unrepresented among the large number of essays received. We also received essays from supporters living in the Southeast Asian archipelago, Thailand, and Japan. *May twenty-first* aroused the hearts of almost all those Chinese able to read who are within the country or abroad, who are concerned about the destiny of our motherland, and who are eager to know the whole, true face of our motherland which is at this perilous juncture. They have brought about a general mobilization of minds.

In organizing, editing, and selecting the essays resulting from this great general mobilization of minds, how can we afford to be less than cautious and thorough? Mightn't we make up a little for our shortcomings in mobilizing essays by our editing of the essays received? Shouldn't we have an editorial policy different from that of ordinary periodicals? These were our hopes at the time, and we have exhausted our limited amount of wisdom in the search for a perfect solution.

Just as hard realities shattered our various idealistic plans when we mobilized essays, so too did hard realities hold our ideals in check when we drafted our editorial policies. The publishing house responsible for printing this book[1] has limited financial strength, and we couldn't help but take this into account. In addition, we had to pay still greater attention to the low purchasing power of readers. In a situation where the two both had to be considered, we, at first, decided on an editorial principle: The number of characters in the entire book was to be between 500,000 and 700,000, and the price was not to exceed one dollar and sixty cents.

This restriction—limiting the number of words because of the limitation on the price—made it impossible for us to use a free hand as ideally as we would have liked in selecting all the essays that carried social significance or reflected every corner of life on one day in China. The essays that we first selected totaled more than 860 pieces and approximately 1,300,000 words. This was almost twice as many as our projected upper limit (which was 700,000 words). What was to be

---

1. The publisher of *One Day in China* was Life Publishing Company. On it, see Appendix A above.

done? It was almost impossible to carry on. Recognizing that there was no way out, we decided upon a second set of criteria for selection, as follows:

(1) Categories were established geographically, according to where contributors came from. In a region where there were many contributors—for example, Shanghai alone had more than 600 pieces accounting for 20 percent of the total essays submitted, and about 130 of them, consisting of 250,000 words, had been chosen on the first round—they had to be critically screened.

(2) Essays coming from the same region were classified according to content and nature. Essays of the same nature or about the same kind of life were also critically screened.

(3) Criteria for the so-called critical screening were difficult to decide upon. Ordinarily work is judged on the basis of whether the writing is skillful or not, but in this case we couldn't do so. If we had done it this way, this book would have been extremely monotonous—many essays would have been rejected whose literary style is not so good or not even grammatically correct but whose contents are extremely meaningful. Wouldn't this have been a great loss? Therefore our criteria for critical screening were first content and second the skillfulness or lack of it in the writing. If the contents of two or more essays concerned the same subject, we chose the one in the best literary style. Next, even if the contents concerned the same subject but were written by people in two different positions, then, though one's writing style might have been good and the other bad, we still included both. For example, in the section on Shanghai, we included two essays describing life in textile factories, one written by a clerk and another written by a worker. (If there had been an essay by an owner of a textile factory, we would feel better about it. When we first mobilized essays, we had this plan, but unfortunately we got nowhere.) Finally, if we received only one piece on a certain aspect of life, then we used it no matter how badly it was written—and edited it to make it intelligible without changing its original meaning.

(4) With regard to so-called content there had to be some criteria. First, we required that the essay had to deal with an event that occurred on May twenty-first. Next, this event had to have social significance or at least reflect the living conditions of a segment of society. At the very least, it should offer a basis for comparison with another serious social phenomenon.

(5) Besides the above points, a special criterion was added (in fact it cannot be said to be a criterion but rather an exception) which is that in the case of frontier provinces from which relatively few or exceedingly few essays were submitted, we used almost all of them without exception. For example, among the essays from Yunnan, we included a piece by a middle school student. Both in content and in literary style, this piece is far inferior to essays from Shanghai, Jiangsu, and Zhejiang that were rejected. But we felt that One Day in China should not be One Day in China of the few provinces and areas which have a comparatively high degree of culture, so the same standards were not appropriate for the frontier provinces.

(6) We also included essays about the utterly irrational and superstitious without exception. Isn't irrationality also an aspect of Chinese life?

We decided upon these criteria for lack of any other alternative. However, even though we were under restriction upon restriction and abandoned many appealing essays, the total remaining number still reached about 490[2] consisting of about 800,000 words, exceeding our upper limit by about 100,000. This number of pieces and words was less than half of what it had been after the first screening, and we deeply regret having to make a second screening. But we feel that we can almost justify it to the readers because we have made the greatest effort to produce a book of 800,000 words in which the aspects of life that have been encompassed are wide-ranging and complex. Isn't it possible to say without exaggeration that it can lay bare a cross-section of China? Moreover, perhaps precisely because realities have forced us to wear "tight shoes," the weaknesses of repetitious material and sloppy organization are almost entirely absent from this book, which is composed of nearly five hundred short essays. In this we also feel we have done justice to the readers.

Once the materials were selected, the next question was how to arrange them. Should they be arranged according to the contents of the essays? Should they be arranged according to geographical areas? We decided upon the latter. If they had been arranged according to the essays' contents, many essays would not fit into any one category, or those able to fit might belong in more than one category. Furthermore, an arrangement by geographical areas can make the special features of Chinese society's uneven development more or less readily apparent. For example, in the section on Shanghai we received essays that describe poverty in the lives of elementary school teachers, and, from Shandong, Hebei, and other provinces we also received essays of the same nature. However, although poverty is the same, the social causes of it are quite different. We feel that placing the essays from Shanghai together with other essays describing other aspects of life in Shanghai is more meaningful than placing the essays in a category such as "The Lives of Elementary School Teachers" and can further illustrate the complicated relationships in the social life of a given area. This also applies to materials of the same nature from Shandong, Hebei, and other provinces.

But even when we arranged them according to geographical area, it was still difficult to fit some essays very neatly into place, such as those written about what was seen or heard from a train or boat. We have specifically put this kind in one place and borrowed a rather interesting term for its title: "Sea. Land. Air."[3] We only received one piece from the "Air," and it could have been put in the section on Zhejiang, but we have used it to fill the category of "Air."

Our fellow countrymen living overseas have shown considerable interest in the plans for this book. Many essays have come in, especially from Hong Kong. We have also put this kind in a separate section entitled "The Trail of the Over-

2. Apparently Mao Dun miscounted, or else he deleted some pieces from *One Day in China* after writing this introduction and before publishing the book, for the actual number appearing in it was 469, not 490.

3. This phrase "Sea. Land. Air." (*Hai. Lu. Kong.*) is perhaps a reference to a patriotic slogan of the 1930s calling for China to resist foreign aggression by building a new and powerful navy, army, and air force.

seas Chinese." This is similar to the so-called "outer section" which the ancients added to the books that they wrote after having completed the "inner section." We feel that the flaw in this otherwise beautiful idea is that too few essays came from Overseas Chinese, on the Southeast Asian archipelago.

All of the above refers to the essays that came in. Besides these we also have sets of materials that we have compiled ourselves.

One set deals with politics, economics, foreign relations, military affairs, education, and sports at the national level for May twenty-first. All of these either appeared in the newspapers on the twenty-first or occurred on the twenty-first. Most of what appeared in the newspapers on the twenty-first took place before the twenty-first, but since these reached all readers through newspapers on the twenty-first, these deserve to occupy a place in this "one day history" of the twenty-first. We have therefore incorporated them. For this kind of material we have established a separate section, "A Bird's-eye View of the Entire Country," which appears at the beginning of the book as a whole. This section was arranged and edited by Mr. Zhang Zhongshi.[4]

A second set of materials is a list of newspapers in various places throughout the country. We have collected nearly one hundred newspapers for this day from each locality throughout the country. According to reliable statistics, there are over 400 major and minor newspapers throughout the country, and what we have collected is, therefore, not quite complete, but we do have all the major newspapers. For the sake of indicating as much as possible what kind of public opinion organizations exist in each locality throughout the country, we have written a simple summary of each of the newspapers that we have collected. We paid attention to editorials, headlines (it is very interesting to compare the various headlines, for they reflect the different viewpoints of the various newspapers), and essays from literary supplements. This task was the responsibility of Mr. Kong Lingjing.[5] We have also established a separate section for these, entitled "The Newspapers of One Day."[6] Because so few periodicals and books were published on this day, they were noted at the end of this section rather than being allocated a section of their own.

A third set of materials is on the entertainment in each locality: movies, plays, radio programs, etc. This section, which is limited to the major cities of each province, is also under a separate title, "The Entertainment of One Day."[7]

Originally we planned to include various statistics of this day—for example, imports and exports from the Maritime Customs, production figures on various major industries, numbers of passengers and loads carried by each railroad and

4. Zhang Zhongshi, a journalist and editor, was a member of the the editorial board of *One Day in China*. None of the section on the events of the day has been translated here.

5. Kong Lingjing, a dramatist, essayist, and specialist on early Chinese fiction, was the assistant editor of *One Day in China*. On him, see Gálik, *Mao Tun and Modern Chinese Literary Criticism*, p. 4.

6. None of the section on newspapers has been translated here.

7. None of the section on entertainment has been translated here.

Chinese commercial or foreign commercial shipping line throughout the entire country, amounts of money in people's savings throughout the entire country, etc. But in China it seems especially difficult to find these quantitative statistics, and since we obtained only one or two incomplete statistics, we threw up our hands and abandoned the idea.

Finally, let us comment on our reflections now that the book has been edited.

If the essays we received are classified according to the social backgrounds of the authors, then 34.9 percent came from students, 15.5 percent from teachers, 1.7 percent from workers, 9 percent from merchants, 0.4 percent from peasants, 4.7 percent from professional writers, and 33.8 percent from free-lance professionals, soldiers, police, and people of undetermined vocations. If classified by sex, only 4 or 5 percent came from females. (Since we could not determine whether a female or a male had done the writing in many essays, this is only an estimate.)

If these were what we received, what did we draw upon most heavily? We drew most heavily on the essays written by those who had never before written for publication (that is, the non-professional writers). This is because their essays conformed most closely to our criteria, and they are the reason why the material in this book is unmonotonous and lays bare the many faces of life on one day in China.

One thing especially worth noting is that most of those who have never before written for publication (that is, the non-professional writers) such as shopkeepers, small businessmen, public servants, soldiers, policemen, military police, elementary school teachers, etc., write with literary skill that is above average. Some of them whose writing is not very fluent have a simplicity that is very appealing. Conversely, most students and even a few professional writers could not in their essays avoid much of the so-called "jargon of the new literature." From this we came to the profound realization that our people have latent talent which, if conditions improve, will bloom and produce literary blossoms several times more beautiful than anything that we have ever seen before.

This is no fantasy. Most of the materials in this book are a guarantee that it is true. The five hundred pieces included in this book come from almost every literary genre. In it there are short stories, reportage, short essays, diary entries, letters, traveler's journals, sketches, impressionistic jottings, and short plays, with quite a few truly good ones in almost every genre. Most of the good ones were written by "untried people" "making their debut." If it were not for "One Day in China," would they ever have picked up a pen and written for publication literary works about things outside their vocations? (In the letters to us that they attached, they all said that they would not have.) Their names are unfamiliar, the material that they have written about is fresh, but it may certainly be said that their technique is refined.

They show us how from south to north and from west to east Chinese farming villages have deteriorated and collapsed under all kinds of domestic and foreign destruction and invasion. They also show us how local bullies and evil gentry have exploited public means for private gain to the extent that wherever there is "reconstruction"[8] it has inflicted suffering on the common people. They cry out in pain at the extent to which the greatest enemy of our race has extended its antennae into poor villages and remote areas. They heroically recount that they have received inhumane treatment as a result of their seeking liberation of the people. They decisively and courageously issue a challenge to those Chinese traitors who have become "claws for the tiger." They show us how many hot-blooded patriots, suffering bitterly and steadfastly under severe oppression, are painstakingly and patiently carrying out sacred work—from promotion of the National Salvation Movement, which has deeply penetrated among the people,[9] to help for the masses in learning their own written language, and from bloody struggles to disciplined and open-minded study of theory.

Truly, here there is everything: the dissipation and indulgence of the rich, the writhing masses on the edge of starvation, the patriots devoting their lives to the people's revolution, the backward and insensate classes, the rampant religious superstitions, the degeneracy of the public servants, the overbearing swagger of the local bullies and evil gentry, the oppression of women, the hesitancy of the petty bourgeoisie and intellectuals, the bitter pain and enduring spirit of the martyrs. Truly! From the main streets and back alleys of cities, from the tall buildings and thatched huts, from the deserted little marketplaces of small towns, from the broken-down walls and dilapidated houses of farming villages, from the schools, from the sleeping quarters of the unemployed, from the army barracks, from the prisons, from the companies and the government offices, from the factories, from the markets, from the small shops, from the old families governed by strict family rules—from every single corner of China there have arisen anguished and strong calls to arms, grief-stricken utterances, bitter cursing, tearful smiles, restrained but boiling passions, the sleeptalking of those leading lives without a sense of purpose, the charlatanism of religious converts, the sardonic laughter of heartless ones! This is the spectacular orchestra heard on one day in today's China, but it is not confined only to this one day!

However much this cross-section may have intertwined the ugly and the evil, the sacred and the pure, and the light and the darkness, we can see in it optimism, hope, and awakening of the masses of people. This is because although on the one side are dissipation and shamelessness, on the other side is work being done in earnest!

Mao Dun   August 20, 1936

8. Rural reconstruction during the 1930s consisted of experiments in several localities designed to improve life in rural China. See "A Comedy in the Midst of Sorrow," n. 1.

9. The National Salvation Movement was an attempt to mobilize popular support for a broad consensus that would bridge the gap between the Guomindang and the Chinese Communist Party and thus unite all Chinese against Japanese aggression. Originally under student leadership at the end of 1935, it grew rapidly during 1936, causing women, workers, professors, and merchants as well as students to form National Salvation Associations and to join in boycotts, strikes, and other anti-Japanese protests. See Israel, *Student Nationalism in China* pp. 158–62; Eastman, *The Abortive Revolution*, pp. 249–51; and Lyman P. Van Slyke, *Enemies and Friends*, pp. 68–74.

Passages Translated

The pieces translated in this book appeared in the original *One Day in China* on the following pages:

	Part I		Part II		Part III		Part IV
A.	1. 3.36–37	A.	1.12.11–13	A.	1. 4.4–5	A.	1. 10.4–5
	2. 9.8–9		2. 9.9–11		2. 4.31		2. 10.10–12
	3. 9.18–20		3. 4.49–50		3. 11.53–54		3. 10.6–7
	4. 12.17–20		4. 6.12–14		4. 9.31–32		4. 10.19–21
	5. 6.37–39		5. 7.30–31		5. 14.34–37		5. 10.12–13
	6. 4.89–90		6. 4.18–19		6. 4.84		6. 10.21–23
	7. 6.21–22	B.	7. 4.81–82		7. 6.34–35	B.	7. 8.41–42
	8. 11.14–17		8. 4.87–89		8. 5.32–33		8. 12.6–7
B.	9. 7.10		9. 4.46–47	B.	9. 12.31–32		9. 13.61–62
	10. 4.60–62		10. 4.47–49		10. 5.37–38		10. 13.4–5
	11. 4.82		11. 11.32–33		11. 6.11		11. 8.45–46
	12. 6.5–6		12. 9.22		12. 6.33–34		12. 11.43–44
	13. 6.19–21		13. 14.16–17		13. 4.68		13. 2.25–27
	14. 13.53–55		14. 9.20–21		14. 5.8	C.	14. 8.7–9
	15. 4.51	C.	15. 13.21–24		15. 12.39		15. 3.14–15
C.	16. 5.49–51		16. 7.32–34		16. 4.58–59		16. 12.2–4
	17. 3.45–47		17. 4.44–46		17. 4.25–26		17. 3.48–50
	18. 5.21–22		18. 6.39–40	C.	18. 5.44–45		18. 5.48–49
	19. 6.2–3		19. 13.43–44		19. 13.40–41		19. 13.64–65
	20. 11.22–23		20. 14.29–33		20. 4.29–31		
	21. 14.13–14				21. 3.90–91		
	22. 3.13				22. 5.30–31		
					23. 13.17–18		

Bibliography

Agee, James, and Walker Evans. *Let Us Now Praise Famous Men*. New York, 1941.

Alitto, Guy S. *The Last Confucian: Liang Shu-ming and the Chinese Dilemma of Modernity*. Berkeley, 1979.

Bagish, Martin, and Hilary Conroy. "Japanese Aggression against China: The Question of Responsibility." In Alvin D. Coox and Hilary Conroy, eds., *China and Japan*, pp. 325–33.

Baker, Hugh D. R. *Chinese Family and Kinship*. New York, 1979.

Bates, M. Searle. *Missions in Far Eastern Cultural Relations*. New York, 1943.

Berninghausen, John. "The Central Contradiction in Mao Dun's Early Fiction." In Merle Goldman, ed., *Modern Chinese Literature in the May Fourth Era*, pp. 233–59.

Bisson, T. A. *Japan in China*. New York, 1938.

Bodde, Derk. *Festivals in Classical China: New Year and Other Annual Observations during the Han Dynasty, 206 B.C.–A.D. 200*. Princeton, 1975.

Bodde, Derk, and Clarence Morris. *Law in Imperial China*. Cambridge, Mass., 1967.

Boorman, Howard L., and Richard C. Howard, eds. *Biographical Dictionary of Republican China*. 4 vols. New York, 1967. Vol. 5, *A Personal Name Index*, compiled by Janet Krompart. New York, 1979.

Cao Xueqin. *Hong lou meng* [Dream of the Red Chamber], translated by David Hawkes under the title *The Story of the Stone*. 3 vols. Harmondsworth, England, 1973, 1977, 1981.

Catalogue of Copyright Entries (Cumulative Series), Motion Pictures, 1912–1939. Washington, D.C., 1951.

Chan Wing-tsit. "Chinese Terminology." In *Encyclopedia of Religion*, edited by Vergilius Ferm, pp. 143–58. New York, 1945.

———. *Religious Trends in Modern China*. New York, 1953.

Chen Bulei. *Chen Bulei Huiyilu* [Memoirs of Chen Bulei]. Shanghai, 1949.

Chen Yu-shih. "Mao Dun and the Use of Political Allegory in Fiction: A Case Study of His 'Autumn in Kuling.'" In Merle Goldman, ed., *Modern Chinese Fiction in the May Fourth Era*, pp. 261–80.

Chen Yuan-tsung. *The Dragon's Village*. Harmondsworth, England, 1981.

Chi, Madeleine. "Ts'ao Ju-lin (1876–1966): His Japanese Connections." In Iriye Akira, ed., *The Chinese and the Japanese*, pp. 140–60.

Chien Tuan-sheng. "Wartime Local Government in China." *Pacific Affairs* 16.4 (1943): 441–60.

Chow Tse-tsung. *The May Fourth Movement: Intellectual Revolution in Modern China.* Cambridge, Mass., 1960.

Ch'u T'ung-tsu. *Local Government in China under the Ch'ing.* Cambridge, Mass., 1962.

Coble, Parks M., Jr. *The Shanghai Capitalists and the Nationalist Government, 1927–1937.* Cambridge, Mass., 1980.

——. "Suppression of the Anti-Japanese Movement in Nationalist China, 1931–1937: Tsou T'ao-fen and His Associates." Unpublished paper presented at the Midwest China Seminar. Chicago, 1982.

Confucius. *Lunyu* [The Analects of Confucius]. Translated by Arthur Waley under the title *The Analects of Confucius.* New York, 1938.

Coox, Alvin D., and Hilary Conroy, eds. *China and Japan: Search for Balance Since World War I.* Santa Barbara, Calif., 1978.

Croll, Elisabeth. *Feminism and Socialism in China.* New York, 1980.

Crowley, James B. "A New Deal for Japan and Asia: One Road to Pearl Harbor." In James B. Crowley, ed., *Modern East Asia*, pp. 235–64.

——. "Intellectuals as Visionaries of the New Asian Order." In *Dilemmas of Growth in Prewar Japan*, edited by James William Morley, pp. 319–73. Princeton, 1971.

——. *Japan's Quest for Autonomy: National Security and Foreign Policy, 1930–1938.* Princeton, 1966.

Crowley, James B., ed. *Modern East Asia: Essays in Interpretation.* New York, 1970.

Davidson-Houston, J. V., and R. V. Dewar-Durie, eds. *Chinese and English Modern Military Dictionary.* Beiping, 1934.

Davin, Delia. "Women in the Countryside of China." In Margery Wolf and Roxane Witke, eds. *Women in Chinese Society*, pp. 243–73.

De Bary, William Theodore, et al. *Sources of Chinese Tradition.* New York, 1960.

de Groot. See Groot.

Diamond, Norma. "Women under Kuomintang Rule: Variations on the Feminine Mystique." *Modern China* 1.1 (January 1975): 3–45.

Dietz, F. C. "The Roman Catholic Church, 1936." In *The China Christian Yearbook, 1936–37*, edited by Frank Rawlinson, pp. 112–24. Glendale, Calif., 1937.

Dirklik, Arif. "The Ideological Foundations of the New Life Movement: A Study in Counterrevolution." *Journal of Asian Studies* 34.4 (August 1975): 945–80.

Diyi jituanjun zongsiling bu [Headquarters of the Commander-in-Chief of the First Group], ed. *Fagui huibian* [Compilation of Regulations]. 4 vols. N.p., 1933.

Dorris, Carl E. "Peasant Mobilization and the Origins of Yenan Communism." *China Quarterly* 68 (December 1976): 697–719.

Eastman, Lloyd E. *The Abortive Revolution: China under Nationalist Rule, 1927–1937.* Cambridge, Mass., 1974.

————. "The Disintegration and Integration of Political Systems in Twentieth-Century China." *Chinese Republican Studies Newsletter* 1.3 (April 1976): 2–12.

————. "Facets of an Ambivalent Relationship: Smuggling, Puppets, and Atrocities during the War, 1937–1945." In Iriye Akira, ed., *The Chinese and the Japanese*, pp. 275–303.

Eberhard, Wolfram. *Chinese Festivals.* New York, 1952.

Ebrey, Patricia Buckley, ed. *Chinese Civilization and Society.* New York, 1981.

Editorial Board of *Izvestiia* (A. Adzhubei, editor-in-chief), ed. *Den mira* [One Day in the World]. Moscow, 1960.

Fairbank, John K. "Introduction: The Many Faces of Protestant Missions in China and the United States." In *The Missionary Enterprise in China and America*, edited by John K. Fairbank, pp. 1–19. Cambridge, Mass., 1974.

————. *Chinabound: A Fifty-Year Memoir.* New York, 1982.

Fei Hsiao-t'ung. *Peasant Life in China: A Field Study of Country Life in the Yangtze Valley.* London, 1939.

Feuchtwang, Stephan, "City Temples in Taipei under Three Regimes." In *The Chinese City between Two Worlds*, edited by Mark Elvin and G. William Skinner, pp. 263–301. Stanford, 1974.

Feuerwerker, Albert. *The Foreign Establishment in China in the Early Twentieth Century.* Michigan Papers in Chinese Studies, no. 29. Ann Arbor, 1976.

Freedman, Maurice. *Chinese Lineage and Society: Fukien and Kwangtung.* London, 1966.

Freedman, Maurice, ed. *Family and Kinship in Chinese Society.* Stanford, 1970.

Funü shenghuo [Women's Life]. Shanghai, 1935–37.

Gálik, Marián. *Mao Tun and Modern Chinese Literary Criticism.* Wiesbaden, 1969.

Gamble, Sidney D. *Ting Hsien: A North China Rural Community.* New York, 1954.

Gewurtz, Margo Speisman. *Between America and Russia: Chinese Student Radicalism and Travel Books of Tsou T'ao-fen.* Toronto, 1975.

Gillin, Donald G. "'Peasant Nationalism' in the History of Chinese Communism." *Journal of Asian Studies* 23.2 (February 1964): 269–89.

————. *Warlord: Yen Hsi-shan in Shansi Province, 1911–1949.* Princeton, 1967.

Goldman, Merle, ed. *Modern Chinese Literature in the May Fourth Era.* Cambridge, Mass., 1977.

Goodrich, L. Carrington, and Fang Chaoying, eds. *Dictionary of Ming Biography, 1368–1644.* New York, 1976.

Gorky, Maxim, and Mikhail Kolzov, eds. *Den mira* [One Day in the World]. Moscow, 1937.

Groot, J. M. M. de. *The Religious System of China.* 6 vols. Leiden, 1892–1910.

Grove, Linda Ann. "Rural Society in Revolution: The Gaoyang District, 1910–1947." Ph.D. dissertation, University of California, Berkeley, 1975.

Hanyu zidian [Dictionary of Chinese]. Hong Kong, 1971; originally published in 1937.

Heercaofu, M. (M. Kolzov). "Shijie di yi ri" [One Day in the World]. Translated by Mao Dun. *Yiwen* [Translations] 1.1 (March 16, 1936): 43–53.

Hofheinz, Roy, Jr. *The Broken Wave: The Chinese Communist Peasant Movement, 1922–1928.* Cambridge, Mass., 1977.

Hou Ching-Lang. *Monnaies d'offrande et la notion de trésorerie dans la religion chinoise* [The Offering of Money and the Idea of the Treasury in Chinese Religion]. Paris, 1975.

Hsia, C. T. *A History of Modern Chinese Fiction, 1917–1957.* 2nd rev. ed., New Haven, 1971.

Hsia Ching-lin et al., trans. *The Civil Code of the Republic of China.* 5 vols. Shanghai, 1931.

Hsiao Kung-chuan. *Rural China: Imperial Control in the Nineteenth Century.* Seattle, 1960.

Hsu Kai-yu. *Chou En-lai: China's Gray Eminence.* Garden City, N.J., 1968.

Hsu Kai-yu, ed. and trans. *Twentieth Century Chinese Poetry: An Anthology.* Ithaca, N.Y., 1970.

Ichiko Chūzō. "The Role of the Gentry: An Hypothesis." In Mary Clabaugh Wright, ed., *China in Revolution*, pp. 297–317.

Inlow, Burke. "Japan's 'Special Trade' in North China." *Far Eastern Quarterly* 6.2 (February 1947): 139–67.

Institute of International Relations. *Chinese Communist Who's Who.* 2 vols. Taipei, 1971.

Iriye Akira. *After Imperialism: The Search for a New Order in the Far East, 1921–1931.* Cambridge, Mass., 1965.

Iriye Akira, ed. *The Chinese and the Japanese: Essays in Political and Cultural Interactions.* Princeton, 1980.

Isaacs, Harold R., ed. *Straw Sandals: Chinese Short Stories 1918–1933.* Cambridge, Mass., 1974.

Israel, John. *Student Nationalism in China, 1927–1937.* Stanford, 1966.

Israel, John, and Donald W. Klein. *Rebels and Bureaucrats: China's December 9ers.* Berkeley, 1976.

Jansen, Marius B. *Japan and China: From War to Peace, 1894–1972.* Chicago, 1975.

Johnson, Chalmers. A. *Peasant Nationalism and Communist Power: The Emergence of Revolutionary China, 1937–1945.* Stanford, 1962.

———. "Peasant Nationalism Revisited: The Biography of a Book." *China Quarterly* 72 (December 1977): 766–85.

Jones, Susan Mann, ed. *Select Papers from the Center for Far Eastern Studies, University of Chicago*, no. 3. Chicago, 1978–79.

Kahn, B. Winston. "Doihara Kenji and the North China Autonomy Movement, 1935–1936." In Alvin D. Coox and Hilary Conroy, eds., *China and Japan*, pp. 177–207.

Kim, Ilpyong J. *The Politics of Chinese Communism: Kiangsi under the Soviets.* Berkeley, 1973.

Klein, Donald W., and Anne B. Clark. *Biographic Dictionary of Chinese Communism, 1921–1965.* Cambridge, Mass., 1971.

Kolzov, Mikhail. "Den mira" [One Day in the World]. In Maxim Gorky and Mikhail Kolzov, eds. *Den mira*, pp. iii–v.

Kong Chong. *Xian zheng jianshe* [The Reconstruction of County Administration]. Shanghai, 1937.

Kuhn, Philip A. "Local Self-Government under the Republic: Problems of Control, Autonomy, and Mobilization." In *Conflict and Control in Late Imperial China*, edited by Frederic Wakeman, Jr., and Carolyn Grant, pp. 257–98. Berkeley, 1975.

———. "Local Taxation and Finance in Republican China." In Susan Mann Jones, ed., *Select Papers from the Center for Far Eastern Studies*, no. 3, pp. 100–36.

———. *Rebellion and Its Enemies in Late Imperial China: Militarization and Social Structure, 1796–1864*. Cambridge, Mass., 1970.

Kuhn, Philip A., and Susan Mann Jones, "Introduction." In Susan Mann Jones, ed., *Select Papers from the Center for Far Eastern Studies*, no. 3, pp. v–xix.

Kulp, Daniel H. *Country Life in South China: The Sociology of Familism*. New York, 1925.

Lang, Olga. *Chinese Family and Society*. New Haven, 1946.

Lao She. *Huozang* [Cremation]. Shanghai, 1948.

Lee Chong-Sik. "The Chinese Communist Party and the Anti-Japanese Movement in Manchuria: The Initial Stage." In Alvin D. Coox and Hilary Conroy, eds., *China and Japan*, pp. 143–72.

Legge, James. *The Four Books*. Hong Kong, 1960; originally published in Oxford, England, 1893.

Levenson, Joseph R. *Liang Ch'i-ch'ao and the Mind of Modern China*. Cambridge, Mass., 1953.

Leyda, Jay. *Dianying: Electric Shadows, An Account of Films and the Film Audience in China*. Cambridge, Mass., 1972.

Li Wenhui. *Zhongguo difang zizhi zhi shiji yu lilun* [Realities and Theories of Chinese Local Self-Government]. Shanghai, 1936.

Lin Yutang. *A History of the Press and Public Opinion in China*. Chicago, 1936.

Ling Yongkang and Fu Zhengyu. "Kang Ri yingxiong Yang Jingyu" [Yang Jingyu, Hero of the Resistance against Japan]. In *Lishi renwu ji* [Collected Essays on Historical Figures], pp. 56–74. Shanghai, 1976.

Liu Bao, ed. *Xiandai Zhongguo renwu zhi* [Directory of People in Contemporary China]. Shanghai, 1941.

Liu T'ieh-yün. *The Travels of Lao Ts'an*. Translated by Harold Shadick. Ithaca, N.Y., 1952.

Liu Yiling. *Song Shangjie zhuan* [The Life of Song Shangjie]. Hong Kong, 1962.

Lu Xun (Lu Hsun). "Wu Chang or Life-Is-Transient." In *Dawn Blossoms Plucked at Dusk*, translated by Yang Hsien-yi and Gladys Yang, pp. 43–52. Beijing, 1976.

———. "The True Story of Ah Q." In *Selected Stories of Lu Hsun*, translated by Yang Hsien-yi and Gladys Yang, pp. 65–112. Beijing, 1960.

McDonald, Gerald D. et al., *The Films of Charlie Chaplin*. New York, 1965.

McDougall, Bonnie S. "The Impact of Western Literary Trends." In Merle Goldman, ed., *Modern Chinese Literature in the May Fourth Era*, pp. 37–61.

Mao Dun et al., eds. *Zhongguo di yi ri* [One Day in China]. Shanghai, 1936.

Mao Zedong (Mao Tse-tung). "Report on an Investigation of the Peasant Movement in Hunan." In *Selected Work of Mao Tse-tung*, vol. 1, pp. 23–59. Beijing, 1967.

Maritime Customs. *The Trade of China, 1936: Introductory Survey*. Shanghai, 1937.

Maruyama Masao. *Thought and Behavior in Modern Japanese Politics*. Edited by Ivan Morris. London, 1965.

Maspero, Henri. "The Mythology of Modern China." In *Asiatic Mythology*, by J. Hackin et al., pp. 252–384. London, 1932.

Meicun (pseud.). "Shen Zijiu." In Yang Yiming, ed., *Wentan shiliao*, pp. 250–51.

Meisner, Maurice. "Yenan Communism and the Rise of the Chinese People's Republic." In Crowley, ed., *Modern East Asia*, pp. 265–97.

Mencius. *Mencius*. Translated by D. C. Lau. Bungay, England, 1970.

Menzel, Johanna M., ed. *The Chinese Civil Service: Career Open to Talent?* Boston, 1963.

Min bao [The People's Journal], 1905–1910. Vols. 1–4 in photolithographic reprint, Beijing, 1957.

Miyazaki Ichisada. *China's Examination Hell: The Civil Service Examinations of Imperial China*. Translated by Conrad Schirokauer. New Haven, 1981.

Morohashi Tetsuji, ed. *Dai Kan-Wa jiten* [Dictionary of Chinese]. 12 vols. Tokyo, 1960.

Myers, Ramon H. *The Chinese Peasant Economy: Agricultural Development in Hopei and Shantung, 1890–1949*. Cambridge, Mass., 1970.

Naquin, Susan. *Millenarian Rebellion in China: The Eight Trigrams Uprising of 1813*. New Haven, 1976.

Needham, Joseph et al. *Science and Civilisation in China*. 5 vols. Cambridge, England, 1954–1979.

Osgood, Cornelius. *Village Life in Old China: A Community Study of Kao Yao, Yunnan*. New York, 1963.

Pa Chin. *Family*. New York, 1972.

Parish, William L., and Martin King Whyte. *Village and Family in Contemporary China*. Chicago, 1978.

Perry, Elizabeth J. *Rebels and Revolutionaries in North China, 1845–1945*. Stanford, 1980.

Poems from China. Translated by Wong Man. Hong Kong, 1950.

Potter, Jack M. "Cantonese Shamanism." In Arthur P. Wolf, ed., *Religion and Ritual in Chinese Society*, pp. 207–31.

Rawski, Evelyn Sakakida. *Education and Popular Literacy in Ch'ing China*. Ann Arbor, 1979.

Roberts, Moss. *Three Kingdoms: China's Epic Drama*. New York, 1976.

Rühle, Jurgen. *Literature and Revolution: A Critical Study of the Writer and Communism in the Twentieth Century*. Translated and edited by Jean Steinberg. London, 1969.

Ruhlmann, Robert. "Traditional Heroes in Chinese Popular Fiction." In *The Confucian Persuasion*, edited by Arthur F. Wright, pp. 141–76. Stanford, 1969.

Schell, Orville. *"Watch Out for the Foreign Guests!" China Encounters the West*. New York, 1980.

Schiffrin, Harold Z. *Sun Yat-sen and the Origins of the Chinese Revolution*. Berkeley, 1968.

Schram, Stuart. *Mao Tse-tung*. Harmondsworth, England, 1966.

Selden, Mark. *The Yenan Way in Revolutionary China*. Cambridge, Mass., 1971.

Shandong tongzhi [Shandong Province Gazetteer]. 1934; originally published in 1911.

"Shanghai: January 28, 1932." *Pacific Historical Review* 9 (1940): 337–43.

Shen bao. Shanghai, 1872–1949.

"Shen bao" nian jian [*Shen bao* Yearbook]. Shanghai, 1936.

Sheridan, James E. *China in Disintegration: The Republican Era in Chinese History, 1912–1949*. New York, 1975.

Shi Naian and Luo Guanzhong. *Shuihu zhuan* [Water Margin], trans. by Sidney Shapiro under the title *Outlaws of the Marsh*. 2 vols. Bloomington, Ind., 1981.

Shih, Vincent Y. C. *The Taiping Ideology: Its Sources, Interpretations, and Influences*. Seattle, 1967.

Shijie zhishi [World Knowledge]. Shanghai, 1935–37.

Shillony, Ben-Ami. *Revolt in Japan: The Young Officers and the February 26 Incident*. Princeton, 1973.

Shryock, John. *The Temples of Anking and Their Cults*. Paris, 1931.

Shu, Austin C. W. *Modern Chinese Authors: A List of Pseudonyms*. East Lansing, Mich., 1969.

Skinner, G. William. "Introduction." In *The Study of Chinese Society: Essays by Maurice Freedman*, edited by G. William Skinner, pp. xi–xxiv. Stanford, 1979.

———. "Marketing and Social Structure in Rural China." *Journal of Asian Studies* 24.1 (November 1964): 3–43.

———. "Regional Urbanization in Nineteenth-Century China." In *The City in Late Imperial China*, edited by G. William Skinner, pp. 211–49. Stanford, 1979.

Snow, Edgar. *Red Star over China*. New York, 1938.

Snow, Helen F. (under pseud. Nym Wales). *Notes on the Chinese Student Movement, 1935–6*. Stanford, 1959.

So Kwan-wai. *Japanese Piracy in Ming China during the 16th Century*. East Lansing, Mich., 1975.

Spence, Jonathan D. *The Gate of Heavenly Peace: The Chinese and Their Revolution, 1895–1980*. New York, 1981.

Ssu-ma Ch'ien. *Records of the Grand Historian of China: Translated from the Shih Chi of Ssu-ma Ch'ien*. Translated by Burton Watson. 2 vols. New York, 1971.

Storry, Richard. "The Mukden Incident of September 18–19, 1931." *Far Eastern Affairs* (Saint Anthony's Papers, no. 2): 1–12.

Tai Yen-hui. "Divorce in Traditional Chinese Law." In *Chinese Family Law and Social Change: A Historical and Comparative Perspective*, edited by David C. Buxbaum, pp. 75–106. Seattle, 1978.

Tanaka Masami. "Ahen sensō jiki ni okeru kankan no ichi kōsatsu" [An Examination of Chinese Traitors during the Opium War]. *Shigaku kenkyū* [Historical Research] (March 1959): 1–14.

———. "Ahen sensōzen ni okeru 'kankan' no mondai" [The Problem of "Chinese Traitors" before the Opium War]. *Shigaku kenkyū* [Historical Research] (March 1964): 1–37.

Thomson, James C., Jr. *While China Faced West: American Reformers in Nationalist China, 1928–1937*. Cambridge, Mass., 1969.

Tien Hung-mao. *Government and Politics in Kuomintang China, 1927–1937*. Stanford, 1972.

Ting Hsu Lee-hsia. *Government Control of the Press in Modern China, 1900–1949*. Cambridge, Mass., 1974.

Topley, Marjorie. "Marriage Resistance in Rural Kwangtung." In Margery Wolf and Roxane Witke, eds., *Women in Chinese Society*, pp. 67–88.

Union Research Institute. *Who's Who in Communist China*. 2 vols. Hong Kong, 1969.

van der Valk, M. H. *An Outline of Modern Chinese Family Law*. Peking, 1939.

Van Slyke, Lyman P. *Enemies and Friends: The United Front in Chinese Communist History*. Stanford, 1967.

———. "Liang Sou-ming and the Rural Reconstruction Movement." *Journal of Asian Studies* 18.4 (August 1959): 457–74.

Wakeman, Frederic, Jr. *Strangers at the Gate: Social Disorder in South China, 1839–1861*. Berkeley, 1966.

Waley, Arthur. *The Opium War through Chinese Eyes*. London, 1958.

Wang Yao. *Zhongguo xin wenxue shigao* [A Draft History of China's New Literature]. Shanghai, 1954.

Welch, Holmes. *The Practice of Chinese Buddhism, 1900–1950*. Cambridge, Mass., 1967.

Wen Juntian. *Zhongguo baojia zhidu* [China's Watch-Group System]. Shanghai, 1935.

Wenxue [Literature]. Shanghai, 1933–37.

West, Philip. *Yenching University in Sino-Western Relations, 1916–1952*. Cambridge, Mass., 1976.

Williams, Raymond. *Keywords: A Vocabulary of Culture and Society*. New York, 1976.

Wilson, David Clive. "Britain and the Kuo-min-tang, 1924–28." Ph.D. dissertation, University of London, School of Oriental and African Studies, 1973.

Witke, Roxane. "Transformation of Attitudes toward Women during the May Fourth Era of Modern China." Ph.D. dissertation, University of California, Berkeley, 1970.

Wolf, Arthur P. "Gods, Ghosts, and Ancestors." In Arthur P. Wolf, ed., *Religion and Ritual in Chinese Society*, pp. 131–82.

———. "Introduction." In Arthur P. Wolf, ed., *Religion and Ritual in Chinese Society*, pp. 1–18.

Wolf, Arthur P., ed. *Religion and Ritual in Chinese Society*. Stanford, 1974.

Wolf, Margery. *Women and the Family in Rural Taiwan*. Stanford, 1972.

———. "Women and Suicide in China." In Margery Wolf and Roxane Witke, eds., *Women in Chinese Society*, pp. 111–41.

Wolf, Margery, and Roxane Witke. "Introduction." In Margery Wolf and Roxane Witke, eds., *Women in Chinese Society*, pp. 1–11.

Wolf, Margery, and Roxane Witke, eds., *Women in Chinese Society*. Stanford, 1975.

Woodhead, H. G. W., ed. *The China Year Book, 1935*. Shanghai, 1935.

Wright, Mary Clabaugh. "Introduction: The Rising Tide of Change." In Mary Clabaugh Wright, ed., *China in Revolution*, p. 1–63.

Wright, Mary Clabaugh, ed. *China in Revolution: The First Phase, 1900–1913*. New Haven, 1968.

Wu Tien-wei. *The Sian Incident: A Pivotal Point in Modern Chinese History*. Michigan Papers in Chinese Studies, no. 26. Ann Arbor, 1976.

Wu Zuguang. *Fenghuang cheng* [Phoenix City]. Chongqing, 1939.

Xianggang wenxue yanjiu she [Hong Kong Literary Research Society], comp. *Zhongguo xin wenxue daxi xubian* [Supplement to the Compendium of the New Literature of China]. 10 vols. Hong Kong, 1966.

Xin min hui zhongyang zhidao bu diaocha ke [Investigative Section of the Central Control Department of the People's Renovation Society], ed. *Jinzhi tushu mulu: Kang Ri zhi bu* [A List of Censored Books: Section on Resistance to Japan]. N.p., 1939.

Xin nüxing [New Woman]. In Xianggang wenxue yanjiu she, comp., *Zhongguo xin wenxue daxi xubian*, vol. 10, pp. 363–405.

Xu Zhucheng. *Jiu wen zha yi* [Miscellaneous Recollections of Things Said in the Past]. Hong Kong, 1980.

Xuanmo (pseud.). "Wenxue yanjiu hui ji qi zhongyao fenzi" [The Literary Research Association and Its Important Elements]. In *Sanshi niandai wenyi luncong* [Essays on the Art and Literature of the Thirties], edited by Sun Ruling, pp. 229–38. Taibei, 1966.

Xunlian zongjian bu [Superintendent of Military Training], ed. *Junshi jianghua* [Lectures on the Military]. Nanjing, 1934.

Yang, C. K. *Religion in Chinese Society: A Study of Contemporary Social Functions of Religion and Some of Their Historical Factors*. Berkeley, 1961.

Yang Yiming, ed. *Wentan shiliao* [Materials on Literary Circles]. Dalian, 1944.

Yong sheng [Everlasting Life]. Shanghai, 1936.

Young, Ernest P. *The Presidency of Yuan Shih-k'ai: Liberalism and Dictatorship in Early Republican China*. Ann Arbor, 1977.

Zhao Shuli. "Dadao Han jian" [Down with Chinese Traitors]. In Xianggang wenxue yanjiu she, comp., *Zhongguo xin wenxue daxi xubian*, vol. 9, pp. 907–17.

Zhu Zuotong et al., eds. *Shanghai yi ri* [One Day in Shanghai]. Shanghai, 1938.

Index

Xi Shi, 26n.1
Xiamen, 196, 235, 236
Xin County, 76
Xinwen bao, 182, 182n.1
Xu Daolin, 91n.5
Xu Maorong, 234

Ya Dongyang, 257–59, 257n.1
Yamen, 18, 18n.1, 21, 45
Yan Xishan, 73, 75, 76, 76n.1, 77, 78n.2,
    107n.2, 255, 255n.3
Yang Guifei, 26n.1
Yang Jingyu, 257–59, 257n.1
Yen, James Y. C., 12n.1
Yi County, 22
Yin Rugeng, 212, 212nn.6 and 7, 216, 234,
    239n.3

Yingkou, 207
Youth Corps, 259, 260
Yue Fei, 229, 229n.1
Yutian County, 210

Zhang Naiqi, xii n.4
Zhang Xueliang, 209nn.7 and 8, 254, 255n.2
Zhang Zhongshi, xiin.4, 274, 274n.1
Zhang Zuolin, 107n.2
Zhao Shangzhi, 259, 259n.1
Zhao Shuli, 202n.1
Zhengzhou, 152
Zhouping, 61
Zhu De, 260, 260n.6
Zou Taofen, xiin.4